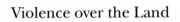Violence over the Land

Violence over the Land

INDIANS AND EMPIRES IN THE
EARLY AMERICAN WEST

◆ ◆ ◆

Ned Blackhawk

HARVARD UNIVERSITY PRESS

Cambridge, Massachusetts

London, England

2006

Library of Congress Cataloging-in-Publication Data

Blackhawk, Ned.
Violence over the land : Indians and empires
in the early American West / Ned Blackhawk.
p.   cm.
Includes bibliographical references and index.
ISBN-13: 978-0-674-02290-4 (alk. paper)
ISBN-10: 0-674-02290-4 (alk. paper)
1. Indians of North America—Great Basin—History.
2. Indians of North America—Wars—Great Basin.
3. Great Basin—History.   I. Title.

E78.G67B53   2006
979.004′97—dc22   2006043477

Dedicated to my grandmother, Eva Charley (1912–1987)

to my father, Evan Blackhawk (1941–),
who showed me that one need not live a life in pain

and to the Kanesatake and Kahnawake Mohawk Communities, whose
articulate and defiant voices in the summer of 1990
helped me discover my own

Contents

Illustrations

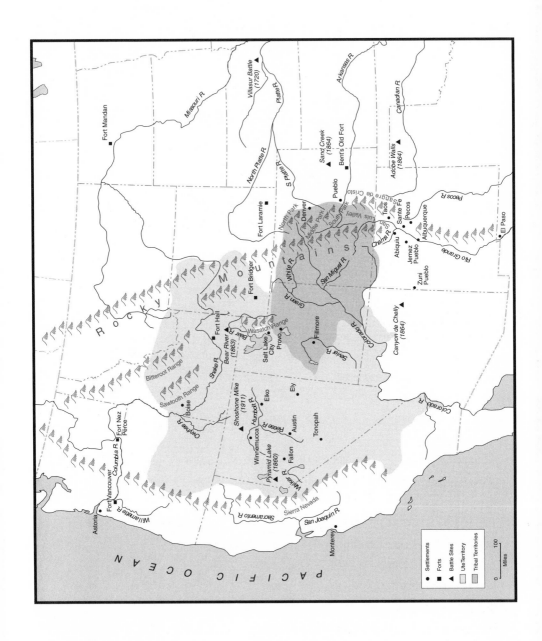

PACIFIC OCEAN

Settlements ●
Forts ■
Battle Sites ▲
Ute Territory
Tribal Territories

0   100
Miles

Astoria
Fort Vancouver
Columbia R.
Willamette R.
Fort Nez Perce
Boise
Owyhee R.
Snake R.
Sawtooth Range
Bitterroot Range
Rocky
Fort Mandan
Missouri R.
Platte R.
North Platte R.
Villasur Battle (1720)
Fort Laramie
Fort Bridger
Green R.
White R.
San Miguel R.
North Park
Middle Park
South Park
Denver
Pueblo
San Luis Valley
Sangre de Cristo
Taos
Santa Fe
Pecos
Abiquiu
Jemez Pueblo
Albuquerque
Pecos R.
Rio Grande
El Paso
Zuni Pueblo
Canyon de Chelly (1864)
Colorado R.
Sand Creek (1864)
Bent's Old Fort
Adobe Walls (1864)
Canadian R.
Arkansas R.
S. Platte R.
Chama R.
Mountains
Wasatch Range
Fort Hall
Bear R.
Bear River (1863)
Salt Lake City
Provo
Sevier R.
Fillmore
Shoshone Mike (1911)
Humbolt R.
Elko
Ely
Reese R.
Austin
Tonopah
Winnemucca (1860)
Pyramid Lake
Fallon
Walker R.
Sierra Nevada
Sacramento R.
San Joaquin R.
Monterey
Colorado R.

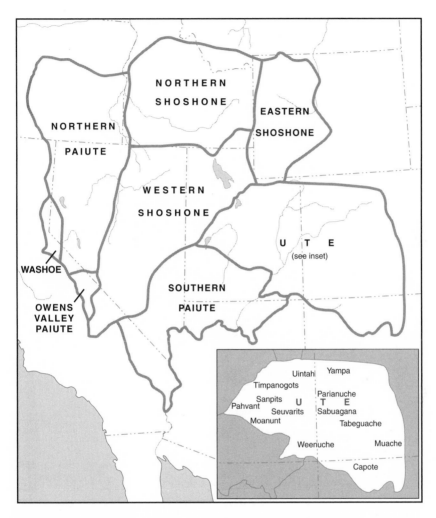

Above: Tribal territories of the Great Basin. Courtesy of the Wisconsin Laboratory of Cartography, Madison.

Facing page: The Great Basin and the American West. Courtesy of the Wisconsin Laboratory of Cartography, Madison.

INTRODUCTION

❖ ❖ ❖

The Indigenous Body in Pain

"All of us, readers and writers, are bereft when criticism remains too polite or too fearful to notice a disrupting darkness before its eyes." So concludes *Playing in the Dark,* Toni Morrison's forceful exposition of American literature's deep "association with race." Published in 1992, the year of the Columbian quincentenary, Morrison's collection locates African Americans at the center of American cultural development, fusing "black" and "white" into a seemingly inescapable imaginary bond. As she and so many others have come to acknowledge, definitions of America are embedded in racial constructions: "the American self knows itself as not enslaved, but free; not repulsive, but desirable; not helpless, but licensed and powerful; not history-less, but historical; not damned, but innocent; not a blind accident of evolution, but a progressive fulfillment of destiny."[1]

This book attempts to add to these equations. The narrative of American history, it argues, has failed to gauge the violence that remade much of the continent before U.S. expansion. Nor have American historians fully assessed the violent effects of such expansion on the many Indian peoples caught within these continental changes. Following Morrison's critique, this work suggests that American history is considered a place of comfort, not one of pain; a realm of achievement rather than one of indigenous trauma.

Compared with Europe, Africa, the Middle East, and Asia, North America, in particular the region that would become the United States, has a short and linear history. Beginning in the early seventeenth cen-

1

tury, scattered groups of Anglo settlers discarded the constraints of Europe for the promises of a new land. Along the Atlantic, these economic and religious outposts grew and eventually united against England. A new polity and nation were formed, and a revolutionary experiment in politics and culture began, an experiment that not only continues to the present but also has spread through much of the world.

These are among the founding truths of American history, as are the United States' subsequent development and expansion as a superpower. Such truths are important. They underscore the achievements of a fledgling nation, and most indexes of American history support and reinforce this narrative. Cities sprouted where forests once stood, immigrants amassed great wealth, and industry grew and grew and grew. By the early twentieth century, such truths had become so accepted that many simply regarded American history as a process of nature: a promised "virgin land" uninhabited before European contact had supinely awaited its natural awakening, the fulfillment of its "destiny." On a narrative and discursive level, America represented the promise of prosperity, and the toil and suffering involved in achieving it simply confirmed the overarching potential and goodness of the nation. *Give us your tired, your poor, and your huddled masses yearning to be free,* and we shall turn them into prosperous citizens and adorn them with the vestments of the rights of man.[2]

Narratives about the past are in constant flux, and it is now commonplace to reject such portrayals as prejudiced and incomplete. Women, workers, racial and ethnic minorities do not fit easily into such contained mythologies. The primary function of myth, as Roland Barthes has argued, is to turn history into nature, and the past two generations of scholars have attempted to reconcile discordant views of our nation's past, to reconcile the mythic promise of America with its past and contemporary inequities, opening new fields of inquiry and reinterpreting canonical subjects. A deluge of scholarship on nearly all aspects of American life and culture now fills university press catalogs and the convention halls of our nation's academic gatherings.[3]

Yet a glaring absence remains at the heart of the field. Still missing from most narratives of American history are clear and informed analyses of our nation's indigenous peoples. Although "Indians" are emblematic of America and continue to excite the imaginations of the young both here and abroad, Indian history is no mere curiosity or sideshow in the drama of the American past. The two remain interwoven. North America was already inhabited when Europeans arrived, and from their first days on this continent, Europeans relied on Native peoples for guidance, hospitality, and survival. American historians since the days of the Puritans have tried to rationalize Europeans' takings of Indian lands and lives, and all Indian peoples have endured the many traumas of contact and colonization. Native and European peoples have interacted, intermingled, and coexisted since the first moments of encounter. They have also come into bitter and deadly conflict. Reconciling the dispossession of millions with the making of America remains a sobering challenge, an endeavor that requires re-evaluation of many enduring historical assumptions. A generation of scholars has already begun this large task, and this book aims to contribute to it.[4]

Historicizing Colonialism

Despite an outpouring of work over the past decades, those investigating American Indian history and U.S. history more generally have failed to reckon with the violence upon which the continent was built. Most scholarship has focused on colonial and early American history or, west of the Mississippi, on the decades of exploration and expansion in the nineteenth century. The Indians of the American Great Basin—the vast interior portions of the American West between the Sierra and Rocky Mountains—still figure little or not at all in the nation's vision of its past. The many Ute, Paiute, and Shoshone groups who have inhabited this region since time immemorial generally appear as distant shadows in historical texts, faint nameless traces of America's primordial past. Whether as hostile combatants against American migrants or as peaceful desert dwellers, Great Basin Indians are rarely seen as agents in histories of the region. They appear passive objects as history essentially rolls over them, forcing them into minor roles in a larger pageant, understudies in the very dramas remaking their homelands. From the first moments of conquest to the present day, the experiences of these Indian peoples remain overlooked and bypassed on the thoroughfare of historical inquiry. These Indians, like so many others, remain nonparticipants in the epic of America.[5]

Such historical oversight is surpassed only by anthropology's treatment of these Native peoples. For nearly a century, many of those who have studied Great Basin Indians have consigned them to the distant netherworlds of "prehistory," to the very margins of "civilization." Because of their sparse technologies and migratory economies, anthropologists, including the influential ethnographer Julian Steward, have represented Great Basin Indians as the quintessential "peoples without history," the most "primitive" peoples in the world. Steward pioneered the field of Great Basin as well as American anthropology, using his research among the Nevada Shoshone to construct elaborate models of human organization in which Great Basin Indians supposedly remained the least "developed" cultures in the world. They represented antitheses of modernity and lived "simple" unchanging lives as endless desert wanderers, the first and definitive "hunters and gatherers." An entire language of cultural development arose from Steward's study of these Indian peoples, who became the sediment upon which others attempted to understand "Man's Rise to Civilization."[6]

Such environmentally determined cultural hierarchies have now become discredited, replaced by more relativistic and discursive notions of culture. In the Great Basin, however, as in many other parts of the Americas, the intellectual residue of primitivism remains. The region's indigenous peoples remain fixed within static definitions of culture, imprisoned in notions of essentialism. As a result of the pernicious, self-perpetuating logic of timelessness on the one hand, and of primitivism on the other, these groups remain outside of history, and any changes or adaptations they have made become only further evidence of their demise. When Native peoples adapt to foreign economies or utilize outside technologies, they are assumed to abandon their previous—that is, inferior—ways while in the process losing parts of themselves; they lose the very things that according to others define them. Once adaptation becomes synonymous with assimilation, change over time—the commonplace definition of history—becomes a death knell. The more things change, the greater the loss.[7]

This study takes direct aim at the intertwined ahistoricism and essentialism that pervade understandings of the Intermountain West. It offers an alternative to this overlooked and overdetermined past. Far from being marginal actors in American history, Great Basin Indians in fact remain central to the development and course of western history. Furthermore, beneath the discourse of primitivism lie painful and traumatic pasts that defy summary analysis. From the spread of epidemic diseases, to the introduction of new economies, to the loss of lands, lives, and resources, these indigenous peoples, like so many others, have experienced epic ordeals. Moreover, they have done so largely outside the view of America's settler and immigrant populations. From their earliest recorded interactions with Europeans in the 1600s to their nineteenth-century struggles within an expansionist state, Great Basin Indians have witnessed the rise of new worlds and the collapse of old ones. Such challenges and changes remain fundamental to understandings of the region's past and are linked to larger imperial and national currents.[8]

These are not, however, simply *peoples with history* whose experiences can be molded or incorporated into common narratives of American history. As the pioneering Indian studies scholar Vine Deloria Jr. noted almost forty years ago, it does little good to add Indians into a flawed mosaic of American history without first reworking the temporal and spatial boundaries of the field. This book extends Deloria's critique and suggests that the experiences of Great Basin Indians force reconsideration of large portions of North American history, histories that after excavation offer far from celebratory portraits of America. Harrowing, violent histories of Native peoples caught in the maelstrom of colonialism define this and other regions and remain necessary foundations upon which other narratives must contend. Such painful histories also have contemporary legacies that continue to influence these communities and their descendants.[9]

Violence as both a subject and a method is at the heart of this book. That Native peoples endured violent attacks or responded to such attacks with force is not news. Indeed, the history of Indian-white relations, particularly throughout the eighteenth and nineteenth centuries, reads like a series of constant wars. The following pages examine the nature of such chronic conflict—the seemingly endless raids, battles, massacres, and numbers lost on all sides. Ultimately, however, violence becomes more than an intriguing or distressing historical subject. It becomes an interpretive concept as well as a method for understanding these understudied worlds. By charting the region's changing relations of violence, this work seeks to open up historical landscapes already altered by European contact, as violence provides the clearest and at times only windows into them. Violence provides the threads that weave Great Basin Indian history together and organizes the discussion in the following four ways.[10]

First, the earliest moments of postcontact Great Basin history become accessible only through analyses of the shifting relations of violence that remade the Intermountain West during the Spanish colonial era. As the first colonial power in North America, Spain initiated imperial intrusions that disrupted the everyday lives of Indian peoples throughout the continent. The demographic, economic, and environmental changes unleashed throughout northern New Spain have received much analysis, but few have considered the central role and effects of violence in these transformations. While many recognize the effects of Spanish horses, trade networks, and diplomacy, few link these changes to broader patterns of everyday life in the Spanish borderlands. Focusing on the easternmost Great Basin groups, principally on bands of Ute Indians in northern New Mexico and in Colorado, Chapters 1 through 4 examine worlds revolutionized by the irruption of new forms of colonial violence. From the earliest explorations and settlements in colonial New Mexico to the varying frontier successes of Spanish and later Mexican regimes, Ute bands adopted changing strategies of survival in response to colonial disturbance and remained critical to the region's balance of power. In response to the waves of violence engulfing their homelands, Utes became feared combatants, courted allies, and eventually gracious hosts whose changing economic and political decisions contributed to the composition of the Spanish borderlands.[11]

Ute adaptation in the face of imperial expansion is, however, neither celebrated nor glorified. Utes responded in kind to the shifting relations of violence sweeping throughout their homelands, redirecting colonial violence against their neighbors, Spanish and Indian alike. Carrying violence to more distant peoples in New Mexico's expanding hinterlands, Utes attempted to monopolize the trade routes in and out of the colony while besieging neighboring groups, particularly those without horses. As their power north of Santa Fe increasingly weighed upon the minds of colonial rulers, Utes forged generations of ties to New Mexico that wedded these societies together in new and surprising ways. However, Spanish-Ute accommodation carried high and deadly costs for Ute neighbors, particularly non-equestrian Paiute and Shoshone groups in the southern Great Basin, whose communities were raided for slaves by Utes, New Mexicans, and later Americans. Like their neighboring Indian and Spanish rivals, Utes remade themselves in response to the region's cycles of violence and did so at the expense of others, as violence and Indian slavery became woven into the fabric of everyday life throughout the early West. While sparsely documented, evidence of Great Basin Indian captivity and Ute slave trafficking underscores the transformative and violent nature of Great Basin Indian history. In short, before their sustained appearance in written records, Great Basin Indians endured the disruptive hold of colonialism's expansive reach, brought to them first by other Indian people.[12]

Violence organizes this study in a second and related way. The shifting relations of violence that remade Native worlds throughout the early West did so largely outside of colonial settlements and the purview of authorities. Often only faint traces remain of the waves of violence that swept out of New Mexico and transformed Native peoples from the Sierras to the Mississippi. Accessing the effects of such waves of violence is a fragile endeavor, the results of which must be viewed with skepticism. As in other contact zones and imperial hinterlands, Utes and other Great Basin Indians inhabited "new worlds for all," the genesis of which remains lost to historical inquiry. The history of these groups becomes, then, a history without clear or fixed origins. The earliest documentary histories of Great Basin Indians remain unfixed and untied to specific moments or locales. They remain histories in motion, accelerated by the revolutionary and violent impacts of European contact and colonialism. As Utes ferried Great Basin Indian captives into New Mexico, for example, colonial officials knew little of the natal origins of these slaves, often classifying them as "Yutas" on the basis of shared linguistic ties. These renamed Great Basin captives—overwhelmingly young women and children—provide the earliest sustained references to nonequestrian Great Basin peoples while also revealing the violence intrinsic to the region's history.[13]

Such attention to violence and motion, however, by no means discredits Ute and other tribal traditions that for strategic reasons emphasize the permanent and immemorial existence of each nation in their respective homelands. Forged against narratives of erasure, such histories have often countered policies aimed at denying Indians access to lands and resources. Emphasis on these Native groups' changing relations of violence is intended here to recast the received categories of analysis that have so readily frozen these Native people. As the following pages suggest, understandings of Indian history, culture, and identity remain historically determined, located not in essential cultural traits but in the violent postcontact time and space of American history. No timeless ethnographic categories or political definitions characterize these Native peoples. Indeed, in this region, precise band names, territorial locales, and stable political designations are often unreliable, particularly given the violent shock waves that engulfed these Indian homelands before their sustained documentation. Hybridity, adaptation, and exchange more clearly characterize these histories than do fixed ethnographic categories, let alone the convenient dichotomies so common to narratives of American Indians. Colonial violence, in sum, characterizes these Native worlds as the violence that saturated communities on the margins of empire has also destabilized the categories of analysis used to describe them.[14]

While violence emerges as the overarching theme of this book, pain remains its implied object, particularly as experienced by Indian peoples. Elusive yet omnipresent, pain remains an uncommon subject in historical inquiry, partly because of language's inability to capture the experiential nature of another's pain. As Elaine Scarry has argued, bodily pain not only resists representation but also destabilizes it, casting this most elemental human experience into the realms of medical and biological sciences.[15]

While Scarry's work focuses primarily on the psychology of pain, several historians have utilized her findings in assessing, in Barbara Young Welke's words, "the irony that the tools of civilization were themselves the instruments of acute suffering." Colonialism's effects upon such indigenous "bodies in pain" necessitate deeper documentary and interpretive attention. Underrecognized corollaries to Europe's expansion into the Americas, violence and pain remain essential, if destabilizing, prerequisites in the study of American history.[16]

Third, violence weds the history of these Native groups to larger imperial histories. Despite accounts to contrary, Europe's colonization of

North American Indian lands defines much of American history. In fact, pioneering American historian Frederick Jackson Turner was partially correct when he declared the process of American expansion as the foundational experience of American history. Although Turner's insistence on the self-democratizing attributes of "frontier" settlement has been recast, few have claimed the effects of such expansion on Indian peoples as equally foundational to, if not representative of, the American experience. This book attempts such suggestion. The violent transformation of Indian lands and lives characterizes European and American expansion. Neither natural nor inevitable, the violent deformations of Native communities locate these indigenous pasts within the broader field of European global colonialism. Historicizing the violent effects of colonialism and suggesting how enduring such effects have become remain objectives in the chapters to come.[17]

Finally, violence and the history of Native influences on imperial and national borderlands require alternative paradigms for understanding the nineteenth-century processes of American expansion. As Chapters 5 through 7 reveal, the United States expanded into worlds already affected by generations of European disruptions and remade these worlds through its own agents of empire. From the use of the U.S. Army to combat and confine Indian peoples, to the state-sanctioned theft of Indian lands and resources, violence both predated and became intrinsic to American expansion. Violence enabled the rapid accumulation of new resources, territories, and subject peoples. It legitimated the power of migrants, structured new social and racial orders, and provided the preconditions for political formation. From the initial moments of American exploration and conquest, through statehood, and into the stages of territorial formation, violence organized the region's nascent economies, settlements, and polities. Violence and American nationhood, in short, progressed hand in hand.[18]

American political formation in the Great Basin occurred through violence in the homelands of Native peoples, many of whom had forged generations of relations with colonial societies. In the 1800s such shared or mutually constructed worlds were overturned. Following a rapid succession of events, newcomers swarmed throughout the region, seizing the most fertile lands and resources for their own. Fur trappers, traders, and explorers either wrought the initial traumas or laid the basis for subsequent ones. In the Great Basin, trappers vied with one another in scorched-earth trapping practices, emptying fragile watersheds of small game, while traders ferried resources into and out of the region, enmeshing Native communities in webs of economic dependency. Explorers and cartographers like Lewis and Clark initiated less immediate forms of violence, performing the geographical measurements required for subsequent disruptions. Armies, settlers, migrants, and their herds soon followed, forever altering the region's ecology and societies. In the span of one generation, from the Rocky Mountains to the Sierras immigrants became settlers, settlements became towns, and Indians became outsiders. Surveying the pre-reservation history of Colorado's and Utah's Native populations, the second half of this book highlights the divergent paths of diplomacy, warfare, and survival initiated by equestrian Utes and Shoshones in response to the pandemic relations of violence engulfing their communities.

Great Basin Indian Struggles for Survival

Amidst such demographic and environmental turmoil, Great Basin Indians struggled to survive. Colorado Utes navigated political channels to protect territories within their familiar yet changing world, while Utah's Utes and Shoshones escalated their use of violence in response to settler and emigrant disruptions. Others became overwhelmed by the onslaught, as many Indian families migrated out of the region to neighboring areas where the federal government had created federally protected Indian lands called reservations. Such enclaves, or "laboratories" as later government officials viewed them, became intertribal refugee centers where previously unrelated peoples joined together in diaspora. Despite the U.S. Senate's ratification of treaties mandating the creation of reservations throughout the region, many Great Basin groups, particularly nonequestrians, received few federal protections and faced the ordeal of conquest on their own.[19]

In Nevada, eastern California, and central Utah, survival often necessitated integration into the region's evolving settler economies. Facing enduring economic and environmental crises, many Indian families attached themselves to white farms, mining communities, or ranches where Indian men and women worked in the most degraded sectors. Great Basin Indian impoverishment—a common trope in American literary and travel narratives—became the clearest expression of such disruption, as everywhere Indian peoples appeared to be on the verge of extinction, impoverished beyond the hope of survival. Mark Twain's infamous comments about the Goshute Shoshone of eastern Nevada encapsulate such perceptions: "It was along in this wild country . . . that we came across the wretchedest type of mankind . . . the Goshoot Indians. From what we could see and all we could learn, they are very considerably inferior to even the despised Digger Indians of California, inferior to all races of savages on our continent . . . Our Goshoots are manifestly descended from the self-same gorilla, or kangaroo or Norway rat, whichever animal-Adam the Darwinians trace them to." What America's most celebrated nineteenth-century writer failed to "learn" was that Indian poverty—masqueraded as "wretchedness" and "inferiority"—remained intimately linked to American colonization; these Native peoples were not relics of an ancient past but products of the most rapid territorial expansion in world history. Racial and cultural difference, however, more easily explained Indian misery.[20]

In the face of such impoverishment, Great Basin Indians fought to retain control over their communities and access to their homelands. Comparing the unique, though parallel, economic adaptations initiated by equestrian Utes and Shoshones, Chapters 6 and 7 link the region's colonial period to the violent aftermath of American expansion. Surveying pre-reservation efforts of Native communities to maintain control over their subsistence lands while also highlighting their growing tensions around settler communities, it ends where many narratives of Indian history end, in bloodshed, with an examination of the January 1863 Bear River Massacre, when 500 Northern Shoshones fought for survival against Civil War volunteers, more than half dying in the morning snow.

The Epilogue meditates on the region's divergent historical narratives. Contrasting Julian Steward's seminal ethnographies with Western Shoshone family histories, it highlights the power of narrative both to define a people's essence and to instill a deep sense of cultural pride. Steward, as powerfully as any American anthropologist, classified his subjects into reified cultural hierarchies and failed to see how the very people he interviewed and traveled among had responded to the challenges of conquest. More concerned with his evolutionary typologies than with the everyday struggles of his informants, Steward went so far as to petition against Western Shoshone attempts to gain federal recognition and reservation lands under the auspices of the Indian Reorganization Act of 1934. He believed that the "traditional" political institutions of the Shoshone were so undeveloped that they could not manage as a "tribe"; their attempts to reinvent themselves politically were antithetical to, and thus threatened, their culture.

Shoshone Beggars at the Railway Station, Carlin, Nevada. Lithograph in *Frank Leslie's Illustrated Newspaper* (New York), November 8, 1873. Images of Western and Goshute Shoshone impoverishment captured the attention of Indian agents, journalists, and travel writers throughout the 1800s, most famously by Mark Twain.

Steward and other American intellectuals, the Epilogue suggests, have perpetuated one of the most lasting legacies of conquest: they have erased violence and colonialism from discussions of the region's past, performing acts of representational violence whose power continues to misinform assessments of these Native people.[21]

Western Shoshone and other Great Basin groups have resisted such intellectual and political racism in many ways. Denied the guarantees of nineteenth-century treaties, particularly the 1863 Treaty of Ruby Valley, the Western Shoshone, for example, spent the entire twentieth century fighting for implementation of the treaty's articles, particularly its provisions for the establishment of Indian reservations in Nevada. Despite Steward's protests, Shoshone groups used the mechanisms of the Indian Reorganization Act to receive some new lands and federal recognition. After World War II, they navigated the equally complicated legal channels established by the Indian Claims Commission to file for their outstanding land claims, and throughout the 1970s, 1980s, and 1990s Shoshone groups fought for the return of Indian homelands. Unlike any other state in the union, over 90 percent of Nevada is "owned" by the federal government, which manages tens of millions of acres through Department of Defense and Bureau of Land Management offices, using the region for everything from nuclear testing to wildlife preserves. The origins of these (sometimes contradictory) policies date to 1863 and to the unconstitutional failure of the federal government to receive title from Shoshone groups. As the final chapter and the Epilogue detail, Shoshone political struggles mirror the social and economic ordeals of other Great Basin groups, in which the threat and legacy of violence also remain ever present.[22]

The Epilogue ends with two nonreservation Shoshone family histories, including my own. The young Shoshone woman in the photo, Mamie Andrews, was my great-grandmother, born in the 1890s in central Nevada during the second generation after American conquest. While Nevada acquired statehood relatively early in the West, institutionalizing the mechanisms of statehood took decades. Many Native peoples continued to live "outside the state," speaking their own language, living to themselves, and traveling, as they always had, seasonally for food, work, worship, and recreation. Their migratory and cultural practices contravened government policies aimed at confining and classifying Native peoples and prompted increased surveillance through institutions of state control, particularly the Bureau of Indian Affairs.

Born on a white ranch in Smoky Valley, Nevada, Mamie from her earliest days learned from her mother and aunts to cook and clean for white families, later becoming a domestic servant herself. Like the other Indian families who lived on ranches and in nearby mining towns, she grew up in intimate familiarity with whites, played with white and Indian children, and remained part of a community of ranchers and their Indian laborers. Never knowing her father, many

Mamie Andrews, about 1919. Eva Charley Family Collection. Photographed in a Nevada studio shortly before her confinement in the Nevada State Mental Hospital, Mamie Andrews left behind four Shoshone children in Smoky Valley, including Eva Charley, the author's grandmother.

believed her to be the result of the often nonconsensual sexual relations between Indian women and white men, which became commonplace in mining and ranching communities, where unequal gender ratios and racial hierarchies converged. Like most Indian laborers, Mamie received an English name. She married a handsome Indian man, Sam Johnson, and had one child with him, Eva, before leaving him for his half-brother, Bob Snooks, and having three more children.

Working hard with four children, Mamie and Bob became increasingly combative, especially during times when Bob drank with his friends and cousins after long days harvesting hay or mending endless cattle lines. Bob's excessive drinking and the aggressive behavior that followed from it paralleled that of other Indian men, whose poverty seemed only more glaring in contrast with the material possessions of whites and the countless images of fancy goods advertised in stores and newspapers. White insults, jokes, and generally disdainful manners fueled the need for escape. Whites owned just about everything, and the creation of liminal spaces outside of white control became as seemingly natural as Indian subjection. Indians traveled to regional Native festivals, called "fandangos," worked in seasonal labor groups, and migrated throughout the region.

After his return from one summer's fandango, Bob's attacks on Mamie became more severe, requiring her to seek assistance from local Indian healers as well as white doctors. Everyone in the community recalls that her second husband's abuse rendered Mamie unstable. Her crying and outbursts continued after Bob left, and her relatives grew concerned about little Eva and her two younger brothers and sister. Local authorities determined that Mamie required mental treatment, and in 1919, at the age of twenty-four, she was institutionalized in the state mental hospital, where she lived alone for her remaining fifty-seven years. The Epilogue traces the lives of Mamie and her parentless children and contrasts them with narratives emanating from anthropological, literary, and other outside commentators.

Mamie's oldest daughter, Eva, was my grandmother, and like her mother's, Eva's life was filled with poverty and hardship, testimony to the enduring challenges wrought by colonial expansion. As Native groups continue to recover from the aftermath of such collisions, these regional and personal histories bear witness to enduring historical truths. Throughout what we now call America, the nature of everyday life was forever transformed as violence swept over the land.

ONE

Spanish-Ute Relations to 1750

Once the battle had ended, their work was nearly done. Spoils still needed to be divided, wounds bandaged, and men and horses accounted for. Now they would also need their knives. Approaching the victims and pulling up their heads by the hair, they swiftly removed tender cartilage from the skulls of all the dead. After filling their sacks with the lightweight, bloody harvest, the attackers returned to camp and prepared for another campaign or for their return into the colony, where the familiar smells of piñon smoke and roasted chilies awaited, as did their bounty for services on behalf of the Spanish crown.

What happened next is unclear. The trophies were either brought into the colony by the attackers themselves or by military leaders who already had exchanged something of value with those ferrying the small satchels. Perhaps a few horses, *fanegas* (bushels) of wheat, and some additional knives sufficed. Guns, powder, and lead would have been desired, though rarely offered. Any clergy witnessing these transactions would have frowned upon this peculiar trade, which like so many practices in this corner of empire shocked and appalled those who clung faithfully to the kingdom of both cross and crown. Resident Pueblo Indians and the low multiracial *castas* (castes) who formed part of the colonial society would have grown accustomed or desensitized to such matters. They had seen, and some had experienced, worse. And the colony's settlers, particularly its male patriarchs, would have understood the need for what was to follow. They too knew frontier warfare and had fought alongside *presidio* (garrison) soldiers and their

Indian auxiliaries in the contests of the north. They had seen family and friends attacked, their settlements and ranches overrun, and on rare occasions their daughters and even wives taken captive by Indian raiders. Communicating the strength of the crown, they knew, necessitated displays of unrestrained power.

Where exactly the trophies were assembled is also unknown. Perhaps they first came out of the sacks when the attackers tallied their harvest. Bringing them out into the air, however, attracted flies, so they were probably dried before transport. By the light of the campfire or under a glowing seasonal sun, these corporeal coins may have been counted and laid out to dry. Whatever their origin, they eventually arrived in Santa Fe, the center of power in the region. Carried into the Governor's Palace, or *Palacio,* and displayed before the governor and his lieutenants, the cargo was finally relinquished, with some payment or reward bestowed upon these uncommon providers.

Next came another, albeit less dramatic, form of labor. As the governor ordered someone to employ a palace servant or an Indian slave from a nearby estate, the small bag again changed hands, and its contents were emptied onto a workbench and neatly arranged. After many days and weeks of transport, the stench nauseated, and the bag was quickly disposed of in one of the building's many fires. A needle was also threaded and run through each shriveled medallion, securely lacing all the victims' ears into strands that resembled the strings of dried chilies, or *ristras,* that adorned city streets, Pueblo homes, and ranches throughout the province.

If a slave performed this task, she may once have known life outside the colony in one of the northern societies where these mute objects originated. She may even have been related to one or more of the victims. Remembrances of her childhood before her abduction may have been stirred when she saw these ears, and she may have wondered about her former family and friends. Some she may have seen at summer trade fairs or heard about when tribal leaders visited. But those days were gone. She now had a new home, possibly family and children, and godparents, as well as a new name.

Unless the trophies still needed drying, the servant carried her finished product to one of the governor's men, who then presented it to the governor. Deciding where he wanted this most recent symbol of his authority exhibited, the governor perfectly understood the many lessons this uncanny prize communicated; for in colonial New Mexico, power, prestige, and influence emanated from the Governor's Palace. The focal point of the city's plaza, housing much of the colony's administrative records, and home to the representative of the crown himself, the *Palacio* dominated the political landscape of North America's oldest permanent colony. Because of the constant threat of equestrian raiders, many buildings throughout New Mexico had small windows with heavy shutters on the inside and occasionally iron grills on the exterior. The *Palacio* had neither; its unprotected windows consisted of large panes of handblown glass. The *Palacio's* architecture spoke of dominance and power, but even more eloquent was the macabre decoration hanging in its portal: strings of dried ears of indigenous peoples killed by parties commissioned by the governor to punish Indian neighbors.[1]

These ears provide a grim yet useful introduction to the history of colonial New Mexico. Terror, horrific violence, and nameless victims characterize much of Spanish relations with indigenous peoples outside the colony. Surrounded on all sides, colonial New Mexico became engulfed in centuries of "endemic warfare" with peoples who came to be classified by names that often subsumed different, and at times competing, territorial and cultural groups under single identities. Spanish authorities often grouped these peoples as *indios bárbaros,* or "savage Indians," and when they did distinguish among them they often did so inconsistently. It thus remains difficult to pinpoint the identities of New Mexico's many Indian neighbors, particularly those killed in battle beyond the colony. One thing is certain: Spanish contact altered the fabric of those neighbors' lives. Within a generation of colonization, Native peoples along New Mexico's immediate borders had remade themselves, assimilating Spanish technologies and goods into their societies while coping with the interrelated disruptions from trade, disease, and warfare.[2]

New Mexico's relations with its Comanche and Plains Indian neighbors to its north and east, Navajos to its west, and Apaches throughout have received examination. The colony's northwestern neighbors largely have not. Though sparsely documented, Spanish colonization first in New Mexico and later in California forever transformed the lives of indigenous societies living between the Colorado Rocky and Sierra Nevada mountains. From the introduction of the horse and other European trade items to the establishment of networks of trading relations, particularly the trade in human slaves, Spanish influences reverberated north and west from Santa Fe, sweeping into the Great Basin in steady and often powerful waves.[3]

As in other zones of encounter and along other slaving frontiers, assessing the impact of these waves of influence presents theoretical and methodological challenges. In the documentary record, such waves are often imperceptible. Spanish authorities following the 1694 Reconquista, for instance, became aware of newly formed equestrian bands of Ute peoples to the north, but they had never mapped or traversed their territories. New Spain, the richest and most prestigious colony of the world's largest empire, ended where Ute and New Mexican societies met, and the earliest documentary references are scattered and confusing. They shed little light on the nature of the revolutionary changes that accompanied Spanish influences north of Santa Fe. Unrecorded paradigmatic shifts in Indian cosmology, for example, remain lost to historical inquiry, while the social and demographic revolutions unleashed by the spread of Spanish horses, microbes, and economies are only faintly visible. But although the exact details of such encounters remain blurred, traces of interactions between Great Basin Indians and colonial New Mexico litter the documentary record.

When Spanish traders, missionaries, outlaws, and armies ventured north, they entered worlds in the midst of dramatic change. Though generally unconcerned with the cultural landscapes through which they traveled, New Mexicans went north with clear motivations that led them to notice narrow but critical details about the peoples there. Missionaries proselytized; traders searched for hides, horses, and slaves; and armies and colonial authorities attempted to enforce imperial decrees. The traces left by these contacts present at best a fragmented and one-sided picture of the colonial encounters in this vast area, but they offer a partial beginning to the history of the northernmost reaches of Spain's American empire.

The peoples to the north inhabited a world of constant movement, interaction, and exchange. Bands who lived along the Sangre de Cristo and San Juan Mountains of northern New Mexico and Colorado, who later came to be known as Muache and Capote Utes, traveled onto the Great Plains in search of game. They migrated in search of resources, and more and more ventured south to gain new and increasingly indispensable goods brought by Spanish newcomers. By the eighteenth century, the horse had become such an integral part of their lives that a nonequestrian existence must have seemed distant or inconceivable. While many peoples, principally those known as Comanche, had adopted the horse and moved out of the Great Basin onto the Plains, Ute bands straddled the Basin's easternmost borders, migrating seasonally to trade, hunt, and raid. Neighboring Ute bands farther north and to the west remained nonequestrian much longer than their eastern relatives, while the peoples farther west and in the heart of the Great Basin, who are now known as Paiutes and Shoshones, lived in lands that remained largely unknown, unmapped, and unexplored by New Mexicans. Their existence in the Spanish record is so limited that few interpretations can be definitive. Although Spanish and later Mexican authorities claimed much of their homelands, these peoples and their lands were outside the direct spheres of European imperialism for centuries after the arrival of Europeans in the American Southwest.[4]

Although they lived on the distant peripheries of New Spain, these nonequestrian Great Basin Indians became enmeshed in the violent networks of trade and slavery that forged the Spanish borderlands. After the 1598–99 subjugation of the resident Pueblo Indian population, Spanish-introduced technologies and economies of violence soon engulfed all surrounding people. Different Ute bands as well as Navajos from south of the Colorado River initially withstood and then displaced the horrors of Spanish colonialism onto the peoples of the Great Basin, and lightning slave raids and warfare came to characterize Indian relations throughout the region. These initial violent colonial influences, then, came not from European marauders but from equestrian Utes, whose complicated struggles to survive the maelstrom of Spanish colonialism form a necessary introduction to their subsequent violent relations with Great Basin peoples. Although one can only speculate about the precise identities of those lost to colonial violence, through partial reconstruction of these changing relations we can see better into the making of the oldest permanent colony in North America. This chapter traces the origins of Spanish-Ute relations and uncovers worlds made of violence throughout the early West.

The Founding of Spanish New Mexico

Spanish expeditions into the Southwest during the sixteenth century encountered various Great Basin peoples along the Colorado River, in northern New Mexico, and on the Plains. Throughout the century, as Spaniards ventured farther into the American interior, the Coronado, Espejo, and Oñate expeditions described various "Querechos" peoples who lived along the eastern fringes of the Rockies and seasonally migrated onto the Great Plains before the spread of the horse. In 1598 east of the Rio Grande, large parties of Indian "Vaqueros" met an offshoot of Juan de Oñate's party under Oñate's nephew, Vicente de Zaldívar. "They are powerful people and expert bowmen," reported Zaldívar, who lived off the "hundred thousand" of "cattle" northeast of New Mexico and journeyed to northern Pueblos to trade. Taken aback by the unfamiliar bison, the Spaniards attempted unsuccessfully to corral a large herd. "They are cattle terribly obstinate, courageous beyond exaggeration, and so cunning that if pursued they run," lamented Zaldívar. Disgusted with, yet fascinated by, these "marvelous and laughable" creatures, Zaldívar returned to the main expedition after noting the existence of more herds and "Vaqueros" to the north: "These cattle have their haunts on some very level mesas which extend over many leagues . . . The Indians are numerous in all that land. They live in rancherías in the hide tents . . . They always follow cattle . . . They kill them at the first shot with the greatest skill, while ambushed in brush made at the watering places."[5]

Seasonal migrations from the "very level mesas" of the Colorado Plateau onto the Plains characterized eastern Great Basin Indian life for generations before Spanish arrival. As bison migrated from mountain park valleys onto the Plains, Ute, Eastern Shoshone, and later Comanche Indians traveled in mobile communities, or *rancherías,* harvesting hides and meat for their long mountain winters as well as for trade. Throughout the seventeenth century, Spanish chroniclers classified these northern peoples in ever more specific ethnographic and political terms, often relying upon Pueblo informers whose communities had long-standing trading relations with northern Indians. Citizens of Jemez Pueblo, for example, had kinship ties with Pecos Pueblo—the "gateway to the Plains"—and offered Spanish friars valuable informants about the mysterious northern people who ventured into the colony. Gerónimo de Zárate Salmerón in his 1626 *Relaciones de las cosas de Nuevo México* identified several bands of "Gawuptuh," "Guaputa," and "Qusutas" peoples at Jemez. Salmerón also used the term "Yutas" for these different bands, a designation that subsequent Spanish chroniclers followed. Both Juan Amando Niel and Alonso de Posados in their chronicles of early New Mexico extended Salmerón's usage and also reclassified some of his generic "Querecho" and "Vaquero" references as "Yuttas" peoples. How exactly Niel and Posados made such connections is unclear; however, it is certain that at the time of Spanish colonization, the indigenous peoples to the north included different bands of "Yuttas" peoples, some of whom migrated seasonally while all began to learn about the Spanish newcomers to the south.[6]

The strangers to the south brought dramatic changes to the everyday lives of Native people as Spanish colonialism and its attendant forms of violence transformed the nature of indigenous social relations. Violence characterized Indian relations before Spanish conquest, but its use and destructive capacities remained comparatively localized before the arrival of Spanish-introduced metals, horses, and the ever more urgent necessity for all to acquire them.

Before conquest, violence remained a largely local phenomenon. While archaeologists demonstrate the prevalence of conflict within precontact communities, their research focuses chiefly on sedentary groups, like those who once lived at Chaco Canyon, Mesa Verde, and other "cliff-dwelling" communities. After contact, sedentary Indian communities entered into worlds of missionization and Spanish dominion; however, the region's migratory groups soon dominated the West's military affairs. The transformation, then, of migratory peoples within the expanding orbit of New Mexico remains both an essential and violent component of U.S. history, as the changes emanating from New Spain remained destructive to their core. Moreover, recent attempts to explain the course of Spanish-Indian relations through the lens of reconstructed precontact indigenous institutions have proved controversial because they minimize the diversity within both migratory and sedentary communities while also mitigating the violent shock waves accompanying colonial expansion, shock waves that obstruct current attempts to form an exact picture of precontact Native North America. Migratory peoples, like the Utes, and sedentary groups, like Pueblos, experienced colonialism in divergent ways, and while their standings within the emergent colonial order eventually overlapped, their initial encounters with Europeans were markedly different.[7]

Initially, Spanish military superiority, forms of punishment, and terror accomplished the subjugation of Pueblo communities, and to understand the dynamics of colonial violence outside the colony it is necessary first to consider the nature of Spanish violence against New Mexico's resident Indian communities. In 1599, to cite one well-known example, following Acoma Pueblo's resistance to Oñate's conquest, dozens of Acoma warriors had their feet publicly cut off in front of neighboring Pueblos, who had been assembled and ordered to witness their brethren's torture. Others were enslaved and sent south to Mexican mines, while Acoma children became personal servants to Spanish leaders. Such lessons were quickly learned and communicated as Pueblo families throughout the province coped with the many traumas of Spanish rule. Violence and terror also ordered settler society, underpinning complex codes of honor and patriarchy while also disciplining Spanish soldiers and Indian laborers from Mexico. The hands, for example, from two captured deserters from Oñate's expeditionary force were severed, preserved in salt, and brought back to the governor for display, while other deserters were rumored to have been beheaded. Such trophies initially reinforced colonial power and over time became institutionalized within more elaborate forms of social control.[8]

Despite subsequent debate about the form and extent of Spanish brutalities in the Southwest, colonial authorities clearly understood the importance of violence in solidifying colonial rule. Beginning with Oñate, all New Mexican governors attempted to arrogate the use of violence as their exclusive privilege, deploying public and ritualized violence to communicate their power. After subduing Acoma, for instance, Oñate continued consolidating his rule. Near the confluence of the Rio Grande and Chama Rivers, he dispossessed Pueblo Indians at San Gabriel and established his administrative center in their former homes. Where Pueblo parents and children had greeted the morning sun, the new governor and his men conversed in their foreign tongue, their shiny weapons propped against cool adobe walls. Oñate, further, levied punishing taxes from surrounding Pueblos and sent soldiers to collect tribute in the form of blankets, hides, or corn.

These and subsequent Spanish policies remained predicated on the threat of violence. Even if unused, Spanish muskets and swords stood ready for use against Indian bodies, and everywhere colonial authorities traveled, the potential for violence and pain followed. As in other parts of the Americas, the new regime made the threat of violence an ordinary part of colonial rule, and resisting rape, abuse, and punishment became everyday forms of resistance for resident Pueblo and soon neighboring Indian peoples.[9]

After conquest, the new Spanish colony incorporated Pueblo and surrounding Indian peoples into northern New Spain's primary economy—mining. Mexican mines constantly hungered for Indian labor and resources, and despite the distance, New Mexico provided mines with Indian-produced supplies as well as Indian slaves. Oñate's father, Cristóbal, had engineered the colonization of Zacatecas, the leading mining district in Mexico, and his more famous son extended northern Mexico's patterns of violence into the American Southwest. As in Mexico, Indian lands were expropriated for agriculture and ranching. Pueblo labor and tribute were allocated to Spanish officials and settlers, and both at the pueblos and in the new capital of Santa Fe, commercial workshops, or *obrajes,* used tribute and captive Indian labor. As John Kessell suggests, in these "bustling, dark, and dirty textile workshops at Santa Fe, unfree Apaches toiled alongside purported orphans and levies of Pueblo Indian laborers." Producing blankets and other marketable commodities such as hides, ropes, and leather, such forced-labor centers traded with Mexico's burgeoning mining districts.[10]

More and more, Indians themselves became profitable commodities throughout the colony. As also in Mexico, exiles from various missions, captives taken from outlying tribes, and others unfortunate enough to fall prey to Spanish slaving provided a steady stream of Indian slaves to the colony's settlements. As Ramón Gutiérrez argues, "For the Spaniards who so relished warfare, eschewed labor, and disdained the thought of commerce, Indian slavery was the only way they would realize dreams of lordship and leisure on the banks of the Rio Grande." As in other parts of the Americas, Spanish settlement and Indian slavery went hand in hand.[11]

The dreams of lordship and leisure particularly appealed to Governor Luis de Rosas. Arriving in Santa Fe in 1637, Rosas took over gubernatorial power from his troubled predecessor, Francisco Martínez de Baeza. Like many early governors, Baeza failed to satisfy both his own economic interests and the religious concerns of the Franciscan clergy, who objected to the enslavement of Indians, a practice that undermined their conversion efforts. Although the colony's ostensible purpose was to explore uncharted lands and to missionize Indians while protecting Mexico's northern border, many governors were more concerned with amassing fortune. Such wealth, Rosas realized, came only from Indian labor. Turning a deaf ear to incensed Franciscans, he pursued his own financial ends, establishing more Indian workshops, launching slave raids, and even jeopardizing frontier security by exacerbating Apache-Pueblo conflicts, all in order to oil the colony's economic wheels.[12]

With little concern for what happened beyond his four-year appointment, Rosas helped perpetuate cycles of violence that characterized the next century of Spanish-Indian relations as neighboring Navajos, Apaches, and more distant Indians bore the brunt of Spanish aggression. At an unrecorded location to the north, for example, he led a punitive slave campaign that brought previously unidentified Indians into the colony's violent orbit. According to a 1639 petition, Rosas launched "an unjust war against the 'Utaca' nation." This attack against people "from whom neither Spanish nor Christianized Indians [Pueblos] had received any injury . . . killed many and brought . . . eighty people in capture." Many of these captives ended up in Rosas' workshops, while others were taken farther from their homelands to Mexico's slave and mining centers.[13]

As the first documented encounter between Spanish and "Ute" Indians, Rosas' slave raid marks an appropriate and inauspicious beginning to Spanish-Indian relations in the Great Basin. "Unjustly" enslaved at the hands of Spanish soldiers, bands of Ute Indians over the next generations exacted punishing reprisals and conducted raids of their own against these violent newcomers. Skillfully adapting to the region's new violent economy, Utes soon became accomplished and dreaded antagonists. By the mid-1700s, their power over the colony's northwest would become unrivaled as Utes and their Comanche allies dominated New Mexico's perimeter, dispersing villages along both sides of the Rio Grande.

As in other zones of colonial encounters, Spanish colonialism reconfigured indigenous societies before their lands became the actual sites of colonization, linking imperial peripheries and colonies in dialectics of trade, enslavement, and warfare. Within such pandemic relations of violence, however, remained the seeds of both destruction and creation. For, just as New Spain needed Ute and other Indian slaves, Utes soon came to rely on New Mexico not just for trade but, ironically, for military protection. A little more than a century after Rosas' raid, an uneasy, fluctuating, yet ultimately enduring coexistence developed between Utes and New Mexicans as the exchange of goods, peoples, and knowledge altered both the boundaries and the distinctions between their societies. In this new world of perpetual and seemingly apocalyptic violence, deep-seated animosities remained unstrategic as the *realpolitik* of Spanish colonialism turned enemies into allies, former nemeses into needed friends. Utes survived the largely undocumented arrival of colonial violence into their homelands. Reorganizing and reorienting their societies, they endured by adopting the new technologies initiated by Spanish colonization, eventually carving out profitable roles within the colonial world. They became courted, feared, and powerful actors along this edge of empire and soon dictated the pace and scale of colonial expansion to the northwest. They helped to create and sustain, as some might suggest, "a middle ground" outside the reach of imperial power.[14]

While Utes did indeed become dominant actors in the Spanish borderlands, they often did so at the expense of their neighbors, particularly those without horses. The currents of colonialism prompted such dominion, as Ute privilege and accommodation carried high and deadly costs for others within New Mexico's growing orbit. As Utes and New Mexicans built forms of alliance in the second half of the 1700s, the relations of violence intrinsic to the region's political economy did not end. Instead, they became displaced onto more distant and, to the Spanish, unknown peoples, groups without horses, metal weaponry, and, most important, without the means to acquire them. Nonequestrian Great Basin Indians, now known as Southern Paiutes and Western Shoshones, became incorporated into the violent world of European colonialism by Utes, many of whom by 1800 lived in migratory slaving societies. The origins of such violence and trauma are found in the economies of violence engendered by Spanish intrusion.

For those who have struggled to reconcile visions of Indian-imperial accommodation with the levels of warfare and enslavement that were engulfing colonial America, the study of Great Basin Indian history may provide some insight. Indian peoples simultaneously could, and did, achieve coexistence and shared social relations with colonial societies. They often did so, however, through the subjugation of others and because of their own previous, violent experiences. Enmeshed within the painful fabric of global colonialism, Great Basin Indians shaped the world around them, doing so under conditions not of their choosing.

The "Yutas" Peoples to the North

Powerful though the Spanish were following Oñate's conquest, they did not have military supremacy throughout New Mexico. Besides, they had another, less costly path for gaining wealth: they had trade. While conquest and colonial authority rested upon the use and threat of violence, perpetual conflict crippled Spanish rule. Despite the greed-driven activities of select governors such as Rosas, most Spanish settlers, clergy, soldiers, as well as governors attempted to mitigate the cycles of violence swirling around them. Unleashing, often unknowingly, microbes, technologies, and motivations, colonial leaders attempted as best they could to minimize disruption. The reins of imperial control, however, often slipped through their fingers; throughout the 1600s, the inability of the Spanish regime to quell Indian raids underscored the unstable and paradoxical nature of colonialism in northern New Spain. Spanish authority necessitated force and brutality, but the technologies of violence needed for colonial rule could be neither fully regulated nor monopolized. The monopolization of violence, a prerequisite for colonial authority, remained elusive. While the distribution of guns and ammunition was monitored, the spread of metals and especially horses was not.[15]

Unable to restrict the flow of goods or fully defend the colony's borders, Spanish leaders attempted to incorporate surrounding nations into trading and political alliances. It became far easier to trade with neighboring Indians than it was to destroy them, especially after surrounding communities had withstood the displacement of colonial violence and assimilated Spanish technologies of violence into their societies. Once allied with Spanish leaders through trade and diplomacy,

powerful Indian "allies" could also more easily obtain the new resources that had become essential to their survival. Over time, the
most effective forms of revenue in the province came from the incorporation of distant Indian peoples into the empire as traders, allies,
consumers, as well as potential slavers. Although the first century of
Spanish rule included countless examples of Spanish brutality, the
New Mexican economy came to rest on the numerous trading relations conducted with local and distant Indians.[16]

For neighboring Indians, these new trading relations became lifelines. Spanish-introduced metals, tools, weapons, and horses augmented
and replaced previous weaponry, currency, and transportation. They
became the oxygen for the community body's survival. Acquiring
these items, however, required tremendous and often violent labor;
for, by offering new trade items, the Spanish provided powerful incentives to those who most consistently brought in items of worth, most
notably slaves, horses, and hides, as the competition both to trade and
to raid reshaped Indian economies. As a result, intense militarization
and internecine warfare accompanied Spanish trade goods out of the
colony, plunging New Mexico's expanding hinterlands into conflict.[17]

While Pueblo Indians received certain legal protections from the
Spanish, outlying tribes had only their own strength and numbers
for protection. As Elizabeth John states, "Missionaries vigorously protested the enslavement of Indians and could largely protect their
Pueblo charges from that illegal fate, but no power on the northern
frontier could prevent the enslavement of 'wild' Indians." These *indios
bárbaros* had to defend themselves not only against Spanish slave incursions but also against each other as raids, counterraids, reprisals, and
counterreprisals came to plague every Indian society throughout the
region. Violent cycles of destructive frontier relations characterized
New Mexico's relations with Native peoples throughout the colonial
era and affected the subsequent course of Indian relations with Mexican and American republics. Generally unrecorded, such warfare and
conflict brought heightened levels of trauma to the everyday lives of
Native peoples throughout the early West.[18]

In the seventeenth century, different Athapaskan-speaking peoples,
referred to as "Vaqueros Apaches" and "Apaches Navajos," appeared
on both ends of the violent spectrum of Spanish slavery, raiding
Pueblos and Spanish settlements while falling prey to Spanish military

expeditions. In the 1650s, for instance, Navajos attacked Jemez Pueblo, killing 19 and capturing 35. New Mexican governor Juan de Samaniego y Xaca responded by invading Navajo territories to the west, killing countless warriors and enslaving 211. While many Athapaskan groups traded with both the Spanish and the Pueblos, the increasing raids and reprisals eroded the little confidence between these codependent yet antagonistic neighbors. Governor Bernardo López de Mendizábal in the 1660s, for example, murdered peaceful Navajo traders who had come to trade at Jemez, enslaving their women and children, and did the same to unsuspecting Apaches at Taos. Carrying campaigns into Apache and Navajo homelands, Mendizábal sold hundreds of slaves to the south. By January 1664, Apache and Navajo reprisals had become so fierce that then Governor Diego Dionisio de Peñalosa Bricezo y Burdiso forbade the entrance of any *bárbaros* into the colony, thereby further eroding the prospects for peaceful exchange while enhancing incentives for raiding.[19]

It was within this world of valued trade items, Spanish and equestrian raids, as well as unrecorded diseases that the "Yutas" peoples of the north struggled to survive. As more Apaches and Navajos obtained Spanish metals and horses, Utes had to contend with powerful Native peoples in addition to the Spanish on their southern borders. They also faced powerful Plains and mountain peoples to their east and north, respectively. With few sources remaining from the seventeenth century, only brief glimpses of their dramatic struggles remain.[20]

Most scholars agree that trading and warfare increased throughout Ute homelands in the 1600s. Besides Salmerón in 1626, Alonso de Posados, who served as Franciscan custodian of New Mexico from 1661 to 1665, provided brief but telling mentions of the lands and peoples to the north. Posados described a northern "kingdom and province which we call Teguayo":

> Crossing the said Grande River [San Juan] one enters the nation of the Yutas. Crossing this nation some 60 leagues in the same northwesterly direction one arrives at some hilly country; through this 50 leagues more or less one arrives at the land which the Indians of the north call Teguayo . . . There are many people and diverse nations in Teguayo . . . all the nations to the north affirm it, especially an Indian named Don Juanillo from the town of Jemez. When I was minister of that frontier

he told me several times of having been prisoner in the said provinces
. . . and that there are many people in the region.

Like Salmerón before him, Posados learned from Pueblo informants
about the cultural diversity along the northern frontier. Posados also
began identifying political and territorial distinctions among these
indios bárbaros. Noting also the presence of slavery, he described lands
and peoples outside the colony's immediate physical borders but already part of its growing consciousness.[21]

In his *Apuntamientos que a las Memorias del P. Fr. Gerónimo de Zárate
Salmerón,* Father Juan Amando Niel analyzed Salmerón's 1626 *Relaciones* and determined that many of Salmerón's "Vaqueros" were Utes
rather than Apaches. Additionally, Niel noted that these "Yuttas" traveled in large bands of up to a thousand, divided into squadrons for
protection, with the elderly and young in the center, and used dog
travois and horses to help carry their many supplies. Niel's reference
to the introduction of the horse corresponds with scholars' estimates
for its initial dispersion during the 1640s and 1650s and also sheds
light on other changes occurring throughout the easternmost regions
of the Great Basin.[22]

Besides the adoption of the horse as an initial supplementary form
of transportation, the band organization and military travel formation
indicated by Niel signal examples of Ute adaptation to colonial disruptions. Both suggest an increased prevalence of warfare in the region.
With Rosas' slave raid in living memory, Utes responded to the escalation of conflict in their homelands with the best deterrent they could
muster: numerical strength. Anthropologists have long argued that
small-scale band organization remained the predominant form of social organization for Utes into the contact period. Niel's reference
implies that such small-scale bands consolidated, at least temporarily,
into larger forms of political and military organization. Summarizing
Niel's findings, S. Lyman Tyler states: "As these groups traveled they
marched in squadrons or files. The women went in files at the front
and along the sides of each squadron, carrying shields made of three
thickness buffalo hide stretched over a frame . . . Close by the
women, and also in files, went the men with their weapons in hand
and ready for use." Such increased militarization and mobilization in-
dicate heightened violence and warfare in Ute homelands, not only

against the Spanish but also against Navajo, Apache, and even Pueblo raiders.[23]

Although most of the earliest references to Utes came from missionaries, colonial authorities noticed their increasing power throughout the last decades of the seventeenth century. Governor Antonio de Otermín, for example, referred to the Utes in his report to New Spain's viceroy in the aftermath of the 1680 Pueblo Revolt, when allied Pueblo groups expelled the Spanish for over a decade. Writing from his refuge in El Paso, Otermín detailed how for several years before the uprising frontier relations to the north had calmed. New Mexico, Otermín reported, had "finally found itself . . . at least in more peace and tranquility than had been experienced in these parts for many years, and on the eve of having more than ever, with the hopes of the reduction to our holy faith of the innumerable and warlike nation of the Yutas, assured by the strong friendship and union that we have had in the period of three years during which we have been treating with them." Otermín's acknowledgment that the Spanish had "been treating with them" in "strong friendship and union" referred to formalized trading relations with unspecified Ute bands. Like surrounding Apache and Navajo groups, Utes attempted to acquire Spanish goods as well as favor, and Ute leaders ventured to northern New Mexico trade fairs to court Spanish authorities. They even agreed to accept missionaries into their communities to hear of the Spaniards' "holy faith" while expecting open and fair markets for Ute trade goods. Although the precise nature of this partnership remains unclear, Spanish and Utes achieved a three-year period of coexistence before the revolt.[24]

Entering into treaty relations with the Spanish brought privileges in addition to trade. Spanish military protection ensured safe and easy travel into the province as well as potential aid in the recurring wars in the north; soldiers often accompanied Spanish friars in their travels to distant encamped Indian villages. Many Apache groups on the borders of the colony had extracted such protection, and they reminded Spanish leaders of their pledged assistance in times of need. By wedding their communities to New Mexico, different Native groups attempted to mitigate the cycles of violence engulfing their homelands, and the Utes in the late seventeenth century saw the Spanish similarly, as inhospitable yet powerful and potentially malleable newcomers. With

Rosas' slave raid and other treacheries in living memory, these Utes needed Spanish goods and protection, and they now shared forms of economic, military, and social relations with New Mexico. Utes accepted Spanish traders and soldiers into their territory, while Spanish authorities welcomed Ute traders to the northern Pueblos and trade fairs.[25]

Such moments of Spanish-Ute accommodation would not endure. The 1680 Pueblo Revolt reconfigured not only Spanish-Ute relations but also the political landscape of New Mexico. Deposing Otermín, chasing Spanish settlers and soldiers out of Santa Fe, and sacking churches and settlements, Pueblo communities regained autonomy lost during Spanish rule. They enjoyed renewed religious freedoms, had greater mobility and communication, and no longer faced imposed economic and labor drafts. Pueblo women were no longer subject to Spanish sexual abuse, and parents raised their children without the scrutiny of Spanish friars.[26]

This reprieve from Spanish colonialism, however, by no means led to a reduction of violence in the region; instead, throughout the 1680s, surrounding Indian peoples, who had endured decades of perpetual warfare on New Mexico's frontiers, used the Spanish absence to enhance their own fortunes. Apaches, Navajos, Utes, and more distant Great Plains groups intensified their raids into the province. Raiders came primarily for horses and possibly to regain former captives. During the Spanish absence, the region's cycles of violence continued as competing Native powers vied for supremacy and survival.[27]

As Pueblo communities paradoxically became more susceptible to equestrian attacks, they responded in kind. Equipped now with seized Spanish arms, armor, and horses, Pueblo groups, like the Spanish before them, initiated military campaigns of their own against surrounding Indian communities. They traveled in mobile equestrian units, used Spanish military technologies and strategies, and combined such advantages with their existing familiarity with the land to deal crippling blows to their adversaries. Such reprisals, however, could not entirely eliminate outside raids. Horses, metals, and other trade items had become so intrinsic to survival that no amount of retribution could extinguish the need to raid. After the revolt, then, raiders increasingly targeted Pueblo horses and herds, so much so that by the dawn of the eighteenth century the horse had spread throughout the

West into distant regions unknown to colonial authorities. No matter how extensive or aggressive Pueblo reprisals, their communities attracted raids. Without the protection of Spanish soldiers and home to critically need supplies, Pueblos endured repeated invasions as Utes, Navajos, Apaches, and other Indian newcomers besieged the northern Rio Grande.[28]

In 1693 the Spanish reentered this world of internecine indigenous warfare. To the north, after retaking Santa Fe, Diego Vargas and his expeditionary force sacked Taos Pueblo in the summer of 1694 both to punish Pueblo inhabitants and to feed his troops. Fearing Pueblo reprisals along the return to Santa Fe, Vargas decided to head north along the Rio Grande, move west to the Chama River, and then descend toward Santa Fe through more open territory. Vargas knew that former Spanish allies, including Utes along the present-day Colorado border, might also come to his aid, and on July 8 he recorded: "in order that the Utes, whom we are seeking, may know of our arrival . . . I ordered that large smoke signals be raised." Traveling through the territory of their former allies, Vargas hoped for renewed Ute hospitality and alliance. His hopes were never fully realized; as his party encamped along the San Antonio River, it was ambushed by Utes. After a brief skirmish, the Utes retreated across the river, signaling for peace. Reminding a startled Vargas of their previous friendship, the Utes apologized for their attack, stating that they had mistaken the Spanish for their enemies—Tewa, Tano, Picuris, Jemez, and Taos Pueblo warriors—who had recently invaded their territory dressed in Spanish armor and hats and mounted on horses. Receiving some of the stolen food from Taos as well as other gifts, the Utes reacquainted themselves with the Spanish after fourteen years of separation, and the meeting ended with Vargas inviting Ute leaders to Santa Fe "as had been their custom prior to 1680."[29]

Vargas' expedition provides a useful window into Ute-Pueblo relations during the years of Spanish absence. Utes raided from Hopi mesas in Arizona to the Rio Grande, and Pueblos responded with campaigns of their own. The Spanish absence, moreover, reshaped Ute diplomacy in response to new exigencies. For more than twelve years, Utes wondered when and, more important, whether the Spanish would return, and with each passing year they increased their raids against Pueblo communities. As Vargas noted, against "the Tewa,

Tano, Taos, Picuris, Jemez, and Keres nations," Utes "have continued the war against those nations with great vigor." During the Spanish absence, then, Utes gained not only greater knowledge of the region but also increased confidence in their capacity to attack settlements along the Rio Grande.[30]

Armed only with "bows and arrows and warclubs," Utes were no match for Vargas' forces. They also fared poorly against raiding Pueblo warriors, who, according to Vargas, "had often come to this region to hunt buffalo disguised as Spaniards, mounted, and with leather jackets [armor], leather hats [helmets], firearms, and even a bugle." Nonetheless, despite such comparative disadvantages, Utes continued raiding in even greater capacity in the ensuing years. Also noting the presence of Apaches, whom "the Ute nation . . . does not countenance . . . in their land," Vargas entered lands abundant with game as well as contested by Indian rivals.[31]

While some Utes took up their former trading relations with the returned Spanish, others escalated their raids. Despite their long-standing hatred of the Spanish, many Pueblos welcomed renewed protection. New Spanish settlements and frontier outposts were established as garrisons moved to quell remaining resistance and to protect villages against equestrian attack. In April 1696, for example, near the confluence of the Chama and Rio Grande, Vargas led a procession of settlers to the former Tanos Pueblo and established the village of Santa Cruz, then the northernmost Spanish settlement on the continent. Gathering the sixty-six families around the chapel of the former pueblo, he led the assembly in rejoicing: "Long live the King, our Master, may God spare him, Señor Don Carlos the second, King of the Spains and of all this New World, and of this new villa which is founded in his royal name." Despite the initial enthusiasm, settlers at Santa Cruz soon suffered Ute and Apache raids that forced its near abandonment in 1703.[32]

The reestablished Spanish colony faced not only recurring raids but also renewed threats of rebellion. Numerous reports of Pueblo plots as well as Pueblo–Plains Indian alliances surfaced following the Reconquista. Vargas, for instance, discovered and subverted a Jemez-Acoma plot involving equestrian groups in 1696 and skillfully played upon Pueblo divisions to consolidate colonial rule by 1700. Regions outside the immediate vicinity of Spanish settlements, however, remained beyond control. Moments of peaceful coexistence and trading relations with neighboring Indians continued to be disrupted by raids, reprisals, and counterattacks from all sides.[33]

The northern lands surrounding the reestablished Spanish colony remained not only outside Spanish political and military control but also generally beyond the realm of Spanish knowledge. In 1700 the northern peoples and lands were unmapped, unexplored, and generally unknown to Spanish authorities. While the seventeenth-century reports of missionaries and of governors such as Otermín produced residual traces of Indian interactions, twelve years of Spanish absence and the changes wrought by the revolt left the political topography of northern New Mexico reconfigured in new ways.[34]

In the first decade of the new century, Spanish campaigns brought back important news of changing northern developments. In 1706, during a campaign to the Apache town of El Cuartelejo near the present-day Colorado-Kansas border, Juan de Ulibarri learned of an alliance between Utes and a new people, the Comanche. En route to the Apache *ranchería,* he heard rumors of an impending Ute-Comanche attack at Taos. Along the Arkansas River in Colorado, the party met Apache warriors moving to fight Utes and Comanches, and on their return to Santa Fe the Spaniards camped among Jicarilla Apaches who were recovering from recent Ute-Comanche raids. Unknown to the Spanish before the Pueblo Revolt, the Comanche newcomers now fought alongside their Ute allies for control of the north, and within a generation their joint raids would further reconfigure the composition of New Mexico. Utes and Comanches together soon dominated New Spain's northernmost hinterlands. In response to the displacement of colonial violence upon their societies, these related Indians formed the region's most powerful indigenous alliance.[35]

The Ute-Comanche Alliance

As with the Utes, Comanche origins in New Mexico remain unknown. Linguistically, Comanches and Utes speak related Shoshonean dialects and once shared similar cultural practices and institutions. According to anthropologists, loosely affiliated Comanche bands migrated out of the eastern Great Basin onto the Plains in the sixteenth century. The spread of the horse in the seventeenth century accelerated their territorial expansion, consolidated their band structure, and brought them into contact with the Utes. Facing new enemies, Ute bands needed allies while Comanche groups at distance from New Mexico needed trading partners and trading goods, and all the earliest references to Comanches also specifically mention Utes. Comanches now accepted Ute invitations to join them at trade fairs, followed Ute trails in and out of New Mexico, and learned the customs of their Ute guides, Spanish hosts, and Pueblo traders. Indeed, Comanche familiarity with northern New Spain would only grow, and these "lords of the South Plains" soon controlled more territory than any other equestrian people.[36]

Although strategic self-interest and preexisting linguistic commonalities drew Utes and Comanches together, such explanations of the origins of their alliance must also acknowledge the heightened cycles of violence affecting these societies. As trade networks and goods militarized their societies, Indian communities faced growing pressures that increasingly prompted violent decisions. In 1694, for instance, a Navajo trading party journeyed onto the Plains and returned with dozens of captives to sell. When the Spanish balked, the Navajo traders grew so enraged that they reportedly beheaded the captives in front of their Spanish hosts. As Alfred Barnaby Thomas states, "The atrocity so shocked the Spanish king that he ordered thereafter the use of royal funds to save such unfortunates." These "unfortunates," however, remained only a symptom of larger relations of violence that both drew and compelled equestrians into the region. In search of trade goods, particularly horses, northern peoples came.[37]

Bolstered by their early raids, Utes and Comanches increased their control at the expense of surrounding Indian peoples. As Ulibarri reported, Apache communities at La Jicarilla, El Cuartelejo, and other sedentary villages northeast of Santa Fe faced repeated alliance attacks. To the northwest, Navajo raids along the Chama and Rio Grande dropped off as Utes and Comanches fanned into the province. Coupled with Captain Roque de Madrid's campaigns against the Navajo in 1705 and 1709, Ute-Comanche presence curbed Navajo movements into the province, leading one historian to conclude:

An unprecedented period of peace, lasting more than fifty years, followed the campaigns of 1709. During this time, known Spanish documents record not a single Navajo raid upon Spanish settlement. Occasional depredations by Navajos against their Pueblo neighbors . . . resulted in punitive expeditions by Spanish and Pueblo forces, but the Navajo clearly and earnestly wished no war with the Spaniards. Indeed, their desire for peace went deeper: they wanted Spanish protection against a deadly alliance.

The scourge of seventeenth-century New Mexico, Navajos and Apaches no longer dominated the north and now turned to the Spanish and to each other for protection against this new and "deadly alliance."[38]

Coming to trade at the northern pueblos, Utes and Comanches often also made off with food, horses, and captives. While trading and raiding appear antithetical—the former as peaceful exchange, the latter as violent seizure—in colonial New Mexico trading and raiding represented complementary sides of the violent equation of Spanish-Indian relations. Northern Pueblos such as Taos, Picuris, and Pecos held growing trading fairs that attracted northern peoples. Bringing slaves, horses, hides, foods, and other items to trade, surrounding Indian peoples often quarreled with their hosts over fair and equitable exchange. Since trade goods represented lifelines for these communities, all traders, Pueblo hosts, and New Mexican entrepreneurs recognized the importance and potential severity of these exchanges. Spanish authorities, accordingly, attempted to regulate these negotiations in order to quell potential violence. In 1714, for instance, Governor Juan Ignacio de Mogollón intervened in a dispute at Taos between local Pueblos and Utes, ordering the Utes to return stolen property, which they did rather than risk bloodshed. Such instances of resolution and nonviolent exchange, however, by no means signaled sustained peaceful relations, as aggrieved Indian parties often pillaged settlements and Pueblos on their return. All who journeyed to New Mexico to trade also had the capacity to raid, and sometimes they did both. These traders thus provoked anxiety as they moved through the mountain passes toward the colony's settlements.[39]

Coming into trade, Ute and Comanche bands also increased their raids throughout the first decades of the eighteenth century. In 1716, while Governor Félix Martínez was visiting Zuni and Hopi Pueblos, Utes and Comanches attacked again, and at Taos, *alcalde mayor* Cristóbal Tafoya rushed two reports to Martínez. The first stated: "the Indians of the Yutas have taken from said pueblo the greater number of their horses and a herd of mares . . . and . . . [Tafoya] is starting in their pursuit." Any optimism was dashed by the second letter, which relayed that Tafoya's reprisal forces "pursued them up to the hill called San Antonio where, he says, the said Yutas were camping and that he did not dare to enter there because their people were many and ours few."[40]

Following Martínez's return, additional reports of alliance depredations came into the Governor's Palace, prompting the governor to call together the region's leading settlers to decide how to punish these alliance members. "I have decided to have a council of war," he wrote. The council's mandate: "whether or not I should declare war against them." Following its decision to retaliate, Martínez's secretary of war, Félix de la Serna, marched north and "attacked the foe at the Cerro de San Antonio, thirty leagues north of Santa Fe," capturing dozens and killing more. "The captives were divided between Don Félix and his brother, and sold on joint account in Nueva Vizcaya." Spanish authorities diverted subsequent Ute inquiries into the whereabouts of their family members with lies, reporting them dead from smallpox.[41]

As the second recorded slave raid against identifiable Utes, Serna's campaign provides another brief glimpse of the heightened warfare engulfing Ute and Comanche communities. The death of dozens and the enslavement of others invariably reconfigured social relations within this decimated Ute *ranchería*, forcing many to migrate to neighboring villages or bands. Such losses reveal how brutalities on all sides now characterized Spanish-Ute relations, because, though violent, Serna's campaign failed to halt Ute-Comanche advances. In fact it only exacerbated Ute and Comanche raids. Soon alliance reprisals would fuel the need for settlement protection while compelling governors to curtail all trading in the north. Aware of the alliance's dependency on trade goods, Governor Mogollón, for instance, in 1712 had banned trading parties out of the province. Others required written permission for the sale and removal of any horses and forbade the sale of any weapons, armor, or ammunition by garrison soldiers, who, like New Mexican governors, often came north for short terms and to line their pockets.[42]

Such were the dialectics of raid and reprisal. Within two decades of Vargas' Reconquista, Utes and Comanches had driven Navajos and Apaches into alliance with New Mexico, secured access to territories from which to launch their attacks, and prompted Spanish retaliatory campaigns. They now controlled horses by the hundreds, if not thousands, and inhabited the homelands of their enemies. In the next generation they consolidated their dominance further, besieging Native and settler communities alike. In fact, in the next decades Ute and Comanche warriors redrew the colony's landscape. By midcentury their raids had become so severe that centuries-old Apache trading centers north of Taos along the Arkansas and Canadian watersheds were forever displaced. Never again would Indians live in horticultural villages

New Mexican Indian militia. Courtesy of the Museum of New Mexico, Santa Fe. Known as Segesser I, an extraordinary hide painting of an unidentifiable battle offers insight into the internecine forms of indigenous warfare sweeping across the American continent. The attackers' use of Spanish armor, horses, and metals gives them a clear advantage over the defenders. Probably commissioned by Governor Antonio Valverde y Cosío in the 1720s, Segesser I provides the earliest known visual representation of the displacement achieved by Spanish colonial violence.

along these rivers; the descendants of these communities soon became among the first diasporic peoples of the Southwest. Ute and Comanche control in the north, in short, became unparalleled.

As Utes and Comanches fanned into New Mexico, they attempted to dislodge Spanish settlements and allied Indian villages that provided buffers against their raids. Apache communities northeast of Taos became particularly vulnerable because they were outside the sphere of Spanish settlement. In the early 1700s alliance raids prompted increased Apache alliance with New Mexico. In 1718, for example, as Jicarillas fled into Taos, one priest pleaded their cause to the viceroy in Mexico City: "A tribe of heathen Apache, a nation widely scattered in these parts . . . have come to ask for holy baptism." Requests for baptism meant allegiance not only to the cross but also to the crown, which provided protection, and New Spain's Viceroy Marqués de Valero responded enthusiastically: "Let a dispatch be prepared for the governor ordering him to employ with the greatest efficiency all his care to allure and entertain them extensively . . . Warn him that it is necessary to hold this nation because of the hostilities which the French have launched among the Tejas . . . As the Apache nation aided by ourselves could inflict considerable damage on the French . . . the governor must assist with all the people he can." Fleeing from their homelands, refugee Apaches soon became crucial Spanish allies in the escalating conflicts in the north.[43]

As the viceroy indicated, tensions in the north came not only from Indians but also from French rivals, and as imperial rivalries unfolded throughout North America, Indians became central actors in European contests. Since Indians controlled the majority of territory between scattered colonial settlements, their movements and potential alliances, not only with each other but also with other powers, concerned the Spanish crown. "The right combination of Indians and Frenchmen," as David Weber states, "could easily destroy New Mexico," and in the first decades of the 1700s the Ute-Comanche alliance represented such a threat. Their growing power now drew Spanish troops north, soon prompting a calamity for New Mexico and its expectant Apache allies.[44]

In August 1719, additional reports of alliance raids and murder arrived. The *alcalde mayor* of Taos, Miguel Thenorio de Alva, reported that "on the eighth day of the present month ten Indians, Utes, came upon Diego Romero, a Coyote, and shot him with arrows," nearly killing him. That evening the same group "ran off four animals and a boy belonging to Captain Xptoval de la Serna." As Father Juan de la Cruz, also of Taos, added, "all that valley of Taos is harassed by a growing number of Utes." At Cochiti, Father Manuel de la Pena reported the murder of a Cochiti Indian by twenty Utes; a company with forty Pueblo soldiers pursued the party north, where "they found the tracks of the Utes, some hundred Indian [*sic*] more or less, and six tracks of women and of dogs which they were using." Traveling in semi-equestrian groups of at least a hundred and raiding in parties of ten and twenty, Ute raiders infiltrated the colony's porous borders. These raids convinced Governor Antonio Valverde y Cosío once again to "command the military chiefs and the rest of the intelligent and experienced settlers . . . in a council of war . . . to give me, each one, his opinion" on whether or not to declare war on the alliance.[45]

Ute and Comanche raids had again forced a meeting of the leading Spanish men in New Mexico. Arriving from Taos, Santa Cruz, Cochiti, and other northern settlements, twenty-eight military chiefs and "intelligent and experienced settlers" testified before Valverde's war council. Each acknowledged the gravity of the situation. Sergeant Juan de Pineda of Santa Fe, for one, argued that "war should be made upon the Indians of the Ute nation . . . [For] they intend to destroy [Taos] and . . . they may go on to more excesses." Echoing similar sentiments, twenty-six of the twenty-eight gathered agreed to the governor's request for war "upon the Ute nation and Comanche nations, who, always united, have been committing robberies." Summing up the council's thinking, Governor Valverde wrote: "It appears to all, since their own lands are more than two hundred leagues away from this kingdom . . . they are coming to attack us on sight . . . I concur with the opinions that war should be made upon them . . . that they may be driven to their lands, and these frontiers freed." Recruiting a force of Spanish settlers and Pueblo auxiliaries, the governor assumed personal command of the campaign.[46]

Deliberations within Valverde's war council revealed a wealth of information about alliance relations. So too did the governor's fall campaign that "numbered some six hundred with as many horses," be-

fore swelling larger as it incorporated refugee Apaches, including Sierra Blanca Chief Carlana, who recounted his people's plight to the
governor: "he had come fleeing from his country . . . with half his
peoples . . . because of the continual war that the Ute and Comanche
make upon them." Responding enthusiastically to invitations to join
the campaign, Carlana soon grew impatient as the massive force
inched along the eastern slopes of the Rockies, finding evidence of recent alliance forces but unable to engage them. Carlana, Valverde
reported, expressed "great irritation . . . in not having found the enemy . . . He wanted the enemy restrained from the attacks they
were making each day on his rancherías, killing many and capturing
women and children." Carlana's "irritation" would only grow as alliance *rancherías* retreated before the slow New Mexican advance.[47]

In the final days of the campaign, Valverde learned of an Apache
who was recovering from a gunshot wound received not from Utes or
Comanches—who did not yet possess firearms—but from French soldiers from the Mississippi. Showing the governor his wound, the victim
"answered that while he and his people were in his land . . . the
French, united with the Pawnees and the Jumanos, attacked them
from ambush while they were planting corn." French colonists were
rumored to have "built two large pueblos, each of which is as large as
that of Taos," somewhere on the Plains. With the looming outbreak of
the War of the Quadruple Alliance, French threats to New Mexico created much worry throughout New Spain, and soon French-Spanish engagements brought major setbacks in New Mexico's defenses—setbacks that ultimately contributed to the abandonment of all Apache
communities northeast of Santa Fe and to the escalation of Ute and
Comanche attacks from that region.[48]

After Valverde's return in 1719, the viceroy ordered him to establish
a *presidio* and mission among the El Cuartelejo Apaches. Arguing that
the distance was too great and the surrounding enemies too many,
Valverde suggested that La Jicarilla was a closer, more appropriate can-
didate for colonization. Dreams of expanding New Mexico, however,
were soon dashed after the defeat of Pedro de Villasur, Valverde's lieu-
tenant-general. Ordered in 1720 to travel north to engage the French
and their Indian allies, Villasur and his cadre of Pueblo auxiliaries
were routed by a Pawnee-French ambush near the junctions of the

Platte and Loup Rivers in present-day Nebraska. The setback cost New Mexico thirty-two soldiers, a third of the trained Spanish garrison of New Mexico, and a dozen Pueblo warriors. The defeat crippled New Mexico's defenses and curbed all plans to expand. The Villasur setback along with the end of war in Europe left the Plains northeast of New Mexico outside European imperial control, contested by Utes, Comanches, and besieged Apaches.[49]

News of the Villasur debacle spread quickly throughout New Spain. In addition to the loss of life, "what grieves me most," lamented Valverde, "is the need for thirty men, the best trained and most experienced in the engagements of this warfare which is constantly active in this kingdom. The great number of heathen, the Utes [and] Comanches . . . invade the kingdom with death and robbery." Upon receiving news of the setback, Viceroy Valero ordered an inquiry into the causes of the defeat as well as ways to stabilize the northern regions.[50]

In the wake of Villasur's defeat, Spanish officials began debating the future of New Mexico's northern frontier. Initially many agreed with Valverde's proposal to missionize the Jicarilla. Juan de Olvian Revolledo, New Spain's auditor of war, recognized that nomadic groups "can without impediment penetrate into [New Mexico] if our allies, the Carlana Apaches, do not block their passage." Apache delegations also came to Santa Fe, recounted sorrowful tales of alliance raids, and pleaded for assistance. Governors such as Carlos de Bustamante visited La Jicarilla, witnessed the extent of Apache sufferings, and urged the viceroy to establish the needed garrison. "The nations Ute and Comanche had attacked them a second time," Bustamante reported to the new viceroy, "and abducted [sixty-four of] their women and children." Unlike Valverde, Bustamante would lead a successful campaign against the alliance, taking an untold number of captives and lives.[51]

As the Spanish debated to colonize La Jicarilla, Apaches endured the wars of the north. A Jicarilla delegation offered the following assessment: "They have decided, since their persons are not being protected, to go to the province of the Navajos," who shared similar grievances against the alliance. Such Jicarilla resettlement, Bustamante worried, would complicate colonization efforts, particularly as royal envoys questioned the piousness of New Mexico's recently won Apache allies. In 1727 New Spain's *visitador*, Pedro de Rivera, inspected the northern frontier and issued his recommendations to the viceroy. Noting the proximity of the Apache communities to Taos, Rivera wrote: "there is not a case of baptism [in Taos] because it is so obvious, that they have no other aim than the purpose of their safety" in requesting missionization. "Safety," Rivera concluded, was insufficient grounds for colonization. "With the cost alone of the tools and the corn," he suggested, "they could be settled in the cited spot [near Taos] at the greatest security for them and without the increased expenditure . . . of a *presidio*."[52]

In November 1727 Bustamante journeyed over the mountain passes to La Jicarilla. Carrying the burden of Rivera's recommendations, he informed these loyal allies of their fate. They could either move to New Mexico or stay at La Jicarilla and El Cuartelejo and endure Ute and Comanche onslaughts. Having served as scouts, traders, and repeated hosts, these Jicarillas undoubtedly felt betrayed. But permanent settlements beyond the protection of Spanish soldiers had now become untenable, and the Apache had little hope of remaining in their homelands. After Bustamante's visit and Rivera's report, the Jicarillas abandoned their cornfields and adobe homes and "came to live near Pecos and about 12 miles north of Taos, where a mission was briefly established among them in 1733. Soon after, however, the greater part fled . . . though the remnants joined the Taos against the Comanches."[53]

The abandonment of La Jicarilla and shortly thereafter of El Cuartelejo signaled the end of sedentary communities northeast of New Mexico, and Pecos, Picuris, and Taos Pueblos now endured the brunt of Ute-Comanche attacks. Historians have long questioned the reasoning of Rivera's recommendations. As Alfred Thomas states, "Rivera . . . was apparently oblivious to the fact that the Jicarillas were in effect a buffer in the northeast between the Utes and Comanches and Spanish New Mexico . . . Later governors . . . lamented the disappearance of the Jicarillas and the use of their lands by the Comanches as a raiding base against the Pueblos and Spanish towns." While events along this imperial periphery may appear tangential to the machinations of the world's largest empire, viewed from the perspective of the Indian communities that saw their warriors killed, women and children enslaved, and pleas for protection unheeded, such attacks represented the end of their former lives. Deliberations in Santa Fe and

Mexico City, let alone in Spain, were of little comfort for these Apache "remnants" who moved out of their homelands to seek stable lives along this violent edge of empire.[54]

The Last Years of the Ute-Comanche Alliance

While Ute and Comanche raids in and around New Mexico are visible in Spanish sources, the same is not true of Spanish and Native reprisals. While some governors, such as Valverde, kept detailed accounts of their expeditions, most did not, or their accounts have not survived. Rosas (1639), Serna (1716), and Bustamante (1724), for example, all led campaigns against Utes, returning collectively with hundreds of captives while killing countless others; however, few details of these conflicts endure. No precise locations, dates, or even numbers engaged tell us about these conflicts. As in much of early Western history, mystery shrouds these encounters.[55]

On a few occasions, Spanish authorities recorded moments from the internecine conflict swirling throughout the north. Like New Mexicans, Apache communities retaliated as best they could. Sometimes they had success. In 1726, for example, Bustamante recounted to the viceroy, the Marqués de Casa Fuerte, that Apache allies had returned to New Mexico with "prisoners who were Comanches . . . a great force of Apaches . . . [went] to look for the Comanches to see if they could force them to leave these regions." Successful in enslaving some, Apaches could never force the alliance out of the region.[56]

Ute and Comanche captives also begin appearing in colonial records from this period, a fact suggesting an increased traffic in alliance members. In 1725 an unidentified Ute was married at El Paso del Norte to another captive. In 1733 another unidentified Ute captive along with other *genízaros* (a term applied generally to exiled Indians, ransomed captives, prisoners of war, and their children) appeared in a court case brought before Governor Gervasio Cruzat y Góngora. This specific group of "detribalized Indians," according to Malcolm Ebright, had unsuccessfully petitioned the governor for lands at Belen, a settlement south of Albuquerque. Despite many pleas on their behalf, Governor Cruzat y Góngora "wasted no time in denying the petition without providing a reason."[57]

New Mexicans were not the only ones taking Indian slaves. Throughout the 1700s, Utes and Comanches raided into neighboring communities while continuing to suffer from others' slave raids. In his 1727 report, for example, Pedro de Rivera offered the first ethnographic observations on the Comanches that include accounts of slaving:

> Each year at a certain time, there comes to this province a nation of Indians very barbarous, and warlike. Their name is Comanche. They never number less than 1,500. Their origin is unknown, because they are always wandering in battle formation, for they make war on all the Nations. They halt at whichever stopping place and set up their campaign tents . . . And after they finish the commerce . . . which consists of tanned skins, buffalo hides, and those young Indians which they capture (because they kill the older ones), they retire, continuing their wandering until another time.

"Always wandering in battle formation," Comanches, like their Ute allies, traveled in militarized bands, constantly prepared to defend themselves as well as to attack weaker neighbors. For Rivera, their "barbarous and warlike" nature explained their enslavement, not their annual "commerce" with New Mexico.[58]

By the time of their earliest sustained appearance in Spanish sources, then, colonial violence had become woven into the fabric of Comanche society. Rivera's claim that Comanche slavers simply killed older captives rather than risk their enslavement was influenced by his many racial and cultural prejudices. Yet chauvinism alone cannot explain these slaves from the Great Plains.

Like their many neighbors, Utes and Comanches adapted to colonial violence in kind, redirecting it against New Mexico while also displacing it onto more distant Native groups. Also like their neighbors, they became irresistibly attracted by the power to trade. Rivera's descriptions after all recount moments of commerce. The "certain" traffic that northern peoples brought into New Mexico consisted of northern resources: furs, hides, eventually horses, and also slaves, who provided a growing pool of laborers in the colony. As James Brooks has demonstrated, New Mexicans "ransomed" Indian captives from surrounding traders, "adopting" captives into settler families, while eventually granting *genízaro* requests for land. Captives were overwhelmingly young women and children whose sexual and reproductive labor became essential to the colony; as a result of constant Indian raids, borders remained unstable, and colonial officials encouraged settlement to buffer against Indian attacks. As equestrian raids destabilized the colony, New Mexican leaders in the 1740s began granting *genízaro* requests for land at towns like Abiquiu along the Chama and farther south at Belen, allowing the children of captives, and even former captives themselves, a modicum of rights within colonial society. New Mexican patriarchs, however, employed Indian slaves not only for needed domestic labor but also for psychological and sexual "comforts," as the presence of *genízaros* and their "illegitimate" children over time underpinned colonial hierarchies of honor, patriarchy, and race. New Mexico's Indian trade fairs thus became epicenters in the West's evolving slave networks, and violence became gendered as raiders competed for captives in an effort, partially, to populate the colony's unstable borders. New Mexico's relations of violence extended far beyond military affairs and shaped intimate forms of everyday life both within and outside colonial society.[59]

New Mexican as well as Indian captors generally found adult males too difficult to enslave and transport, and, as Rivera implied, they often killed them in battle. Although some male captives were sent south in the 1600s to the mining centers of northern Mexico, throughout the 1700s settlement, defense, and economic development dominated New Mexico's colonial affairs, and the vast majority of captives became women and children. Moreover, whereas in the 1600s Spanish slavers, like Rosas, procured slaves directly from surrounding nonequestrian Indians in military campaigns, in the 1700s outlying Native groups became the region's primary traffickers. Although some scholars maintain that these patterns of servitude originated in precontact Native America, the violent transformations engendered by colonial technologies, economies, and warfare—combined with New Mexicans' growing proclivity for female and young captives—suggest that the gendered nature of the Indian slave trade stemmed from colonial disruptions, not from precontact Indian "culture." Eighteenth-century Indian groups, themselves recalibrated by violent changes, adopted and extended the patterns of enslavement flowing from Spanish colonization. Although few sources directly reveal the Ute and Comanche alliance's involvement in the slave trade, by midcentury colonial settlements facilitated the traffic of alliance captives into New Mexican families.[60]

Rivera's identification of the Comanche mobile band organization testifies not only to the region's levels of violence but also to the difficulties in identifying the precise ethnographic distinctions among these eighteenth-century peoples. Such bands often consisted of hundreds of tents that when seasonally camped became small villages, or *rancherías*. Within such encampments, ethnographic distinctions remained unclear to Spanish chroniclers. As Captain Sebastián Martín had told Governor Valverde in 1719, "squads of armed men and Indians of the pueblos should be placed where the Ute nation commonly enters in order to ascertain whether those who come to commit hostilities are Utes or Comanches . . . Utes . . . may be many times Comanches." At the same war council, Captains Miguel de Coca and Tomás Olguín echoed, but then blunted, Martín's uncertainty: "the two nations, Utes and Comanche . . . are to be understood as one with respect to their speaking the same language and going about together, and to be punished as one." Speaking, traveling, and fighting together seemingly resolved the confusion between these "two" nations.[61]

By midcentury, as Ute and Comanche bands shifted allegiances, New Mexican authorities began to use more precise territorial and band designations. Projecting these classifications back onto earlier periods, however, is problematic. The bands that raided New Mexico after the Reconquista were classified unspecifically and inconsistently. Their changing locations, relations with each other, and cultural practices went largely unrecorded. Assigning ethnographic distinctions to their worlds remains not only difficult but also dangerous, potentially categorizing unidentifiable peoples into static cultural topologies. Whether the Ute-Comanche alliance was a composite of different allies, tribal groups, bands, or even a fused amalgam of all three, it affected the course of borderlands history.[62]

In the 1740s, then, unspecified Ute bands continued to live to the west of the Comanches in the Colorado Plateau, migrating seasonally and during war. Although little evidence survives about the nature of Ute-Comanche relations during this period, Utes and Comanches probably intermarried, seasonally encamped together, and continued to strategize for ways to gain horses, metals, and trade goods. Whether the distinctions between them remained as blurred as the Spanish perceived remains an open question. In the coming years, however, as

New Mexicans noted the distinctions between and within these north-ern nations, they also noted growing tensions.

As Ute and Comanche raids continued throughout the north, New Mexicans became more knowledgeable about these northern raiders, particularly at the settlements that suffered from their attacks. Indeed, in the coming decades New Mexico's northwestern perimeter would become a flourishing "Ute frontier." But for the time being raids by the alliance continued along the Chama River northwest of Santa Fe. In 1736, for example, an unspecified "Yuta" band attacked along a trib-utary of the Chama, killing and capturing livestock. Residents held a war council and unsuccessfully pursued with a force of settlers and Pueblo allies. The cycles of attack, attempted reprisal, and constant loss of animals continued to characterize northern Indian relations.[63]

Ute raids along the Chama and to the west against the Navajos soon produced the first documented Ute band designations. In a 1745 re-port on the "Conversion of the Pagan Indians of the Province of Na-vajo," Governor Joachín Codallos y Rabál interviewed a dozen settlers who had traded among the Navajo. Many noted that the current Span-ish-Navajo peace was a direct result of Ute-Comanche aggression; alli-ance attacks, settlers testified, had forced Navajos to "live on the tops of the mesas in little houses of stone. And . . . the reason for their living in those mountains is [that] the Yutas and Comanches make war upon them." Don Manuel Saens de Garbisu, a Castilian *presidio* soldier in Santa Fe, further noted that raids by the "Yutas and pagan Taguaganas who live close to them" had also forced Navajos into the mountains.[64]

"Taguaganas" was the name given the first recorded Ute band—also later referred to as "Chapuapuas," "Aguaguanos," "Chaguaguas," and "Sabuaganas"—that New Mexicans came to identify. Soon after the governor's report in 1747, Rabál campaigned against "los Enemigos Gentiles Yutas y Chapuapuas" in what would be the last Spanish slave raid against Ute communities. As with many encounters, however, only fragments of evidence remain. Afterward *presidio* soldier Antonio Santiestevan was convicted and banished for a year "because he was standing guard" when "an enemy Yuta Indian who was seized during the campaign" escaped.[65]

Like most campaigns against the Utes, Governor Rabál's 1747 attack came after a period of alliance raids. In 1746 Comanches raided Pecos, killing twelve, while also attacking Galisteo and other settlements. In the same year Rabál forbade trade with the Comanches at Taos and threatened a mandatory death penalty for anyone going more than a league from the pueblo without a license. Later that summer, along the Chama River at Abiquiu—the colony's northwesternmost settlement—unidentified raiders again attacked. As Father Juan Sanz de Lezaún recounted, the raiders "carried off twenty-three women and children, besides killing a girl and old woman for having defended themselves . . . a few settlers went out to follow their trail and found three women dead and a new-born child; the rest having been carried off." One of the captives returned after seven years and reported that her abductors had been Comanches, not Utes. Ute bands, however, suffered the governor's immediate reprisal.[66]

In October, with over 500 soldiers and Indian auxiliaries, Rabál's campaign engaged a large "Yutas y Chapuapuas" *ranchería*. After a Spanish ambush, a reported 107 Ute deaths, 206 captured, and nearly 1,000 horses seized provided ample cause for New Mexican rejoicing. Four Utes were also publicly executed, notwithstanding Rabál's 1744 gubernatorial edict, or *bando,* "prohibiting cruelty to defenseless women and the children of savages . . . during campaigns." Whether any of the 206 captives suffered additional punishments from Spanish and Indian soldiers is unknown.[67]

One of the enslaved became the focus of a property dispute shortly after the governor's return. In December 1748, General Juan Domingo Bustamante presided over a trial in Santa Fe concerning the ownership of "a pagan Ute Indian woman." "Before me," Bustamante noted, "Antonio de Salazar . . . promised to tell . . . if he knew *una India Grande de Na[tion] Yuta* who belongs to his brother Pablo. He said that yes he knew that his brother bought her last year." Antonio's testimony helped establish his brother's claims to property that had become a part of a contract dispute brought against Pablo. Antonio's testimony aided his brother, whose ownership of this woman offers further insight into New Mexico's relations with alliance members.[68]

Pablo de Salazar's ownership of this unidentified Ute woman provides one of the earliest sustained references to a Ute captive in colonial New Mexico. Tellingly, recent warfare characterized her arrival in New Mexico; purchased only months after Rabál's summer raid, she was brought in along with other captives. She had lost not only family

members during the governor's attack, but also her former community. Three hundred killed and enslaved was more than most bands
could withstand, so too 1,000 horses to the Ute economy.

Over time, captives such as Salazar's Ute slave may have forged ties
to northern Indian communities through language, cultural familiarity, and kinship, but not always with their original communities, which
had suffered retaliatory campaigns. As we shall also see, in the coming
decades mention of "Ute" captives referred not always to Utes but
more often to distant Great Basin Indians, further complicating any attempt to identify captives' precise identities. For now, this woman *was*
property: "an Indian woman of Pablo de Salazer who is his and has no
other owner." Whether she endured labor, forced acculturation, or
sexual "comfort," she could be controlled, exploited, and her ownership disputed.[69]

As Ute survivors mourned their dead and enslaved, alliance reprisals escalated. In January 1748 Comanches attacked Pecos with significant losses on both sides, while Ute and Comanche raids along the
Chama became so severe that in March Juan Beitta, the *alcalde mayor* of
Santa Cruz de la Cañada, whose jurisdiction covered these settlements,
asked Rabál to heed his residents' requests to relocate. "The inhabitants of the places of Ojo Caliente, Santa Rosas de Abiquiu, and El
Pueblo Quemado have come before [me]," Beitta reported, "stating
that . . . they find themselves in imminent danger of losing their lives
. . . against the invasions . . . [from] the pagan Indian enemies, Yutas,
Aguaguanos, Comanches . . . who appear in said places, daily." "There
is no other remedy," he pleaded, "except for the petitioners to move
. . . until the said enemies become pacified."[70]

Governor Rabál concurred, though soon diplomacy and not pacification would remedy the Chama's plight. "I . . . allow the petitioners to move to the places that may be more convenient to them," he responded, "without thereby causing injury to the land and houses they
have in said places which for the time being they leave." Abandoning
their houses, lands, crops, and roaming livestock, these settlers hurried toward Santa Fe, displaced "for the time being" by northern attacks, their villages now empty with fallow, untended fields.[71]

Rabál's tenure from 1743 to 1749 encapsulated paradoxes endemic
to Spanish-Indian frontier relations. While successful military campaigns punished and enslaved, they also exacerbated northern insta-

bility. Indian reprisal parties in turn struck at smaller towns and pueblos, usually fleeing before Spanish forces were mobilized. As outlying
settlements knew far too well, policing nomadic mobility and aggres-
sions remained beyond the scope of colonial power. The institutions of
Spanish violence were effective against northern Indians in concentrated and sustained forms, and while Spanish campaigns often devastated Indian communities, ensuing Indian reprisals continued to terrorize smaller settlements. Cycles of violence, in short, characterized
Spanish-Ute relations.[72]

Having driven Apaches and Spanish communities out of the north,
Utes and Comanches seemed at the zenith of their power. Their militarized bands moved largely with impunity along the peripheries of
the colony, raiding livestock and communities before large campaigns
were mobilized. As Rabál's successor, Tomás Vélez de Cachupín,
quickly learned, "It is extremely easy for this numerous nation [Utes]
to consort with the other two, Chaguaguas and Moaches, to commit
upon this province the greatest hostilities because of their proximity
and because the extremely rough terrain which shelters them makes
it difficult to attack them." Identifying a third major Ute band, the
"Moache," Cachupín also recognized how military relations had affected the region's physical landscape. He understood that after generations of raids, the "rough terrain" of the numerous canyons, mesas,
and arid mountain regions northwest of New Mexico had taken on additional strategic value; the violent transformation of Utes had also imbued the region's topography with new meanings readily discernible
to colonial authorities. The new governor's reflexive recognition of
the terrain's capacity to simultaneously protect and impede testifies to
the imperial militarization of landscapes. By the mid-eighteenth century the colony's relations of violence had become so normative that
the physical and natural worlds were now imbued with violent meanings.[73]

Although Ute and Comanche strength still coursed throughout the
north, their alliance had begun to unravel. Consummate diplomats
and raiders though they were, the Utes were able to achieve only a precarious security, particularly as their homelands north of New Mexico
grew increasingly isolated from the dynamic Great Plains. After raiding seasonally in the Arkansas, Canadian, and other watersheds with
their Comanche allies, eastern Ute bands returned to their mountain

valleys until the next season. After the Apache dispersal, however, the Plains northeast of Santa Fe did not remain vacant. Instead, they became home to growing trade centers that linked multiple Indian, New Mexican, and French traders from the east. During the 1730s and 1740s the Comanche came to dominate these lands, occupying former Apache territories while consolidating their control over the rich grazing grasslands of the southern Great Plains. While the Utes to the west migrated from mountain parks to Plains river valleys, by 1730, if not sooner, the Comanche had become, as Rivera noted, entirely a Plains people. Utes dominated northwestern New Mexico, but Comanche control over the colony's northeastern plains soon proved more advantageous. Soon the Comanche would no longer need their Ute allies. Indeed, the Utes, despite their long-standing ties, soon threatened both Comanche diplomacy and Comanche trade.[74]

The first hint of Ute-Comanche tensions surfaced in 1735. For the first time, Comanches coming into the colony to trade hides for knives expressed animosity toward unspecified Utes, and in response Spanish authorities described the Utes as "enemies" of the Comanche. Although there were no direct accounts of Ute-Comanche hostilities until the 1750s, evidence of Comanche disengagement from the alliance recurred throughout the 1740s. In the summer of 1748, for example, just months after Bietta's report from the Chama, 600 Comanches entered Taos and assured their hosts of their lack of involvement in any of the year's previous raids. Comanche interests, as Pekka Håmålåinen argues, now centered on their Great Plains trading centers and on monopolizing trade between New Mexico and French Louisiana. The Comanche were quickly becoming imperialists on their own account; over the next generation they extended their power over a constellation of subject peoples, including New Mexicans. The Ute-Comanche alliance had developed, expanded, and was now dissolving in a multipolar world.[75]

For the Utes, the changing imperial economies of the southern Plains, Comanche fortunes, and a new reformist governor in Santa Fe ushered in dramatic realignments in the northwest, realignments that eventually wedded New Mexico and Ute communities for the next half-century. After taking office in 1749, Cachupín launched a series of initiatives to incorporate Indians into a more stable regional economy. Committing to punish northern raiders as well as Spanish settlers who abandoned their villages, he made force and discipline cornerstones in his policy of détente with northern peoples. In a minor but representative move, the governor responded to renewed signs of settler abandonment along the Chama. "Many of the residents of the settlement of Chama," reported a group of concerned settlers, "have determined to abandon their houses and to come, some to Rio Abajo, and others to the Capital Villa of Santa Fe." Only one year after the abandonment of the other Chama River settlements, the loss of these settlements would have left "only [la] Cañada and Chimayo" north of Santa Fe. Cachupín responded: "the Alcalde Mayor . . . will notify all the residents . . . that under no consideration must they abandon and depopulate that locality, nor their houses or lands which the King has granted them." The punishment: "two hundred dollars fine and four months in jail, and the loss of their house and land." If caught again, "the further penalty of being vanished from this Kingdom, and sent to a prison . . . for four years."[76]

Cachupín's firm commitment to weathering these Ute raids represented an alternative vision of frontier relations. Comanche and Ute raids did continue during the first years of his rule, and they were often met with brutal counterattacks. Cachupín, however, followed up such responses with overtures of peace. As Comanche fortunes flourished with their trade networks, Ute stability in the north became compromised. Generations of raiding, subjugation to Spanish campaigns, and countless Indian reprisals had taken a toll on these Ute bands, and by the end of his revolutionary tenure, terms of endearment would flow from the governor's lips about these once "pagan," "barbarous," and "savage" people. In his report to his successor, Cachupín implored: "You should show [the Utes] the greatest kindness . . . Protect them in their commerce and do them justice . . . to their captain, named Thomas, show all courteousness, great friendship, and love." Flowery terms of affection indeed characterized much of the next generation of Spanish-Ute relations, while in practice the emerging Spanish-Ute détente heralded turbulent changes for more distant lands and peoples along New Mexico's northern borderlands.[77]

TWO

The Making of the
New Mexican–Ute Borderlands

Following the erosion of the Ute-Comanche alliance, the various "Yutas" peoples to the north struggled to survive. For generations, New Mexican, Navajo, Apache, and Pueblo raiders had besieged Ute communities, leaving hundreds dead and enslaved while forcing others to consolidate with neighboring *rancherías* for protection. Now, faced with additional threats from their former Comanche allies, Ute bands along the eastern slopes of the Rockies faced an uncertain future. A century after the first sustained contacts with Spanish invaders, Ute Indians in northern New Mexico and Colorado continued to endure the many challenges of colonialism.

New Mexico in the 1740s and early 1750s similarly faced the constant threat of attack. Having engendered cycles of violence that now swept back into the colony, Spanish settlers and Pueblo groups stood guard against equestrian raiders whose incursions sometimes forced the complete abandonment of villages. Along the Chama River in the northwest, at Pecos and Galisteo Pueblos in the northeast, and even in the shadows of the *Palacio* in Santa Fe, Indian raiders attacked farmers in their fields, took women and children captive, and ran off with countless horses and sheep.[1]

Within this violent world, Ute and New Mexican leaders initiated a series of agreements that bound the former enemies together in new and surprising ways. Decades of violence had proved that neither Utes nor New Mexicans could impose their will on the other through force alone. For generations, Utes had withstood and redirected colonial violence back against New Mexican settlements, using the forces of destruction unleashed in the 1600s to secure economic and military control. Now, in alliance with the Spanish, they recreated themselves and the worlds around them.

Initially the evolving Spanish-Ute alliance recast the boundaries between these former enemies. In lands where they had once met as combatants, new forms of exchange, diplomacy, and protection now bonded Ute and New Mexican communities as the militarized landscapes between their homelands became a landscape of peace with fluid and permeable borders. Ute leaders became welcomed guests in Santa Fe while New Mexican traders and soon missionaries ventured into Ute territories. These newly created bonds became the foundation for an evolving alliance that soon reconfigured both imperial and indigenous communities.

While trade, gift exchanges, and other forms of reciprocity mitigated the levels of violence between these former combatants, such activities by no means diminished the levels of violence in the region. In fact, as they stabilized the relations between themselves, New Mexicans and Utes fought to secure territories adjacent to their homelands. Such efforts increasingly spread Spanish colonial influences into previously unincorporated regions and among previously unidentified peoples.

Beginning in the 1760s, New Mexican traders, explorers, and missionaries extended Spain's colonial empire toward the Pacific, and such extension remained predicated upon stable relations with Utes. As the colonization of California brought efforts to expand the territory of New Mexico, dreams of imperial growth necessitated compliance, hospitality, and, above all, peace with New Mexico's northern Ute neighbors. Although many have studied Spanish attempts to link Santa Fe and California, few have recognized the political relations intrinsic to such designs. Expansion came through Ute homelands, followed Ute trails, and relied on Ute guides, hosts, and communities. Ute bands meanwhile often regulated, profited from, and oversaw this expansion and trade, extracting tribute from New Mexicans passing through their homelands. The centrality of Utes to the making of colonial New Mexico was never more evident as the Spanish-Ute alliance accelerated the growth of New Spain's northern borders and economies.[2]

Caught amidst an increasing stream of Ute and New Mexican explorers and traders, the nonequestrian peoples of the southern Great Basin in the late 1700s began to endure the high and deadly costs of colonial expansion. As Utes ferried goods to New Mexican trade fairs, they increasingly displaced the violent political economy of northern New Spain onto more distant Great Basin peoples. Utes had horses, metals, and generations of trading relations with New Mexico. More distant Great Basin peoples living in environments less suitable for equestrianism did not. They lacked not only horses but also the means to acquire them. With the Navajo to their south, the Comanche to their east, and increasingly powerful Plains peoples to their north, Utes in the mid-1700s began enslaving Indians to their west in southern Utah, Nevada, and California, exchanging them for horses, weapons, and wares. Great Basin Indians, who are now known as Southern Paiutes and Western Shoshones, were incorporated into the violent orbit of Spanish colonialism, not by Spanish conquistadors or soldiers, but by Utes, whose alliance with New Mexico spread slavery into the Intermountain West. The offspring of colonialism, Great Basin Indian captives became central to the creation and endurance of the New Mexican–Ute borderlands.[3]

Like other captives, enslaved Great Basin peoples remain largely voiceless in the Spanish colonial record. Within moments of their purchase, Spanish masters, or *dueños,* began the processes of Hispanicization. Slaves were initiated both into the households of their captors and into larger New Mexican society. They became part of the holy family of Christianity through baptism, acquired the badges of New Mexican identity and honor with Spanish names, and labored within the New Mexican economy. These captives and their children became neither tribally identified Indians nor Spanish settlers nor *vecinos* (citizens). They constituted a separate, racialized ethnic group of detribalized, sometimes mixed-blooded Indians, referred to as *genízaros,* who at adulthood often secured limited forms of legal protections and land ownership. Over time, *genízaros* constituted upward of a third of many northern towns and played central roles in the fortification and defense of the colony. Indeed, the sustained incorporation of Indian captives into colonial society led to the eventual creation of northern villages capable of buffering New Mexico from nomadic attack. Originally born into or descended from northern Indian societies, *genízaros* helped defend colonial society from raids from northern communities.[4]

The New Mexican communities closest to Ute homelands received the most Great Basin slaves. At the *genízaro* community of Abiquiu northwest of Santa Fe, these captives were overwhelmingly Indian girls and children, as Spanish and Indian slavers targeted Indian women and children who were considered more assimilable and compliant than Indian men. Unlike other captives, whose bands regularly attempted to reclaim enslaved members, nonequestrian Great Basin communities had little hope of retrieving their former family members. Without the horses and weapons acquired through trade, nonequestrian Paiutes endured Ute hegemony over New Mexico's northwestern borderlands.[5]

By the early nineteenth century, raiding Utes and New Mexicans had spread throughout the southern Great Basin, opening the Old Spanish Trail linking California and New Mexico. Trade along the trail began in Abiquiu, ranged northwest through Utah, ended in Los Angeles, and then returned to New Mexico. The Paiute and Shoshone bands in these regions often became enslaved or displaced from their homelands. Besides introducing slave trafficking to the Great Basin, Ute control and knowledge of these lands enabled the first Spanish, Mexican, and later Anglo-American explorations into this *terra incognita*. This incorporation, initiated by Utes, would prove more traumatic for Paiutes and Shoshones throughout the nineteenth century. Utes, in short, precipitated radical changes in the lifeways of Indian peoples well before their lands became sites of direct colonial encounters, as the violence of Spanish colonialism became further displaced throughout the colonial era.[6]

The Forging of the Spanish-Ute Alliance

By the middle of the eighteenth century, Spanish-Ute relations remained as tense and unpredictable as they had since the Reconquista. Raids, counterraids, and reprisals characterized the bulk of relations between Santa Fe and Ute groups. In 1749, immediately after his inauguration, Governor Tomás Vélez de Cachupín began formulating ways to protect the colony's precarious borders. Unlike his predecessor, he outlawed the abandonment of settler communities along the Chama

River northwest of Santa Fe. In the northeast, at Pecos and Galisteo, he additionally created, according to Elizabeth John, "veritable fortresses, surrounding them with entrenchments, erecting towers at the gates, and posting thirty presidials." These fortified northern settlements, he hoped, would deter nomadic movements into the colony. With limited initial success, later governors would soon lament the failure of settlers to comply fully with Cachupín's orders that "the resettlement must be made with a union of houses and formation of squares so that it would be respected by the enemies and capable of defense by the inhabitants thereof." Just as Ute and other Indian societies had become concentrated bands constantly prepared for war, social space throughout northern New Mexico remained similarly militarized.[7]

As Ute-Comanche fortunes unraveled, Spanish officials developed strategies either to incorporate these northern groups into alliance or to annihilate them altogether. In April 1750 Cachupín received such advice from New Spain's counselor general of war, the Marqués de Altamira. Hoping that "the said Governor will continue his Christian fervor . . . in protecting and guarding that Government, its settlements and inhabitants . . . from the . . . treacherous invasions and hostilities of the infidel enemy Indians," Altamira encouraged Cachupín to adopt one of two strategies for dealing with the Comanche and Ute bands. For the Ute "enemy . . . nations: Utes, Chaguagos, and Moaches," he suggested "trying . . . all of the most reasonable terms and methods to induce them to become converted . . . until they shall be able to support themselves by the fruit of their labor. We only desire their greatest good," he continued. In case such hopeful plans to missionize the Utes failed, however, Altamira envisioned a violent alternative. "If they do not agree . . . they shall be destroyed and exterminated by campaigns which shall be carried on . . . in their own country . . . so that . . . there shall not remain a single enemy of them that may disturb the said Navajos or the Christian population of the said Government of New Mexico."[8]

Altamira's call for Ute missionization or extermination highlighted continued anxieties about northern defenses. New Mexicans feared Comanche, Apache, and Ute attacks, and with French traders from Louisiana making inroads into the region, Spanish authorities further worried about growing foreign influences among their many Indian "enemies." As John writes: "All that amity among Frenchmen and Indians on the plains seemed to Governor Vélez Cachupín to threaten the very existence of New Mexico." By reducing the dependence of northern groups on New Mexican trade as well as offering new trade items, including guns, expanded French influences would indeed further jeopardize Spain's northernmost colony. Exterminate, missionize, but above all keep the region's Indians from falling into alliance with rival imperialists—these were the principal anxieties facing the crown's representative.[9]

It was within this environment of anxiety and fear that Cachupín attempted to curb Indian attacks and to counter French imperial designs. By arresting French traders who ventured into New Mexico and appealing to Iberia to enforce international laws against French expeditions, Cachupín helped limit French expansion into New Mexico. Ending the cycles of Indian attacks upon the province, however, was beyond his control. Despite calls, such as Altamira's, for exterminating northern groups, Cachupín realized that northern Indians remained far more capable and resilient than many Spanish leaders assumed. Indians, not New Mexicans, controlled the colony's hinterlands, often dictating the nature and pace of frontier relations. The future stability of the province lay not with the governor, the viceroy, or the Spanish crown, but around the campfires of equestrians, particularly those of the Utes and their former Comanche allies.[10]

As much as any other factor, Comanche power helps explain the changing relations between Spanish and Ute societies. New Comanche trading alliances with the French and with Plains Indians had cemented their role as intermediaries between New Mexico and New France. While the Spanish curbed French trade into New Mexico, Indian villages along the Arkansas and the other rivers of the southern Great Plains became vibrant, and often competing, trade centers that attracted traders from the Mississippi to the Rio Grande. And through forceful diplomatic and military tactics the Comanche dominated much of this trade. As Pekka Hämäläinen suggests, the Western Comanche became "not only active traders, but also operated a major trade center," a factor that strengthened the basis of their emergent power.[11]

As the Comanche fanned onto the Great Plains, they increasingly dominated the lands east of New Mexico, relying less on their former Ute allies. Although Ute control over the eastern slopes of the Rockies and its string of mountain parks remained strong, by 1740 it also had paradoxically become less advantageous; for, having facilitated the rise of Comanche equestrianism, Utes had failed to consolidate their own control over the abandoned Apache communities northeast of New Mexico. Combining their equestrianism with seasonal trading and hunting in the mountain valleys of central Colorado and New Mexico, Utes left abandoned Apache territories to their Comanche allies. Such decisions fatefully altered the course of Western history, as by 1730, if not sooner, Comanches had become entirely equestrian societies. As the spread of the horse remade Native economies and polities, then, those who controlled not only horses but also horse-grazing ecologies initially prospered. Although the Utes had horses, they had not taken advantage of the ecosystems most suitable for large-scale horse trading. They chose to continue to live in the mountainous homelands of their ancestors, leaving the grasslands of the Great Plains to others.[12]

The southern Great Plains with its verdant grasslands became an economic and political hub west of the Mississippi, and through their trade centers the Comanche expanded their power exponentially. Unknown to New Mexico in the seventeenth century, by the 1760s the Comanche dominated the plains east of Taos. Few details survive to explain why the Utes and Comanches turned from alliance to enmity, but the Comanche probably no longer depended upon New Mexican trade as much as Utes did. In fact, the more the Comanche consolidated their control over the Plains, the less they relied upon New Mexico altogether. Once the exclusive source of needed trade goods, by the mid-1700s New Mexico no longer monopolized the horse and metal trade. Indeed, by 1770 the Comanche stole more horses from New Spain than they traded, and they eventually controlled horse herds larger than those of New Mexicans. In short, the emerging imperial borderlands between New Spain and French Louisiana became the primary centers of the Comanche world, and their former Ute allies lost the influence they had once achieved with their Comanche kinsmen.[13]

The most direct evidence of these changing fortunes appears in letters from Cachupín to his successor, Don Francisco Marín del Vallo. Cachupín noted that before he took office Utes were "counting upon peace and support [with New Mexico] against another tribe, the Comanche." Utes had additionally seized "an Indian woman of twenty-five or thirty years of age . . . from the Comanches." Such fragmentary traces of conflict suggest larger and more complicated hostilities. Before Governor Rabál in 1747 had "captured and put to the sword a [Ute] ranchería of more than one hundred tipis," Cachupín continued, "the Utes were doing their best to advance their good relations" and seemed likely to counterbalance the Comanches' growing power. The subsequent Ute counterattacks in 1748 along the Chama, Cachupín noted, had resulted from "their just indignation" over Rabál's slave raid. So, while these Ute raids had left the Chama settlements "ruined and completely deserted," Utes still searched for potential allies in a world surrounded by enemies.[14]

Unlike many of his predecessors, Cachupín grasped some of the dilemmas confronting neighboring nations. His recognition of the Utes' "just indignation," for example, reflected an understanding of northern politics in which revenge was rational, if not justifiable. Initiating a series of policies that attempted to accommodate New Mexico's Indian enemies, the reformist governor tried to mediate outstanding grievances, to forgive as well as punish acts of vengeance, and to incorporate rivals into the Spanish empire. Such frontier policies contrasted with the half-century of warfare since the Reconquista. Although the governor's initial attempts at reconciliation with the Comanche stalled, Spanish overtures of peace became more attractive for Utes.[15]

On August 17, 1752, the *alcalde mayor* at San Juan Pueblo hastened a letter to the governor about the appearance of several Ute bands on the outskirts of town. Different Ute bands had periodically raided as well as attended trading fairs around this village near the confluence of the Chama and Rio Grande Rivers, but this day's activities were unusual. As Juan Joseph Lobato described them, "There appeared today at this pueblo the three chiefs who compose the superior triumvirate of the nations of the northwest: Don Thomas, chief of the Utes, Chief Chiquito of the Muachis, and Chief Barrigon of the Chaguagua. They came to state their desires, to see your lordship, and to talk to you. They brought more than one hundred tipis with their pelts for trade."[16]

Representing their respective bands, these Ute chiefs had come to meet the new governor, whose reputation for forgiving New Mexico's enemies had spread throughout the northwest. According to Lobato,

the Ute leaders had reason to believe that the new governor had for-
given their previous attacks. Reportedly, they had just attacked a Navajo encampment, and when the surrounded Navajos surrendered,
they did so "carrying a wooden cross above which was this almanac on
a pole." The Utes recognized the peaceful symbolism of the cross but
were less certain about this "almanac"—possibly a parchment or piece
of paper. The Navajos, Lobato continued, told the Utes: "'The great
chief of the Spaniards sent you this letter and the cross and ordered
you to be our friends' . . . The [Ute] chiefs held their conference there
and agreed that since your lordship punished the Comanches severely
and afterward pardoned them benignly when they sought peace by
carrying another cross, it was but proper that they should do the
same." The Utes subsequently returned their captured Navajo goods
and captives and decided to "submit their action at the feet of your
lordship" with the almanac in hand.[17]

Upon receipt of Lobato's letter, the governor "went at once to meet
the three chiefs of the nation." He upheld the fiction of his supposed letter to the Navajo and, more important, "showed them great
kindness and friendship." Here was an opportunity both to mitigate
Ute raids and to secure potential allies against the Comanche. As
Cachupín later explained: "As the ranchería was left sixteen leagues
away where they could pasture their large herd of horses, it was necessary for me to visit it, where I remained two days." Although the details
of his stay are unknown, this meeting initiated forms of communication, exchange, and protection that would soon characterize relations
between Utes and New Mexico.[18]

Such relations, as Utes knew, already existed for other Indians in
alliance with New Mexico, and while each of these leaders had likely
traded in the colony before, now, in a confederation, they brought
their bands together to negotiate the terms of alliance. Representing different territorial areas, they simultaneously initiated talks
with Cachupín and strengthened the ties between their bands. Soon a
delicate détente emerged. Concluding these eventful deliberations,
Cachupín recalled: "They held in this neighborhood the exchange of
pelts from which all parties derived much pleasure and satisfaction."
Such forms of reciprocity would soon become increasingly common.[19]

The 1752 accord brought immediate relief to northern New Mexico. Peace with Utes enabled Cachupín to repopulate the Chama Val-

ley settlements of Abiquiu, Ojo Caliente, Embudo, and Quemado. Additionally, Ute trade, particularly in hides, jump-started many village economies, benefiting "the province in such a way that it stimulates . . . its settlers . . . to go to La Vizcaya and Sonora to purchase whatever effects they may need." As Cachupín noted, "Without this trade [settlers] could not provide for themselves . . . when . . . the trade with the Utes ceases, that of these neighborhoods also ends." Ute peace, then, enabled not only the resettlement of northern New Mexico but also its replenishment.[20]

Cachupín's peace process centered upon using alliance members to discipline hostile neighbors, and Utes understood their new responsibilities as allies. They soon undertook campaigns against the Comanche while also, importantly, allowing governors the freedom to conduct campaigns without worrying about potential invasions from Utes. Although northern settlements along the Chama and west of the Rio Grande continued to suffer Comanche and Apache raids, over time Ute alliance protections afforded increased stability. Previously displaced by Utes, northwestern villages soon developed what James Brooks refers to as "borderlands communities of interest" with their Ute allies, doing so within the violent currents of colonial relations. The Spanish-Ute alliance, in short, became a cornerstone for New Mexican growth and stability in the northwest. As Cachupín emphasized to Marín, "it is necessary that the zeal of your grace be completely applied to maintain with these four nations of Utes, Chaguaguas, and Payuches [and Moaches] the best friendship and good relations, treating them with generosity . . . be very humane in your contacts with them." Seven years after Rabál destroyed a Ute *ranchería*, then, governors now implored local officials to be "very humane" with their Ute neighbors.[21]

The specific benefits and meanings of Spanish alliance for "these four nations of Utes" remain less certain. With so little known about the composition and practices of these bands, only speculative sketches of their motivations are possible. As for the Spanish, the attractions of the alliance undoubtedly centered upon peace, trade, and protection. Utes had long come to rely upon Spanish horses, metals, and trade goods, and peaceful attendance at northern trade fairs now assured Ute traders regular access to New Mexican weapons, foods, and supplies. Regular and peaceful trade now became possible in outlying northern settler communities, which became annual migratory stopping points for Ute bands. Welcomed into New Mexico after fall harvests, Ute bands were even invited to stay the winter. In 1794, for instance, Governor Fernando de la Concha told his successor, Fernando Chacón, that the "Sahuahuanes" Utes from Colorado "usually come once a year in . . . October . . . and they remain . . . until the following May, when the melting of the snows in the mountains allows their return." Camping outside Pueblo confines, Utes solidified the many ties that bound them to New Mexico, their *rancherías* teeming with New Mexican guests.[22]

The hot steel of combat also forged the bonds between Utes and New Mexicans as shared hostilities against the Comanche brought Ute and New Mexican warriors into the field. As Mexican Bishop Pedro de Tamarón noted during his 1760 visit of New Mexico, "The Ute tribe is very numerous . . . Formerly they waged war, and now they are at peace because of their fear of the Comanches." Fear of the Comanche indeed pervaded both New Mexico and Ute communities, whose warriors now acted in concert with Spanish leaders. In 1761, for example, Governor Manuel Portillo Urrisola reported to Tamarón how a New Mexican campaign with Ute allies had surprised and routed a Comanche *ranchería*. Such success, however, was mixed, as after the initial rout the Utes dropped back and began to plunder. As Urrisola bemoaned, "while we were occupied in pursuit of the fugitives, they sacked the camp. They carried off more than a thousand horses and mules and more than three hundred Comanche women, large and small." Unable to prevent this plunder, the governor continued his "pursuit of the fugitives . . . [until] fields were covered with their bodies." Though united, Utes and New Mexicans held varying ambitions when campaigning together against Comanches.[23]

Urrisola's complaints notwithstanding, Utes assisted New Mexico in the escalating Comanche wars, usually with valor and determination. The bloody victories were short-lived, however; Comanche raids persisted through an entire generation. According to Ross Frank, more than 100 Comanche raids were reported from 1767 to 1777, and not until the late 1770s would Spanish leaders achieve some stability in relations with these Great Plains rivals. Although the exact toll of Comanche raids on Ute villages is unknown, it was surely as severe as the Utes' momentary 1761 enslavement.[24]

While providing access to Spanish trade items and protection, alliance with New Mexico also brought new pressures. Internal dissensions and tensions, for example, plagued Ute leaders. Ambitious warriors attempted to assert their prowess and authority over those who sought accommodation with New Mexico, while many eyed the herds of their new allies. Others must have second-guessed the alliance during its many setbacks. An unspecified Navajo band, for instance, had used the cloak of shared alliance with New Mexico to surprise a Ute band. "The Navajos," Cachupín wrote, "failed to keep faith in the friendship which my good offices concerted between them . . . [and] killed a ranchería of this tribe, and stole everything they had." Ute counterattacks, he continued, "have been frequent . . . punishing the Navajos, whom they have forced to abandon the province." Despite such retaliation, the loss of a *ranchería* and its many families dimmed the luster of alliance with Santa Fe.[25]

Ute leaders' commitment to the sustaining alliance overcame such setbacks and internal dissension. After some warriors continued stealing from New Mexican herds, for example, Ute leaders agreed to return stolen horses and to punish the guilty parties. "When a Ute displeases by stealing some horses," Cachupín told Marín, "a general threat should not be made against the whole tribe, nor their chiefs advised of the fact with harshness. Give them notice of it as I have done so that they may punish the culprit and return the property. I have succeeded in securing peacefully the return of some horse herds." Spanish leaders' abilities to make such distinctions between "friendly" Ute leaders additionally strengthened the authority of alliance chiefs, and by returning stolen horses and disciplining "guilty parties," Ute leaders now acknowledged forms of political authority, rooted in the alliance, over their own tribesmen. As in other parts of colonial America, imperial and indigenous leaders moderated tensions not only between groups but also among them, as leaders understood the necessity of maintaining reciprocity in order to preserve social stability.[26]

Spanish leaders also came to recognize forms of authority, rooted in the alliance, over their subjects. Just as the Spanish expected Ute leaders to punish those who had stolen horses, Utes expected similar treatment from Spanish officials. In one of the most illustrative examples of

Spanish-Ute accommodation within New Mexico, Cachupín adjudicated Ute complaints against a *genízaro* horse thief; the loss of a single horse occasioned correspondence, punishment, and insight into these overlapping dimensions of imperial and indigenous authority.

After taking a second term as governor, in 1762 Cachupín reviewed the testimonies taken by Santa Fe's *alcalde mayor* Manuel Gallegos about a *genízaro* accused of stealing a horse from Ute visitors. At San Juan Pueblo on March 29, a Ute complained "that a 'coyote' of that villa [Santa Fe] has taken a bay horse with a white spot on its face." Gallegos found the accused Juan de la Cruz Valdez already "in custody with two sets of chains in the royal guardroom." After interviewing the defendant, Gallegos recounted the crime: "he said that he left his house and came to the Bosque of San Juan and there were two horses . . . 'and there I caught the bay one and I mounted . . . I came to the home of the soldier Isidro Martín [in Santa Fe] and sold him the bay horse for fifteen pesos.'" Corroborating Valdez's confession with Martín, Gallegos sent the testimonies to the governor for a verdict and sentence of punishment.[27]

"Having seen the confession of the culprit," Cachupín began, "about the sale and purchase of a horse stolen from a tribal Indian of the Ute nation who came to Pueblo of San Juan [and] who I am certain suffered great anguish . . . I pass sentence . . . that the Indian culprit *genízaro* Juan de la Cruz Valdez be exiled for four years . . . and sent for that whole time to the workshop of the Hacienda of Encinillas . . . without salary." Cachupín ordered that Valdez additionally be given "fifty lashes . . . when the Utes are present, when they normally come to celebrate their fairs and captive exchanges."[28]

Valdez's conviction and punishment underscore forms of power that Spanish and Ute leaders increasingly constructed. A twenty-year-old *indio genízaro* and "coyote," Valdez occupied a stigmatized racial caste within colonial society; however, despite his status, Valdez lived as a Christian, spoke Spanish, and was entitled to legal representation. He had enough freedom to circulate freely and engage in commercial activity, and he understood that he had committed a crime, to which he confessed. He understood moreover that he was also now to be punished. As *indios bárbaros*, Utes held none of these inherent rights or honors. Their language, dress, and appearance together stood out against New Mexico's social and racial landscapes. While equestrian allies were welcomed into New Mexico, they remained visitors, their appearance the subject of simultaneous fear and fascination. Like all Spaniards, Cachupín also maintained notions of cultural supremacy, telling Marín, for example, not to show "repugnance at their rude clownishness and manners." As allies, however, Utes enjoyed greater participation in the colony's political and social institutions than has been previously recognized. Their ability to retrieve a single stolen horse, to track the thief into the capital without hindrance, and then to use the Spanish legal system for redress reveals a social tapestry of intricate detail.[29]

Furthermore, the governor's insistence that corporal punishment occur "when the Utes are present" reveals the unfolding of further reciprocities between these former enemies. As Spanish authorities enforced and expanded the institutions of violence within colonial society, they used public and ritualized forms of punishment to communicate and legitimate their rule. A century and a half old, the Spanish regime now included more presidial soldiers, greater authority and jurisdictions for *alcaldes,* and larger penal institutions. Yet the right to use violence remained restricted to a select few. Indian captives, honorable women, and successful men all knew their respective status and the boundaries that they could and could not cross—boundaries that when violated often brought a severe and painful response. Valdez's punishment occurred within the parameters of such institutions of honor and authority. For Cachupín did not order the aggrieved Utes to witness Valdez's whipping; he ordered the whipping to be witnessed by the Utes. By observing such spectacles, Utes reinforced their status as allies while also helping to legitimate the governor's as well as their own authority. Sanctioning the governor's decision to resolve this and later disputes, they participated in public displays of violence that communicated their own status and honor. Ute leaders remained respected guests, not *indios bárbaros,* and they expected their power and rights to be recognized. The degrading social hierarchies (and the concomitant threat of violence) that structured colonial society with its "infinitesimal distribution of power relations" did not include these Indian visitors. As they watched the whipping of Valdez, then, Ute leaders viewed a common, everyday ritual, witnessing it from a negotiated position of privilege.[30]

De genizaro y mulata Gíbaro (Of the *genízaro* and *mulata* Gíbaro), by Francisco Clapera, ca. 1785. Oil on canvas. Courtesy of the Denver Art Museum. An example of *castas* painting that communicates the social hazards associated with *genízaro* intermarriages.

Abiquiu and the Great Basin Indian Slave Trade

Regular Ute attendance at trade fairs and their traffic in slaves became primary features of the New Mexican–Ute alliance. Peripheral to Spain's Atlantic empire, New Mexico's economy centered upon the production of domestic goods as well as trade with surrounding

Indios bárbaros, attributed to Juan Rodríguez, ca. 1715. Oil on canvas. Courtesy of Breamore House, Hampshire, England. *Castas* (caste) paintings communicated the racial and social hierarchies within Spanish colonial society, highlighting the stigmatized consequences of interracial relations. In New Mexico, although *genízaros* had low social status, they received legal representation in the colony's legal system and played increasingly important economic and social roles in the second half of the 1700s. *Indios bárbaros* existed outside the framework of domestic institutions and were often targeted by Spanish military and slave campaigns. Throughout the colonial period, *bárbaros* nations adapted to the waves of Spanish violence and became powerful actors throughout northern New Spain.

peoples. Before 1750, Utes had come to trade in New Mexico, but they came just as often to raid. Beginning in the 1750s, Utes brought trade goods and captives to northern trade fairs, and they did so peacefully. From 1752 until the end of the Spanish empire in North America, Utes and New Mexicans carved out a peaceful coexistence. "They bring captives to sell, pieces of chamois, many buffalo skins, and, out of the plunder they have obtained elsewhere, horses, muskets, shotguns, munitions, knives, meat and other various things," noted Tamarón in 1760. For nearly a century, this trade served as the main axis on which the alliance revolved.[31]

As the "gateway to the northwest," Abiquiu recorded the highest number of identifiable "Ute" captives. Situated astride the Chama River, Abiquiu remained New Mexico's northwesternmost settlement throughout the second half of the eighteenth century. After initial attempts at colonization failed in the 1740s, Abiquiu became a critical outpost in the north, its stability inextricably linked to Spanish-Ute fortunes. The traders, missionaries, and explorers who ventured to the northwest and soon to California left from Abiquiu, while northern Indian groups, particularly the Utes, came every season to trade, solidifying their ties through exchange, diplomacy, and gift-giving. And for the Utes, Indian captives became primary commodities of both trade and diplomacy. Eventually such human exchanges enmeshed Ute and New Mexican societies to such an extent that linguistic and intercultural fluency blurred distinctions between "Indian" and "New Mexican."

Such hybridity characterized northern *genízaro* settlements like Abiquiu, and prominent New Mexican interpreters and eventually even Ute leaders hailed from the colony's north. The Colorado Utes' most famous nineteenth-century statesman, Ouray, shepherded at Abiquiu as a teenager, mastering the Spanish language; while *genízaro* guides like Manuel Mestas and later Atanasio Trujillo similarly learned Ute there. As captives, traders, and guides, borderland residents crossed the boundaries between New Mexican and Ute homelands, linking the two into a common social landscape.

After 1750 an emergent slave trade increasingly structured relations between northern villages and Ute communities. As Francisco Atanasio Domínguez noted at Abiquiu in 1776, "many heathens of the Ute nation come [every fall] to the vicinity of this pueblo . . . Sometimes there are little captive heathen Indians [for trade]." Between the time of the repopulation of the Chama River Valley in 1754 and 1866, 152 identified "Ute" captives were baptized at Abiquiu (see graph). Though representing less than 2 percent of the approximately 8,000 baptisms there from this period, these captives offer telling insight into the nature of Spanish-Indian relations throughout the north. They also mark the first sustained appearances of nonequestrian Great Basin Indians in colonial sources.[32]

As a *genízaro* settlement established to help buffer the north from equestrian attacks, Abiquiu was composed of Indian captives and their children. "Ransoming" or "adopting" captives from northern Indian traders, colonial authorities bought them in exchange for Spanish goods. Local officials and clergy then initiated the process of Hispanicization through baptism and the imposition of Spanish names, followed by the selection of local settler godparents, or *padrinos,* and then the placement of captives in settler families. Such strategies of assimilation were particularly common at Abiquiu and are partially visible through Abiquiu's baptismal indexes. Of the 152 "Ute" captives baptized at Abiquiu, for example, the vast majority, 139, or 91.4 percent, had no known or identified parents. Since parentage and lineage, as Ramón Gutiérrez elucidates, remained primary markers of social status, children of unknown parentage came from slavery; of the remaining 13 captives (8.6 percent) with identified mothers, only one had a known father. As Gutiérrez argues, "Names were marks of social status . . .

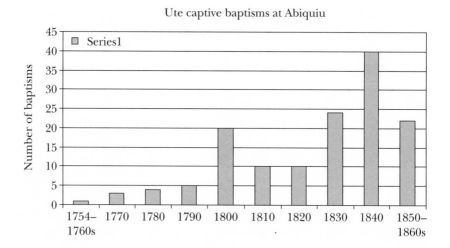

Ute captive baptisms at Abiquiu

those lofty slave compound names . . . far from a trivial act or a simple legal formalism, indicated a natal origin in slavery . . . Children born in wedlock carried a patronym. Slaves did not and everyone knew that." To be baptized without a patronym became, then, synonymous with degradation, and most slaves, *genízaros,* and their children lived so stigmatized.[33]

The identified "Ute" captives at Abiquiu were not from Ute bands who were at peace with New Mexico. The resettlement of Abiquiu, the cessation of Ute hostilities in the northwest, and the Spanish-Ute alliance all coincided with the beginning of baptismal recordkeeping at Abiquiu. Indeed, Abiquiu's existence was tied to stable relations with Utes, and although Spanish-Ute relations often fluctuated over the ensuing decades, their alliance endured. Abiquiu and the Chama River settlements, in turn, continued to grow. Moreover, the alliance system prohibited Ute raids against New Mexico, and colonial governors repeatedly issued *bandos* forbidding unlicensed trading and slaving in Ute homelands. Surely, Ute children sold at Abiquiu, whether stolen by unscrupulous New Mexicans or Ute enemies, would be recognized by visiting Ute bands and returned to their families. Successful Ute redress for a lone stolen horse in 1762 and Valdez's subsequent trial highlight their comparative power and security within New Mexico. Utes traveled into the colony as guests, and they received gifts and protection from New Mexican leaders. Unless Ute leaders had their children purposefully baptized at Abiquiu as forms of alliance maintenance, or selectively placed their children into colonial society in forms of cultural exchange, then, it appears unlikely that the Utes would have permitted the capture and enslavement of their children. The appearance of the Ute bands together in 1752 at San Juan additionally suggests forms of interband alliance and cooperation that would seemingly have precluded interband slaving. From where, then, did these "Ute" captives come?[34]

As with the history of the African slave trade or the southern Indian slave trade, identifying the exact community backgrounds of captive children remains an impossible challenge, and these identified "Ute" captives offer only fleeting traces of larger, violent processes. When viewed in the context of the Spanish-Ute alliance, the presence of identified "Ute" captives in New Mexico suggests that as Spain incorporated neighboring Indian peoples into alliances, these Native groups in turn further displaced the violence and slavery of Spanish colonialism onto more distant, less powerful peoples. With powerful Navajo and Apache groups to their south, Comanche and other Great Plains peoples to their east and north, Utes primarily enslaved semi- and nonequestrian Great Basin peoples in the arid and mountainous terrain of southern Utah, Nevada, and eastern California. Such indications become more readily apparent in nineteenth-century sources, when traders, trappers, and Mormon settlers confronted Ute traffickers who insisted on trading children.[35]

Only a fraction of the total number of Great Basin captives survives in documentary records. Of the approximately 8,000 total baptisms at Abiquiu, for example, an estimated 1,000 were performed on children and young women without any identified ethnographies or parentage—telling hallmarks again of enslavement. Spanish clergy and officials probably documented the tribal origins of those whom they could identify, using general ethnographic and linguistic designations for classification. Since Utes, Southern Paiutes, and Western Shoshones speak related dialects of Southern Numic of the Shoshonean language family, New Mexicans classified these northwestern peoples as "Yutas," as Navajo historian David Brugge has suggested. Identifying a total of 527 "Ute" captives in New Mexico's church records from 1700 to 1849, Brugge notes that "the term *Yuta* . . . was obviously used as a general term for all Utes and Paiutes," a scholarly contention that many have followed. When viewed in the context of Spanish-Ute relations, Brugge's conclusions become even more pertinent. Utes in sum ferried semi- and nonequestrian Paiute bands into the colonial world after the 1750s during the consolidation of their alliance with New Mexico.[36]

These undifferentiated Southern Paiutes came from small, patrilineal bands from the low deserts of eastern California to the headwaters of the Colorado River. When exactly Paiute groups became enmeshed in the violence of Spanish colonialism is uncertain. The extent of colonial influences in these lands before the colonization of California remains undocumented. Like all Native peoples throughout New Mexico's hinterlands, Paiute groups experienced heightened levels of war, trade, and violence while enduring invasion by equestrian raiders. Besides destroying Indian families and communities through slavery, increased trade and traffic consumed scarce water supplies, game, and grasses—the staples of Indian survival in the region. While select moments of coexistence between "Payuche" and "Ute" bands are evident, by the nineteenth century many Ute bands had become predatory slavers who dominated nonequestrian communities. Such enslavement would last throughout the early decades of U.S. settlement and precipitate conflict during the Mormon-Ute wars of the 1850s.[37]

As with "Yutas," the term "Payuche" applies to different though culturally related groups, not to a single unified "tribe." Southern Paiutes, furthermore, generally lacked the equestrian economies of their Ute neighbors, living in more arid parts of the Great Basin less capable of sustaining equestrianism. Not forming consolidated bands like their equestrian neighbors, Southern Paiutes remained isolated from the zones of colonial encounter during the first century and a half of Spanish colonization. They did, however, face the growing threat of enslavement, particularly from their Ute neighbors, whose changing fortunes in New Mexico brought increased traffic and enslavement to their homelands.[38]

After their enslavement, Paiute captives, like other slaves, faced the cruel and arduous passage from their former communities to New Mexican markets. Taken by equestrian raiders, tied up and carried on horses or forced to walk, captives languished long before their sale into New Mexico. Women and children particularly suffered, often becoming incorporated into Ute and other Indian societies as wives or servants of their new Indian lords. Such incorporation remains difficult to identify, especially in the early decades of the Spanish-Ute détente; only in the early 1800s does the violent treatment of Paiute captives come into documentary focus, often in exaggerated form. Since few individual Paiute captives appear in eighteenth-century colonial records, inferences about the condition of Great Basin Indian slavery can be gleaned from records of the Utes' treatment of their other captives.[39]

The horrors of enslavement included punishments and abuses of all kinds, and the Utes were no more or less violent than other slave powers struggling to survive the maelstrom of colonialism. Utes responded to enslavement in kind and achieved many of their individual and community goals through violence as violence became woven into everyday life in the early West. Reprisals against other Indian slavers, in particular, provided both economic and personal compensation. In

Abiquiu on August 18, 1805, for example, Father José de la Prada wrote a grief-stricken letter to Governor Don Joaquín del Real Alencaster concerning the plight of a young Navajo woman (re)named María Concepción, who had been maltreated by Ute captors. Long known as bitter enemies, Utes and Navajos fought, raided, and attacked each other throughout the eighteenth and nineteenth centuries. Now one of the young casualties of these conflicts surfaced in front of a desperate Spanish friar. "As a religious, moved by charity," de la Prada wrote, "I . . . saved her from the tyranny of the Utes who took her as a captive in just war . . . but on account of their barbarous nature she was so ill-treated that her body was covered with wounds inflicted by arrow points, and she had been horsewhipped in such a manner that if I had not rescued her from them she would now be in eternity, and perhaps in Hell." Paying her tormentors several horses, a mule, and "about 100 pesos," de la Prada pleaded with the governor to place her in his custody rather than return her to her tribe against her wishes: "having been asked repeatedly . . . if she wished to return to the Navajos, bathed in tears she repeatedly answered, 'I do not want to.'" Notwithstanding the friar's pleas, María's professed wishes to stay at Abiquiu, and the small fortune spent to ransom her, leaders in Santa Fe reported that they found little "reason why she should not be surrendered to the Chiefs of the Navajo tribe." Spanish concerns about sustaining Navajo peace now outweighed concerns about an unfortunate casualty of war.[40]

María's treatment at the hands of her Ute captors was brutal but not extraordinary. Slavers often if not routinely abused their captives. Heated arrow points, whippings, and outright killings were among the most extreme forms of maltreatment recorded by Spanish observers. Such treatment was often deployed to exact greater sympathy as well as higher prices from colonial officials, and it extended into the Mexican and U.S. national periods, disquieting travelers, explorers, and settlers well into the 1860s.

Visitors, especially priests, left a long trail of angry denunciations of both Indian traders and Spanish authorities complicit in the slave trade. Describing the *genízaro* settlements along the Chama River, for example, Father Miguel de Menchero in 1744 noted that slavers "sell people of all . . . nations to the Spaniards . . . by whom they are held in servitude, the adults being instructed by the fathers and the children baptized. It sometimes happens that the Indians are not well treated in this servitude." In 1761 Father Pedro Serrano was far more extreme in his condemnation of what he witnessed at northern New Mexican trade fairs:

> Among many other infamies is one of such a nature that if I did not so desire a remedy I would remain silent . . . It is the truth that when these barbarians bring a certain number of Indian women to sell, among them many young maidens and girls, before delivering them to the Christians . . . if they are ten years old or over, they deflower and corrupt them in the sight of innumerable assemblies of barbarians and Catholics . . . and saying to those who buy them . . . "Now you can take her—now she is good."

The serial rape of captive Indian women became ritualized public spectacles at northern trade fairs, bringing the diverse male participants in New Mexico's political economy together for the violent dehumanization of Indian women. Such control over Indian women's bodies had become by the mid-1700s part and parcel of the region's slave networks. Colonial violence, in sum, recalibrated social relations within and between the region's many populations as the recovery of cultural dignity amidst such treatment became increasingly compromised.[41]

Coupled with the statistical information on "Ute" captives at Abiquiu, these brief glimpses of Indian slavery emphasize that enslavement, though violent, was not indiscriminate: it remained heavily gendered, with adolescent girls among the prime targets. As Pedro de Rivera noticed among the Comanche in the 1720s, raiders often killed adult male captives rather than attempting to enslave, transport, sell, and then incorporate them into colonial society. New Mexicans, furthermore, feared adult male captives, whose loyalties to crown and cross could not always be trusted. The Abiquiu "Ute" baptismal records reveal such intertwined gendered and age-based disparities. Of the 152 identified "Ute" captives at Abiquiu, 116 were also given approximate ages upon baptism, though how clergy and Spanish authorities assessed such age remains unclear. Of these 116, only 6.9 percent were fifteen years or older, and of these only 2 were males. Less than 2 percent of the "Ute" captives at Abiquiu, then, were adult males.[42]

The Spanish bought enslaved young Indian women not only for domestic and agricultural labor, but also for "sexual comfort" and reproductive labor. Nonconsensual sexual relations between female captives and New Mexican patriarchs assured demographic growth and male sexual pleasures. According to Ramón Gutiérrez, the "sexual comforts" of slavery created generations of *genízaros*, "coyotes," and other mixed-blood people, many of whom became wards or "children of the Church." Of the thirteen children baptized at Abiquiu to identifiable Ute mothers, only one, María Antonia Pfeffer, had an identified father. The rest did not. Perhaps their mother's *dueños, padrinos,* or other men who did not want to be acknowledged were their biological fathers. Since colonial hierarchies privileged the chastity and "virtue" of women, Indian children born out of wedlock became further stigmatized. Indian slavery thus not only reduced the numbers of surrounding Indian groups and strengthened the ties between New Mexico and its many Native allies; it also promoted a larger colonial population.[43]

At Abiquiu, "Ute" captive records additionally reveal another chilling aspect of Spanish slavery. Of the 13 "Ute" captives born to identified "Ute" mothers, the average age upon baptism was 1.6 years, an indication that these children of slaves, like their mothers, retained enough vestiges of tribal identities to be baptized as "Yutas"; whether they had ever lived in their mother's tribal communities remains uncertain. The balanced gender distribution of these 13 (7 males and 6 females) suggests that they were not brought into the colony as slaves, because the overwhelming majority of "Utes" baptized at Abiquiu were both female and young. Of the remaining 139 "Utes" baptized at Abiquiu, 90 (64.7 percent) were girls, as slave raiders targeted "Ute" girls nearly two to one over "Ute" boys. Such a high proportion of infants and young children further reveals that the political economy of Indian slavery prized the very young just as much as Indian women.

Although it is possible that neighboring Ute families had their own children baptized by Spanish friars at Abiquiu as part of the alliance system, baptismal records from nearby villages do not contain commensurate numbers of "Ute" baptisms. If Ute leaders had sought out baptism for their children, then such evidence should appear at neighboring communities like Santa Cruz de la Cañada or Taos, home to more prominent colonial religious and political leaders. Additionally, if Ute leaders sought access to their allies' spiritual power, surely they would have gone directly to those who exercised it in the colony's largest settlements and churches. Abiquiu remained on the margins of the colony.

Combined with the fleeting accounts of Ute traffic in captives at Abiquiu, comparative analysis of "Ute" baptisms in northern communities suggests that the threat of violence and enslavement remained both heavily gendered and age-based, with the most vulnerable members of Indian societies as targets. Baptized as "Utes" on the basis of their traders' language, these children may have never known their tribal origins. Some may have never learned, or soon forgotten, their native languages and customs, while others clung tight to memories of lost families and friends.

Inducted into the institutions of colonial society, captives lived at the lower levels. But though marginalized in New Mexico's caste system, the "Utes" at Abiquiu grew up among similarly diasporic peoples. They adapted to the racial and class inequities around them, eventually carving out autonomous spaces for themselves, their families, and future generations. For Abiquiu was a gateway community. As Pecos was to the Plains, Abiquiu was to the northwest. In the shifting dialectics of warfare, alliance, and enslavement between Utes and New Mexico, *genízaros* increasingly bridged these communities and regions. Over time, Indian captives and their descendants played central roles in the development of New Mexico's borderlands, becoming, for example, reliable militia members whose cultural familiarity and knowledge of northern societies helped mitigate border conflicts.[44]

Life at Abiquiu also differed from the experiences of other captives in settler homes in Santa Fe or Albuquerque. Although all felt the loss of family and experienced the horrors of enslavement, captives at Abiquiu and in Chama settlements entered communities composed largely of displaced peoples. Repopulated in the early 1750s, Abiquiu from its outset included exiled Indian peoples from Hopi and other pueblos as well as northern Indian captives. Though often indentured to work as ranchers, herders, and domestic servants, *genízaros* at Abiquiu eventually received land grants and raised their own crops and herds, forms of autonomy uncommon in settler households. Governors granted such property rights in order to increase the population of northern communities and to create fortified buffers along New Mexico's borders. Cachupín, for example, in May 1754 toured Abiquiu, appointed the first resident priest in the town, and asked the viceroy to recognize the "permanent establishment . . . of the recently congregated nation of Genizaros." Living in the village in their own adobe homes, *genízaros* herded, produced goods for market, and eventually secured more freedom than most other captives. Over time, Abiquiu's *genízaros* married, served in the colony's defenses, and helped explore northern hinterlands. The relationships between Abiquiu's *genízaros* and Ute allies, then, facilitated the colony's reach to California, expansion that brought Spanish traders, missionaries, and explorers for the first time into the Great Basin.[45]

Abiquiu and Great Basin Exploration

Abiquiu's population increased after the creation of the Spanish-Ute alliance. From an abandoned village of forty-four families in 1744, Abiquiu had grown by 1760 to 733 inhabitants (16 percent *genízaro*). In 1798 its denizens numbered 1,749 (10 percent *genízaros*), and in 1821, 3,275 (8 percent "Indians"). While identifiable Indians and *genízaros* constituted an ever smaller percentage of Abiquiu's total population, the rapid growth of the *vecino* population suggests a high degree of acculturation and Hispanicization as captives and *genízaros* acquired new ethnic classifications. Abiquiu's heterogeneity reflected its proximity to northern Indian nations, its security and demographic growth indelibly tied to stable relations with the Utes.[46]

The peace that was carved out by Spanish and Ute leaders centered upon mediated trade fairs, gift exchanges, and other negotiated protections and privileges. Unsanctioned trading by New Mexican settlers in Ute homelands jeopardized the peace, because unlicensed traders sought economic and carnal temptations provided by Indian slavery. Spanish leaders constantly worried when unscrupulous traders antagonized Indian communities either by trading at grossly inflated rates or by seizing unprotected goods and children, thereby eroding the bonds of reciprocity that had developed between allies. While turning a blind eye to aspects of the slave trade within the colony, colonial governors attempted to monitor trade outside, requiring licenses for those who wished to venture north. In 1778, for instance, Governor Francisco Trébol Navarro issued a *bando* stating that "no goodman, Indian or *genízaro* shall go nor send another . . . to the Ute country to trade, under the penalty of losing all the effects sent or received . . . a fine of 100 'pesos de la tierra' . . . [and] if [the transgressor] is Indian or *genízaro* . . . 100 lashes." New Mexican traders, according to Navarro, had transgressed earlier *bandos*, "going again and again to the Ute country."[47]

Despite such proclamations and threatened fines, northern trade continued to entice, and many New Mexicans went illegally in search of the Utes. Between 1770 and 1800 five expeditions were caught and their members tried; David Weber notes that "illegal *entradas* into the Ute country . . . may have occurred as frequently as once a year." Not surprisingly, the majority came from Abiquiu and surrounding communities. In 1783, for instance, Santiago Martín, the lieutenant to the *alcalde mayor* at Abiquiu, "got up a posse of ten Spanish men and two Indians to go . . . and pursue . . . certain settlers who went fugitive to trade with the Utes." Catching eight settlers from Abiquiu, Martín imprisoned the party and seized its goods, which consisted of awls, knives, bushels of corn, and tobacco, as well as a few horses and mules. Under interrogation, three of the traders testified that Abiquiu's *alcalde mayor* himself had given them permission to go north and sent one of his *genízaro* servants to accompany them. When questioned by his lieutenant, Salvador Martín indeed confessed to having allowed the party to venture north in open violation of the law, as the benefits of Ute trade tempted normally dutiful citizens and authorities alike.[48]

As the 1783 trial indicated, Indian servants and *genízaros* often accompanied and guided trading expeditions. Identifiable "Ute" *genízaros* often participated in this illegal trade as guides, translators, or intermediaries. They also served in officially sanctioned expeditions, the first of which occurred in 1765 under Juan María Antonio Rivera. Rivera described his companion as "the interpreter Joachín, *indio genízaro* of the Pueblo of Abiquiu." According to Joseph Sánchez, Joachín was probably "of Ute origin," and his service on Rivera's behalf nearly brought the expedition imperial fame. Fantastic rumors had circulated throughout the colony after a Ute named Cuero de Lobo had traded a piece of silver to an Abiquiu blacksmith, who made two rosaries and a cross out of this precious metal. Could additional mines be found in New Spain's most northern province? Coming a little more than a decade after the formation of the Spanish-Ute alliance, Rivera's two expeditions initiated a half-century of exploration as dreams of fame, wealth, and mythic waterways lured New Mexicans into the Great Basin.[49]

Assembled in late June 1765, Rivera's party consisted of eight men, mainly from the Chama Valley region. Traveling past familiar Ute paths and landmarks, Rivera observed, recorded, and renamed much of the landscape. Entering the present limits of southwestern Colorado, for example, the party forded rivers, several of which still bear Rivera's names, and on July 4, along the Rio de las Animas, they encountered their first Ute *ranchería* since departing:

> After we had presented them with food, tobacco, corn, and pinole [a warm and probably fermented beverage], Gregorio Sandoval began to talk about our reason for being there. They were well aware that the Yuta we sought, *Cuero de Lobo,* was not at that settlement. He was the one who showed us the piece of silver or metal [he had found]. We were told that he had gone to a settlement of the Payuchis to visit his mother-in-law. They added that about five leagues down the river was a[nother] settlement . . . Among them was an old Yuta woman who knew about other silver outcroppings. They suggested that we should go see her instead.

After finding this woman and getting directions to the silver deposits, Rivera and a few men rushed "to the said place . . . having run our horses at a quick trot and gallop." The party then spent three days searching unsuccessfully for the deposits and became "so angry . . . at the Yuta woman, that . . . thoughts to kill her . . . crossed our minds."[50]

Deciding instead to find Cuero de Lobo among the Payuchis, Rivera's party traveled for several days west through the dry, relatively open terrain near the current Four Corners region. Under a newly enlisted Ute guide, the party's forward scouts on July 14 encountered "about ten small settlements of unruly Payuchis," traveling back to meet the main party two days later, "accompanied by the Payuchis." As Rivera recounted:

> I received Captain Chino and his Payuchis in our camp and we gave them gifts of tobacco, pinole, flour, and corn . . . That done, *Captain Chino* ordered that we communicate. He began by asking about what we Spaniards were doing [passing] through such rough country. What

was it we sought? To which we responded that we hoped to find a Yuta called *Cuero de Lobo* . . . We also said that we wanted to know where was the largest river in the area, called *Río del Tizón.*

The Paiute leaders responded that Cuero de Lobo "had returned to his land" and that "the said river was too far" away in a "waterless country with little pasturage." Encouraging the Spanish "not to be foolish," Captain Chino suggested that they return to New Mexico and come again in the fall, when "there would be pasturage and some water."[51]

Receiving additional geographical information, Rivera returned east, where he finally located Cuero de Lobo. The Ute trader guided him to mineral deposits that Rivera hoped would soon rival the mines of Peru. "It can be said without exaggeration," he reported, "that the entire mountain is made of pure metal." Unfortunately for Rivera, "what the Yutas thought was silver was actually lead." Collecting several of these less valued minerals, the party departed south disappointed. For local Utes and Paiutes, the trip had failed to satiate the Spaniards' never-ending hunger for precious metals and its accompanying demand for Indian labor.[52]

Rivera's first expedition produced a wealth of information about the northwest, and Cachupín granted his request to survey and prospect the region further. After nearly two centuries of colonization, the governor entertained visions of another Potosí that might transform his colonial backwater into a land of fabulous riches. And failing that, the great Río del Tizón identified by Rivera offered the potential of irrigable lands for future settlement as well as possible waterways to the Pacific. The northwest, in short, could now be colonized. And these unknown peoples, the Payuchis, "of which there are seven or eight" tribes, might be potential converts, though they had warned about seasonal shortages of water and forage. So Rivera returned to the northwest in October 1765.[53]

The lands northwest of New Mexico had of course already been named by and were intimately familiar to Paiute and Ute peoples. To Rivera and the Spanish, however, Ute and Paiute homelands presented imperial possibilities—new lands, mines, waterways, and peoples to control—and Rivera yielded to such fantasies as he and his party trudged over difficult terrain, the pain and sweat of their toil only further reminders of potential fortune. Unlike the illegal traders from Abiquiu, Rivera had received sanction for his expedition from the highest levels in the empire. The glory they achieved would be not contraband.

Although Utes had interacted with New Mexicans since the 1600s, Paiute groups had lived outside the realms of European knowledge, settlement, and cartography. Their everyday worlds, and the changes that came to them, thus went unrecorded. But their absence from the constellation of documented peoples by no means shielded them from the effects of colonial expansion. Like all Indian peoples surrounding New Mexico, Paiutes witnessed increased warfare, the spread of epidemic diseases, and forms of violent capture. These colonial influences affected Paiute groups before Rivera's arrival, and their encounters with Rivera and subsequent explorers provide glimpses of such disruptions.

Rivera's party traveled during a period of peace between Utes and New Mexicans when Ute and Spanish leaders received respectful treatment in each other's territories. Consequently Rivera's party moved freely into Ute homelands, surveying lands and peoples. Rivera found the Paiutes different from, and more "unruly" than, New Mexico's Ute allies. Unruliness, for Rivera, signaled critical differences: Utes traded annually in New Mexico, held counsel with the governor, and fought aside Spanish forces; semiequestrian and nonequestrian peoples did not.

The boundaries between Paiute and Ute societies were, however, porous; the Colorado Plateau remained a landscape of territorially organized bands, not "tribes." Rivera, after all, had encountered Chino's Paiute band while in search of the Ute guide Cuero de Lobo. Like many Utes, Cuero de Lobo had traded at Abiquiu, moved between New Mexican and Ute homelands, and guided Spanish parties into Ute territory. He had guided Rivera to the mountain of metal. He was familiar and comfortable negotiating with Spanish traders. He also had a Paiute wife and "was said to be among" her people when Rivera arrived. Cuero de Lobo carried such familiarity into his wife's community, telling them about his experiences with their southern neighbors. Chief Chino's band of Paiutes, then, had ties to Ute bands and included families who had traveled, traded, and lived with New Mexicans.[54]

Clearly, Chino's Paiutes as well as the "seven or eight" bands who were their neighbors to their west, knew about the Spanish before their arrival in Paiute territory. His band was possibly a part of the "Payuchi" nation referred to by Cachupín during the 1752 Ute treaty negotiations. They were also among the first Paiute groups to acquire horses; for, as Rivera recorded two days after their first meeting, "Our men, whom we quickly recognized, arrived accompanied by the Payuchis." Accompanying Spanish scouts meant riding alongside them on horseback. Organized under the leadership of a chief, or "captain," who spoke for his band, received guests, and traveled to meet their leaders, this Paiute group remained allied to some degree with Utes to their east, living on the distant border of the equestrian frontier of northern New Spain. By the nineteenth century, however, few Paiute groups would achieve a comparable coexistence with their Ute neighbors; waves of enslavement, warfare, and increased foreign traffic soon positioned equestrian groups over others.[55]

Rivera's journal of his October 1765 return provides initial insights into the growing disparities between equestrians and nonequestrians. Again, select Ute and Paiute bands responded differently to his journey. Having never received Spanish leaders into their communities, for example, Ute bands in western Colorado joyfully welcomed his party, emulating the ways in which Spanish leaders welcomed Utes. A Tabehuachi village, for instance, "came out to happily receive" Rivera's party. They shared foods, danced, and gathered together to smoke, enacting the shared rituals of the Spanish-Ute alliance. Dependent upon Ute guidance, Rivera responded cordially though unenthusiastically: "As a test of friendship, they implored us to stay with them . . . to celebrate and trade with us . . . as we did not wish to make them unhappy, we accepted . . . [even though] we did not like wasting two days." His party's time, food, and staples were critical to their project of exploration, not to maintaining the Spanish-Ute alliance.[56]

For other communities, Rivera's party occasioned not celebration but danger. In southern Colorado, for example, a party of Muache Utes were "determined not to let us pass, saying that we were going to reconnoiter their lands and could ruin their trade." As the closest allies and intermediaries between New Mexico and the northwest, the Muache feared losing their comparative advantage: the spread of Spanish trade networks might threaten not only their control over their lands but also their trade with other groups, and they resisted

Rivera's calls for guides. Negotiating instead with nearby Paiutes for guides, Rivera hurriedly left Muache territory, venturing into lands previously unmapped by New Mexicans. After several days the party met "five Payuchi settlements [in] which, when their people saw us, they sounded alarms and fled our intrusion." Persuading these Paiutes that they came to trade, not to plunder, Rivera's guides convinced these frightened people to come down from their hideouts—defensive maneuvers increasingly noted by subsequent expeditions. The initial Paiute reactions, the use of well-positioned alarms and flight into the hills, suggest that these people had experienced intrusions into their community before. Apparently they had reasons to fear the presence of unknown horsemen in their homelands.[57]

In mid-October, after weeks of travel and anticipation, Rivera's party reached the fabled Río del Tizón. After their Ute guide sent "two boys who had accompanied him to call the people down from the other side so that they could trade," Rivera and his party turned to him and expressed doubt: "We communicated with our guide, telling him that this was not the Río del Tizón which we sought and that he had misled us. To that, he responded sadly that there was no other major river in the area than that one." When the peoples across the river arrived to trade, Rivera immediately "asked them" about the river. Even the following day, after meeting some Sabuagana Utes, Rivera continued to doubt what everyone had told him. "They confirmed the same," he wrote, "and we were then persuaded that it was the river we sought . . . I judge that it is the Colorado River that empties into the Gulf of Mexico." For months Rivera had traveled through Ute and Paiute homelands hoping to find a fabled river that flowed into the Pacific. His imperial fantasies were slow to evaporate; expecting to find marvelous possessions, he doubted the veracity of the Indian peoples who lived in lands where he had never been. Having found neither silver deposits nor a Northwest Passage, before the party returned to New Mexico Rivera made his most enduring mark of discovery: "In the meadow of the Great Río del Tizón, on a white poplar, I carved a large cross with the words 'Long Live Jesus' at the top and my name. At the foot of the tree, I carved the year so that it could be verified at a future time that we had gotten that far."[58]

Rivera's journeys to the northwest offered little justification for expanding the crown's authority into these northern lands. Poor min-

eral resources, few sites for missionization, and difficult waterways offered Cachupín little incentive for colonization. The governor's more
immediate concerns in 1765 involved maintaining peaceful relations
with Comanches, relations that his successors failed to sustain. Soon
New Mexican–Comanche conflicts escalated to critical levels, devastating New Mexico and even extending farther south into Mexico.

In the wake of these conflicts, larger imperial processes in the 1770s
would refocus on the northwest as the paths charted by Rivera eventually broadened into a larger regional network of trade. Such trade and
traffic would remain dependent upon Ute compliance and wreak further terror and devastation upon the region's nonequestrians. Soon
numerous equestrian raiders would dominate the interior between
New Mexico and California, as Paiute community alarms became increasingly sounded.

THREE

✦ ✦ ✦

The Enduring Spanish-Ute Alliance

Because it ventured hundreds of miles farther than any previous Spanish party, crossing into central Utah, the 1776 expedition of Francisco Atanasio Domínguez and Francisco Silvestre Vélez de Escalante is often viewed as the first event in Great Basin history. Far from moving into societies previously untouched by European influences, however, the expedition traveled through homelands already affected by the imperial contests remaking North America in the late eighteenth century. The party's interactions with a dozen Ute and Paiute bands in Colorado and Utah provide glimpses into the nature of these transformations. For example, the friars' repeated promises that Spanish missionaries would return to "live among them," to instruct them in the teachings of the Gospel, and to show them the benefits of agriculture and settlement met with much enthusiasm. Plagued by equestrian raiders, many viewed the friars as potential allies in their violent homelands. Such promises, however, went unfulfilled as Spanish dreams of Great Basin missionization faded with the disintegration of Spain's New World empire.[1]

Following Domínguez and Escalante, the last half-century of Spanish rule in the Southwest brought not peace but increased trade, disruption, and slavery to Great Basin peoples. By the end of the 1780s, New Mexico's Comanche conflicts, which had helped forge the Spanish-Ute alliance, had ended, and a rapprochement ensued between these former enemies. As New Mexican–Comanche antagonisms dissipated, New Mexicans and Utes solidified their alliance in new ways.

Through trade and diplomacy these allies expanded the ties developed during the Comanche crisis as the cessation of Comanche raids brought prosperity to both New Mexican and Ute communities. Growing *vecino* settlements teemed with activity throughout northern New Mexico, furnishing Utes with additional metals, foods, cloths, and other trade items in exchange. Utes in turn increased their trade with the northern valleys. But what benefited the Utes did not necessarily benefit their neighbors. As they had since the beginnings of the Spanish-Ute alliance, Utes continued to raid neighboring Indian communities for slaves whom they sold at New Mexican trade fairs. Throughout the late eighteenth and early nineteenth centuries, trade and slave routes expanded into the Great Basin as Ute and New Mexican traders ferried goods between their communities. Such trading, exploring, and slaving went through Paiute homelands and incorporated these communities into New Mexico's hinterlands.[2]

With the collapse of Spanish New Mexico and the creation of independent Mexico in the 1820s, New Mexican–Ute relations began to erode. Three generations of social relations between New Mexico and its Ute allies had centered upon negotiated privileges and protections. Mexican independence, however, presented new challenges. Beset by perpetual instabilities, with the many different peoples of the north often ignoring or disobeying national authority, Mexico failed to incorporate its northern borders into a unified nation. New Mexico's growing autonomy and concomitant weakening state structure, in turn, heralded the dissolution of the Spanish-Ute alliance. As Mexican officials failed to ensure and enact the ritualized relations of the Spanish-Ute alliance, Ute bands developed alternative and violent strategies of survival. Growing Ute militarization and weakening political ties with Santa Fe ensued with the collapse of Spain's American empire.[3]

Mexican independence accelerated a second change to the New Mexican–Ute borderlands. In their attempts to encourage economic growth and liberalize the national economy, Mexican officials encouraged greater trade with British and American traders. Whereas Spain had attempted to police its colonies' borders and regulate foreign traffic, Mexico envisioned increased international trade and even foreign immigration in its north. New Mexicans, desperate themselves for more material goods, welcomed and participated in this new trade, and after 1821 Anglo-American traders streamed into the region. Entering and passing through Ute homelands, these agents from a different empire carried imperial designs that would soon bring even greater changes to the peoples of the north.

Domínguez and Escalante in Great Basin Indian Homelands

As northern New Spain suffered increased indigenous raids in the second half of the eighteenth century, debates about expanding, solidifying, or even abandoning the north preoccupied the Spanish monarchy, which soon initiated sweeping reforms. When King Carlos III dispatched Spain's most prominent military advisers to inspect New Spain's defenses, few knew what recommendations would be forthcoming. The Marqués de Rubí, assigned to tour the northern *presidios* in 1766–1768, reported on the dismal failure of nearly all missions and *presidios* north of Durango to control resident as well as outlying Indian populations. In order to protect Mexico's valuable mines, he suggested that a defensive line from the Gulf of California to El Paso be established to ward off Indian invasions. Such redrawn imperial boundaries would have left Spain's settlements in New Mexico and Texas unprotected altogether. Rubí's call for essentially abandoning the north, according to Elizabeth John, suggested "to the Crown that much of its empire in the north was a sham . . . the northern presidios were military mockeries." Powerful Indian societies controlled most of the territory that New Spain claimed within its northern boundary. With England's growing control over North America following the Seven Years' War and Russian exploration down the Pacific coast, Spanish officials, notwithstanding Rubí's suggestions, reaffirmed their commitment to New Mexico, and in a bold move even planned to expand colonial settlements northward along the Pacific.[4]

The colonization of California, begun in 1769, quickly spread north to Monterey, where local Indians were subdued and missionized by Spanish soldiers and friars. Along with the calls emanating from Spain for reinforcement of its colonial frontier, the California missions spawned efforts to link the two northernmost colonies of New Spain—New Mexico and California. Spanish leaders envisioned two sets of trails linking the Rio Grande and the Pacific. The first would travel from Santa Fe due west past Hopi and Zuni Pueblos, before heading south into southern California. The second would leave New Mexico from Abiquiu, where a decade of traders had developed intimate ties with northern peoples. This second route was envisioned to pass through the unknown lands of the Utes, toward a fabled watershed that Spanish leaders believed flowed to the Pacific from the Rocky Mountains, whose slopes received the heaviest snowfall in all of New Spain.[5]

Spain's greatest cartographic and geographic minds affirmed that such a river flowed west to California. Both the Sacramento and San Joaquín Rivers of central California drain into the San Francisco Bay north of Monterey, and early explorers believed that the headwaters of these rivers originated in the mountains north of New Mexico. Franciscan Francisco Garcés, for example, who traveled under Indian guides through central California, the Mojave Desert, and then to Hopi Pueblo in Arizona, wrote: "If from the said Yutas be taken the direction northwest . . . it is certain one could go to Monte-Rey and also to the Puerto de San Francisco." Direct and "certain" travel meant following western rivers, and the most experienced Spanish explorers, like Garcés, believed that Ute homelands were key to any exploration to California. The great distances, vast and dry lands, and peoples in between remained unmapped as the Spanish began their efforts to link the two colonies.[6]

As with Rivera, such imagined geographies seemed entirely credible to Spanish explorers. They motivated passage through difficult terrain, and traders, missionaries, and explorers planned their expeditions in anticipation of finding potential metals, converts, or important geographic information. To travel and explore became synonymous with empire-building as all the earliest licensed travelers to the northwest extended the influence of the crown into uncharted lands.

Such imperial logic propelled the first expedition from Abiquiu to the Pacific. Commissioned in 1776 to chart the lands of the northwest and to search for routes to Monterey, Franciscans Domínguez and Vélez de Escalante assembled a party of ten and left Santa Fe on July 29. Unlike previous trading parties out of Abiquiu, theirs would be a journey not of weeks, but of months, designed not to yield profit but to establish links with Monterey.

The party followed the familiar paths out of Abiquiu that Rivera and other traders had charted. In it were two brothers, Andrés and Antonio Lucrecio Muñiz, who had accompanied Rivera. These experienced traders both spoke Ute and had traded several times in Ute territory in violation of gubernatorial *bandos*. This expedition, however, as Domínguez and Escalante repeated to their party, was not for personal gain, but for the greater glory of God and His appointed servant, His Majesty King Carlos III. Spreading the truth of the Gospel to unconverted Indian gentiles, identifying fertile sites for new settlements, and finding an overland path to Monterey were their primary objectives.[7]

To these ends, Domínguez and Escalante faithfully recorded their journey, noted changing geographic and ethnographic landscapes, and enlisted the services of cartographer Bernardo Miera y Pacheco. Miera had come to El Paso from Spain in 1743, and his cartographic skills had already expanded the geographic knowledge of northern New Spain. The friars' journals and Miera's maps make their travels among the best-documented Spanish campaigns in North America, providing focused insights into the nature of Great Basin history in the late eighteenth century.[8]

As with other trading expeditions to the northwest, Domínguez and Escalante's voyage came only with the compliance and hospitality of Utes, as the Spanish-Ute alliance provided the mechanisms for their guidance through Ute homelands. Domínguez had arrived in New Mexico in March 1776, and Escalante a few years earlier. Neither, then, had had much previous contact with Ute leaders, and they sometimes misunderstood the political and social landscapes into which they ventured. The friars, for example, had heard fanciful tales about the north, including cryptic stories of a "lost" tribe of Spaniards. This unknown group reportedly lived north of the Colorado River, used metal weapons and armor, and wore long beards. The friars believed them to be offshoots of the California settlements or even marooned sailor communities from the galleon fleets from Manila to Mexico. Such tales fueled their belief that Monterey was only a short summer's travel away, a mistake that nearly cost them their lives.[9]

Setting out from Abiquiu on August 1, the party under the Muñiz brothers' guidance traveled weeks before locating Ute guides. The lands immediately northwest of Abiquiu remained controlled by no single Native group and were used by Navajo, Ute, and Comanche bands as a corridor into New Mexico; heading southeast along the Chama, hostile Native groups often launched raids from distant *ran-*

cherías where women and children anxiously awaited the return of fathers and sons. Allied Native groups, such as the Utes, brought their bands farther into the colony and camped along the Chama and its tributaries, pasturing their herds and preparing their goods for market. New Mexican traders knew these lands and their hazards well, referring to them simply as "lands of war." Traders used natural and manmade landmarks to make their own way back and forth, and such mentally recorded cartographies became invaluable for official expeditions. The Muñiz brothers and Miera no doubt spent long hours discussing the features of these northern lands, and Miera drew them for the first time on paper.[10]

The first month proved far more difficult than anticipated. The trails out of Abiquiu were well worn, but the passage through the canyons of southwestern Colorado taxed the party's supplies and horses. After passing into recognized Ute territory, the expedition traveled two weeks before finding Ute guides. Domínguez also grew ill after an evening of "excessively cold" weather along the Mancos River. Following the trails of Rivera and earlier traders, the party was overtaken on August 14 by a *genízaro,* Juan Domingo, and a "coyote," Felipe, both from Abiquiu, who had come "so as to wander among the heathen. They had run away without the permission of their masters." Reluctantly accepting these newcomers, the party, now twelve, became further lost as they followed tracks into dead-end canyons and sought pasture and water for their horses. On August 23 they finally found a Ute guide and persuaded him "to guide us as far as the encampment of a Sabuagana chieftain who our interpreter and others said was very fond of the Spaniards." This guide was reluctant to take the foreigners to distant Ute *rancherías,* but he agreed after receiving a few of the trade goods the party carried. Because trade had become so intrinsic to Spanish-Ute relations that it overshadowed other potential purposes, the Ute's small band "did not wholly believe" that the Spaniards had not come to trade.[11]

As Rivera had learned earlier, Utes expected explorers to enact the rituals of the Spanish-Ute alliance. Gift-giving, shared celebratory offerings, and above all trade wedded these northern peoples to Santa Fe. Domínguez and Escalante, however, had not brought extensive gifts or trade goods. Theirs was a divine mission. The friars did understand the need to share ritual food, tobacco, and some trade items, but they were not prepared to trade for cumbersome deerskins, buffalo hides, or horses. At first their failure to enact a trade ritual remained of limited consequence: on August 30, for example, a Ute community celebrated the party's arrival, enjoying "the kindness we were doing them." But the Spaniards' failure to engage in sustained exchange soon brought increased tensions with their hosts.[12]

The friars' first attempt to convince Ute leaders to convert came on September 1. After arriving in a Sabuagana *ranchería* of approximately thirty tents and eighty warriors, Domínguez explained their purpose. Sharing the Gospel with the assembled Ute leaders, he promised to return "to instruct them and set them in a way of living that would lead them to baptism." The friars noted sites for possible Spanish colonization and hoped to return the following year to missionize these allies. Missionization, however, would require that Utes discontinue many cultural practices. Some Ute leaders, for instance, reportedly took multiple wives and, according to the friars, often named themselves "after wild beasts—thus placing themselves on a par with them, and even below them." Such practices, they instructed, must end when the friars returned. Hundreds of miles from the closest settlement, the friars' conviction and chauvinism surprised Ute leaders, who were accustomed to less-than-pious traders. Whether Utes found such prescriptions offensive or simply abnormal, they nonetheless marveled at the party's resilience, a resiliency that confounded and soon jeopardized established protocols for diplomacy. For the friars' travels through Ute homelands brought unanticipated hazards for their Ute hosts, who worried that the expedition's potential demise might threaten their own standing in Santa Fe.[13]

As Sabuagana leaders weighed the benefits of Spanish missionization, they strenuously discouraged the expedition from traveling farther, warning them of "Comanche" raiders to the north. "A little before sundown," the friars noted, "the chief, some very old men, and many others . . . began trying to persuade us to turn back from here, exaggerating anew and with greater effort the hardships and perils to which we were exposing ourselves." Thanking the Ute leaders for their concern, the friars reiterated their faith and resolve. To which the Utes "said that since we wished to go ahead . . . we should write to the great chief of the Spaniards telling him that we passed through their country, so that, in the event that we had some mishap and did not return, the Spaniards would not think that they had taken our lives." Dismissing these warnings and requests, Domínguez and Escalante failed to realize how they threatened the very communities among whom they traveled. Already concerned about losing possible Spanish gifts to their northern enemies, these Utes worried even more about losing their standing in New Mexico. Comanche grievances with the Spanish were well known, and the Ute leaders knew well the dangers of traveling in a small, unarmed party through adjacent lands. Having warned the party each time "with greater effort" not to continue, Ute leaders now requested written proof of such warnings. The power of Spanish documentation, they hoped, might absolve them should misfortune beset the expedition. Such appeals first to Spanish rationality and then to documentation reveal the Utes' understandings of colonial technologies of power, understandings solidified by generations of trading and now alliance with New Mexico.[14]

As Ute requests fell on deaf ears, several members of the expedition, much to the friars' displeasure, began to trade. The Muñiz brothers, in particular, shared their hosts' fear of northern enemies, and after failing to convince Domínguez and Escalante to turn back, the brothers began trading for weapons that they knew would be needed in the territories ahead:

> Ever since La Villa de Santa Fe, we had reminded all . . . not to take along any goods for trading . . . All agreed not to bring a thing, nor to have any purpose other than the one we had, which was God's glory . . . But some of them failed in their promise by secretly carrying some goods . . . We had just been telling the Sabuaganas that we needed neither arms nor men because we placed all our safety and defense in God's almighty arm . . . [when] Andrés . . . with his brother . . . peddled what they secretly brought along and most greedily sought weapons from the infidels.

The Muñiz brothers exchanged hidden goods to better equip themselves for potential battle, an irony lost on the Spanish friars. The brothers had traveled among northern peoples before and believed the Utes' heeds and warnings. They also traded to demonstrate respect for their Ute hosts. While Domínguez and Escalante entertained lofty religious and imperial ambitions, other members of their party better understood the practicalities of defense and alliance diplomacy.[15]

After leaving the Sabuaganas, the expedition secured two "Laguna" Ute guides to take them farther west toward Monterey. These Utes, one renamed Silvestre, another Joaquín, "still a boy," came from communities to the west that lived near several large lakes. Believing these waters to be headwaters of rivers to the Pacific, the party traversed for two weeks through western Colorado. While Silvestre fearfully noted "Comanche" tracks along their paths, the party eluded enemies—the friars' piety and judgment proven in the face of *genízaro* and Ute experience. Passing the westernmost chain of the Colorado Rockies, known as the Wasatch, the expedition soon emerged from the mountainous valleys of the Colorado Plateau into the expansive horizons of the central Great Basin, and as they neared Utah Lake in early October, the distances and unknown lands to the west became ever more daunting. Surrounded by tracts of arid lands in western Utah, the party debated returning to New Mexico, fearing the evening cold and distant sierra snows. The *terra incognita* to their west, they knew, must lead to the Pacific, but just how distant their objective was and what societies existed in between they could not tell.[16]

Unlike their distant Ute neighbors in Colorado, these "Laguna" Utes lived in less concentrated and mobile settlements. They had few, if any, previous relations with New Mexicans. They lived hundreds of miles from Santa Fe and weeks of arduous travel from their Ute neighbors in Colorado. Outside of the Spanish-Ute alliance system, they lived not in militarized equestrian *rancherías* but in semisedentary villages on the banks of Utah Lake and its rivers. They fished seasonally and in 1776 lacked the horse herds needed for extensive hunting and travel. The cycles of violence swirling throughout New Mexico's hinterlands, however, had already affected their homelands. They repeatedly expressed their fear of equestrian attack to the friars, and as the expedition emerged into the Utah Lake Valley, it encountered Laguna defenses: "Through where we came we found the meadow's pastures recently burnt and other adjacent ones still burning. From this we inferred that these Indians had taken us for . . . hostile people and, perhaps seeing that we brought horses, had tried to burn the pastures along our way so that the lack of them would make us leave." While burning may have ordinarily been an agricultural practice, these Utes knew the dangers posed by equestrian intruders and scorched their own homelands accordingly. As for so many peoples around New Mexico, the threat of equestrian violence had become a part of the Lagunas' everyday lives.[17]

Assuaging Laguna fears through their interpreter, Silvestre, the expedition spent several days spreading their message of a beneficent king and heavenly father. As Domínguez explained: "For, by submitting themselves . . . our Great Chief whom we call King would send them everything . . . He would . . . [regard] them as His children." The Laguna chiefs gathered the following day, "and all unanimously replied that the padres should come . . . adding most earnestly that we must not tarry long in returning." Excited about the potential benefits as well as the protection of missionization, the Lagunas expected to see the padres the following fall, and as the party departed the Utes "bade us farewell most tenderly, especially Silvestre, who hugged us tightly, practically in tears."[18]

Despite their successes among the Laguna, the route toward Monterey still eluded the expedition. Securing a new guide, the party continued southwest for two weeks despite the Utes' remarks "that none of them knew much of the territory in the direction . . . we were about to take," though they recommended "we would go on making inquiries among the nations along our route." The nations along their route, however, had never heard of any Spaniards to the west. Small bands of Paiutes encountered south of the Sevier River lived in scattered settlements and in much smaller numbers than the Lagunas. Some were so fearful that they ran away upon sighting the strangers. Others agreed to guide them only to get them away from their families, then fled. They also spoke dialects difficult for the New Mexican translators to interpret. The party, in short, was nowhere near the Pacific, becoming more desperate every day. Such desperation soon bred desperate acts as the party's men forcibly detained Paiute men and women in attempt to secure guides. "We tried to take away their fear," they reported on October 12 after encountering a group of twenty Paiute women and a few men out gathering: "They were running so fast that they [the scouts] were barely able to get hold of one." One captive became "so intimidated that he appeared out of his mind," but slowly began to comply with his captors' requests. When asked about other Spaniards and the lands to the west, "he answered that there weren't any, that although many peoples lived all over these areas, these were of his very own language, and Indians like himself." Leading them back to his small band, he and another guided the party farther south, into a tight canyon where, promptly, "they vanished from our sight."[19]

Unable to retain guides, the party wandered through southern Utah. As the weather, terrain, and environment worsened, the friars realized that Monterey was not as close as imagined. The arid lands of Utah contrasted with the lush Californian splendor that they had anticipated, and their hopes not only of reaching California, but also of ever returning to Spanish settlements, receded further every day.

With no guides, little food and water for themselves and their herd of animals, and beset by cold, the friars decided near present-day Cedar City to return to New Mexico. In an attempt to judge their position better, they climbed a small peak in the Black Mountains and gazed along the valley floor to the west: "We . . . saw that from here toward the southwest it stretched for more than thirty-five or forty leagues, for where it ends in this direction one could barely discern the sierras, those being very high." Gazing toward Nevada, the friars saw a landscape of seemingly endless mountain valleys, home to Indian peoples who offered little or no help in reaching California. Berated by their nearly mutinous crew, who still wanted to continue, the Franciscans put their faith in divine judgment, decided to cast lots, and finally secured consensus to return to New Mexico.[20]

Despite encountering lands of scarcity, Domínguez and Escalante envisioned future missions and settlements throughout the region, and their visions of empire centered upon Utes and Paiutes as servants to crown and cross. These groups, they noted, had no prior exposure to Christianity or "settled" life, and their receptiveness confirmed the friars' determination and sense of purpose. Shortly after they crossed the Rio Santa Ysabel (Sevier River), for example, a group of Paiute leaders approached the party. "Very early, twenty Indians arrived in the king's camp . . . all covered with blankets of cottontail and jackrabbit furs . . . Now these ones, more fully bearded than the Lagunas . . . more resemble the Spaniards than they do all the other Indians known in America." These "Bearded Utes," as they became known, quickly won the Spaniards' affection and epitomized the urgency of missionization. Their friendly manners, beards, and industry reminded the friars of followers from strict religious orders and suggested that even in such a remote region the common humanity of all God's children could be found. After receiving the Gospel "very joyfully," the Paiutes replied that the padres must "come back . . . [and] that they would do whatsoever we taught them." Afterward the parties exchanged tearful goodbyes: "They touched our hearts so much that some of our companions could not hold back the tears."[21]

Though no doubt embellishing their journals to convince imperial officials of their achievements, Domínguez and Escalante offered Paiute and Ute communities throughout the region beneficent visions and promises of colonization. They kindly received local leaders, shared emotive visions of the glories of salvation, and offered whatever material items they could spare as gifts. They recognized shared social values and engaged in moments of cultural exchange that, as they noted, contrasted with many of these bands' previous experiences with New Mexican traders. A few weeks after their October 12 capture of Paiutes, "thoughtless companions" in the party wanted to take a Paiute "by force" to guide them across the Colorado River; such forms of seizure were apparently commonplace for New Mexicans arriving in Paiute homelands. Although they often condemned Ute and Paiute cultural practices and insisted on rigid adherence to Catholic orthodoxy, the Spanish missionaries imagined a peaceful incorporation of these distant peoples into the services of both Majesties.[22]

Paiute and Ute enthusiasm for Spanish proselytizing sprang not only from notions of spiritual salvation but also from the everyday realities and material needs confronting these different groups. The missionaries promised wondrous fortunes, and their horses, material items, and weapons confirmed their wealth. Such promises contrasted with these groups' previous understandings of New Mexican traders, who, according to the friars, came into the region engaged in "the despicable fur trade." Such traders often stayed for months on end and hindered colonization through their avarice and immorality: "The infidels who have most dealings with the Spaniards and Christians in these parts show more resistance to the truth of the Gospel, and their conversion becomes more difficult . . . When some go to the Yutas and remain among them in their greed for pelts, others go after the flesh which they find here for their bestial satisfaction. And so, therefore, they blaspheme against Christ's name and impede or, to put it better, oppose the spreading of the faith." Going "after the flesh" of Indian women's bodies remained, then, a prime motivation for traders in Ute and Paiute homelands. Condemning such practices, the friars presented, indeed embodied, alternatives to the trading, raiding, and slaving cycles that pervaded the region. Theirs was a vision of empire rooted in a different form of conquest: the friars promised to build and lead communities rooted in and organized around shared beliefs and practices, and such visions of harmony generally met with welcome throughout their months-long expedition.[23]

The return of the Domínguez and Escalante expedition to New Mexico in December was a momentous event for the weary party and for colonial villagers and authorities alike. Returning with little Joaquín, the friars had traveled over 1,700 miles and been gone nearly half a year. The events of their journey were officially presented in their journals while fantastic stories of bearded Indians, of the friars' crossing of the Colorado, and of their repeated sufferings circulated throughout the colony.

The expedition proved the unlikelihood of a northern route to Monterey while offering a wealth of experiential knowledge. Miera's maps soon became the standard cartography of the region, offering generations of explorers and chroniclers the only existing geographic view of the Intermountain West. Such visions persisted well into the nineteenth century, perpetuated by cartographers Alexander Von Humboldt and William Clark. Miera's geographies, like the friars' promises of the future, however, remained highly imaginative. Miera connected, for example, the Utah and Great Salt lakes while also suggesting that the two remained linked to the Pacific by a mythical western waterway, a fallacy perpetuated by later mapmakers. Unpublished for a century, Miera's vision of the Great Basin nonetheless circulated throughout New Spain, eventually filtering throughout the Atlantic World.[24]

The friars' diligence in recording different Ute and Paiute band names and territorial limits also provided the first overview of the cultural topography of the eastern Great Basin. In a "brief account of the peoples whom . . . we saw, had dealings with, and learned about from reports," the friars identified five major Ute bands and six Paiute groups, about whom they concluded: "In this land there reside a great number of people, all of pleasing appearance, very engaging, and extremely timid . . . The name of each comes from the area it inhabits, whereby they are distinguished according to several provinces or territories—not according to nations, as all the Yutas known heretofore compose a single nation, or let us call it kingdom."[25]

The different Paiute bands, then, remained loosely organized, not confederated like their eastern Ute neighbors, whose "kingdom" New

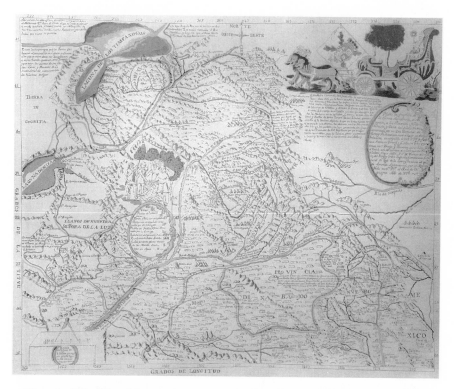

"Bearded Ute Map," by Don Bernardo de Miera y Pacheco, 1778. Pen and ink on paper. Courtesy of the Utah State Historical Society, Salt Lake City. One of the most influential map of the Intermountain West ever produced, Miera's map from his travels with Domínguez and Escalante provided a wealth of information about Ute and Paiute homelands, influencing western cartography for generations. The Franciscans' journals along with Miera's maps highlight forms of mutual accommodation achieved between New Mexican and Ute communities in the late 1700s.

Mexicans readily identified. Although these groups' "timidity" was obviously linked to their fear of equestrian invaders, Paiutes, like the northern Laguna Utes, remained on the margins of the larger military, economic, and political relations that had characterized northern New Spain. Some Paiute groups in southern Utah had, as the friars noted, developed seasonal corn crops, and others had incorporated metals, vessels, and other material items from their southern neighbors. In general, however, these Paiutes lived mostly off subsistence gathering and hunting and in small bands. Like Rivera before them, Domínguez and Escalante noted that Paiute bands often consisted of extended families under the control of male chiefs. In the next two generations, however, these small, patrilineal family bands were subjected to increased external influences. As Paiute and neighboring Ute societies became further enveloped in the violent transformations remaking the north, some became migratory and predatory bands while others became subjugated and nearly vanquished societies. After their initial encounter with these Spanish missionaries, subsequent generations of Utes and Paiutes in Utah faced immeasurably greater and violent challenges. By the 1820s and 1830s, when the region once again became "opened" to outside expeditions, Utah's Indian societies would bear little resemblance to those encountered in 1776, as the West's larger imperial contests crashed upon the region with increasing fury.[26]

New Mexican–Ute Relations, 1780–1810

Within a decade of the friars' return, New Mexico's northern borderlands underwent major realignments. The Comanche conflicts of the 1760s–1780s had ended, and a new era of stability developed throughout the north. Common animosity against the Comanches had brought Ute leaders to New Mexico seeking peace, and joint military campaigns and protection became primary expressions of their alliance. After the Comanche peace, however, institutions of diplomacy, trade, and redress became more central to the Spanish-Ute alliance, for although Utes maintained their animosity toward western Comanches, they could no longer turn to Santa Fe for military assistance.

Before peace with the Comanches, New Mexico had been in crisis. The internecine wars swirling throughout the north demanded attention and resources. Comanche and other Indian depredations threatened the colony to such a degree that they preoccupied colonial authorities from Santa Fe to Mexico City, and in 1778 new policies, greater resources, and firmer commitments from the crown accompanied Governor Juan Bautista de Anza's succession to office. His mission: to incorporate or subjugate the Comanches into alliance or submission. He accomplished both. His defeat and slaying in 1779 of the Comanche leader Green Horn ushered in an unprecedented rapprochement between Comanches and New Mexico while bringing demographic and economic growth to both New Mexican and Comanche communities. The peace also recalibrated Spanish-Ute relations, drawing these allies closer through forms of trade, diplomacy, and gift-giving.

The Spanish triumph and the terms of the subsequent Spanish-Comanche peace came with the assistance of New Mexico's Ute allies, who remained central actors in the region's balance of power. Like other allies, they followed the governor into battle, received weapons, horses, and spoils, and fought alongside the diverse social and ethnic groups that composed New Mexico's military forces. As he was riding north to engage Green Horn, for example, more than 100 Ute warriors intercepted Anza's party. The Utes, Anza noted, "ever since my assumption of this government have asked me . . . that they be admitted into my company in confirmation of our friendship, provided I should go on a campaign against the Comanches." They now had their chance provided that they remained subject to "my orders as to what of spoils belonged to them in case of encounters and defeats of the enemy." Accepting this provision, the combined force passed the site of a recent attack against a Ute *ranchería:* "At this place, on the 10th of July of the present year a large number of Comanches attacked a force of Utes who were camped there with their families . . . bodies with other evidences proved the fact." As the force prepared for battle, then, Ute warriors carried powerful reminders of the stakes of such violent encounters.[27]

Anza's defeat of Green Horn initiated the second hallmark of his rule: the Spanish-Comanche peace of 1786. Ute leaders again played influential roles in these deliberations, protecting their alliance with New Mexico while extracting concessions from both their Spanish allies and Comanche enemies. Ute leaders had initially been outraged by Anza's decision to offer peace to Comanche leaders. Arriving in Santa Fe in January 1786, two of the Utes' "most authoritative chiefs called Moara and Pinto . . . heatedly declared against the attempted peace . . . stating . . . that [Anza] preferred frequent, unfaithful rebels to friends always obedient and faithful." Arriving from their winter camps, Moara and Pinto knew that a Spanish-Comanche peace could bring dire consequences for their communities. Their years of "obedient and faithful" friendship and the negotiated terms of their alliance could be jeopardized by Anza's plans, because without guaranteed Spanish protections, the Utes might not withstand Comanche onslaughts. As they had suffered at the hands of Navajo allies in the 1750s, Utes feared comparable retaliation from New Mexico's other Indian allies. "They were so inflamed," continued a Spanish official, "that for more than four hours while they repeated their arguments, they did not wish to smoke or accept any other present." Failing to enact their most common rituals of alliance became a means of protesting the governor's actions.[28]

Although Anza did not heed Moara and Pinto's admonishments and made peace with Comanche leaders, he addressed several of their concerns. Initially Anza "tried to dissuade them gently . . . explaining to them the many reasons which united to make impossible adherence to their arguments." Though failing to convince the governor, the Utes subsequently positioned themselves in the unfolding negotiations, demanding to be included in the peace talks. "In regard to this request . . . [Anza] promised to interpose all his meditation with the Comanches in proof of the appreciation which he had of their faithful and ancient friendship" and invited Ute leaders to stay. As the recently ascendant Comanche chief Ecueracapa marched into Santa Fe and extolled the virtues of Anza and the peace process, he did so under the watchful eye of not only Anza but also Moara and six other "authorized individuals of his nation." Ute leaders, in sum, helped sanction the Comanche peace and participated in the evolving Spanish-Comanche détente, participation underrecognized in many accounts of these fateful days.[29]

Despite Ute fears, the negotiations of 1786 did not compromise their position as Spanish allies. Whereas alliance with New Mexico had centered upon shared grievances against the Comanches, it now came to rely on other forms of trade, hospitality, and protection. Spanish

leaders understood these fragile institutions and attempted to preserve them after the Comanche threat no longer loomed. The commander general of the northern interior provinces of New Spain,
Jacobo Urgate y Loyola, for example, when informed of the Comanche peace, instructed Anza to ensure the stability of the Ute alliance by
requiring the return of Ute captives. "Another article [of the treaty],"
he dictated, "must include the freeing of all the Christian prisoners
that they captured and also those pagans that belong to the Ute Nation and other friends of the Spanish." The plight of Ute captives and
the stability of the Spanish-Ute alliance, then, concerned authorities
throughout colonial Mexico.[30]

As the shifting world of northern New Mexico stabilized, Anza and
subsequent governors also sought to curb Ute, Navajo, and Comanche
raids against New Mexico as well as one another. New Mexico soon increasingly used these allies in ongoing wars against Apaches, who now
bore the brunt of the region's cycles of war; and while previous animosities never fully dissipated, the strategic deployment of gifts, resources, and favors provided governors additional leverage with the
colony's Indian powers. Stability within as well as outside the colony, in
short, flowed from the Comanche peace. As Elizabeth John writes: "All
in all, Urgate set for Anza an extraordinary task: to nurture a political
structure where almost none had existed before and to foster social
and economic revolution among an alien people; to prepare a nation
of warriors for peace, even while inciting them to war; to make fast
friends of tribes long hostile to one another; and, perhaps hardest of
all, to restrain his own people from abusing the interests of the new allies." Although these former enemies did not become "fast friends,"
Spanish leaders mitigated the levels of violence outside New Mexico,
realizing that colonial security remained, as it had for generations,
linked to the many Indians on its borders; and officials soon began recording the "peaceful conduct" between these Indian rivals. From
1790 to 1793, for example, a chain of letters traveled between Governor Fernando de la Concha and Commander General Pedro de Nava,
the successors of Anza and Urgate respectively, nine of which specifically noted the "good conduct" of the Utes. Each also wrote to Viceroy Conde de Revilla Gigedo in Mexico City, who responded enthusiastically to news of the Utes' continued alliance.[31]

Thus the Utes weathered the incorporation of their enemies into alliance with their closest allies, and by the beginning of the nineteenth century they began to enjoy the prosperity that accompanied the Comanche peace. For, as Ross Frank demonstrates, stability brought increased northern settlement and economic development. Population growth generated taxes and tithes for provincial coffers, and the flow of goods and currencies filtered throughout the region.[32]

New Mexico also received increased funds destined for its Indian allies, establishing important economic avenues for many Indian bands. In 1786 Viceroy Bernardo de Galvéz ordered that individual Indian warriors and chiefs be given monetary payments for their friendship, financial incentives to sustain alliances. Such payments, in turn, brought growing revenues to the colony, as the Comanche peace, as Urgate wrote to Anza, necessitated an increased overall budget for New Mexico: "The measures . . . required for clinching the general establishment of peace with the Comanches . . . demand indispensably various expenses which cannot be met with one thousand pesos, four hundred horses, twenty mules, and two carbines which were sent to your lordship in the last caravan . . . I have resolved to consign for the present six thousand pesos each year for all the extraordinary attentions of this province." In one sense, then, allegiances became cheaper to purchase than to lose, as New Mexico poured gifts and currency into former enemies' hands. Such forms of alliance created expectations of permanent beneficence.[33]

Such annual funds were expended on New Mexico's Ute allies. An inventory of yearly rations provided to guests at the Governor's Palace in 1806–07, for example, included those for 145 unidentified Ute "captains," "roamers," and their families, who stayed an average of four days and consumed a total of 588 rations, or 20 percent of the year's "2,897 rations furnished to allied heathen." Such gifts and annual visits to New Mexico had already become integral to many Ute communities as alliance privileges provided regular access to goods, protection, and trade. The end of Spanish rule would, however, bring an end to such gifts and rations. Their disappearance would splinter the diplomatic ties initiated by Cachupín, Anza, and the Bourbon reform effort.[34]

As the fortunes of Ute bands in Colorado and northern New Mexico remained tied to Santa Fe, the trade of captives—so central to their alliance—also flourished. In the four decades following the defeat of

Green Horn, 311 "Utes" were baptized in New Mexico, over 40 percent of all the colony's 769 nomadic Indian baptisms during this
period. At Abiquiu, 40 "Utes" were baptized between 1800 and 1820,
triple the total "Ute" baptisms since its resettlement in 1754. The escalation in "Ute" baptisms reflected an increased number of captives
brought by Utes to New Mexican trade fairs in exchange for Spanish
goods. The majority of these captives came from the Great Basin. "By
1800," as David Brugge writes, "the New Mexicans were looking for
captives who might be more easily exploited. Attention shifted [away
from Plains Apache and Comanche groups] to the Shoshonean speak-
ers of the north." As the Comanche peace stabilized relations with
New Mexico's Indian neighbors, then, the traffic in nonequestrians accelerated.[35]

The well-worn paths leading to New Mexico's slave markets also witnessed outbound traffic as traders went in search of Utes. In 1811, for
instance, the postmaster of New Mexico, Don José Rafael Sarraceno,
traveled three months in Ute territory and traded, according to Pedro
Bautista Pino, for "a large shipment of beautiful pelts which he had
purchased very cheaply." A respected settler, Sarraceno traded in
accordance with gubernatorial decrees, returning without captives.
Slaving, authorities knew, exacerbated cycles of warfare and jeopardized the alliance system, but decrees prohibiting unlicensed trading
carried less weight on the colony's perimeter, requiring constant enforcement. In 1812, for example, Governor Joseph Manrrique had to
remind *alcaldes* of the colony's laws against Indian slavery. Reiterating
earlier statutes, he wrote: "It is prohibited the acquisition of Indians as
slaves, also their sale, exchange and possessing them even though
other Indians will have captured them during times of war among
them. Those who break the law will be punished . . . and the Indian or
Indians will be returned and restituted to their own lands, and environment with whole and natural liberty." The slave trade remained
technically illegal in late colonial Mexico, and Manrrique ordered that
his new *bando* be read throughout the colony. Slaves, the governor declared, would be returned to their tribes, and unscrupulous New Mexican traders would be punished. Captives taken in war, children bought
and "ransomed" at trade fairs, and the hundreds of illegal captives
smuggled into New Mexico, however, became familiar exceptions to

the loose prohibitions against Indian slavery. While the law outlawed its traffic, the temptations and benefits of the Indian slave trade remained.[36]

The first documented New Mexican slaving party in the Great Basin came the summer following Manrrique's *bando*. Eight men from Abiquiu and adjacent settlements traveled to Utah Lake and back under Don Mauricio Arze and retired soldier Lago García. Traveling in less than half the time of Domínguez and Escalante, upon return the parties' members were caught and brought to trial. Their testimonies provide clear evidence that routes to the Utah Lake and the many Ute and Paiute groups along the way had become familiar to New Mexican traders. Their testimonies also reveal some of the effects of such slavery upon nonequestrians. Purchasing twelve unidentified captives and more than 100 hides, the expedition revealed how common slaving had become among these northwestern bands and how central slave trading remained to Spanish-Indian relations in the Great Basin.[37]

Domínguez and Escalante in 1776 had not recorded examples of captive-taking among the Utes and Paiutes of Utah. The Laguna Utes, or Timpanagos, remained fearful of equestrian raiders, but they did not attempt to sell captives to the friars' party. The "Bearded Utes" and other Paiute groups similarly remained "timid" around the friars and did not attempt to sell children to them. The Franciscans had commented extensively on the "pleasing appearance," enthusiasm, and peacefulness of Utah's Laguna and Paiute groups and noted few adverse trading or military relations among them. Though these communities had feared equestrian attacks, they had still been isolated from cycles of enslavement. As the friars had deplored New Mexicans' "going after the flesh," they also probably would have condemned examples of slave-taking in these communities. At the time of their expedition, then, captivity and slavery seem not to have been institutionalized within these communities.

At some point after 1776, things changed. By 1813 many of these same groups had not only experienced slave raids into their communities but also conducted raids of their own on their Indian neighbors. Evidence of such escalating violence abounds in the transcripts of Arze and García's trial.

When asked what places they visited, whether they were welcomed by the Utes, and how many captives and furs they bought, the party's translator, José Velásquez, recounted the expedition's harrowing experiences. Among the Timpanagos, he said,

> They were welcomed . . . but after their trade talks, in which they did not want to buy Indian boys or girls which the Utes offered to sell them for horses, the Spaniards did not buy them . . . The Utes, then, moved their *ranchería* angrily towards the closest mountain . . . [The party] then left for the *laguna* [Lake Utah] where they stayed for three days . . . Other Utes came to them to make the trade . . . They offered seven captives, males and females, that they have to sell as they have done on other occasions. He and his companions [again] refused . . . The Utes replied "but you bought our children before" and then four of the same Utes got up and went angrily to the party's horseherd and started to kill them, the animals.[38]

Had not the Timapanagos' leaders intervened, their warriors would have continued killing the New Mexicans' horses. Leaving the Timpanagos and heading south toward the Sevier, the party encountered a lone Ute trader from the "nation Sanpuche" who agreed to guide them to other "unknown Utes" to trade. Leaving two behind with their herd, Velásquez and the others traveled west for three days, where "they arrived to one nation of warlike people with hairy beards whom they found to be upset already. The Utes received the group noisily and screaming and with weapons in their hands telling the group that what they would trade were arrows." Velásquez and the others tried to reassure the frightened Paiutes, but that evening small groups of armed Paiutes congregated around them, threatening to kill them. Sneaking away that night, the New Mexicans rushed back to their companions and finally headed south to "the [Ute] Ranchería of Guaracher which was on their way waiting for them to trade as it was custom." This Ute leader also offered captives for trade. "The Utes offered first 'Indias' and 'Indios,' and the *comandante* [Arze] did not permit [the party] to buy them. So the Utes considered the trade over." Arze, however, reconsidered and allowed the purchase, "clarifying that they were at the disposal of the Señor Governor who will make good use of them or not." Velásquez reported that although he did not buy any captives, he "saw that Don Mauricio Arze bought four." Two others each bought three women, and two others one apiece. "Of these women bought . . . three belonging to Tenorio died," as did two others. Upon return to Abiquiu, the party had seven slaves and 109 hides to show for its time away.[39]

Velásquez's testimony paralleled those of Arze, García, and the other members of the expedition. How carefully they had rehearsed their testimonies in the days preceding their court appearance went unasked. Clearly, each feared the fines and punishments that befell convicted slave traders, and each probably fabricated portions of his story. The party had traveled north, in violation of Manrrique's *bando*, to trade profitably. Wealth from trade came only from Indian hides, furs, and especially captives. It is therefore unlikely that they purchased a dozen captives to place at the "disposal" of the governor. And when the Lagunas offered to sell them seven captives "as they had done on other occasions," their refusal to buy them did not stem from law-abiding pricks of conscience; they later purchased twelve slaves, nearly all women. The subsequent deaths of half of their slaves belied their alleged concern about putting the fate of these twelve "at the disposal of the Señor Governor." There was no inquiry into what happened to these women.[40]

The fragments of information about the Arze-García expedition into Utah present incomplete but important glimpses into the changes remaking these northern peoples. The Timpanagos wanted Spanish horses and reportedly offered their own children—"sus propios hijos"—in trade. Although these children possibly came from the Timpanago communities, it is more likely that they had been taken as captives from neighboring Paiute, Shoshone, and other Indian peoples. The New Mexicans may have mistaken the children for Timpanagos because the Utes, like other slave traders, commonly incorporated captive children into their own societies for extended periods before selling them. In the next generation, the incorporation of Paiute captives into Ute society would intensify as multiple trade networks extended into the region.

Since hosting Domínguez and Escalante, the Timpanagos had not only traded with New Mexicans but also become dependent upon horses. In 1805, for example, "Yutas named Timpipas" had gone to New Mexico, stolen horses, and subsequently agreed to return them to the "Ute interpreter" Manuel Mestas, a *genízaro* trader from Abiquiu who had gone to Utah Lake to retrieve lost horses and mules. In 1813 these Utes reacted angrily to Arze's decision not to trade horses for captives, as traders had "done on other occasions." Outraged, they attempted to force the party to comply by killing its horses. These acts of intimidation masked deeper motives. The equestrian attacks reported to Domínguez and Escalante had accelerated throughout the region, and the Timpanagos had become engaged in hostilities with Indian peoples north of Utah Lake who coveted the valley's grazing lands, which Miera had described as "the most pleasing, beautiful and fertile site in all of New Spain." In their struggles to retain control over their homelands, the Timpanagos needed Spanish horses, goods, and weapons. They also needed slaves to trade for such goods and acquired them in raids against their less powerful Paiute and Shoshone neighbors.[41]

The New Mexicans' visit among the "Bearded Utes" also revealed the increased prevalence of violence in these lands. These Paiutes' immediate hostility stood in contrast to their forefathers' relations with Domínguez and Escalante. Their "warlike" and desperate reaction frightened and confused the traders. Organized in less concentrated and diversified societies than their Laguna neighbors, Paiute groups had fallen prey to more mobile bands of equestrian raiders. Raiders primarily took children and women, either for trade or incorporation, and often killed Paiute men. These Paiutes' hostility and refusal to trade with the New Mexicans stemmed from years of such raiding. They had reasons to fear equestrian intruders and mobilized themselves accordingly.[42]

The Ute *ranchería* of Guaracher, "which was on their way waiting for them to trade as it was custom," offered the expedition a safe and familiar reprieve from these "bearded and annoyed" Paiutes. This familiarity likely included rituals of the Spanish-Ute alliance such as exchanges, smoking, and feasts. It also included the offering of Indian slaves, as Guaracher led a *ranchería* in southern Utah in a region where Domínguez and Escalante had encountered only scattered Paiute bands. This Ute band now congregated in lands where wood, food, and water were scarce and did so in order to trade with New Mexicans.[43]

The migration of Ute bands into Paiute homelands increased throughout the last decades of Spanish rule. Displacing and subjugating local Indians, Ute intruders spread their control over lands and peoples once outside their territorial range. Domínguez and Escalante had encountered no Ute groups south of Utah Lake in 1776, but now, in 1813, Guaracher commanded a *ranchería* in the region and traded Indian slaves with New Mexicans, a practice that increased throughout the first half of the nineteenth century.

New Mexicans who traveled into Utah entered from Ute communities in western Colorado as well as from the south beyond the Colorado River. Domínguez and Escalante's harrowing crossing of the Colorado without Indian guides remains among the only documented accounts of passage through this mighty river. Traffic to Utah was, however, common enough that authorities did not inquire during the Arze-García trial about the exact routes taken. In fact, as Joseph Hill wrote after analyzing the transcripts of this trial, "None of the accounts gives any particulars as to the route followed between Abiquiu and the lake of the Timpanagos, possibly because that route was so well known." Timpanagos Utes had raided New Mexican herds. New Mexicans such as Manuel Mestas and the Arze-García party had traveled to the Utah Lake, and intermediary trade posts like Guaracher's *ranchería* had developed in between. Despite the illegality of such activities, these few examples suggest larger patterns of trade, exchange, and enslavement. As David Weber notes, "Decrees and punishments notwithstanding, illegal entradas into the Ute country continued with furs and slaves as the main objectives. These entradas may have occurred as frequently as once a year, but we only know of those persons whom authorities apprehended." Thus Utah's Indian homelands were opened to New Mexicans in the last decades of Spanish rule. Such incorporation only increased with the collapse of New Spain as institutions of alliance crumbled under the weight of Mexican national rule.[44]

A Ute Family in the New Mexican–Ute Borderlands

In the summer of 1820, as the struggle for independence reached its climax in central Mexico, José María Sandoval of Abiquiu went to court to seek return of a lost horse. Sandoval charged that the *alcalde* of Abiquiu, José García, had illegally ordered that Sandoval give one of his horses to Juan Trujillo, also of Abiquiu, in compensation for the loss of one of Trujillo's servants. Trujillo's servant was a former Ute

slave sold into captivity by "Caigua" warriors at Taos. Baptized, given a
Spanish name, and eventually placed in Trujillo's home, the captive
became the subject of debate when her father came into New Mexico
in search of his lost daughter.[45]

Sandoval was not involved in the theft and sale of this captive. He
had traveled earlier that year to central Utah to trade with Timpanagos
Utes, where he had accepted the services of a Ute guide on the condition that he help this bereaved father find his stolen daughter.
Sandoval accepted the Ute's assistance, but as the party grew closer to
Abiquiu he became reluctant to uphold his agreement. "I did not try
to enlighten the Ute to the fact that his daughter was in our community," he told officials, "but rather tried to conceal it." Though knowing Trujillo and the girl's whereabouts, he simply told the Ute that he
believed Timpanagos captives had recently been sold at Taos. With the
help of a New Mexican translator, the Ute traveled to Taos and some-
how learned of the fate of his daughter. Arriving back at Abiquiu, he
located the girl and returned to Utah Lake to reunite his daughter
with her family.

Trujillo meanwhile had asked the *alcalde* at Abiquiu to compensate
him for the loss of his servant. Holding Sandoval responsible for
Trujillo's loss, García ordered that Trujillo receive a horse from Sandoval in compensation—a standard measure of a captive's value.
Sandoval then appealed to the governor to overturn the ruling. Governor Facundo Melgares, however, upheld García's decision and reiterated official decrees against the traffic and sale of Indian captives. Although slavery remained technically illegal, the loss of Trujillo's
servant and her labor, Melgares rationalized, necessitated compensation. The exigencies of New Mexican slavery continually required such
peculiar justifications.[46]

Sandoval's unsuccessful lawsuit sheds light on the processes of exchange and slavery that bound Great Basin Indians to the violent
world of the Spanish borderlands. Villages such as Abiquiu and Taos
were crucial links in the growing web of relations in the north. Raiders
from the Plains attacked and enslaved Utes, and on their return they
sold their captives at Taos. Such Plains Indian–Ute hostilities, like so
many of the region's Indian wars, went largely unrecorded by New
Mexicans but became partially visible through such visits to New Mexi-

can settlements. Relations among Great Basin peoples, Plains equestrians, and New Mexicans often reflected such triangular networks of trade and war.

The close ties and familiarity between Timpanagos Utes and New Mexico further demonstrate the evolving and enduring nature of the Spanish-Ute alliance. Though more distant than Colorado Utes, the Timpanagos welcomed New Mexican traders in Utah, returned with them to New Mexico, and knew the cultural landscape of colonial society well enough to conduct inquiries and retrieve stolen children. The Spanish-Ute alliance enabled such exchanges and redress. Whereas captives from hostile tribes were often exchanged only in return for Spanish captives, horses, or goods, the aggrieved Ute father did not make, nor was he expected to make, such compensation. Sandoval was held responsible for Trujillo's loss, not the girl's father or her family or community. Utes were also able to retrieve children taken by hostile neighbors. Smaller, nonequestrian bands, however, lacked the resources and power to launch such ventures. With their range limited by dependence on subsistence seasonal gatherings, foods, and game, they also often became prey to Ute and New Mexican raiders. Thus the experiences and fate of this young Timpanagos girl remain only partially applicable for Great Basin Indian captives, because Utes had achieved privileges and power uncommon for nonequestrians.

The End of Spanish New Mexico

The networks of alliance and exchange identified in the Sandoval trial grew weaker with the collapse of New Spain. Mexican independence transformed the region's political economy, redefined the system of Indian alliances, and ushered in an era of unprecedented foreign influence. These changes reshaped and soon unraveled the Spanish-Ute alliance, sending reverberations throughout the Great Basin.

The prosperity spawned by the Comanche peace had accelerated settlement, trade, and demographic growth throughout the colony. Spanish colonial policies, reformulated under the Bourbon reforms, had also stimulated prosperity while curbing administrative inefficiencies. The Spanish military presence had, for example, expanded throughout New Spain, rising from 3,000 soldiers in 1758 to 29,000 by 1800, with substantial increases in the north. During these last decades of Spanish colonialism, then, New Mexico's economic and population growth combined with relatively peaceful Indian relations to generate prosperity. Spanish imperial rule had finally become stable and moderately prosperous in this corner of empire. While illegal trading and slaving occurred, authorities regulated trade fairs, maintained Indian alliances through gifts and exchanges, and policed New Spain's borders for foreign intruders. Though tenuously linked to the empire, the Spanish state in New Mexico, particularly the army, church, and legal systems, had become institutionalized and powerful. The crisis of Mexican independence, however, reconfigured state control in fundamental ways.[47]

With Mexican independence, imperial control in Santa Fe gave way to economic and political uncertainty. Initially New Mexicans remained removed from the civil wars and expulsion of Spanish landowners that characterized Mexico during these pivotal decades. Indeed, news of independence traveled slowly to Santa Fe, where political confusion and sporadic conflicts soon broke out.

Although it was on the peripheries of the independence struggle, the north too felt the winds of independence. Institutions of Spanish rule in the north, particularly the army, grew underfunded and understaffed and were sometimes abandoned altogether. "To a great extent," Ana Maria Alonso writes of Chihuahua, "the responsibility for frontier defense became displaced onto provincial governments . . . The main burden of defense fell on the civilian population . . . Part-time specialists in violence operated with a considerable degree of autonomy." The "burden of defense" shifted from Spanish governors, soldiers, and officials to citizen-settlers whose loyalties to national policies were often uncertain. As David Weber describes the "new politics" of the north, "Frontier officials could never be certain which Spanish regulations were still in force or if they conflicted with the new laws of the Republic. Each side in a controversy could usually find a law to support its position." Critical matters of Indian trade, diplomacy, and warfare now became the domain of the local citizenry. Local and regional exigencies determined Indian relations and frontier management more than ever before.[48]

For Indian peoples outside the colony, New Mexico's transition from empire to nation brought two principal changes: the unraveling of Spain's many alliances and the influx of foreign traders. The erosion and expulsion of the colonial state led to a breakdown in New Mexico's alliance system and initiated a concomitant escalation in warfare, especially as the struggle for independence depleted critical resources used for frontier defense and Indian alliance. Governor Melgares in 1818, for example, implored his superiors for additional funds for New Mexico's Indian allies: "Your Lordship will already know . . . that if people of some other group come, I shall find myself perplexed to satisfy them. I supplicate that . . . [you] send me whatever your goodness may have best intended for this purpose." After independence, then, not only did resources remain in chronic short supply but officials were also ill prepared for the military and political realities of Indian relations. As Charles Kenner notes, "the rapid turnover of officials (there were no less than ten different governors during the first twelve years of Mexican rule) made it impossible to maintain any continuity in [Indian] policy." Navajo, Apache, Comanche, and ultimately Ute conflicts increased throughout the national period.[49]

Accustomed to the loyalties and rituals of trade and alliance, many Indian peoples found the erosion of Spanish diplomacy confusing. After the Comanche peace, carefully maintained institutions of Indian diplomacy had successfully mitigated the levels of violence between the region's powerful neighbors. For Utes and other peoples, Mexican national rule now undermined these institutions and reignited simmering antagonisms both among themselves and with New Mexicans. Resorts to violence soon followed.

The collapse of institutions of Spanish-Indian diplomacy paralleled the second radical change in frontier relations. Growing numbers of Americans had streamed west of the Mississippi following the Louisiana Purchase in 1803, remaking the West's social landscapes. In 1806 Zebulon Pike became the first American official to travel to New Mexico. Identified by Spain's Ute allies in Colorado, members of his party and then Pike himself were escorted to Santa Fe, where Governor Real Alencaster cautiously welcomed him. When asked by Alencaster, "You come to reconnoiter our country, do you?" Pike replied: "I marched to reconnoiter our own." Though not laying claim to Spanish territory, Pike asserted U.S. dominion over the recently acquired lands of Louisiana, whose boundaries, as Pike made clear, remained open to interpretation.[50]

The ambiguities of American and Spanish claims were momentarily resolved with the Adams-Onis Treaty of 1819, which for the first time settled Spanish and American claims in the West. While Spanish and American officials negotiated boundaries, Indian societies still controlled these territories. Many of these lands, particularly west of the Arkansas, remained unmapped and unknown to imperial officials in either Mexico City or Washington.[51]

Spanish authorities had confronted rival imperialists in northern Mexico before. French, British, and Spanish rivalries had constantly spilled into the interior of North America. American imperialism however, proved far less ephemeral. Following Pike, U.S. traders swarmed throughout New Mexico, supplying manufactured goods, especially guns and ammunition, to Indian tribes as well as to New Mexican settlers, whose demographic growth had created markets for eastern goods. Spanish leaders had attempted to curb this trade by policing their borders and imprisoning traders whose presence undermined Spanish monopolies. Trading parties were caught, their goods auctioned off, and their members imprisoned. Other traders were denied access to New Mexico and forbidden to trade along the northern Rio Grande in Colorado. Governors even sent expeditions onto the Plains in search of foreign traders; Governor Melgares, for instance, dispatched Don José María de Arce on such a campaign in 1818.[52]

With Mexican independence, foreign trade not only became legal; it was encouraged. Trade routes between American outposts on the Mississippi, particularly St. Louis, and northern Mexico now flourished. As Thomas Hall argues, "While the value of this trade [was] quite small . . . Missouri now displaced Chihuahua as the major source of manufactured goods." Santa Fe and Taos became links in an economic chain connecting the United States and central Mexico. The 1821 inauguration of this trade route, known as the Santa Fe Trail, by William Becknell reflected this sea-change in economics. Traveling west from St. Louis before news of Mexican independence had spread, Becknell hoped to trade in Taos and to escape without fines or imprisonment. He did both. Melgares, who had become the first Mexican governor of New Mexico, informed Becknell that foreign traders were not only now welcome but also would be encouraged to settle in the region. "Had Becknell arrived a year earlier," David Weber wryly notes, "Melgares probably would have arrested him."[53]

Mexico's liberalization of foreign trade brought a flood of traffic through Ute and other Indian homelands. Growing numbers of traders operating out of centers along the Arkansas, Platte, and Missouri Rivers flowed back and forth between Mexican and American outposts, drawing ever more distant lands and peoples into their orbit. For eastern Ute bands in New Mexico and Colorado, American traders would bring critically needed trading goods and resources, while the Utes establishing their hegemony in Utah and the southern Great Basin would soon depend upon American traders both as sources of weapons and other manufactured goods, and as markets for stolen horses and slaves. Through such traders and their trade posts, Indian peoples across the West experienced the growing pull and capacity of the American economy.[54]

Spanish imperial hopes and dreams withered and died before this onslaught of newcomers. Domínguez and Escalante never returned to live among their Ute and Paiute hosts. Instead, their vision was soon followed by a different movement of faith, one bent on turning Ute and Paiute homelands into settler farms within a new religious order.

FOUR

Crisis in the New Mexican–Ute Borderlands

The revolution of Mexican independence was also a revolution for neighboring Indian peoples, who used the opportunities afforded by the weakness of the Mexican state to pursue other forms of economic gain. As Mexico's attempts to establish control in New Mexico waxed and waned, social relations outside the province remained haphazard and violent. Throughout northern New Mexico, western Colorado, and southern Utah, trading relations between Utes and New Mexicans continued, but many of the institutions of the Spanish-Ute alliance unraveled. Whereas New Spain had prohibited unlicensed trade and exploration in the north, Mexico permitted, indeed promoted, trade, travel, and even settlement outside the province. Mexican settlers, for example, moved as far north as the San Luis Valley in Colorado and laid claims to land grants within Ute territories, often creating tense, hostile relations. Mexican-appointed governors arrived in Santa Fe with little appreciation of the respect, gifts, and reciprocity demanded by Ute allies. And, most powerfully, the circulation of foreign goods and traders undermined Mexican influence. With ambiguous national boundaries inherited from Spain, Mexico's northernmost borders remained undefined, unconsolidated, and contested, and as the nascent republic's Indian policies foundered, the Spanish-Ute alliance crumbled.[1]

The erosion of the Spanish-Ute alliance escalated cycles of violence throughout the Great Basin. New Mexican and Indian traders now traded with even greater impunity as the few negotiated forms of diplomacy and redress established under Spanish rule dissolved. Raiders

119

along the Old Spanish Trail between Santa Fe and Los Angeles increased their capture of Indian women and children, acting without reproach or punishment from colonial governors. Ute and other raiders traveled to California, stole horses and mules from *Californio* settlements, and then returned to New Mexico to trade their spoils. One Timpanagos Ute leader, Walkara, became according to many accounts the "greatest horse thief in history," taking and trading horses by the thousands. Such theft and travel came through Southern Paiute homelands and became intimately linked with Paiute slavery. On their journeys to and from California, Ute raiders forced Paiute bands to trade their women and children or be killed, and at Abiquiu "Ute" captive baptisms reached record heights. Mexican and American traders conducted similar transactions, and by the end of the Mexican national period, officials reported Paiute bands with staggering gender disparities. Paiute women also recounted harrowing tales of enslavement.[2]

The inability of Mexico to consolidate national control over these borderlands generated competing territorial claims. After Mexican independence, Anglo and American traders increasingly moved into the Great Basin, taxing local Indian communities' foods, resources, and energies. British and American trappers exhausted many of the region's fragile river valleys of furs, often also depleting Indian subsistence foods. These traders represented competing designs, and throughout the first half of the nineteenth century, England and the United States enveloped many Great Basin Indian peoples in their imperial contests.[3]

With the influx of many foreigners, Great Basin peoples struggled to maintain order over their homelands. Some migrated away from frequently traveled trade routes, others consolidated with neighboring groups, and many provided assistance and guidance to trading and exploration parties in exchange for needed foods, goods, and weapons. Throughout the nineteenth century, these Native people increasingly lost control of what their lands would become. Outsiders' visions of what exactly constituted "the Great Basin," who had access to the region, who had control over its resources, and most indelibly who planned the region's future became deeply contested in the decades following Mexican independence. Domínguez and Escalante had offered ethereal promises of a shared subservience to a distant king and spiritual father. Mexico inherited New Spain's institutions of trade, diplomacy, and alliance but lacked sufficient resources to secure them. Anglo-American traders, explorers, and soon settlers carried different imperial visions that assumed a priori the dispossession of Native communities.[4]

Foreign Traders and the Unmaking of the Spanish-Ute Alliance

Initially Ute leaders responded to the crisis of Mexican independence by attempting to reestablish the economic, military, and diplomatic privileges of the Spanish-Ute alliance. When Spanish and, later, Mexican leaders failed to ensure such privileges, Utes began searching for new avenues of trade, alliance, and accumulation. In 1818, for example, Utes joined Navajos in raids on New Mexican settlements. They also raided with Jicarilla Apaches on the Great Plains. While such raids had been by no means uncommon earlier, their steady increase throughout the Mexican period contrasted with the half-century of Spanish-Ute stability since the 1750s. Most Ute bands also began directly trading with, or extracting tolls from, American traders in their lands, and some occasionally attacked foreign parties on the Plains. While some bands grew more distant from New Mexico, others attempted to remain faithful allies as the turbulent storms of independence swept into their homelands.[5]

Before independence, New Mexican leaders had expected Utes not to raid settlements, to help protect New Mexico from its enemies, and also to assist Spanish missionaries, explorers, and traders in the north. Although similar patterns of diplomacy and exchange endured after independence, they became less ritualized, less reciprocal, and much more commercial. Only two years into the independence struggle, for example, in 1812 Pedro Bautista Pino noted that among the Utes, "money is all powerful . . . It is the only thing that has induced them to make peace with us and to permit us to cross their territory." Money and wealth were indeed becoming increasingly central to Ute economic and social relations. From glass beads to guns and from horses to slaves, new trade goods flowed into Ute communities, and as this trade transformed the region's political economy, the Spanish-Ute peace began to unravel. Pino's insights seemed ever more prescient.[6]

Ironically, northern Mexican officials believed that such commercialism would benefit the young republic, not jeopardize it by fueling American expansion. As Andrés Reséndez explains, "Far from discouraging Anglo-American settlers or attempting to control the U.S.-Mexico border, New Mexican officials sought to attract enterprising foreign settlers to promote industry and agriculture and above all facilitate New Mexico's commercial exchange with the Untied States." Hungry for increased foreign trade and markets, New Mexico's burgeoning populations sought to establish new commercial links, offering favorable immigration as well as settlement terms to westward-streaming U.S. traders. Far from unwelcomed, foreign men quickly gained both economic and social mobility within the region, often amassing enormous tracts of land along the way.[7]

American traders like Thomas James not only helped accelerate this new commercialism but also began recording it, and, in the north, traders recognized Utes as powerful warriors and partners, as well as potential enemies. As New Mexicans had known for generations, to trade and travel in the north required an understanding of the region's Indian peoples. During his travels from St. Louis to Santa Fe in 1821 and 1822, James witnessed spectacular displays of Comanche power, Ute defiance, and Mexican state weakness. Comanches had severely taxed his resources, taking, as many Indian peoples did, "presents" in return for safe passage through Indian homelands. Like many traders, James did not fully recognize, or ignored, the customs of reciprocity and gift-giving on the Plains. After threatening to kill the party, the Comanche band relented only upon the arrival of a New Mexican trading party that carried the important news not only of the colony's new independence but also that the former Spanish policy of interdicting American traders was to be abandoned. James and his fortunate party now followed the New Mexicans south and entered the newly independent Republic of Mexico, where he became the first U.S. citizen to establish commercial networks and offices in Santa Fe.[8]

While James busied himself in his new environs, word of independence spread to Ute villages throughout the north, and Ute leaders responded in kind to the dramatic news. They particularly wanted the attention of the newly arrived Americans. Under the leadership of Chief Lechat, as James later recalled, "a deputation of fifty Indians from the Utah tribe" rode into Santa Fe in February 1822: "They came riding into the city, and paraded on the public square, all well mounted on the most elegant horses I had ever seen. The animals were of a superior breed . . . The Indians alighted at the Council House and sent a request for me to visit them. On arriving I found them all awaiting me in the Council House, with a company of Spanish officers and gentlemen." Lechat and the Utes came to Santa Fe not to meet with Spanish leaders, but to attract American traders: "He told me in the Spanish language, which he spoke fluently, that he had come expressly to see me and have a talk with me. 'You are Americans, we are told, and you have come from your country afar off to trade with the Spaniards. We want your trade. Come to our country with your goods. Come and trade with the Utahs. We have horses, mules, and sheep, more than we want. We heard that you wanted beaver skins. The beavers in our country are eating up our corn. All our rivers are full of them . . . Come over among us and you shall have as many beaver skins as you want.'"[9]

Lechat's remarks about the bountiful skins, horses, and furs in his homelands enticed James. Having arrived in Santa Fe to build commercial links in the region, James was more than happy to accept the northerners' offerings, and after their meeting, "Lechat produced the *calama,* or pipe, and we smoked together . . . I sent to my store and produced six plugs of tobacco and some handkerchiefs, which I presented to him and his company, telling them . . . to remember the Americans, and treat all who visited their country from mine as their own brothers." The Utes accepted these conditions as well as the presents, proudly displaying the scarves on their lances as they rode out of town.[10]

James's recollection of Lechat's visit underscores the growing influence of foreign traders in northern Mexico. Utes had already learned much about American traders. They had escorted members of Zebulon Pike's party into New Mexico, had traded with Jacob Fowler and other forerunners of the Santa Fe Trail, and knew that such traders represented a powerful nation to the east. These foreigners, Utes understood, brought guns, ammunition, and powder needed by Indian peoples. While New Mexico had begun trading Spanish muskets to Indian allies in the late eighteenth century, Spanish governors had sought to use the gun trade for political leverage and traded old guns prone to need repair and longer rifles that were unwieldy on horseback. Most of all, governors regulated the amounts of gunpowder and lead in order to foster economic and political dependence. Early American traders did not operate under such constraints. They came to profit, and everywhere the Americans went, the gun trade flourished. Utes recognized such advantages and attempted to draw traders away from New Mexico and into their lands.[11]

Indian economic and political fortunes had long been intertwined. As Utes courted American traders they grew less interested in remaining aligned solely with New Mexico, and evidence of Mexican-Ute tensions abounds in James's narrative. The arrival of Indian delegations in Santa Fe was a common occurrence, but James was taken aback by Lechat's contemptuous attitude to his Mexican hosts. After inviting James to come to trade, for example, Lechat turned and began insulting his hosts:

> in [a] most contemptuous manner and with a scornful look he said, "What can you get from these? They have nothing but a few poor horses and mules . . . They are poor—too poor for you to trade with. Come among the Utahs if you wish to trade with profit. Look at our horses here. Have the Spaniards any such horses? No, they are too poor. Such as these we have in our country by the thousand . . . These Spaniards . . . What have they? They won't even give us two loads of powder and lead for a beaver skin, and for good reason they have not as much as they want themselves. They have nothing that you want. We have every thing that they have, and many things they have not." Here a Spaniard cried out: "You have no money." Like a true stump orator the Utah replied, "and you have very little. You are *depicca* [despicable]." In other words you are poor miserable devils and we are the true capitalists of the country . . . He looked like a King upbraiding his subjects.[12]

The Utes' entrance and harangue left lasting impressions on James and provide insight into the changing nature of Ute diplomacy on the morning of independence. The Spanish-Ute alliance had enabled such familiarity that Ute leaders felt comfortable not only in visiting Santa Fe, but also in public displays of power and defiance. They boldly announced their arrival in the city's plaza on horses of "superior" strength and then left parading their lances adorned with James's scarves. Like Chiefs Mora and Pino before them, Lechat commanded respect. He and his warriors were welcomed into town, given symbolic gifts as well as supplies, and seated in centers of governance. Unlike in the days of Anza, however, Lechat did not reciprocate the hospitality.

Indeed, his insults (in their native tongue no less) offended the honor of the New Mexicans. Despicable, poor, and powerless to control the region's "true capitalists," Lechat displayed little of the graciousness that had underpinned previous Spanish-Ute deliberations. Descriptions of "friendship," "allies," and "peace" and concerns with diplomacy, protection, and redress had characterized Spanish-Ute relations since the 1750s. Though not yet broken, the alliance was clearly weakening.

The exact sources of the Utes' displeasure toward New Mexico remain unclear. As the prosperity following the Comanche peace leveled off during the independence struggle, so too did Spanish expenditures for troops and Indian gifts. Governor Melagres had noted in 1818 that funds for Indian gifts had run out, leaving him "little or nothing of that used as Indian presents." Spanish funds to northern *presidios* had declined approximately 25 percent from 1798 to 1811, with a decline of 43 percent for Indian gifts. By 1825, Santa Fe's year-end balance for its *presidios* account was 41 pesos—95 percent less than its balance ten years earlier during Spanish rule. Despite New Mexico's economic boom in the late colonial period, then, the independence struggle and subsequent economic chaos drained funds used to protect New Mexico as well as to provide gifts to Indian allies. With New Mexico low on funds, troops, and supplies, Utes no longer relied as heavily on Santa Fe for gifts and protection. The growing number of foreign traders, the region's proliferating livestock, and expanding trade networks all provided greater avenues of wealth than New Mexican benevolence. Utes had secured privileges befitting powerful allies. They continued to enjoy such protections and privileges but had achieved self-sufficiency during the collapse of New Spain. Like many Indian peoples in the Southwest, they developed alternative forms of access to wealth after Mexican independence.[13]

New Mexican leaders initially responded to Ute defiance and disrespect with moderation. As the dust from Lechat's horses settled, authorities collected themselves. They had sat patiently as Lechat berated them. Such tirades had become more common during the lean years of independence, and many now wondered whether the promises of the new republic would bring more stable Indian relations. As David Weber notes, "New Mexicans feared a general Indian attack from all directions, and danger from potentially hostile Indians probably weighed more heavily on the minds of frontiersmen in 1821 than did the political uncertainties accompanying independence." Governor Melagres and his subordinates understood the realities of state control in the region and accepted Lechat's berating. They had few other options. As Navajo hostilities continued west of the Rio Grande, New Mexican leaders realized that Lechat and Ute bands were still critical to frontier stability. A full-scale Navajo-Ute attack or alliance would cripple the province, and Utes had in 1818 shown signs of joining Navajo raiders. During Lechat's visit, officials inquired "with considerable interest what the Navahoes were doing, and whether they were preparing to attack the Spanish settlements. They had been at war with this tribe for several years, and seemed to fear that the Utahs might take part in it as allies." For the first time since the Comanche peace, Indian hostilities threatened to overwhelm the province, and for the first time since the 1750s, Ute availability and alliance were uncertain.[14]

The precariousness of the Spanish-Ute alliance contributed to New Mexico's tumultuous transition from empire to nation. Chronic funding shortages, civil wars in central Mexico, and turbulent frontier Indian relations undermined Mexican state power, and throughout the 1820s few successful efforts were made to expand territorial control or to explore the region's vast hinterlands. New Mexico's immediate borderlands to the northwest remained, as they had for generations, the domain of the Utes.[15]

Ute wealth and power, as James detailed, had also reached considerable proportions. Not only were their horses "of a superior breed," but the Utes had them "by the thousand." With their rivers teeming with beavers, Ute homelands soon became important components in the region's growing fur trade. By hunting, raiding, and trading, Ute bands acquired the precious furs and hides that traders so desired. They also permitted and encouraged foreigners to enter their lands. Such ability to attract traders drew them further outside of New Mexico's orbit, weakening their ties to Santa Fe.

Within months of Lechat's remarks about his homeland's plenitude of beaver, trappers fanned into the region. The Pecos River, the northern Rio Grande, the San Juan, and eventually the Colorado River and its many tributaries all saw extensive trapping. In early 1822, for example, Americans Ewing Young and William Wolfskill joined William Becknell in Missouri for his second trip to New Mexico. That fall, however, they left New Mexico to trap along the Pecos. Two years later, upon returning from the San Juan, Young and Wolfskill entered Santa Fe with an estimated $10,000 worth of fur. Later expeditions that year were rumored to include eighty members, three times larger than any previous trapping party. After his return to Missouri in 1824, Augustus Storrs described these trappers' scramble for fur: "A majority of them left Taos about the first of August, intending to go westward thirty days' journey, probably seven hundred miles . . . They would then diverge . . . where prospects of success might invite them." Tracing New Mexico's western rivers to their headwaters, trapping parties now took as much fur as possible. The hunt for furs would play a central role in Great Basin Indian history for the next generation as trappers flowed into the region from every direction.[16]

As they had for decades, Utes guided, welcomed, and joined trading parties in their homelands. Few records of trappers' travels in western Colorado and southern Utah remain, particularly from before 1830, but evidence of such traffic can be gleaned. For example, following Wolfskill and Young's exploits along the San Juan, dozens of parties moved into the region. The most effective parties established lucrative trade centers with Ute and other Indian peoples, while others suffered and even perished from Indian attacks, cold, and hunger. The most successful, Antoine Robidoux, established two trading posts in Ute territory, one in western Colorado along the Gunnison River, the other east of Utah Lake Valley on the Green River of northeastern Utah. At these outposts and other forts in Colorado and Wyoming, Utes annually traded for guns, metals, beads, and other manufactured goods. These trading centers, however, represented varying imperial and corporate interests; though often operating out of New Mexico, such trade was linked to faraway imperial centers. From Montreal to the mouth of the Columbia River, the Hudson's Bay Company dominated the West's northern fur trade, while American trappers out of St. Louis consolidated control over the Great Plains. New Mexican and Ute homelands remained, then, crossroads within larger economic and imperial contests.

Robidoux's forts encapsulate the experience of much of the last decades of the New Mexican–Ute borderlands. For twenty years, his operations depended upon stable relations with Ute communities. Far from settlements and only moderately fortified, these forts replenished trapping parties in the Intermountain West, purchasing harvested furs and transporting them south to Taos. And whereas many trappers left the region as the fur trade declined, Robidoux's forts remained, provisioning overland travelers until 1844. One of these travelers, Rufus Sage, in 1841 provided one of the few accounts of Fort Uintah:

> The trade of this post is conducted principally with the trapping parties frequenting the Big Bear, Green, Grand, and the Colorado Rivers, with their numerous tributaries . . . A small business is also carried on with the Snakes and Utah Indians . . . The common articles of dealing are horses, with beaver, otter, deer, sheep, and elk skins, in barter for ammunition, firearms, knives, tobacco, beads, awls, etc. The Utahs . . . afford some of the largest and best finished sheep and deer skins I ever beheld . . . These skins are dressed so neatly as frequently to attain a snowy whiteness . . . They may be purchased for the trifling consideration of eight or ten charges of ammunition each.

Robidoux oversaw such operations from Taos, accumulating profits from hides, horses, and furs. Sage's identification of high-quality sheepskins among the trade items highlights the myriad Spanish influences in the region. As New Mexico's sheep population exploded in the early 1800s, Ute and other Indian bands had increasing access to these resources. Estimated at over a million, the Southwest's sheep population surged following the Comanche peace. Though nominally at peace with New Mexico, many Utes raided these and neighboring Navajo herds at will as additional skins, foods, and even wools became part of everyday life.[17]

Robidoux was but one of many foreigner trappers who traded in Utah and Colorado during the years of Mexican rule. James Bridger, Jedediah Smith, Peter Skene Ogden, and William Ashley, among others, traveled into the region from the north, tracing the Green, Bear, and other rivers south. Utah had several annual trading sites, or rendezvous, for trappers and Indians in the region. Unlike traders operating out of New Mexico, however, many of these trappers represented distant corporate interests in England and the United States, and in their rush into the Intermountain West, they exhausted the region's furs. A few, such as Jedediah Smith, traced the mountain valleys and smaller rivers, such as the Virgin and Sevier, farther south into the arid landscapes of southern Utah and Nevada, while others, like Ogden, searched for possible river ways to California. Such travels eventually took these traders into the homelands of nonequestrian Paiute and Shoshone peoples and opened the way for later expeditions.[18]

The Ute bands of western Colorado and Utah, then, traded with foreigners on their southern, eastern, and northern borders as throughout the Mexican national period the West became part of a larger continental economy. Such changing economic fortunes ultimately recast the calculus of Ute diplomacy. Following Lechat's tirade, New Mexican–Ute relations increasingly shifted from alliance toward enmity. As Navajo-Mexican hostilities intensified, for example, Utes joined Navajos in attacks against New Mexico. In August 1829, Navajos at Jemez Pueblo reported that "the Utes have come inviting [us] to join the war" against New Mexico. Navajo raids at Abiquiu and other northern settlements often came through Ute lands, and many New Mexican leaders suspected that Utes either participated in or at least condoned such attacks. In July 1832, for example, a Navajo-Ute party raided San Juan Pueblo and made off with ten horses. The year before, Utes had captured an unidentified Indian woman and sold her to the Navajos. In 1835 Navajo and Ute *rancherías* were reported encamped together in the La Plata Mountains along the Colorado border, and in 1839 Ute leaders requested a meeting with New Mexican leaders for their Navajo allies. In short, throughout the 1830s joint Navajo-Ute depredations fell upon the province. By 1840 New Mexicans increasingly feared Ute attack, and many considered Ute lands dangerous.[19]

American traders also recorded the Utes' growing bellicosity toward New Mexico. As Josiah Gregg in 1837 explained, "The Yutas are one of the most extensive nations of the West, being scattered from the north of New Mexico to the borders of the Snake River and Rio Colorado, and numbering at least ten thousand souls . . . Although these Indians are nominally at peace with the New Mexican government, they do not hesitate to [rob] the hunter and traders . . . and on some occasions they have been known to proceed even to personal violence." Gregg additionally recounted his party's conflicts with a Ute band on the Arkansas River. When Utes stole and failed to return a horse, the two parties readied for combat. With "one-third of our party being Mexicans," he noted, "the first step of the Indians was to proclaim a general *indulto* [pardon] to them . . . 'My Mexican friends,' exclaimed [one] in good Spanish . . . 'we don't wish to hurt *you;* so leave those Americans.' To which the Mexicans responded: *'Al diablo!* we have not forgotten how you treat us when you catch us alone . . . expect ample retaliation for past insults.'" Despite the bitterness, the two parties resolved their dispute, though resentment underlay both sides' threatening acts.[20]

Gregg's account reveals the familiarity as well as increasing hostility between many Utes and New Mexicans. Although the Utes spoke "good Spanish" and attempted to use their position as nominal allies to exempt the Mexicans from attack, New Mexican traders no longer trusted the Utes, and for good reason: not long before this incident, as Gregg explained, "A prominent Mexican officer [Don Juan Andrés Archuleta] was scourged . . . by a party of Yutas" for unspecified reasons. Archuleta's humiliation elicited no immediate response from Santa Fe, where "the government has never dared to resent the outrage." New Mexicans in Gregg's party recalled this and other "past insults" and wanted a chance to exact "ample retaliation" on these supposed allies. Their desire for vengeance, however, remained unappeased while Gregg and Ute leaders negotiated the return of the disputed animal.[21]

Juan Andrés Archuleta held prominent military and political positions in New Mexico and was familiar with the north and its peoples. Although the exact moment and location of the Utes' assault upon him is unclear, it probably came during one of his many campaigns in the 1830s against the Navajos and their suspected Ute allies. In the fall of 1839 he again spent three months directing one of two Mexican divisions in pursuit of Navajos. The expeditions ranged from Canyon de Chelly and Zuni in Arizona into southern Colorado, killing thirty, capturing slaves, and taking horses by the hundreds and nearly 10,000 sheep. Three years later Archuleta was ordered by the governor simply to kill any Navajos suspected of stealing outside Abiquiu, and in 1844 the governor again instructed Archuleta to enlist 500 men to campaign against the Navajo as well as to monitor the Utes. Like many "citizen-soldiers" of northern Mexico, Archuleta built a military career around defending settlements from Indian attacks while carrying violence into Indian homelands. And throughout the last decade of Mexican rule, he and fellow New Mexican commanders no longer viewed Utes as allies. They were to be feared, not trusted, and closely monitored during their visits into the province. Such mistrust further eroded the increasingly hollow New Mexican–Ute alliance.[22]

Since many Mexican governors arrived in Santa Fe from central Mexico knowing little or nothing about frontier Indian relations, they relied upon the knowledge and experience of Archuleta and other settlers. Accustomed to the nuances and complexities of Indian politics, settlers often protested the inexperience and performance of these federal appointees. In 1844, for example, Donaciano Vigil complained that Governor Mariano Martínez showed "great ignorance of our situation and relations with neighboring heathen tribes." In addition to exacerbating Navajo hostilities, Martínez further destabilized the frontier with an egregious attack on a Ute delegation in Santa Fe at the Governor's Palace.[23]

In September 1844, only months after Archuleta's most recent campaign against the Navajos, several bands of Utes arrived at Abiquiu demanding a meeting with the governor. Earlier that summer New Mexican soldiers had reportedly attacked a Ute *ranchería,* killed seven warriors, and taken children captive. As they had for generations, Ute leaders expected compensation and redress for such violations of their nominal peace, and they demanded the return of "two small children and two boys." Leaving their *rancherías* north of town, six Ute chiefs and 100 warriors headed into Santa Fe to the *Palacio* to present their grievances. What happened next remains unclear. Apparently, after refusing gifts and offerings, as Ute leaders had historically done to show their indignation, the chiefs were escorted into a room where, according to David Weber, "discussions . . . led to angry words and a fist fight in the governor's office . . . According to his own account, Martínez fought the Utes off with a chair . . . The Utes fled town amidst gunfire, leaving some of their number dead and dying in the streets where their bodies remained unburied for at least a week." On their way out of town, Ute warriors sacked settlements along the northern Rio Grande and then returned north to spread word of the governor's treachery.[24]

As Ute bands mourned their dead and prepared for war, memories of an earlier era of respect and hospitality in Santa Fe grew ever more distant. Martínez's assault violated the norms and rituals of New Mexican–Ute diplomacy and sounded the death knell of the New Mexican–Ute alliance. As they had since the 1750s, Utes had come to Santa Fe to uphold the institutions and privileges of their alliance. Though weakened by recent raids and animosities, they still believed that diplomatic channels existed. Governors Cachupín, Anza, and Melagres, among others, had received similarly aggrieved Ute leaders. These Spanish leaders, however, were steeped in the realities and exigencies of frontier Indian diplomacy. They knew that Indian leaders came to Santa Fe to ensure redress or exact some compensation for the families of fallen warriors. Horses, weapons, and especially captured children were offered or returned to Santa Fe's Indian allies.

The recently arrived Mexican governor lacked such experience and familiarity. He had come north from a republic divided by civil war, and he was without critical resources and vision. Notwithstanding Mexico's growing antagonisms with the United States, frontier Indian policy remained low on the list of national concerns because of insufficient resources and growing indigenous power. Martínez's repeated orders to Archuleta and others to increase their expeditionary campaigns and to kill suspected Navajo and other Indian raiders, and now his inability to receive peaceful Ute delegates reflected ineffectual policies that characterized northern Indian relations. Before the melee, Martínez later rationalized, the negotiations inside the *Palacio* had grown hostile and taken on a personal character. Ute leaders, led by a chief named Panasiyave, had berated the governor and criticized his ability to ensure northern peace and prosperity. Like Lechat before them, Ute chiefs voiced their disdain for New Mexican leaders. They humiliated not simply to offend, but to ensure that their power, authority, and honor be recognized and upheld. Previous governors, such as Melagres and Anza, had waited as Ute leaders displayed such indignation. Ute diplomacy and alliance required such displays of power and, if need be, tirades. The Utes' visit to Santa Fe had been diplomatic; had 100 warriors intended to maraud and plunder, they would have marauded and plundered. But Martínez mistook Ute defiance for animosity.[25]

The once carefully negotiated institutions of diplomacy, protection, and redress between Utes and New Mexico now degenerated into violence. Utes subsequently razed both of Robidoux's forts, killing all his New Mexican employees. Raids along the Chama, at Abiquiu, and throughout the north plunged much of the province into war, prompting Archuleta's return to the field in 1845. Mexican state control outside the province had reached new lows. Not since the slave raids of Rabál had relations with Utes been so dark. Ute and Navajo conflicts would not only cripple the province but also outlast it as Mexico's northern Indian wars were superseded by another, more cataclysmic continental contest.[26]

Violence and Slavery on the Old Spanish Trail

Despite the increasing hostilities, travel and trade continued throughout the New Mexican–Ute borderlands. Although diplomatic relations eroded between Mexican and Ute leaders, the everyday ties of kinship, language, and trade continued to bind these northern peoples together, especially at Abiquiu, "the gateway to the northwest." In fact the erosion of political relations between New Mexican leaders and Utes expanded opportunities for rogue entrepreneurs, traders, and trappers as the vast hinterlands northwest of the province became opened further to illicit trade, traffic, and trapping.

With the collapse of New Spain and Mexico's many weaknesses, state control over northern hinterlands loosened. Governors no longer strictly enforced taxes, licenses, and laws forbidding trade and travel to the north, and local prefects and *alcaldes* similarly grew lax in enforcement of former colonial regulations. Besides, the northern Indian trade and its many temptations remained woven into the fabric of northern society. By the 1820s, for instance, Indian captives had not only provided generations of servile labor but also developed new ethnic identities. Some *genízaros* continued to maintain social relations with northern Indian communities, and when Indian *rancherías* visited, former and now Hispanicized captives and their children reconnected with family and friends, sharing their respective languages and customs, as well as new stories and older memories. *Genízaros* also continued to guide, translate, and trade throughout the north. Northern New Mexican towns, like Abiquiu, and their residents remained, then, deeply connected to northern Indian peoples, and their historical, cultural, and economic connections only intensified during the Mexican period through the expansion of trade, traffic, and slavery in the Great Basin.[27]

The trading route for furs, slaves, and horses out of Abiquiu and eventually to Los Angeles became known as the Old Spanish Trail, although, as David Weber notes, the route "was neither Spanish nor old." Following trails established first by Utes and then by Spanish explorers Rivera (1765) and Domínguez and Escalante (1776), the Old Spanish Trail connected New Mexico with California. Developed after the collapse of New Spain and in the context of ineffective Mexican frontier policies, the trail linked a series of smaller trade routes into a regional, indeed continental, network of trade and supply. The route eventually joined California, Nevada, Utah, and Colorado not only to New Mexico but also to the Santa Fe Trail and American outposts along the Mississippi.[28]

After exhausting most of the region's mountain furs, trappers and fur companies generally abandoned the drier regions of the Great Basin. Some continued to meet at rendezvous in Utah, but trade and traffic in the southern Great Basin came to center on the Abiquiu–Los Angeles axis. Although many claim that it was first "opened" by Americans such as Jedediah Smith, Ute and New Mexican traders predominated in use of the trail. The trail's many traders, however, defy easy classification. Bands of Ute raiders, for instance, often included a hodgepodge of American and New Mexican traders, while Mexican parties relied upon Indian guides and were often financed by foreign traders. Soon New Mexican emigrant parties including Indians, *genízaros,* and peoples from other parts of Mexico would make the hazardous trek to California. The hybridity of the borderlands, then, was reflected in the trail and its many traffickers. Amply evident, as well, was the use of violence.[29]

Dozens of such parties traveled along the trail, and all passed through and relied upon Ute, Southern Paiute, and Western Shoshone communities. In 1830, for example, Americans George Yount and William Wolfskill, who had previously traded in central Utah, left Abiquiu for California with the first licensed foreign party. Upon entering Utah's Sevier River Valley, the party was warmly received in a Ute village. Recognizing Yount from his earlier expeditions, Ute traders shared foods and goods with the party, who witnessed the funeral of a Ute chief. The Utes, according to Yount's testimonies, then granted the traders permission to continue south to "hunt and trap in all the territory of the great Eutau nation." In the territories to the south of this great nation, however, the Americans encountered repeated hardships.[30]

Because of the extreme temperatures of summer, parties departed in the fall or early spring for their months-long expeditions. Even then, however, weather could still influence travel. Wolfskill and

Yount, who left in September, encountered "deep snows and solitary gloom." Having got lost in southern Utah, they eventually traced tributaries of the Colorado River south to Mojave Indian bands, who offered crucial food and guidance. Traveling due west, they then encountered Shoshone bands, or "Digger Indians," in the Mojave Desert, who also provided dried meats and guidance. Finally arriving in southern California in February 1831, they decided to remain in California, becoming Mexican citizens. Their wanderings along the trail had not only depended upon different Indian bands but also tempered these seasoned traders' interests in such future travel.[31]

Wolfskill and Yount thought little of the California Indians who had saved them. Yount considered the Shoshone subhuman, so adapted to their environment that they were indeed animals. "These people are an anomaly—apparently the lowest species of humanity," he later wrote, "approaching the monkey. Nothing but their straight form entitles them to the name man." Yount characterized Shoshones not only as primitive but as the most primitive—a trope continued by subsequent observers. Although his party had relied upon their communities, Yount later disavowed their aid. He represented them not as beneficent hosts, which he knew them to be, but as an anomalous subspecies, because he perceived their limited material conditions as proof of inferiority. Such racism pervades subsequent accounts of the region's nonequestrians; throughout the nineteenth century Great Basin Indians became equated with primitivism, their increasing deprivation evidence not of a changing history but of a permanent state of nature. As we shall see, such deprivation resulted from intertwined environmental and social traumas.[32]

New Mexican trading parties depended less on Great Basin Indian guidance and assistance than did the smaller bands of trappers. Laden with domestic goods, particularly woolen textiles, annual caravans departed in the fall bound for California, where demand for manufactured goods and the region's proliferating cattle and horse herds created favorable conditions of trade: generally two New Mexican blankets for one horse or mule. Horses and mules were then driven back by the thousands to restock the region's diminished herds, heavily depleted for decades by Indian raiders, as well as to supply traders for their return trips east on the Santa Fe Trail.

Small, nonequestrian Paiute and Shoshone bands often either fled from the intrusion of such large parties or greeted the foreigners cautiously. The first commercial expedition to leave Abiquiu in 1829, for example, consisted of sixty men and more than 100 mules and horses under the direction of Antonio Armijo. Expecting possible Navajo, Mojave, and other Indian raids, Armijo encountered small Paiute bands on five occasions and noted their peaceful behavior. Little remains from these encounters other than his terse daily reports: "December 10 . . . on this day there was found a settlement of Payuches, with no mishap; it is a gentle and cowardly nation . . . December 27 . . . We found a settlement of Indians . . . Nothing happened, for these Indians are gentle and cowardly . . . January 14 At the River of the Payuches, where a village was found; nothing happened, for it was gentle."[33]

The fragments from these first expeditions on the Old Spanish Trail highlight the difficulty in accessing Paiute and Shoshone responses to foreign intrusion. An unspecified Shoshone band assisted Young and Wolfskill in eastern California while several Paiute groups nervously received Armijo in southern Utah. The specific details and repercussions of these encounters remain unknown. Only traces exist. Though incomplete, these brief accounts provide suggestive glimpses into the changes accompanying foreign intrusion in the region.[34]

An unspecified Paiute group in Utah, for instance, fled "in terror" upon Armijo's approach. Dozens of foreigners had descended into their homelands with herds that destroyed vegetation and fouled water supplies, and Paiute fear no doubt arose from previous attacks by Ute or New Mexican raiders. As earlier traders had detailed, Paiutes often fled from intruders, sounded well-positioned alarms, or mobilized against unknown equestrian travelers. Now, the size of Armijo's expedition dwarfed that of previous parties. As Domínguez and Escalante and other expeditions had noted, nonequestrian Great Basin Indians lived in small bands, often under the command of a single leader. These "extended family units," as anthropologists describe them, lacked the warriors, horses, and weaponry to resist such intrusion. Sixty horsemen expert in the arts of frontier combat could have laid waste to any nonequestrian societies. Why some groups welcomed Armijo at all remains unclear. Lacking horses and mobility, they perhaps had little choice or hoped for peaceful trade. Whatever the reasons, Paiute apprehensions testify to the levels of terror accompanying exploration and trade in the region.[35]

Additional effects of such traffic in Paiute and Shoshone homelands are also difficult to measure but easy to suggest: disease, starvation, and ecological destruction. Armijo's journey contributed to the intertwined processes of defoliation, starvation, and possibly the introduction of disease. The party's hundreds of horses and mules as well as sixty men consumed game, water, and grasses along their route. Subsequent caravans with even larger herds continued the depletion of local waterholes, grasses, and foods central to Indian subsistence. Such rivers and waterholes were essential for survival, for Paiutes lived along rivers and their tributaries throughout southern Utah, especially the Virgin and Sevier Rivers. As these rivers south from Utah Lake became primary routes along the Old Spanish Trail, their seasonal grasses, game, and fowl were increasingly exploited by foreign traffic. The large mule trains and horse herds along the trail, then, triggered ecological and social change throughout the southern Great Basin as Paiute and Shoshone impoverishment, increasingly conspicuous to outsiders, increased with the passage of each caravan.[36]

Caravans and large herds came into the Great Basin from the west as well as the east. While California's settler, or *gente de razón,* population of 3,000 remained nearly three times smaller than that of Santa Fe and ten times smaller than all of New Mexico, the region's horse herds outnumbered New Mexico's. Feral horses in the San Joaquin Valley of central California were estimated to number in the tens of thousands, and Indian and *Californio vaqueros* drove thousands of them into coastal settlements, often simply to be slaughtered and skinned. Amazed by the size of caravans arriving from the uncharted deserts to the east, Mexican leaders soon grew concerned about the lawlessness accompanying the New Mexican trade. Only three years after Armijo's arrival, for example, a series of laws were passed curbing unlicensed trading, establishing fixed rates of exchange, passport requirements, temporary stays, and duties, and setting specific points of inspection and departure in Los Angeles. New Mexican traders, one early California historian noted, "were as closely watched as if they were foreigners."[37]

Beginning in the early 1830s, horse raiders encroached upon California's southern settlements and began driving more herds into the Great Basin. While feral horses grazed in California's central and coastal valleys, raiders targeted the domesticated herds adjoining missions, settlements, and *Californio* ranches; raiders had little time to break, tame, and then drive feral horses to New Mexican markets. In addition, confederated Californian Indian peoples loosely controlled many of the feral herds, especially after 1833, when Mexican national laws secularized coastal missions and drove thousands of former mission Indians into interior valleys, participating in what George Harwood Phillips calls the "repopulation of the San Joaquin Valley." Horses and mules ready for travel into the desert became the prime

Valley in the Slope of the Great Basin, Leading from the Tejon Pass. Lithograph from a sketch by Charles Koppel, in Reports of Explorations and Surveys, to Ascertain the Most Practicable and Economical Route for a Railroad from the Mississippi River to the Pacific Ocean (1855). At the western terminus of the Old Spanish Trail, equestrian traders, slavers, and raiders entered southern California through its eastern deserts. Initially charted by New Mexican and Ute traders, the Old Spanish Trail wrought ecological and social havoc upon Great Basin nonequestrian Indians.

targets of horse raiders following the creation of the Old Spanish Trail.[38]

In the spring of 1840 California suffered its greatest horse raid. A band of robbers, "who are called the Chaguanosos and are adventurers of all nations," attacked simultaneously at the missions San Gabriel, San Juan Capistrano, and San Luis Obispo. Herding several thousand horses together into a single herd, the raiders struck off east to the desert. According to Leroy and Ann Hafen, "So widespread were the raids and so great the losses that a concerted effort was . . . [made] to recover the stock and punish the thieves . . . Tiburico Tapia, prefect of Los Angeles . . . organized parties for the pursuit . . . [and] resorted to freeing prisoners from jail to augment the forces" as infantrymen.[39]

Accounts of the ensuing pursuit diverge. American trader Thomas "Pegleg" Smith later boasted that after driving their tired horses into the desert 100 miles east of Los Angeles, the raiders split their party, leaving a small contingent in hiding at a local waterhole. According to Smith, after the *Californio* party arrived and watered their horses, the raiders attacked, spooked the herd, and drove them into the desert to augment their spoils. Humiliated, the soldiers retraced their path on foot, waiting for their convict reinforcements to join them for their long walk back to Los Angeles. Commander José Antonio Carillio's account details similar misfortune but suggests that his lost mounts were not stolen but perished from exhaustion. Besides, he contended, the raiders had also lost nearly half of their approximately 3,000 horses to fatigue.[40]

Although Smith and other "American" traders were reported among the band, this "Chaguanosos" party included Ute warriors, particularly the leader Walkara. Walkara, according to Smith, led the raid at San Luis Obispo, sneaking into the mission's corral and making off with its herd of 1,200. His involvement and the identification of these "Chaguanosos" suggest that although these "adventurers of many nations" included Americans, the party was under Ute command. "Chaguanosos" is related to designations of the Sabuagana Utes of western Colorado, who had ties to Laguna or Timpanagos Utes of Utah Lake, from where Walkara came. Whether or not this party included Utes from Colorado, it was identified along existing Ute band designations and included the most famous Ute raider. And one year after Walkara's 1840 coup, California documents again noted "a motley gang of Frenchmen, Utes, Americans, Saguanosos, and Sozones." Whether Walkara was again involved is unknown, but Utes stole from California herds, a form of pride and honor within Utah Ute societies. As one California official succinctly warned, "effective measures [should be taken] to prevent robberies by the *chaguenosos* . . . should entry of these horse thieves take place the country will be totally ruined."[41]

Walkara's exploits in California and to the Pacific reveal both the hybrid and militaristic organization of Ute raiding parties. Operating in tandem with traders such as Smith, these raiders dominated the hinterlands between California and New Mexico. Although New Mexican caravans commanded more men, they traveled seasonally and under the auspices of Mexican-appointed commanders who ordered their men not to "separate from the company." Governors additionally gave commanders authority to administer corporal punishment to members of their own companies and attempted to minimize acts of brutality against local Indian peoples. As New Mexican Governor Manuel Armijo instructed trader Franco Estevan Vigil in 1841, "When they come to a tribe friendly to this Department [Province], the Indians should not be harmed or given any cause for complaint." Ute raiders operated under no such constraints. Besides driving stolen herds through the Great Basin, Ute marauders dominated the region's nonequestrians, and throughout the Mexican period their capture of Shoshone and Paiute women and children increased in scope and scale. Although the specifics of such slave raids are elusive, a few accounts suggest the extent of this growing domination.[42]

The sale of Indian women and children figures in innumerable reports of Walkara's activities. American William Lorton, for example, noted that during his travels in Utah in the 1840s, the "Indian Walker deals largely in Piede children and horse flesh." Trader Daniel Jones offered a similar description: "Walker and his band raided on the weak tribes, taking their children prisoners and selling them to the Mexicans." At annual trapper rendezvous in the 1830s and 1840s, American traders bought Californian horses from Walkara's band and were then offered Indian women. The traders, according to one Walkara biographer, "enjoyed Indian [women] through his hospitality and sought to imitate his successful trafficking in native slaves." Although the identities and treatment of these Indian women remain unknown, repeated observations that Walkara's slave trafficking centered on Great Basin Indians and that he and his band often kept young women as wives suggest that these women were Great Basin Indian captives. Mormon settlers also noted such trafficking beginning in the late 1840s.[43]

Most revealing are accounts by Paiute women enslaved by Utes. In the 1920s, for example, Mary Shem, an elderly Southern Paiute woman, told the historian William Palmer of her abduction as a young girl. As Palmer relayed, "There lives at Santa Clara, Utah, an old [woman] named Mary Shem who was captured by a band of Wah-kar-ar's men. She was a girl of perhaps twelve years old when the raiders carried her away from her tribe—the Shivwits . . . Mary was placed in charge of a woman who was the wife of one of the warriors. This Indian had announced his intention of making this girl his second wife." Fortunate to escape the Utes' camp, Mary spent several days traversing southern Utah before returning to her people.[44]

Generations of Southern Paiutes like Mary Shem have passed along oral histories of nineteenth-century slave raids. For example, interviewers for the American Indian History Project—begun in the 1960s to record tribal histories—interviewed dozens of Paiutes as well as early Utah settlers about Paiute history and culture. Numerous informants recalled stories of Paiute children either enslaved by Utes or placed in Mormon homes. When asked, for example, "Were there any old stories about Utes capturing Paiute children and selling them for slaves and things?" Toney Tillohash of the St. George Paiute community of Utah replied, "Utes? Yes, they did that. I heard that they take especially—they take Shivwit people—get their children and bring 'um up and trade 'um to some white people . . . they got a lot of kids that way, a lot of 'um."[45]

Throughout the 1830s and 1840s, New Mexican, Californian, and American traders all detailed the region's escalating Indian slave trade. The New Mexican governors regulating the caravans over the Old Spanish Trail had little or no control over the stream of illegal trading parties into the northwest. As they had for decades, New Mexicans came in search of hides, horses, and slaves, and became equally complicit in the region's traffic. American trader Dick Wotton, for example, noted that while trapping in the Wasatch Mountains in the late 1830s, he often traded with New Mexicans. "[It] was no uncommon thing in those days," he later recounted, "to see a party of Mexicans in that country buying Indians . . . I sent a lot of peltries to Taos by a party of those . . . slave traders." Taos, Abiquiu, and northern New Mexico received record numbers of "Ute" captives beginning in the 1830s. As David Brugge records, 271 of New Mexico's 626 total identified Indian captives baptized from 1830 to 1860, or 43 percent, were "Utes." More "Ute" captives were baptized during this period than Comanches, Apaches, and Navajos combined. At Abiquiu, 64 identified "Ute" captives were baptized from 1830 to 1850, nearly half of Abiquiu's total "Ute" baptisms from 1754 to 1866. As always, the vast majority were young women and children.[46]

The numbers of such captives are small but significant. They represent larger patterns of enslavement. Unidentified slaves far outnumbered captives with tribal designations, and unidentified Great Basin Indians undoubtedly outnumbered those identified as "Utes." But during the Mexican period, as Mexicans encountered Paiutes on the Old Spanish Trail, padres and *padrinos* also began noting different "Ute" band designations. "Capote," "Chahuahuana," "Pavant," "Saguano," "Timpanago," and "Paiute" are a few of the band names that appear in New Mexican ecclesiastical records. Of the eighty-seven captives baptized with these band designations, sixty-nine were Paiutes.[47]

Paiute captives generated considerable profits for Ute, New Mexican, and American slavers. According to Thomas Farnham's account from 1839, "The New Mexicans capture them for slaves; the neighboring Indians do the same; and even the bold . . . old beaver-hunter sometimes descends . . . to this mean traffic. The price of these slaves in the markets of New Mexico varies with age and other qualities of the person. Those from ten to fifteen years sell from $50 to $100." Trader Daniel Jones summed up the traffic, noting even higher values for Paiute girls:

> So systematic was conduct of the California–New Mexican slave trade it resulted in tremendous profits to its participants. The poorer mounts being reserved for exchange with "Digger" Paiutes, who would often relinquish their children . . . The traders would then continue to California, where Paiute children were bartered . . . On the return trip, the process would be repeated—the women and children being taken to New Mexico and sold as menials—at the current rate of $100 a boy, and

from $150 to $200 for healthy girls, who were in greater demand as household servants.[48]

In California, Paiute captives brought less return. California's settler population remained much smaller than New Mexico's, and labor drafts extracted former mission Indians for servile labor throughout the province. Far fewer Paiute captives appear in California state records than in those of New Mexico. Los Angeles Plaza Church death records, for example, include only scattered references to a half-dozen identifiable Great Basin captives. A few court records detail the sale of unidentifiable Indian children by New Mexicans throughout the 1830s, but generally the sale of Great Basin slaves remained less institutionalized and lucrative than in New Mexico.[49]

As a few of these accounts of Great Basin Indian slavery suggest, raiders did not always resort to physical violence to enslave Paiutes. Many reportedly traded fatigued or injured horses for children. Suffering from the increased diseases and deprivation accompanying foreign intrusion, Paiutes and possibly Shoshones in eastern California reportedly exchanged their children for food. As Daniel Jones noted, "Many of the lower classes [of Indians], inhabiting the southern deserts, would sell their own children for a horse and kill and eat the horse." Moreover, as slave raiders descended upon their bands threatening to massacre them, Paiute leaders often had few options other than to compromise and negotiate with their oppressors. Paiute mothers contested these decisions, violently protesting when their children were pried from their arms. A Paiute woman interviewed by Palmer recalled the fate of one such child sold to the Utes. An unidentified Paiute mother refused to turn her baby over to Ute traders and fled with the child up Thompson's Point along the Virgin River in southern Utah. When finally surrounded by her child's new owners, she threw her baby into the river.[50]

The seasonal and cyclical patterns of the Great Basin Indian slave trade persisted after the United States acquired the region. Through the 1840s into the 1860s, American explorers, settlers, and officials recognized, and some attempted to regulate, the traffic in Indian slaves. In Utah, Mormon invaders were initially horrified by this traffic in children and attempted to purchase captives out of slavery and place them in settler homes. Subsequent attempts to outlaw the trade altogether drew increasing wrath from Walkara and other Utes. Indeed, competing visions of the future of the slave trade became a primary cause of Mormon-Ute hostilities in 1853. New Mexican traders also protested Mormon attempts to outlaw this lucrative trade and were jailed for violating newly formulated Mormon laws. The Great Basin Indian slave trade, in sum, continued to entice and divide Intermountain West communities long after Mexican rule had been extinguished along the Rio Grande, and, as always, its practice and effect remained tortuous beyond measure.[51]

FIVE

Great Basin Indians in the Era of Lewis and Clark

The early nineteenth-century arrival of Anglo and American traders, trappers, and explorers brought not only new challenges to the Indians of the Great Basin but also potential opportunities. The Ute leader Lechat understood as much in 1822, when, in his attempts to attract American traders directly into Ute lands, he belittled his New Mexican hosts, equating New Mexico with poverty. Through the first half of the 1800s, Ute bands under leaders like Lechat and Walkara continued to control vast hunting, trading, and slaving territories, and they hoped that competing Anglo and American traders would facilitate their communities' growth and expansion. How could they expect otherwise? Utes had adapted to the arrival of powerful newcomers since the early seventeenth century and had skillfully reorganized their societies accordingly. Warfare with New Mexico had given way to alliance and stability, and tensions with neighboring Indian powers had eased after the Comanche peace and Bourbon reforms of the 1770s and 1780s. These English-speaking traders now seemed ideally suited to facilitate Ute ends. They traded better guns than New Mexicans. They had more ammunition and supplies, and they came directly into Indian lands to trade. American fur-trading "mountain men" even stayed the winter, some living among Indian communities, while traders out of New Mexico continued to make inroads with the Utes. While New Mexican trade fairs remained important destinations on Ute travels, American traders and their centers in Utah and Wyoming afforded new markets and resources for Indian communities, and in the decades after Mexican independence, these traders introduced new economies, technologies, and motivations that powerfully shaped the fabric of Great Basin Indian societies. By the 1840s, for example, Utes still controlled extensive lands, herds, and subject Paiute vassals. Their growing dependence upon these foreign traders and their goods, however, would soon have seismic consequences.[1]

Unbeknownst to Ute leaders, American trade centered not upon New Mexico or points farther south but upon burgeoning entrepôts along the Mississippi and Missouri, where cities like St. Louis and St. Joseph had come into existence specifically to facilitate American expansion. St. Louis' hyperbolic claim to be the "gateway to the West" only slightly exaggerates its prominence in opening western lands to American development. Primary exploration, trading, and later emigrant trails originated here, extending west like the tentacles of a large octopus. Although Spanish imperial designs had extended beyond *presidio* walls, their reach had grown predictable and was easily outmaneuvered by mobile Indian powers. "Licensed" traders and explorers—Britain's and the United States' initial agents of empire—resembled their Spanish counterparts in form only. They ventured west unencumbered by century-old Iberian imperial decrees that sought to incorporate Native peoples into the religious and political folds of empire; moreover, unlike their British counterparts coming from the north, American traders operated independently of strict trading monopolies like the Hudson's Bay Company. Nominal representatives of a new expansionist state, western American traders worked primarily for market-driven economic interests; national, religious, and political concerns were secondary if not forgotten.[2]

Leaders of the nascent American republic viewed expansion as a necessary though vexed evil. Understanding territorial acquisition to be a fundamental precondition for national development (if not unity), antebellum officials increasingly interpreted expansion along strict sectional lines—"free" versus "slave" labor—and remained largely untroubled by its economic effects on Native groups. Indeed, American democracy, as Thomas Jefferson constantly advocated, required the continuous accumulation of interior lands for conversion into independent freeholdings where virtuous citizens could enjoy the pursuits of life unhindered by the corrupting constraints of centralized power. Following the Louisiana Purchase of 1803, the Adams-Onis Treaty of

1819, and the Mexican-American War of 1846–1848, Jefferson's vision quickly extended across a vast and, to the Americans, largely unknown continent.[3]

Drawn into the currents of empire by a growing dependence upon foreign goods and markets, Utes initially experienced imperial intrusion as a boon. Using the goods offered by small groups of traders, Utes throughout the 1830s and 1840s extended their raiding networks, striking terror into the hearts of *Californio,* Paiute, and New Mexican societies alike. Such goods and markets, however, diminished as local resources were exhausted and, most important, as distant leaders and their armies claimed the region through military conquest. Outside the main theaters of the Mexican-American War, Utes would soon find themselves for the first time under the territorial rule of outsiders whose plans for the region's future conflicted with their own.

The Utes were not the only Great Basin Indian groups affected by the initial phases of American conquest. Like the Utes, equestrian Shoshones—often called "Snakes"—in northern Utah, Wyoming, and Idaho welcomed traders into their homelands, actively shaping the region's growing trade networks. Profiting from rival fur traders, Shoshones allied with other equestrians to draw American traders deeper into the northern reaches of the Great Basin. Such expansion initially brought only select representatives of the republic. Traders, explorers, and trappers plied needed weapons and supplies to equestrian groups but did so individually or in small groups. Only in the 1820s would trappers come into the Great Basin prepared to meet the needs of these Shoshone peoples. For nonequestrian Basin groups, however, such as the Paiutes and Western Shoshones, the arrival of rival Anglo trappers and traders brought more dire consequences. British trappers along the Snake and Humboldt Rivers, for example, quickly exterminated the region's beaver and fur-bearing animals in deliberate attempts to keep American trappers out of the region, while horse traders to the south on the Old Spanish Trail continued to deplete rivers of grasses, water, and game. Everywhere these foreigners went their animals consumed the staples of Paiute and Shoshone survival, launching a series of ecological and social crises in the years preceding American conquest.[4]

Mountain men, New Mexicans operating under weak Mexican national prohibitions, and Ute raiders also participated the Great Basin

Indian slave trade, continuing forms of gendered violence among non-equestrian Basin peoples. Using Indian women for sexual and domestic labor and trading Indian children for horses and other goods, Ute, New Mexican, and American slavers further displaced Paiute and non-equestrian Shoshone groups from their accustomed lands and waterways. Such violent practices had originated in the Spanish colonial era, and they increased in the early 1800s with the annual influx of largely male companies of traders, trappers, and explorers. While licensed parties occasionally complained about one another's treatment of Indian women and children, small groups of renegade horse thieves, slavers, and trappers, often in alliance with Ute raiders, openly touted their masculine honor through the violent subjugation of vassal Indian communities and their women. When the first American migrants and settlers ventured into the region in the 1840s, they were horrified by the violence that characterized the everyday lives of non-equestrian Paiutes and Shoshones, many of whom initially welcomed Euro-American settlement as a reprieve from generations of slaving.[5]

Colonial violence continued to take other forms in these years preceding American conquest. Slavery, rape, and horse-raiding remained colonialism's most visible legacies; Utes, New Mexicans, and Euro-American traders, born into worlds steeped in violence, had become accustomed to and fluent in its uses. For most Native peoples, however, violence would soon begin taking larger and more pernicious forms. As literate traders and explorers ventured into uncharted lands, they carried, often unknowingly, the most critical tools of empire. Everywhere they traveled, they took notes. They located and recorded trails and mountain passes. They renamed waterholes, and, most important, they followed rivers. Waterways became in the first half of the nineteenth century the routes of empire, and those who navigated and mapped the West's major arteries controlled their future. While trappers and rogue traders brought more immediate forms of violence to the everyday lives of Great Basin Indians, state-sponsored explorers laid the foundations of empire. Their maps, reports, and journals ultimately carried greater influence than the thousands of beaver pelts and horses ferried to market in St. Louis. By producing the knowledge from which conquest could flow, those who extended American claims in the region became agents for the most violent forms of imperialism. The settlement, law, policing, and governance—the mechanics of colonial rule—that followed within a generation overturned the worlds of Great Basin Indians forever.[6]

Maps, Furs, and Imperial Rivalry in the Intermountain West

The Great Basin, as eighteenth-century Spanish explorers and traders had painfully learned, was not an easily navigable or traversable region. Bordered by the Rockies to the east, the hazardous Colorado River and Grand Canyon to the south, and the uncharted Sierras to the west, the region remained one of last areas in North America outside the sphere of European colonization. Spanish expeditions and trading routes had bisected the south along the jagged arc known as the Old Spanish Trail, but the western and northern portions of the region, particularly the lands west of Salt Lake and east of Lake Tahoe, remained literally off the map of European knowledge.

In 1776 Domínguez and Escalante and their proficient cartographer, Bernardo de Miera y Pacheco, had provided a wealth of information about the Intermountain West. Though unpublished for nearly a century, Miera's maps influenced subsequent cartographic surveys of the West, particularly through the works of Alexander von Humboldt, the great German naturalist-cum-cartographer who developed his 1811 "Reduced Map of the Kingdom of New Spain" in 1803 at the Royal School of Mines in central Mexico. With dozens of maps from New Mexico to aid him, including at least two that incorporated Miera's famous renditions of the Great Basin, Humboldt crafted what many consider one of the most important maps of the West ever produced.[7]

Whereas Domínguez and Escalante had been concerned primarily with matters of faith, Humboldt and subsequent American cartographers made little effort to identify sites and peoples suitable for missionization. Native peoples and their attitudes toward conversion were of limited concern to Humboldt and other nineteenth-century American mapmakers, whose imperial ambitions overrode religious and ethnographic concerns. These men coveted above all else geographic knowledge. They scoured available charts, reports, and known maps in an effort to identify the remaining uncharted portions of the continent. Following Humboldt, many believed that the West's interior waterways drained from the Rockies to the Pacific, and whoever identified and controlled such a route could more readily exploit the continent. As the nineteenth century began, then, the imperial contests reshaping North America propelled a host of trained geographers west, and their maps, reports, and findings precipitated larger disruptions for Native peoples.[8]

Such geographic imperatives were of course nothing new. Spanish explorers had traversed the perimeters of New Spain for centuries; generations before the founding of New England, Spaniards had crisscrossed and begun mapping the Southwest. But in the late eighteenth and early nineteenth centuries, contests among New France, New Spain, British North America, and the United States redrew the imperial boundaries of North America in nearly every generation. In 1763, French Louisiana, for example, became part of New Spain. Reverting to France in 1801, it was sold to the United States for a song in 1803 after Haiti's bloody revolution doomed Napoleon's ambition to rebuild France's once expansive American empire. Such political competition necessarily centered upon geography. Drawing boundaries, claiming territories, and ultimately controlling them required intimate familiarity with both geographic and cultural landscapes. The failures of Spain, Mexico, and to a lesser extent France to consolidate their influence over western Indians stemmed in part from their inabilities to understand and meet Native groups' changing demands for greater protection, trade, and autonomy. And, as Spanish and French claims to the western half of North America evaporated on eastern battlefields, at the treaty tables at Versailles, and in revolution, British and American agents of empire pushed farther and farther west.

In the mountainous West, British and American exploration had two primary and interrelated goals. The first was to identify the most accessible routes across lands previously uncharted by Europeans. Doing this meant following rivers. As they stood on the outskirts of St. Louis in the spring of 1804, for example, Americans Meriwether Lewis and William Clark and their federally sanctioned Corps of Discovery planned to follow the Missouri River—America's longest waterway—as far as they could. After wintering on the upper Missouri at Fort Mandan, the party traced its headwaters to Montana and began searching for routes west. Judiciously enlisting the assistance of local Native groups to cross the Continental Divide, particularly through the help of Sacagawea, a young Northern Shoshone captive living among the Mandan, the party reached the Pacific at the mouth of the

Columbia River, where they wintered before returning to St. Louis. Unlike most Spanish expeditions beforehand, but much like their British counterparts, Lewis and Clark's assiduously described and mapped the enormous terrain through which they traveled, and upon their triumphant return their maps, journals, and speeches captivated and catalyzed an entire generation.[9]

The second objective of both British and American western expansion was profit. Explorers charted unmapped lands to meet the geographic needs of empire *while also identifying* suitable sites for colonization and resource extraction; they were particularly interested in facilitating the expansion of the fur trade, which in the early 1800s remained one of the primary arenas of economic competition between the United States and Britain. Jefferson's instructions to Lewis and Clark made such imperatives quite clear: "The object of your missions is to explore . . . the most direct and practicable water communication across this continent for the purpose of commerce." Hoping to curb growing British influence among western Native groups, Jefferson increased federal funding for western exploration and commerce, which became guiding twin principles in his and subsequent administrations.[10]

The geographic imperative that fueled westward expansion was initially shaped by a select group of powerful men like Jefferson and Humboldt, most of whom had never seen the West. Influenced by Miera's maps, Humboldt, for example, assumed that the purported Rio San Buenaventura flowed to the Pacific from Salt Lake; Miera and other New Mexicans, after all, had been to the region and lived among its indigenous peoples. How could their findings not be trusted? When visiting the U.S. capital in 1804 after his extended stay in New Spain, Humboldt shared his new cartographic creation with the third American president and even left a copy with the State Department. An avid "student of geography," Jefferson no doubt focused on the portions of the West previously unmapped by Euro-Americans, marveling at his German guest's proficiency at uncovering corners of the continent unknown to the English-speaking world. Humboldt's map ended at the northern limits of Spain's empire, along the 42nd parallel, and it undoubtedly fueled Jefferson's eagerness for information from Lewis and Clark about the lands beyond. Whereas Humboldt's main concerns were to identify mineral resources for foreign extraction, Jefferson's interest in cartography lay in its potential to facilitate territorial acquisition. Like an architect drafting her designs, Jefferson orchestrated the exploration and acquisition of much of the nineteenth-century American West.[11]

Meriwether Lewis and William Clark became essential instruments in Jefferson's enterprise. Traveling through the northernmost regions of the Great Basin via tributaries of the Snake River, the Corps of Discovery gained only vague understandings of the vast, arid region to their south; they learned even less about its Native peoples. After traveling through western Oregon, they mistakenly assumed that the Willamette River, which they named the Multnomah, originated hundreds of miles to their southeast in the northern reaches of New Spain: their 1806 map, produced immediately after the journey, shows the Multnomah extending deep into uncharted southern territory, and Clark's 1810 map borrows from Humboldt, including multiple Ute groups and nearly linking the Multnomah with the Rio Grande. Clark's more famous map of 1814 drops all ethnographic references to Native groups but still suggests a possible overland river connection between the Columbia and the Rio Grande. If such a route existed, it would offer not only a means of entry into these uncharted lands but also an outlet to the sea. The most important American explorers and cartographers of their time, then, believed that a waterway to the Pacific originated in the Great Basin, a belief that drew more and more outsiders into the region.[12]

Humboldt's and Clark's cartographic mishaps become more than mere errata in geography. Their maps not only fueled attempts to modify and expand the cartographic record but also revealed the limits of American geographic knowledge. Lands, and by extension peoples, "off the map" became more than empty spaces on paper; they became indicators of the possibilities as well as the limitations of empire. If basic geographic principles did not apply to territories and peoples in proximity to one's own, then the stability of the nation was cast into doubt: mighty rivers, resources, and peoples not only possibly existed in such landscapes; they also had to be made known, that is, "discovered," in order to facilitate their incorporation into the nation and to curb potential foreign incursion. As historians of cartography have argued for some time, "blank spaces are intolerable to the geographical imagination," and throughout the nineteenth century such intolerance remained at the core of U.S. imperialism as regions adjacent to the republic were systematically explored, mapped, and incorporated into new mental and political regimes.[13]

For those who lived in such uncharted lands, the earliest Anglo and American arrivals hardly heralded the beginnings of a new era. On the contrary, early explorers often wandered in unfamiliar lands, depended upon Native groups for survival, and rarely posed threats. In the northern Great Basin, Lewis and Clark's dependence on

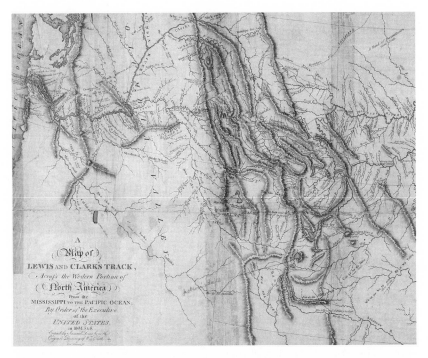

A Map of Lewis and Clark's Track across the Western Portion of North America. Lithograph, drawn and engraved by W. G.Evans, 1814. Courtesy of the Wisconsin Historical Society, Madison. Thomas Jefferson's instructions to Meriwether Lewis and William Clark to ascertain the nature of the recently acquired territories of the Louisiana Purchase took U.S. agents into the northern Great Basin in 1804–1806, and their maps sustained Miera and Humboldt's apocryphal vision that an interior western waterway extended from Ute homelands to the Pacific. Such cartographic and imperial confusion characterized generations of early western American explorers.

Sacagawea and her Northern Shoshone kin, for example, cannot be overstated. Lacking horses in the Great Basin–Plains borderlands of eastern Idaho and western Montana, the river-bound Corps of Discovery spent several weeks in the summer of 1805 looking for Shoshone bands to transport the party and their supplies across the Continental Divide. By early August the search had become desperate. After several of his men's feet had become infected by prickly pear cacti, Lewis took command of a small scouting group to search yet again for possible Shoshone groups, noting on August 8: "it is now all important with us to meet those people." As James Ronda explains, "Without horses the expedition would be stranded. Facing a second winter east of the mountains, on short rations and unsure of the route ahead, the expedition was at a desperate point." Finally finding a Northern Shoshone band under the leadership of Sacagawea's brother, Cameahwait, the Corps enlisted the help of dozens of Shoshone porters and, most important, obtained enough horses to begin tracing the tributaries of the Columbia, whose dried Pacific salmon among the Shoshone enticingly lured the Americans farther west.[14]

Like their Ute neighbors to the south, the Shoshone straddled the ecological boundary between grasslands and mountain valley homelands, migrating seasonally in search of game, fish, and plants. Unlike the Utes, Northern Shoshones had access to the salmon runs of the Northwest and maximized their catch by using nets and weirs along the Snake, Salmon, and Lemhi Rivers. Salmon, berries, plants, deer, rabbits, fowl, and other small game made the summer, ideally, a time of harvest for these northern Basin peoples. The introduction of the horse had expanded their territorial and economic range, facilitating travel, trade, and hunting onto the western plains of Montana, where antelope and bison abounded. As all Basin peoples knew, in moments of scarcity horses could also furnish food when the traditional foods from hunting and gathering were unavailable. This Shoshone band had upward of 700 horses as well as scattered numbers of mules. Why, then, according to Lewis and Clark, were Cameahwait's people so impoverished in the summer of 1805, and why did they live in such a "wretched stait of poverty"? Why was their "extreem poverty" so apparent that Lewis noted several times and at length that he "viewed these poor starved devils with pity and compassion"? How could these peoples face such hardships in lands of apparent bounty?[15]

Cameahwait answered Lewis' queries at their first meeting, on August 14, 1805, and his answers reveal the stresses of life on the distant margins of empire. The leader of the first group of Indian peoples encountered by Lewis and Clark west of the Missouri's headwaters— peoples without whom the expedition surely would have failed—explained that, despite their isolation from Euro-Americans, his people had long felt the destructive influences of European trade. Far to their south, Cameahwait complained, the Spaniards would not allow Native peoples to

> have fire arms and ammunition . . . thus leaving them defenseless and an easy prey to their bloodthirsty neighbors . . . who being in possession of fire arms hunt them up and murder them without rispect to sex or age and plunder them of their horses . . . they were obliged to remain in the interior of these mountains at least two thirds of the year where the[y] suffered as we then saw great heardships for the want of food sometimes living for weeks without meat and only a little fish roots and berries. but this added Cameahwait . . . would not be the case if we had guns, we could then live in the country of buffaloe and eat as our enemies when placed on an equal footing with them.

Shoshone impoverishment, then, stemmed not from culture or ecology but from economic and military disadvantage, particularly from the absence of firearms. Lewis attempted to assuage his hosts' anxieties and sketched a vision of an impending and improved future in which "whitemen would come to them with an abundance of guns . . . that they would be enabled to supply themselves . . . in exchange for the skins of the beaver Otter and Ermin (Weasel) so abundant in their country." Pledging his community's unconditional support to the party, Cameahwait "expressed great pleasure . . . to (finally) see the whitemen that traded guns."[16]

Ensconced in the interior portions of the northern Great Basin, Cameahwait's peoples faced hostile neighbors on nearly all sides. To their east, whence the Corps had recently arrived, Crow, Assiniboin, and northern Plains equestrian raiders made forays into Shoshone territories in search of horses, captives, and game. All of them were better armed than the Shoshone, having procured guns from French and British traders, and they generally rode horses of superior quality raised on the spring and summer grasslands of the Plains. Responding themselves to the expansion of outside aggressors, particularly the Lakota, into their own homelands, these Upper Missouri peoples had long adapted to the many ordeals associated with equestrian warfare, and throughout the 1700s and early 1800s various northern Plains Indians carried the violence from their own worlds into those of their less powerful neighbors in the Intermountain West. To the Shoshone's north, confederated allies of Blackfeet and Piegan bands, as David Thompson detailed after his winter stay in the region in 1786–87, also fought against the Shoshone. In the mid-1700s Shoshone bands had gained an initial equestrian advantage over their northern neighbors, but these advantages were short-lived. By the next Piegan-Shoshone encounter, the Piegans had acquired guns from French traders. As John Ewers explains, "Confused and terrified by the deadly, incomprehensible action of this new weapon, the Shoshone line broke." Guns, more than horses, now decided the outcome of most intertribal conflicts in the region.[17]

To the Shoshone's south, Ute bands had metals, horses, and other wares brought from New Mexico. They did not, however, trade guns, which the Spanish tried to monopolize in the last decades of their rule; and the Utes kept the few firearms they could obtain from Great Plains trading networks for themselves. Only to their immediate southwest and west did the Shoshones not face equestrian enemies. To their southwest, the Shoshone warned, the dry, hostile landscapes of Nevada and northwestern Utah hindered equestrian travel, lands through which Lewis was told "we must suffer if not perish for the want of water," as well as worry that "the feet of our horses would be so much wounded with the stones [that] many of them would give out." The peoples of this region were also to be feared: though they did not have guns or horses, they reportedly "lived like the bear of other countries among the rocks and fed on roots or the flesh of such horses as they could take or steel from those who pass through their country." Like many subsequent accounts of nonequestrian Great Basin peoples, this earliest English description of Western Shoshones linked their culture to nature, representing them as animalistic peoples who "lived like the bear among the rocks." Only to their west did the Shoshone not face enemies. Several Salish-speaking groups, known as Flatheads, were allied with Cameahwait's band and together migrated seasonally onto the Plains near the Three Forks region in western Montana—which was, at that time, the easternmost reach for these seasonal and provisional buffalo hunters.[18]

Far from reaching Indian groups unaffected by the continent-wide disruptions engendered by colonialism, the Corps of Discovery encountered besieged, dependent, and fearful Great Basin peoples. Theirs was a world of desperation born amidst recurring and multiple challenges. Living at one end of the expanding gun trade while enmeshed in the horse trade, Northern Shoshone groups had become enveloped in the pandemic relations of violence that characterized both the northern Spanish borderlands and the northern Plains, where the colonial violence from French influences in the 1600s initiated cycles of trade and warfare similar to those emanating from New Mexico. Indians to the Shoshone's south had acquired horses before they did, while Indians to their north and east had done likewise with guns. Horses could be bred and also gained through trade, raiding, and warfare. Not so guns. Guns in the eighteenth- and nineteenth-century West routinely broke, required constant repair, and, most important, were useless without additional trade items, ammunition and powder, which could not be manufactured indigenously. Cameahwait understood these things, as did Lewis, Clark, and their men, one of whom, John Ordway, noted that the Shoshone had only "2 or 3 guns, but no ammunition." Such dependency bred desperate acts. As Ordway noted one morning, as "our hunter had turned his horse out to feed one of the Indian took his gun and Sprang on his horse and rode off." Minor theft aside, once Cameahwait and his people had an opportunity to trade with the horse-desperate Americans they shrewdly exchanged the one resource they had for the one they most desired. Trading horses for guns and ammunition in late August, when the party needed to depart immediately, the Shoshone raised the terms of their trade, extracting from Clark alone on August 29 "my Pistol 100 Balls Power & a Knife" for a single horse. As James Ronda remarks, "Despite their best efforts, the captains did not prove to be especially astute traders."[19]

More astute traders did follow Lewis and Clark into the region, but they took a while. After the Corps's return to St. Louis in September 1806, motivated and now informed American traders prepared to return to the portions of the West accessed by Lewis and Clark. Not only had the Missouri been navigated to its headwaters, but an overland route to the Pacific had also been identified. A continent beckoned, and eager individuals and entrepreneurs flocked to St. Louis nurturing dreams of western trade and travel. Lewis had also observed that the beaver fur in Shoshone territory was "as good as I ever saw anywhere; and [I] believe that they are never out of season on the upper part of the Missouri and its branches within the Mountains." More than any other resource, beavers now drew outsiders into the Intermountain West. For the next thirty years fur trappers and traders—and not state-sponsored explorers and soldiers—became the primary agents of empire in the territories charted by the Corps of Discovery.[20]

Despite the allure of beaver profits, after 1806 nearly a generation of American traders failed to harvest the fur-rich territories identified by the expedition. A secure overland route west of the Rockies eluded St. Louis–based traders until the 1820s. Traders knew that untouched beaver reserves abounded in the headwaters of the Missouri and in the Snake-Columbia watershed. They had maps or had seen maps tracing the Corps's route. Most important, they had also heard tales of wonder, of bountiful resources, and of challenging but profitable lands. But powerful imperial and indigenous rivals blocked the route along the Missouri. To avoid the British and well-armed Blackfeet who dominated the upper Missouri trade, American traders focused on the buffalo-robe trade farther east, which involved Indian labor and negotiated trade relations. The few American trappers who ventured into the Intermountain West came mainly from the south and east, leaving the northern reaches to the British, whose presence in the Pacific Northwest increased annually in the early 1800s. In the first quarter of the nineteenth century, then, broader imperial, economic, and geopolitical rivalries left the trade resources of the northern Great Basin to the British. After Lewis and Clark, the earliest sustained trading relations in the area came not from the region's eventual conquerors, but from their primary Anglo rivals.[21]

The British Snake River Brigades

The War of 1812 helped to delay American expansion west of the Continental Divide. Before the war, a few American entrepreneurs recognized the economic potential there and began securing capital and labor to venture west. John Jacob Astor's elaborate designs to construct a string of American trading posts extending to the Pacific included plans not only to harvest the interior West's fur supplies but also to lay American claims to the region. Unlike the bison traders who ferried robes to St. Louis for eastern markets, Astor envisioned a market for his goods in Asia, where Cantonese merchants offered the highest returns for American furs.

Building a port at the mouth of the Columbia to outfit interior fur-trading expeditions while also equipping Chinese-bound merchant fleets with furs, Astor set in motion the greatest early nineteenth-century American colonizing scheme in the West. With the arrival of the *Tonquin* at Astoria on the mouth of the Columbia River in March 1811, Astor's Pacific Fur Company constructed the first American port on the Pacific. Simultaneously Astor dispatched an expeditionary party under Wilson Price Hunt to travel to Astoria overland and to identify the most suitable locations for fur extraction. The results were disastrous. The second American overland party to cross the continent, Hunt's expedition nearly ended in ruin in the winter of 1811–12. Lost, exhausted, and impoverished in the maze of steep river valleys that constitute Snake River country, Hunt's experienced *voyageurs* found themselves in a "mountain nightmare" and passed four months inching their way across Idaho and Oregon, believing that Astoria lay only days away. To survive, some drank their own urine and ate their animals. The only woman in the expedition, Marie Dorion, lost her baby thirteen days after its birth on Christmas Day. Dependent upon multiple groups of Shoshone, Flathead, and Columbian Plateau Indians, the Hunt expedition proved the impossibility of making the Lewis and Clark route a commercially viable path to the Pacific; and as Britain and the United States resumed hostilities in 1812, Astor, Hunt, and the Astorians' dreams evaporated. Astoria, its supplies, and its recently harvested pelts were sold in 1813 to the more experienced traders of the British North West Company for a fraction of their total value.[22]

Moving not west, but east from the Pacific, the Pacific Fur Company expanded the fur trade along the mighty Columbia. Many of the beaver-rich headwaters of the Missouri and the Snake, however, remained untapped. While many Columbia River Indians became able trappers and traded furs with both British and Astoria traders, many others farther inland did not. The equestrian Nez Perce in central Oregon, for example, according to Alexander Ross, "spurned the idea of crawling about in search of furs," as did many Native peoples, for whom the daily and communal chores of subsistence militated against the monotonous toils of individualistic trapping. Frustrated by their inability to find reliable Indian partners, British traders began in the second decade of the 1800s establishing interior trading houses from which large trapping expeditions, or "brigades," could be launched inland. Unlike the expansive fur-trading world of the Hudson's Bay Company—which relied primarily upon Indians to procure, tan, and transport the millions of furs that formed the infrastructure of the British empire in North America—in much of the Intermountain West, trappers had to find, process, and carry their own furs. Unable to persuade Indian communities to perform the necessary labor of the fur trade, large companies of men soon began descending from points along the Columbia equipped with their own traps, munitions, and herds.[23]

Initiated in 1818 by Donald McKenzie from the recently established Fort Nez Perce at the mouth of the Walla Walla River, the "Snake River Brigades" formed the initial westernmost arm of a fur pincer enclosure moving into the northern Great Basin. McKenzie trapped for months in Snake country with more than fifty men, 200 horses, and 300 traps, relying for the first time in the Northwest less on Indian labor than on their own sweat and provisions. Reaping bountiful rewards, the party initiated what became not only an increasingly profitable strategy but also an imperial one. For, to the east, across the Rockies, and onto the Plains, St. Louis–based traders were also preparing to make their own inroads across the Continental Divide.[24]

After the War of 1812 and its "status quo" resolution in the Treaty of Ghent, Britain and the United States resumed continental rivalries. In 1818 both agreed to the terms of the Joint Occupancy Treaty, which allowed for shared Anglo-American economic access to the "Oregon Territory." Delaying any political determination on the future of the Pacific Northwest for ten years, the treaty facilitated the reentry of American traders into the region. A race for the furs of the Intermountain West was now under way, the winner of which would ultimately not only control the furs but also determine the future of the lands and its peoples.[25]

Donald McKenzie had served the North West Company for more than a decade before his departure in 1818 from Fort Nez Perce. He had clerked in Montreal, the company's headquarters, but left in 1810 to join Astor's overland party under Wilson Hunt. Breaking off from Hunt's party with a small group and arriving at Astoria a month beforehand, McKenzie learned firsthand of the perils as well as opportunities posed by the Snake River. A man of tremendous girth, McKenzie had fewer problems than others surviving the hardships along the Snake, and he attempted to redirect trading interests back into the interior regions that so many dreaded. In 1818, after rejoining the North West Company, he finally had his chance. Venturing into "a rich field of beaver in the country lying between the great south branch [of the Snake] and the Spanish waters [the Green River]," McKenzie's party soon began trading with equestrian Shoshones, inaugurating economic and diplomatic relations with Shoshone bands throughout the northern Great Basin.[26]

Following Hunt's overland expedition in 1811–12, only scattered traders had ventured into Snake River country, and Shoshone groups remained, as they had in the summer of 1805, desperate to trade with whites. Unfortunately for the Shoshone, McKenzie's 1818 expedition was composed of small groups of trappers who separated from one another to trace the tributaries of the Snake. For many Native groups, this trapping strategy proved problematic on two levels. First, McKenzie could provide only limited trade goods to the communities that hosted him; these were after all trapping and not trading expeditions. Second, controlling the behavior of men away from the main party was nearly impossible. Thus while Shoshone leaders responded favorably to McKenzie's promises to trade the next year, other unspecified Indian groups suffered violence when, after entering "the country of the Snakes," a group of Iroquois traders among the expedition "began their old trade of plotting mischief." Threatening to abandon the expedition and to head toward American markets with their furs, approximately twenty-five Iroquois trappers demanded an early departure from the expedition to begin trapping on their own. Trying to "put the best face on things," McKenzie "filled them out well in everything they required, and with the rest of the party proceeded on our journey, leaving them to work beaver" by themselves.[27]

Like many other employees of the North West Company, McKenzie was adverse to keeping a journal and to corresponding with company officials; shortly before his death decades later, his wife reportedly

threw his uncompleted manuscript autobiography into their lit fire-
place rather than continue watching the self-imposed torture that writing imposed on her aging husband. Hundreds of miles and weeks of
travel away from Fort Nez Perce, McKenzie's three expeditions into
Shoshone territory survive only in documentary fragments, principally
in the accounts by Alexander Ross, the North West Company trader
who ran Fort Nez Perce during McKenzie's absence. From what Ross
wrote, it becomes clear that many of the Iroquois who left the expedition had noncommercial, ulterior motives. Oskononton, for example,
reported to Ross that after leaving McKenzie's main party, he and his
Iroquois trappers "set to trapping and were very successful but had not
been long there till we fell in with a small band of Snakes. My comrades began to exchange their horses, their guns, and their traps with
these people for women! and carried on the traffic to such an extent
that they had scarcely an article left, and being no longer able to hunt,
abandoned themselves with the savages and were doing nothing!" Returning to Fort Nez Perce before McKenzie, Oskononton offered Ross
the first reports of McKenzie's progress in the interior. Fearing that
such sexually aggressive behavior might jeopardize the safety of the entire party, Ross delighted in seeing McKenzie return in early 1819. After recuperating, McKenzie confirmed Oskononton's account, though
without any mention of the Iroquois's sexual transgressions. McKenzie
also reported that instead "of finding the Iroquois together and employed in hunting . . . I found them by two's and by three's all over the
country, living with the savages, without horses, without traps, without
furs and without clothing! perfectly destitute of everything I had given
them. I left them therefore as I found them. Iroquois will never do in
this country."[28]

The first trapping expedition into the "country of the Snakes," then,
included men who traded their material possessions—horses, guns,
and traps—for access to Indian women. Although the details of this
"exchange . . . for women" are lost, it is clear that when left to their
own devices, fur trappers exploited their material and later military
advantages over Indian groups for sexual service. While the culprits
were themselves "Indians"—unspecified Iroquois traders who had
long ago attached themselves to the fur-trading empire of the English—their behavior paralleled that of New Mexicans in the borderlands, where "going after the flesh" remained a prime motivation for

leaving New Mexico. Shoshone bands may have possessed cultural and social practices that sanctioned sexual relations between community members and outsiders, but it is unclear whether the women referred to by Oskononton were even members of this community. As in the New Mexican borderlands, these women may have been captives taken for the purposes of trade and sexual traffic.

Oskononton and McKenzie emphasized the Iroquois's material deprivation—their loss of possessions—and their concerns suggest that the Iroquois acted not only unvirtuously but also against company policies. After all, these were employees, company men. Their business was furs, not wanton self-indulgence, and they were now responsible and indebted for their missing supplies and undelivered furs. The Snake River country, however, remained far removed from the centers of empire, far "beyond the protective reach of the state," as Cole Harris has argued, and forms of European "justice" were often enforceable only through violence. Much like New Mexico's borderlands, the northern reaches of the Great Basin became in the early 1800s a liminal space for outsiders, a zone of encounter, commerce, and exchange distant from the purview and control of colonial administrators. In such borderlands, men acted impulsively, and such impulses often took violent tolls on Native communities, particularly on their women. Rather than risk confrontation, McKenzie left the Iroquois behind, offered his condemnations to Ross, and prepared for his next return inland, seething at the loss of his men, furs, and supplies.[29]

Shoshone leaders responded to McKenzie's return in 1819 with enthusiasm. He had left several members of his party in the interior and had returned to Fort Nez Perce to resupply. Anticipating his return, Shoshone leaders amassed the largest Shoshone encampment hitherto documented by Europeans; after his arrival, the encampment eventually numbered "more than ten thousand souls." Upon his entry into this sizable gathering, McKenzie met with two principal Shoshone chiefs along with fifty-four other leaders in council. According to Ross, he "made known to the chiefs his views as to establishing of a general and permanent peace between themselves and their enemies on the northern frontier . . . McKenzie also signified to them that if the peace [was] met . . . the whites would then open a profitable trade with the Snake nation, and that henceforth they might be supplied with all their wants." Reacting with "universal" approval, these Shoshone leaders pledged their support for McKenzie's peace initiatives and also promised to rein in distant Snake River Shoshones and Bannock bands to the west who raided Nez Perce and other Columbia River peoples in search of horses, captives, and supplies. Equestrian Shoshone leaders now believed that the time when outsiders would come into their homelands to trade had finally arrived. As in the summer of 1805, the Shoshone welcomed whites into their communities, pledged their unconditional support for new trading relations, and also again received desperately needed goods.[30]

Lewis and Clark had promised Shoshone leaders that traders would soon arrive to trade manufactured goods for their furs, but the immediate concern had been horses, not furs. Sporadic groups of whites, like Hunt, had also traveled along the Snake, and they too had been concerned more with safe passage than with trading. McKenzie reversed such equations. Bringing dozens of men and hundreds of traps and horses, his three expeditions initiated the harvest of the Intermountain West's untouched northern beaver reserves. Moreover he communicated to Shoshone leaders that reliable Euro-American traders would now annually venture into their territories. A few of his trappers had also instructed the Shoshone on how to place traps and harvest furs, and during his second expedition the Shoshone excitedly traded furs for whatever manufactured goods they could. Ross probably exaggerated the reported size of this 1819 encampment, but he could not contain his contempt for Shoshone trading acumen: "it was truly Indian-like to see those people dispose of articles of real value so cheap . . . a beaver skin worth twenty-five shillings in the English market might have been purchased for a brass finger ring scarcely worth a farthing . . . Beaver or any kind of fur was of little or no value among these Indians, never having any traders for such articles among them." Such disdain aside, Ross also noted that "axes, knives, ammunition" were "the articles most in demand," and that while the Shoshone had a few firearms "which they might have got from other Indians," nonetheless "they had scarcely an article among them to show that they had ever mixed with civilized man." Metals, weapons, and the imperative to acquire them had preceded trappers in the region, recalibrating the motivations for these Great Basin Indian communities before they "had ever mixed" with Europeans.[31]

Though they still had much to learn about the comparative value

of furs and were, for example, in a state of "astonishment . . . at seeing
two hundred and forty beaver caught by the hunters and brought
into camp all at once," Shoshone bands now acquired the manufactured goods they needed to compete with their rivals. They used both
McKenzie and later British traders to equip themselves. The British
moreover attempted to inaugurate peaceful relations between the
Shoshone and their rivals, also in the interests of oiling the wheels of
trade. Although British traders from the Northwest could do little to
stem the advance of upper Missouri peoples, they not only traded guns
and ammunition to Shoshone encampments but also pledged to help
stem Nez Perce and other Columbia Plateau peoples' raids into the
Great Basin. It is no wonder then that the "Snakes" responded so favorably to McKenzie's visits, one leader even riding "round and round"
the perimeter of this massive encampment "that of itself was almost
the work of a day . . . to harangue the Indians, [to] remind them of the
peace [and] their behavior towards the whites." And, despite the occasional theft of traps and horses, Shoshone leaders now firmly committed themselves to the fur trade and to hosting and trading with whites
annually. The extraction of fur from their homelands would come as
much as possible on their own terms.[32]

McKenzie's Snake River expeditions yielded surprising returns. Upon
his return in 1820, the train of horses into Fort Nez Perce was "said
to have extended for over two miles," each with 120 pounds of fur.
Scholars debate the total quantities of furs harvested during his three
expeditions, but none doubt that the thousands of pelts acquired in
the interior transformed British imperial strategies in the region. For,
while McKenzie was away in 1821 on his third and largest expedition,
the North West Company merged with the Hudson's Bay Company,
creating a North American "monopoly of furs" second to none. After
the merger, company officials decided to expand McKenzie's strategy
further into the Great Basin both to replicate such harvests and to
ward off growing American interests in the region. Finding an effective leader to lead such long and difficult journeys, however, took
some time.[33]

After two less successful excursions, the company in 1824 appointed
Peter Skene Ogden to head the Snake River Brigades. Ogden, more
so than McKenzie, understood both the imperial and the economic
strategies of the British. While McKenzie harvested large amounts of

furs, he failed to extend the company's greater imperial mission. Cementing peaceful relations between Indian groups, extracting fur, and sowing continued goodwill did the British only so much good, because following the 1819 Adams-Onis Treaty between the United States and Spain, which set a southern limit on the Louisiana Purchase at the 42nd parallel, and following the 1821 independence of Mexico, American traders began swarming throughout the West, contesting British claims and claiming lands and resources. British officials increasingly realized that western furs attracted not only their own traders but also these representatives of the American republic. In a deliberate attempt, then, to confine American expansion to the Rockies and to solidify their claims over the Northwest, company officials gave Ogden a larger imperial mandate: eradicate all the furs west of the Continental Divide in the Snake River and adjoining territories. Deplete these territories entirely of their fur. Create a "fur desert" or barrier through which no Americans would venture. For the Native groups of the region, many of whom like the Shoshone now depended upon the fur trade, their survival became secondary to the dictates of empire. For those who lived in even more remote locations and subsisted on the Great Basin's most fragile ecologies, their first documented contacts with whites occurred within such increased imperial competition.[34]

Great Basin Indians and the Rocky Mountain Trapping System

By 1824 the Snake country had gained a reputation as the hardest assignment in the Hudson's Bay empire. The hundreds of miles of travel, winter months spent waiting for rivers to thaw, and the waist-deep harvest of traps in those same thawing waters made for difficult work indeed. Since most of the men who served the company exchanged their furs for provisions provided by company stores, many became enmeshed in a form of debt peonage that lasted for years. As a result most traders going to the Snake River were assigned to do so by the company and had not volunteered, and such traders presented difficult challenges to the British goal of solidifying economic and imperial fortunes. Many indebted employees often fled their own expeditions for American and New Mexican outfits, which generally provided better returns for their furs while wiping their slate of debts clean. Others simply abandoned campaigns to live outside the imperial ambit, to live off the land, or to cohabit with Native peoples. The Iroquois became the clearest expression of such corporate disobedience, while hundreds of others yearned to become "freemen" like their American counterparts. Leading large campaigns away from company trading posts and moving them closer to American traders thus presented serious labor challenges, requiring considerable, often strict leadership.[35]

Peter Skene Ogden eventually developed such skills during his annual Snake Country expeditions, which from 1824 to 1830 carried more than 1,000 trappers across much of western North America. Often returning to northwestern posts for only a few days, Ogden spent nearly every day for six years campaigning in the field. His life came to center upon beaver harvests, and his journal entries often end with simply a tally of the number of beaver each day. Before long rival American traders out of St. Louis and Taos as well as many Native bands emulated the Snake River Brigades, traveling between commercial centers exchanging their resources, and the central Great Basin, particularly the headwaters of the Green and Bear Rivers, became a crossroads for various migratory groups. Some, like Ogden, represented imperial economic interests and maintained rigid social hierarchies during their annual ventures into the region. Others, like the growing numbers of nominally American "mountain men," lived continuously within the region, resupplying seasonally at rendezvous centers, where supplies ferried overland from St. Louis and Taos were brought directly to mountain traders in exchange for yearly fur harvests. At the same time, Ute, New Mexican, and Californian traders migrated along the region's southern margins, exchanging horses, captives, and skins between Californian and New Mexican markets. Whereas the New Mexican–Ute borderlands had come into being amidst eighteenth-century changes emanating from New Mexico, the Great Basin borderlands of the nineteenth century arose amidst influences from all sides. No group held full dominion over these crossroads, though many competed for such ownership.[36]

Ogden learned of such overlapping and contested claims the first time he entered the region. Departing from the Flathead Post in Montana in December 1824 and wintering along the Snake's tributaries in Idaho, by April his party had moved south into present-day Utah to tap reserves along the fur-rich Bear River. The expedition consisted of over 130 men, women, and children, with half as many guns and twice as many horses. Sending scouts off from the main body to prospect streamheads, Ogden reported on April 27 that several of the waterways had been "been trapped by the Americans last Year." Hearing from Shoshone hunters of a large party of nearby Americans, Ogden nevertheless directed the expedition farther south, hoping to continue their good fortune after harvesting their "first thousand" furs by late April. On May 23, however, the party was intercepted by a "Company with 14 of our absent men a party of 25 Americans with Colours flying." Headed by trapper Johnson Gardner, the defiant newcomers "lost no time informing all hands in Camp that they were in the United States Territories & were all free indebted [all indebted were free]." Besides trying to siphon away company traders and their furs, Gardner approached Ogden the next morning and spoke more bluntly: "he questioned me as follows Do you know in whose Country you are? to which I made answer that I did not as it was not determined between Great Britain & America to whom it belonged, to which he made answer that . . . it had been ceded to the latter & as I had no license to trap or trade to return from which I came." Noting Gardner's harsh tone, Ogden's chief clerk, William Kittson, reported that Gardner told Ogden, "if he . . . knew what was good for himself and party he would return home."[37]

Gardner's enticements worked. Within three days Ogden lost nearly half of his trappers, most of his furs, and many provisions. A dispute over a horse nearly cost him his life. As he watched his former crew depart and heeded insults from Iroquois, Mexican, Russian, French, and American trappers, Ogden bemoaned his plight: "Here I am now with only 20 Trappers . . . to remain in this quarter any longer would merely be to trap Beaver for the Americans." Gathering his remaining men and their families, Ogden returned northwest to Fort Nez Perce to begin preparations for a different kind of campaign, one that would leave the beaver-rich reserves of northern Utah to others and search for lands still untapped by the troublesome Americans.[38]

Ogden's encounter with Gardner revealed telling new truths about the region's changing fortunes. In their competition for furs, labor, and allegiances, rival English-speaking leaders understood that the race for furs had become largely a matter of time. Whoever first identified and extracted the region's furs reaped bountiful rewards; those who came too late or could not control their labor force were less successful. Whereas powerful Indian powers on the northern Plains, like the Crow and Blackfeet, attempted to restrict travel into and out of many trapping territories, in northern Utah and southern Wyoming trading outfits established themselves alongside or even irrespective of Indian powers. They came not just to trap and trade. They remained. These individual trappers, or "mountain men" as they are romantically termed, lived off the land and in a sense made it their home. The British had learned a decade earlier that "brigades" were their only mechanism for extracting furs from the interior, and they succeeded temporarily in exploiting untapped beaver reserves. Using not Indian labor but large companies of their own men, British campaigns also lived off the land, often consuming, for example, the meat from their fur harvests for sustenance. American trappers, however, as Ogden now learned, maintained less regimented groups and profited from individual trapping parties, not monopolies. These trappers might annually venture to Taos or to growing American trading centers on the Missouri, but they never had to. For most of the late 1820s and 1830s, these trappers harvested furs year-round. After trapping out a stream in the fall, for example, many cached their furs, wintered among allied Indian communities, and migrated to additional riverbeds in the spring before gathering their furs to await the arrival of the summer rendezvous. After the rendezvous, they returned better supplied (as well as armed) to new trapping locations. Not settlers, these semipermanent occupants succeeded in undermining British imperial control east of the Columbia.[39]

While some of the Iroquois from Snake River campaigns attached themselves to Indian communities, others formed or joined roving groups that moved independently among trading centers. Largely undocumented—Gardner, for example, left no known written records other than an "X" beside his name on an 1831 contract—such autonomous parties straddled multiple imperial zones. Nominally "American," such trapping groups included Iroquois, francophone, anglophone, Russian, and even Polynesian castoffs from the British empire as well as the multiplicity of peoples from the Spanish borderlands, and they used such multicultural fluency to navigate Mexican, British, American, and Indian communities. Far from being loners or social outcasts, these mountain men, in fact, became imperial precursors.

They, and not the Hudson's Bay Company men like Ogden, developed the most effective means of harvesting fur from the mountains, and they helped expand much of the geographic and cartographic knowledge of the West for later American statesmen and settlers. Cutting labor costs and sharing revenues, the "Rocky Mountain Trapping System," as David Wishart demonstrates, served not only to drive out the British monopoly, but also to plant outside territorial claims to the region. For, as neither Gardner nor Ogden suggested in their 1825 encounter, the polyglot Americans with their parading colors and threatening words as well as the disgruntled British were on foreign soil. Not only were they, as Kittson noted, "situated on the borders of the Utas lands"; they also had headed south of the 42nd parallel into territory claimed by neither England nor the United States, but by Mexico, which had inherited Spain's claims from the 1819 Adams-Onis Treaty after its independence in 1821. Anglo and American trappers, in short, ventured into lands visited by Domínguez and Escalante half a century earlier, and vied for resources claimed by the Republic of Mexico. Mexican sovereignty, like Indian land rights, however, mattered little in these borderlands crossroads.[40]

Unlike the trappers who increasingly traversed their homelands, Shoshone and Ute groups gained little from the British retreat. Indeed, the eventual withdrawal of the British monopoly into deeper recesses in the Great Basin foreshadowed ominous changes for these mountain peoples. Shoshone groups, in particular, no longer had British traders, like Ogden or McKenzie, to compete for their goods and against whom to "play off" the Americans. Assessing Native responses to these transformations, however, is difficult. For, while Ogden, Kittson, and some American chroniclers garnered critical ethnographic and historical information about Ute and Shoshone groups, most trappers were either illiterate or kept scattered and often sensationalized accounts of their time "among the Indians." As the most reprinted work in Shoshone history suggests, "Early accounts of the Shoshones are so meager in diaries and memoirs that from time to time they seem to fade from sight," and most studies of the western fur trade relegate these Indian peoples to the margins.[41]

What is clear in the fragmentary accounts from the 1820s is that Ute groups continued to maintain close ties with New Mexicans while Shoshone groups, particularly those along the Snake River known as

Northern Shoshone and Bannocks, lost trading partners and markets for their goods. Utes, reported Kittson, were "indians, belonging to the Spaniards. They are, as we are told, mostly Christians, and three of them whom our men saw, bore the Cross to their necks." Ogden similarly noticed Ute friendliness to whites. Upon his first arrival in the region from St. Louis, William Ashley in 1825 also noticed the Utes' calm, comported ease with outsiders: "I was much surprised at the appearance of these people. I expected to find them a poor lifeless set . . . alarmed at the sight of a white man but to the contrary they met me with great familiarity and ease of manner." Snake River "Snakes" and Bannocks, however, were in a more precarious and less "friendly" position. As Ogden noted in 1826 during his second tour, they "are certainly surrounded on all sides by enemies . . . their resources are not great in such a wretched Country, nor would they remain in this quarter but [for] the dread of loosing their Scalps should they remain in a Buffalo Country." Like Cameahwait's band a generation earlier, Northern Shoshones and their Bannock neighbors remained pinned between more powerful enemies who restricted their access to productive hunting and grazing grounds while also limiting the flow of traders and trade goods into their homelands. For the next half-century, such isolation bred increasingly violent encounters.[42]

Shoshone leaders had told McKenzie in 1819 that they would attempt to control the distant bands to their west along the Snake River, but it is unclear how much influence "Plains Snakes," as Ogden called them, held over the "Lower Snakes." Throughout the 1820s and 1830s, these latter Shoshone and Bannock bands appeared increasingly in American trappers' accounts and usually did so in hostile and vilified form. James Beckwourth, for example, the notoriously self-aggrandizing mountain man whose exploits in the western fur trade remain among the most debated, reported a series of conflicts with Bannock bands in the mid-1820s. An early employee of Ashley's Rocky Mountain Fur Trading Company, Beckwourth attended the first rendezvous and chronicled yearly conflicts between the American trappers and various Indian powers in the region. While usually allied with Shoshone bands against the Blackfeet, Beckwourth noted how many Shoshone bands had become estranged from one another as a result of competition for American resources. Such estrangement now proved deadly. While encamped near the Green River, Ashley's men, Beckwourth recounts, learned "that there were one hundred and eighty-five lodges of Pun-naks [Bannocks] encamped only two miles distant, a discarded band of the Snakes, very band Indians, and very great thieves. Captain Sublet informed the Snakes that if the Pun-naks should steal any of his horses or any thing belonging to his camp, he would *rub them all out,* and he wished the friendly Snakes to tell them so." Having suffered through a series of Bannock horse raids, the American trappers now looked for provocation, and after a small trapper party was attacked for approaching "Pun-nak lodges," a call to arms was issued:

> Volunteers were called to punish the Pun-naks for their outrage. Two hundred and fifteen immediately presented themselves at the call . . . We started to inflict vengeance . . . We followed their trail forty-five miles, and came up with them on the Green River. Seeing our approach, they all made across to a small island . . . the enfilading commenced, and was continued until there was not one left of either sex or any age. We carried back four hundred and eighty-eight scalps, and, as we then supposed, annihilated the Pun-nak band. On our return, however, we found six or eight of their squaws . . . whom we carried back and gave to the Snakes.[43]

"Scalps," Beckwourth explains, "are taken off with greater ease while the bodies are warm." Scholars regard the reported 488 trophies as further evidence of Beckwourth's tendency to exaggerate his own importance as well as the numbers involved in a series of historical events, and western historians since Francis Parkman have considered him an unreliable source. Nonetheless, every scholar of the fur trade and Indians in the Intermountain West relies upon his narrative in some form or another, and his description of the "extermination of the Pun-naks" offers vivid insight into the potential costs for Indian groups at odds with the Americans. Beckwourth's and others' accounts are filled with so many acts of brutality that it is clear that the rendezvous trapping system accelerated the violent deterioration of many indigenous communities. Similar in size and weaponry to Ogden's parties but without as much discipline and authority, American rendezvous communities could easily number several hundred. They constituted, as Beckwourth recalls, "quite a formidable little army, or, more properly, a moving city." Often allied with various Indian groups, such "little" armies surpassed every Native group in the region in collective firepower. Ute, Shoshone, and other Indian groups recognized such mobility and power, which increased annually following the first rendezvous in 1824 and the subsequent expulsion of the British from Utah in 1825. Well-armed American traders had come into the region prepared for violent encounter, and in 1826 the first wheeled vehicle, a cannon, was carried over South Pass, across the Continental Divide, and into the Great Basin. Its intended use: to impress Native people and if need be target them.[44]

Many Shoshone groups attempted to respond cooperatively to the growing power of Americans in the region. Following the "extermination of the Pun-naks," for instance, some "friendly Snake" bands joined in the Americans' celebration. As they had done since the days of Lewis and Clark, Shoshones allied themselves with powerful outsiders and attempted to develop cooperative strategies of survival. Hunting,

Extermination of the Pun-Naks. Lithograph in The Life and Adventures of James P. Beckwourth, Mountaineer, Scout, and Pioneer and Chief of the Crow Nation of Indians (1856). Tensions between "mountain men" and Shoshone equestrians during the Great Basin fur trade often erupted into violent retribution as competing social groups vied for increasingly scarce natural resources. Wisconsin Historical Society, image no. WHi-37663.

hosting, and above all trading with American trappers secured for many Shoshones needed resources and protection, and the gun-desperate, "friendly Snakes" are referred to in positive terms by American trappers, in contradistinction to "enemy Snakes." Beginning in 1825, they attended the summer rendezvous, wintered in close proximity to trappers, fought alongside the outsiders in recurring conflicts against rival Indian powers, particularly the Blackfeet, and occasionally intermarried with them. Throughout the late 1820s and 1830s, then, the headwaters of the Green River, which witnessed half of all the rendezvous, became a central destination in many Shoshone groups' migratory economies. When trappers gathered their yearly caches and hurried to meet their overland supply trains, Shoshone women and men often preceded them. "What first struck our eye," reported one visitor to the Green River in 1839, "was several long rows of Indian tents extending along . . . for at least a mile. Indians and whites were mingled here in varied groups."[45]

The long summer days of the rendezvous were generally times of merriment. Men and women shared tales of their previous year, recounting moments of glory as well as folly. Successful trappers obtained impressive returns on their harvests, while Indian men and women traded horses, foods, skins, leggings, moccasins, and other items for manufactured and other outside goods. "The logic of the rendezvous," as Dale Morgan has detailed, was improvised and developed by William Ashley, who learned not only of the tremendous yields offered by fur harvests but of the varying social and economic needs of the interior West's diverse residents. The desertion of Ogden's freemen, "most of whom had Indian wives and families, with varied wants," particularly revealed to Ashley the potential yields from "fofarraw," as the trappers called Indian domestic trade items. Including silk, sewing supplies, ribbons, combs, earrings, soap, and "slay bells," these trade goods became "fully as important as kettles, ammunition, trap springs, gun locks, rum, flour, sugar, and coffee," which made up the bulk of the trappers' supplies.[46]

The coexistence between "friendly Snakes" and trapping communities was restricted mainly to the summer months. Shoshone hardships continued year-round and were not easily alleviated by American trade, particularly as the Rocky Mountain fur trade exhausted the region's furs. Additionally, equestrian Shoshone groups overestimated their capacities to conduct peaceful trade with trappers while increasing their raids against rival groups. For, emboldened by their growing acquisition of American trade goods, Shoshone warriors exacted retribution on Blackfoot, Crow, and other rivals, paradoxically becoming ever more dependent upon American goods for survival while provoking retaliations. But the hardest days came in winter, when rivers were frozen, snows were deep, and food hard to come by. During times of common deprivation, Shoshone-trapper relations grew particularly strained. In the unusually severe winter of 1828, for example, Ogden wintered along the Snake near present-day Pocatello and recorded a series of increasing Shoshone-white tensions. The "Snakes are now encamped within half a mile of our camp," he noted on February 21, and "are starving and very troublesome." Even the "Plains Snakes" had been engaged in horse theft, which, as everyone knew, was the surest way to raise the trappers' ire. "How long will the Snakes be allowed to steal and murder, I cannot say," Ogden reported, and even though Shoshone impoverishment clearly underlay their raiding, his patience had become severely tested:

> The Americans appear and are most willing to declare war against them, and a short time since requested to know, if they did [so] in the spring, if I would assist. To this I replied if I found myself in company with them at the time I would not stand idle . . . I will not hesitate to say I would most willingly sacrifice a year and even two to exterminate the whole Snake tribe, women and children excepted, and in doing so I am of opinion I could fully justify myself before God and man.[47]

Equestrian Shoshones were not exterminated by Ogden or by American trappers, though many maintained such genocidal ambitions. Such hatreds would foment again in the coming generation, when the Snake and Bear Rivers witnessed some of the bloodiest conflicts in western history. These Shoshone conflicts, however, would be not with trappers and traders, but with emigrant settlers and the growing presence of the American state and its army in the region. Along the region's icy rivers in January 1863, Ogden's ambitions would finally materialize, though Shoshone "women and children" would not be exempted. For now, as the 1830s wore on, new and larger violent forces were gathering as the era of trapping and furs paved the way for larger imperial machinations.

SIX

◆ ◆ ◆

Colorado Utes and the
Traumatic Storms of Expansion

As Anglo and American fur trappers competed for resources, information, and access to the Intermountain West, seismic transformations emanated from the centers of empire. By 1830 Mexico's ineffective Indian policies had disappointed and alienated *vecinos* from San Antonio to Monterey, and organized political rebellions brewed in Taos, Texas, and California. Along the Pacific, Russian, English, and soon American outfits competed for furs from seals and sea otters, establishing small "prized anchorages" from Alaska to Fort Ross in California. These outposts were established not as colonizing epicenters but as commercial entrepôts to facilitate Pacific trade. Throughout the Plains into the eastern reaches of the Columbia River basin, an expanding demicircle of forts, supply centers, and trade routes connected disparate British, American, and New Mexican outposts. From Taos, to Bent's Fort in Colorado, to the string of posts along the upper Missouri and into the Columbia watershed, a network of imperial launching pads mushroomed in a broad jagged encirclement of the Great Basin.[1]

Surrounded by the economic rivalries remaking the nineteenth-century West, the Great Basin remained an imperial hinterland for the first half of the 1800s. Numerous polyglot companies of male traffickers ferried resources into and out of the region, allying with Ute and Shoshone peoples on the eastern and northern perimeters. The formidable Indian powers of California's central valleys and the Colorado River nations, as well as the challenging geographies and cli-

176

mates of the Colorado River and Sierra Nevada, limited access into the region from the west and south. The "Great Basin" in fact did not exist as a geographic entity until 1844, when John Charles Frémont's Second Expedition mapped the region, ending much of the cartographic phantasmagoria about mythic waterways and peoples. For the first third of the nineteenth century, the Great Basin remained home to linguistically related Shoshone-speaking communities, many of which had become incorporated into spheres of European influence but remained outside the zones of direct European colonization.[2]

The 1830s, 1840s, and especially 1850s brought an end to such isolation. Indeed, these decades heralded the beginnings of a new time and of a new world. Equestrian Utes in New Mexico and Colorado had known for generations that the worlds of Spanish and other foreign peoples held tremendous if frightening possibilities. These Native peoples well understood how profound the social variables of European diseases, warfare, trade, and technologies could be. They had endured and adapted to such conditions for some time. They were unprepared, however, for the onslaught of American expansion that accelerated in the aftermath of the U.S.-Mexican War.

As thousands of migrants, soldiers, and settlers moved into New Mexico and Colorado, confederated bands of Ute Indians confronted the American challenge to their homelands with resolve and effective diplomacy. Initially conducting insurgencies against American forces while cementing the ties between their bands, Utes under tacticians like the renowned leader Ouray quickly scaled back their hostilities with the U.S. Army to withstand the brunt of expansion. While they suffered military defeats, by 1868 Colorado Utes had used negotiation, diplomacy, and even service on behalf of the army to retain access to their homelands. They remained unwaveringly committed to staying in their mountain communities and were quite prepared to help "pacify" other indigenous rivals in order to do so.

Upon traveling to Washington in the 1860s, Ouray and other Ute leaders faced the common fate of most nineteenth-century Indians: the transfer of their lands for secured constitutional protection over a territorially bounded reservation. While payments and additional resources often sweetened the Americans' offers, such treaty negotiations inherently involved land cessions. Despite losing access to all their former territories in New Mexico as well as portions of southern

Colorado, ratified Ute treaties by 1868 had created a reservation of over fifteen million acres across western Colorado. Though bounded, reservation lands proffered Colorado Utes the opportunity to continue their hunting ways in their bountiful and beloved mountain territories. The Utes' tactful diplomacy, military service on behalf of the government, and steadfast commitment to preserving their homelands now seemingly assured these Native peoples continued access to their new reservation homelands. Bands of Utes, in short, from the 1840s through the 1860s confronted the decades-long challenge of American state incorporation by navigating institutions and individuals of the American state, notably the U.S. Army and Indian Agency officials like Christopher "Kit" Carson, to preserve territorial integrity. Moreover, they held to such commitments and conducted such negotiations under extreme pressures. For, throughout the early 1800s, the challenge of maintaining equestrian economies in a region of declining game combined with increased indigenous rivalries to make the years before U.S. conquest exceedingly traumatic. Such initiatives would, however, come under unrelenting stress as a series of struggles over the place of Indian peoples in Colorado erupted in the 1860s and 1870s. For these Native peoples, the crisis of American state formation involved not only navigating *national* military and political actors but also placating *regional* white interests, which often cared little about enforcing the nation's Indian policies.[3]

Growing Pressures from Outsiders, 1820s–1840s

Mexican independence unraveled economic and political institutions forged between neighboring Indian peoples and Spanish colonial officials during the trying years of Comanche conflicts. Before independence, Utes had come to rely upon New Mexico for alliance, trade, and gifts while providing hospitality and guidance to representatives of cross and crown. Many forms of accommodation between Plains Indians and New Mexicans developed during the last half-century of Spanish rule, and within the same period a distinctly *vecino* culture emerged in northern New Mexico. Not surprisingly, then, many Utes, *Hispanos,* and other borderlands peoples viewed the chaotic aftermath of independence as affronts to their everyday lives.[4]

Like Navajo, Comanche, and other surrounding Indians, Utes in

New Mexico and Colorado responded to such instabilities by escalating their raids upon settlements while opening trade with Americans. Such Indian attacks as well as growing American trade networks now fueled cycles of conflict throughout the early 1800s as Natives, *Hispanos*, and Anglo-Americans vied for control over lands, resources, and one another. However, unlike Plains Indians, whose dependency upon horses and bison has been well detailed, Utes possessed advantages that augured well in their struggles to control their homelands. First and foremost, Utes were mountain peoples who migrated between alpine encampments, river valleys, and trade centers alongside the Front Range of the Rockies. Intimately familiar with New Mexico's northern trade centers and the routes in between, Utes had learned since their days as Comanche allies that the Plains north of Pecos remained contested by several equestrian nations. Comanches and their Kiowa allies; Cheyennes, who would soon split into northern and southern divisions, and their Arapaho allies; Pawnees and their eastern allies; Lakotas; and to a lesser extent Crow, Shoshone, and Blackfeet from the upper Missouri—all these Indian peoples lived, hunted, or raided on the central Plains. As Elliot West argues, these "contested plains," whose lush grasslands provided pastures for horses and bison, held opportunities for economic power. Such power, however, proved alluring not just for Indians but also for growing numbers of Euro-American hunters, New Mexican *comancheros* (Indian traders) and *ciboleros* (bison traders), and, most ominously, American settlers, who were moving past the Mississippi in waves. Include thousands of eastern Indians pushed west by American "Removal" policies as well as dispossessed *métis* and *creole* populations from Louisiana, and West's contention that "from the 1820s to the 1860s the central plains were probably the most viciously contested terrain of North America" proves convincing.[5]

While influenced by the intertribal conflicts that characterize this epic contest, southern Utes, particularly Muache, Capote, and Tabeguache bands, ventured onto the Plains seasonally and provisionally to graze their herds, hunt bison, and raid, as well as to visit the region's many trade centers. But the Utes remained much less dependent than other equestrians upon the Plains economy. In the 1700s, with the rise of imperial equestrians like the Comanche, their isolation from the Plains cost Utes much of the hegemony they had previously enjoyed when they had displaced Apache, Navajo, and *Hispano* communities along both sides of the Rio Grande. Now, in the early 1800s, such isolation proved advantageous, for the Utes were not drawn inescapably into the Plains' spiraling conflicts.

Mountain isolation also provided economic advantages. Within Ute territories bountiful game, including bison, grazed in the parks and headwater valleys of the Arkansas, San Luis, Rio Grande, and Southern and Northern Platte, while pasturage existed along these watersheds and their many tributaries. West of the Continental Divide, the San Juan, Gunnison, Dolores, and Green Rivers offered fish, fowl, and foods for gathering, while formidable mountains shielded much of the region and its valleys from outsiders. Starting in the 1820s, fur traders had begun arriving in Ute homelands with more regularity than New Mexicans and by the 1830s were offering improved goods as well. After the founding of Bent's Fort, Pueblo, Hardscrabble, and other Arkansas River trading settlements in the 1830s and 1840s, traders like Alexander Barclay traded in Ute country on a monthly basis. Nestled in the diverse ecologies of the Colorado Plateau, Utes had mountain, river valley, and, when needed, Plains territories from which to obtain resources.[6]

Securing their communities and homelands remained a constant preoccupation for the Utes. Their creation of defensive mountain strongholds suggests that they were committed to ensuring that equestrian rivals did not venture too far west of the Front Range. As Domínguez and Escalante had learned, Colorado Utes feared Plains raiders, and throughout the Spanish period Utes secured, as best they could, the entrances to the three great ecological game havens of central Colorado: North, Middle, and South Park. They built stone blinds at the passes into these parks and into the San Luis Valley farther south, which likewise provided game and grasslands. Utes felled trees to solidify these holdings, which when used in combat offered the additional security of defending not only a fortified position but also an elevated one. And year round they traded, manufactured, and accumulated stores of weaponry, both foreign and indigenous. Securing their communities and the lands through which they traveled remained, as always, a constant preoccupation within Ute society.[7]

Despite Ute defenses, rivals did penetrate beyond the Front Range, especially after 1840, when allied Cheyenne and Arapaho bands secured a historic peace with their Comanche and Kiowa adversaries at

Bent's Fort. The year 1840 indeed marked the beginning of a tumultuous time for the peoples of the Plains. Despite establishing peace between their confederacies and agreeing to common hunting grounds between the North Platte and Arkansas, these equestrians soon faced a cascade of challenges. Not only had the Rocky Mountain Trapping System declined, but the formation of emigrant societies out of Missouri brought increased traffic from the east. Fewer trading resources and more emigrants soon spelled economic and environmental disaster. The 1840 settlement also accelerated the destruction of the sheltered bison commons, or "neutral grounds," earlier established between the Platte and Arkansas as a result of indigenous warfare. As West explains, as Native conflicts between the rivers abated, "the great peace suddenly ended the animals' security . . . the pastoral hunters found themselves progressively constricted within a deteriorating environment . . . The central plains region, that vast, open country that had seemed a liberation, was rapidly becoming a cage." In their efforts to restrict emigrant access, central Plains Indians became enveloped in deepening conflicts.[8]

Pushed west by the turmoil on the Plains, Arapaho raiders moved into Ute lands for bison and other resources, conducting raids and reprisals against Ute encampments. Like other Plains societies, the Arapaho raided not only for material and economic gain but also for social honor and distinction, valued norms around which cultural institutions, especially gendered age-grade societies, revolved. In 1840, then, as Plains Indians secured peace, the need for new lands, resources, and opportunities for social achievement brought increased incursions into Ute territories.[9]

Numerous travelers to "Bayou Salado," as New Mexicans called South Park, recounted evidence of Arapaho-Ute conflict. On June 18, 1844, for example, on its return journey east Frémont's Second Expedition encountered signs of an Arapaho encampment near South Park. Aware that "we were coming out of their enemy's [the Utes'] country, and this was a war-ground, we were desirous to avoid them." Unable to elude Arapaho scouts, Frémont braced his party for attack: "We had scarcely made our few preparations, when about 200 of them appeared . . . mounted, painted, and armed for war." The Arapaho along with "about 20 Sioux" were prepared to attack Frémont because they believed that "we had doubtless been carrying assistance in arms and ammunition" into their "enemy's country." Assured that these foreigners were travelers and not traders, the Arapaho party went in search of its primary target. Four days later Frémont's expedition encountered a mourning "party of Utah women, who told us that on the other side of the ridge their village was fighting with the Arapahoes . . . [and] pressed us eagerly to join with their people." Frémont disappointed them as he had the Arapahos: "it was not for us to interfere in such a conflict." As Charles Preuss, Frémont's Prussian subcommander, noted, "a few howling women and fugitive horses were all we could see" of the conflict.[10]

The soon-to-be famous fur trader–cum–guide Kit Carson guided Frémont's expedition, and it was perhaps to him whom these Utes made their final pleas. For Carson was conversant in Ute. He had traded out of Taos and Bent's Fort into Ute territory, had recently purchased a Paiute captive from the Ute leader Walkara in Utah, and was on favorable terms with many Ute leaders; in fact a sickly Carson would accompany the Colorado Ute delegation to Washington in early 1868. Given Frémont's mandate to traverse and map the Intermountain West, however, the expedition's leaders had little time for Indian politics. As Preuss flatly recorded, "It was most advisable for us to remain neutral. Therefore, we hurried past as fast as possible."[11]

Throughout the first half of the 1800s, Arapahos and Cheyennes, along with their Lakota allies, dominated the slopes of the Front Range, a dominion facilitated by their marriage-based relations with traders at Bent's Fort. Several Bent brothers had married daughters of Cheyenne leaders, establishing partnerships between their communities. Cheyenne, Comanche, and other Plains Indians additionally received more trade gifts from New Mexican leaders than from Utes during the waning years of Spanish rule, a fact that has led one scholar to conclude that Utes remained "isolated from the economic developments in the pastoral (Navajo) and Plains borderlands" and that "they gradually fell behind their competitors in military potential."[12]

Since much of Ute trade occurred illegally with New Mexicans and unlicensed trappers, assessing Ute trading relations proves difficult. Clearly, isolation from Plains trading centers cost Utes access to critical resources. Traders like the Bents offered more guns, powder, and better terms of trade than New Mexicans. They could also repair guns and, when needed, participate in military raids or defense. Having newcomers as partners, allies, and even kinsmen, in short, offered many Plains Indians critical advantages over mountain groups.[13]

In an era of growing conflict, mountain isolation could prove a strength as well as a hindrance. Since the 1820s, Utes had been able to attract traders from nearly all directions into their homelands. From the north, "mountain men" and British "brigades" had established trade centers and rendezvous locations along major rivers within Shoshone and Ute territories. From the south, New Mexican and U.S. traders had operated out of Abiquiu and Taos, including Antoine Robidoux, whose two forts on the Green and Colorado lay entirely within Ute homelands and depended upon stable relations with Ute leaders. To the west, Utes in Utah, such as Walkara's band, had accumulated horses by the thousands, collected tolls from passengers along the Old Spanish Trail, held numerous nonequestrian Native captives under their vassalage, and raided as far west as the Pacific. Now, in the 1830s and 1840s, traders from newly formed settlements along the Arkansas were coming from the east.[14]

Notwithstanding Arapaho-Cheyenne ties at Bent's Fort, Arkansas River trading communities also had dealings with Utes. In June 1844 in South Park, for instance, the Arapahos assumed that Frémont was carrying "arms and ammunition" to the Utes. That the Americans traveling east also feared Arapaho interdiction further suggests that trading parties dealing with the Utes risked Arapaho retaliation. And, most tellingly, 200 Arapaho and Lakota warriors had ventured into the jewel of the Colorado bison parks and turned it into a "war-ground." Had the Utes possessed superior military capacity, they would not have permitted such incursions. On the other hand, despite their losses in the initial attack, the Utes were not routed by this war party from the continent's powerful indigenous allies. According to Frémont, "about 300 warriors" chased the retreating raiders, who had driven the Utes' horses "to the end of a hollow, where they had previously forted at the edge of the pines. Here the Utahs had instantly attacked in turn, and . . . were getting rather the best of the day." Their village surprised, several of their leaders killed, much of their herd driven off, and their enemies, presumably armed with superior weaponry, now retreating toward a fortified encampment—that even such advantages did not ensure Arapaho victory reveals the Utes' considerable military capacity as well as their commitment to contesting incursions into their homelands. Far from lacking military potential, Utes by 1840 had positioned themselves within expanding networks and had obtained enough resources to compete with their rivals. Far from being minor actors on the margins of empire, Utes controlled prosperous lands, resources, and territories around which, for them, the world revolved.[15]

Though a watershed event in Great Basin history, Frémont's Second Expedition offered little to Colorado Utes through whose territories he traveled. Aside from the Arapaho conflict, Preuss and Frémont recount little of the region's indigenous peoples. Preuss's diary, for example, devotes more space to the culinary challenges of bison than to the region's Native populations.

The cursory and infrequent mentions of Colorado Utes in many accounts from the early 1840s suggest that they had secured fairly peaceful relations with outside traders. Thus Alexander Barclay, a veteran trader operating out of Hardscrabble who conducted two "Eutau expeditions" in September and October 1846, restricted his account to two phrases—"On Eut encampment" and "In Eut village"—for his entire October activities, and his record of his two-week September expedition contains no mention of the "Eutau" with whom he lived during that time. Although Ute warriors did occasionally mount raids against travelers—including an immortalized wrestling match with Carson after his departure from Frémont—such raids by no means suggest concerted campaigns against outsiders, especially traders. Whereas Martínez's the murderous incident in Santa Fe in September 1844 plunged Ute relations with New Mexico into violence, traders like Barclay and even Carson understood that, minor altercations aside, Utes remained on good terms with whites. Throughout the early 1840s, Utes were anxious about the growing presence of foreigners, both Native and non-Native, in their homelands, but they were also committed to sustaining relations with the traders who provided them with crucial support. Such relations, however, came under increasing strain during the years of American conquest.[16]

The Challenges of American Conquest, 1840–1855

While mountain isolation afforded Colorado Utes some reprieve from the contests occurring on the Plains, incorporation into foreign economies initiated ordeals of its own. Traders carried not only resources to Ute communities but also destabilizing influences. "Arms and ammunition," as Frémont noted, had become necessities for Utes, but acquiring items to trade in exchange remained a constant, difficult exercise, particularly as the region's furs became overharvested and as rates of exchange fluctuated. Utes understood that skins and furs were alluring to traders, but they could not understand how their value could decline so rapidly, especially as the amount of labor needed to acquire mountain beavers increased with every harvest. By 1840 beaver pelts, once so valued and abundant, had grown both unprofitable, as new markets and materials met European demand, and scarcer. They became harder to procure while also becoming less valuable. The downward spiral in value not only lowered rates of exchange for Indians but also wrought havoc throughout the West, terminating supply systems like the rendezvous, driving trappers from the region, and even, teasingly, catalyzing small fur rebounds along many streams. It was, for example, changing economics, not simply coincidence, that led former trappers like Carson to become guides while others like Barclay became settlers. The early 1840s witnessed, in short, rapid economic transformations throughout the West. For Utes, such turbulent economics combined with the incursions from their rivals and their tensions with New Mexicans to make the years of U.S. conquest an especially trying time.[17]

Utes responded to such challenges with violence. Provoked by what they saw as unfair trading practices, belligerent Mexican leaders, and Arkansas Valley traders' favoritism toward their enemies, in the wake of the 1844 Martínez incident Utes unleashed a series of attacks that killed dozens and reconfigured the political geography northwest of Santa Fe, raiding settlements, murdering New Mexican traders at the two forts within their homelands, and, for the first time in western history, burning a fur-trading post to the ground. At Fort Uintah along the Green River in Utah, where he had resupplied his weary expedition, Frémont recounted that Utes had "attacked . . . since we passed it; and the men of the garrison killed, the women carried off." Those at Fort Uncompahgre in western Colorado had met a similar fate as Ute warriors vented their anger at New Mexican traders within their homelands. Utes also increased their grip on isolated settlements. According to George Ruxton, for example, New Mexico's northernmost settlement, El Rio Colorado, fell into a state of vassalage to "the barbarous Yutas . . . by sufferance of whom the New Mexicans have settled this valley."[18]

In a different era, such attacks would have prompted renewed negotiations from New Mexican leaders, for this was not total war, nor was it a blood feud. It was a political and economic dispute to which economic and political solutions existed. In their killings at Fort Uncompahgre, for example, the Utes had spared an American trader and instructed him to send word that the furs at the post would be left untouched, "a clear indication," according one assessment, that the Utes "sought revenge only, not the elimination of commercial ties." But commerce and revenge remained interwoven. In their hostilities at Fort Uintah, for example, Utah Utes, having learned of their eastern brethren's humiliation in Santa Fe, used that betrayal as final motivation to unleash their own simmering resentments against Robidoux's more famous post. A successful fort even after the decline of the fur trade, Fort Uintah had remained capable of supplying large overland parties such as Frémont's. Local Utes, however, had grown so dissatisfied with the worsening terms of trade that a distant outrage in Santa Fe triggered its demise. Had aggrieved Utes in New Mexico sought only revenge from Martínez's attacks, more distant Ute bands in Colorado and Utah would not have risked eliminating the trading centers within their territories, outposts that had long remained dependent upon stable relations with Ute communities. Dissatisfaction with Robidoux and other traders operating within a cycle of diminishing demand underlay the Utes' increasing resort to violence.[19]

Their diplomacy with Santa Fe in shambles, their relationship with New Mexican traders in decline, and their struggles to protect their lands from rivals unabated, Utes used violence not only as a way to release deep-seated resentments but also as a way to forge new strategies in the face of growing challenges. They knew that New Mexican retaliations would come, as they did in the summer of 1845, when General Archuleta's organized militia of over 1,000 chased Utes as far north as the Arkansas, which savvy Ute leaders retreated across in order to move into "foreign" U.S. territory. They also knew that destroying Robidoux's forts would threaten relations with Taos-based trading companies. Utes deemed such risks worth taking. Taos traders and New Mexican officials now seemed incapable of meeting Ute needs. Indeed, their economic and political policies had unraveled generations of close ties between their respective communities. New strategies of survival were now required to cope with their rapidly changing world.[20]

Alexander Barclay's uneventful summer trips to Ute villages in 1846 suggest one dimension of their evolving strategies. George Ruxton's condescending remarks six months later from El Rio Colorado suggest another. In the chaotic months of the U.S.-Mexican War, Colorado Utes were not only incorporating Arkansas River traders into their economies but also establishing profitable ties with breakaway Mexican villagers, allowing them to live within their lands as cohabitant settlers. Securing trade from the Arkansas and opening their lands to *Hispano* settlement became new economic strategies in the years following Martínez's attack. Such strategies, Utes believed, could help shelter them from the fallout from the plummeting fur trade. These initially promising efforts proved abortive after the American conquest of New Mexico as powerful foreign actors moved into the region and recalibrated its balance of power. Though unsuccessful, such adaptations highlight the transitions occurring throughout Ute homelands as Indian peoples responded to the initial phases of state expansion before being drawn further into its turbulent wake.

Barclay's move to Hardscrabble in 1845 came amidst changing Ute fortunes with Arkansas River traders. After the destruction of Robidoux's outposts and their growing relations of violence with New Mexico, Utes increased their trade with Robidoux's rivals, hosting mountain traders from the Arkansas River Valley. Although the Bents were allied with the Arapaho and Cheyenne, dozens of other outposts mushroomed before the U.S.-Mexican War as traders competed for the traffic between the two republics. Before the outbreak of war in 1846, forts on the U.S. side of the river generally traded with Indian groups and American migrants, explorers, and soldiers, while on the other side posts like Hardscrabble and Greenhorn traded in what was still Mexican territory. These smaller posts more readily trafficked contraband, including stolen horses, alcohol, and firearms. Attempting policies of appeasement and isolation with Indians, U.S. officials policed the sale of firearms and alcohol in its western territories. They could do little, however, to stem such traffic within Mexican territory, where state control was ephemeral. Alcohol traders worked out of these nascent settlements, traveling within the folds created by overlapping economic spheres.[21]

Venturing to Taos and New Mexican distilleries, traders trafficked

their potent cargo to outposts along the Arkansas, whence parties ferried supplies into the mountains, exchanging alcohol and manufactured goods for skins and furs. Such trade differed from the rendezvous system, in which distant companies and individuals like Robidoux
and William Ashley set aggressive rates of exchange designed to maxi-
mize profits from Indian lands. These smaller trading units operated
seasonally and supplemented their livelihoods with more sedentary
forms of economic subsistence like agriculture and ranching. Trade of
this sort was run by individual traders, not by company trappers,
though many had once experienced the glory days of the "mountain
men."[22]

Alcohol did not help Ute hunters catch more game, nor did it protect them from their many rivals. While traders supplied staples besides alcohol, such as lead and powder, these avenues of trade hardly
sustained Ute needs. As always, game, not goods, remained the back-
bone of Ute subsistence, and finding secure and consistent forms of
food, particularly in the face of dwindling bison herds, remained the
challenge for Ute communities. Of course, such subsistence depended
in part on functioning weapons, but the vast preponderance of Ute
economics centered upon hunting and gathering, particularly on a
combination of small and larger hunts with seasonal berry and piñon
harvests. Colorado Utes' recent descent into violence with New Mexican leaders had additionally compromised their defenses, creating
more antagonists to their south while depriving them of supplies once
provided at Robidoux's forts. New allies in addition to suppliers were
now needed to enable them to manage their changing fortunes.[23]

George Ruxton's accounts of his travels from Mexico into the Rockies provide incomparable insight into the nature of mountain life. A
decorated officer from European continental wars, Ruxton left New
Mexico in early 1847, risking winter travel in search of heralded places
and peoples. Although he nearly froze to death, Ruxton was indeed
fortunate that he had not heeded others' advice to winter in New Mexico; he ventured north just days before the Taos Uprising cost many
Euro-Americans their lives, including several traders with whom he
had roomed. The Taos Uprising marked a revolt by allied *Hispano* and
Pueblo groups against the U.S. occupation of New Mexico and its
installation of outside political leaders, many of whom, including
Charles Bent, had been early profiteers in the region.[24]

While Ruxton's contempt for New Mexicans bristles throughout his writings, his derision is instructive for understanding Ute motivations during the transition from Mexican to U.S. rule. As he continued defaming the inhabitants of El Rio Colorado, for example, he reached the following conclusion:

> in this remote settlement, anything I had formerly imagined to be the *ne plus ultra* of misery, fell far short of the reality: such is the degradation of the people of Rio Colorado. Growing a bare sufficiency for their own support, they hold the land they cultivate . . . on sufferance from the barbarous Yutas, who actually tolerate their presence in their country for the sole purpose of having at their command a stock of grain and a herd of mules and horses, which they make no scruple to helping themselves to . . . Rio Colorado is a kind of game preserve, where the Yutas have a certainty of filling their bag.

Noticing also the presence of "one or two Yuta Indians" living among the fifty settlers, Ruxton continued north toward the Arkansas, distancing himself "without one regret" from those "under the garb of a Mexican sarape."[25]

As in earlier decades, Ute dominion over New Mexican settlements reflected larger dynamics that Ruxton glimpsed, if not fully grasped. A tiny settlement of fifteen families, El Rio Colorado appeared to the Englishman to be at the ends of the Mexican universe. Nothing could be more humiliating, he concluded, than to live in poverty under the ever-present eyes of "barbarous" Indians who not only helped themselves to the fruits of one's labor but also, reportedly, came to "depend upon procuring a few brace of Mexican scalps, when such trophies are required." Sanctioned theft, impoverishment, and possible murder confounded the sanctimonious veteran of multiple European campaigns.[26]

The fluidity within and between Indian and New Mexican communities, as James Brooks has shown, involved complicated sets of hybrid social relations. Bonds of kinship, captivity, and ritual conjoined "borderlands communities of interest" throughout the late Spanish and Mexican periods, and El Rio Colorado's Ute relations conform to multiple aspects of Brooks's paradigm, particularly the presence of "Utes" within the settlement. Ute "sufferance" also stemmed from economic, political, and military exigencies forged amidst complicated power relations. The Utes' recent decision to "tolerate" New Mexicans on their borders arose from their immediate predicaments, not simply from custom. Diminishing resources, more rivals, and above all economics fueled their realization that they could not survive without incorporating others into their society as potential allies, subjects, and kinsmen. They certainly needed the trade with New Mexico's burgeoning villagers, whose demographic growth had generated their own political dissatisfactions with Mexican leaders. Settlers also provided important buffer zones between Ute mountain strongholds and their rivals, sheltering Utes from raiding parties while also alerting them to outsiders' movements. Most important, Utes materially benefited from the presence of farmers and herders "in their country," helping themselves when needed to horses, cattle, mules, sheep, goats, and grain in exchange for the use of their lands. Becoming in essence indigenous landlords with their own stocked pantry of New Mexican villagers, Colorado Utes, in short, were now adopting practices that Spanish leaders had devised a century earlier to secure their communities from outside incursions. Utes allowed socially marginal New Mexicans such as *genízaros* and former captives a modicum of usufruct rights in exchange for economic and social services, services they regarded as crucial to managing their turbulent world.[27]

If Ruxton condemned those at El Rio Colorado, he would have expressed even greater disdain for Atanasio Trujillo, who six months after Ruxton's visit ventured north from El Rio and began negotiating with Ute leaders to settle along Colorado's San Luis River. As Thomas Andrews argues, the New Mexican settlement of the San Luis created the seeming paradox of equestrian Indians inviting pastoral settlers into a region of diminishing resources. After all, along with South Park, the San Luis was the most prized game reserve for Colorado Utes, a sheltered bison and animal commons the size of Connecticut between the San Juan and Sangre de Cristo Mountains renowned for its winter pasturage. Why would equestrian Utes permit the growth of ranches within their homelands when they knew such settlements would create competition for the valley's flora and fauna? Did Utes not know that New Mexican cattle and sheep herds, soon estimated in the thousands, would undermine the valley's remaining bison populations as well as compete with their own horses and game for valuable grasses?[28]

Of course they knew, or at least they considered that such risks were worth taking, especially following the August 1846 U.S. takeover of Santa Fe. The 1847 Taos Uprising was but one indicator of the resentment fostered by American conquest; its violent suppression also revealed the amount of force that could be brought to bear against insubordinates. Although in this case the targets had been limited to resident New Mexicans, the likelihood of regional conflict continued, especially outside the province, where Ute, Navajo, and other Indians maintained varying degrees of power. The Utes' decision first in 1847, then again in the summer of 1848, to permit Trujillo to begin settling the San Luis Valley contrasted with their earlier resistance to *Hispano* settlement. As Trujillo recalled, before the war Utes had attacked nascent settlements and also turned their herds loose on crops, forcing Trujillo's predecessors to abandon their farms before winter. Now the Utes awaited Trujillo's arrival. Trujillo, whose competency in Ute stemmed from his days in the fur trade, recalled in 1866 the gracious welcome of Ute leaders. After Trujillo greeted them in their language, the Utes assured him in Spanish: "'Come, Antanasio, do not fear. We are the same as sons to you.'" At a time of regional unrest, the Utes' need to rethink their calculus of diplomacy and subsistence clearly influenced their assuring invitation for the Trujillo family to join them in the San Luis.[29]

An important strand in the region's historical tapestry, the settlement of the San Luis Valley occurred during the turbulent years of American rule when foreign armies, officials, and migrants swarmed across the Arkansas and down the Rio Grande. After meeting with U.S. officials in September and October 1846, 100 Ute leaders concluded that the new regime in Santa Fe would meet their communities' needs. The assurances, however, also came with prohibitions. Plied with blankets, gifts, and bons mots, Ute leaders listened to the first of many calls to abate their violence. "Peace" was to be a precondition for diplomatic relations. Ute leaders had conducted negotiations in Santa Fe before, pledging peace to Spanish and Mexican governors. Such times, however, were now gone. While U.S. negotiations with Indians resembled prior gatherings, the distinctions involved more than linguistics, because the pledge of peace that the Americans now required involved more than an end to violence. In September and October respectively, General Stephen Kearny and Colonel Alexander Doniphan conducted negotiations as agents of an expanding national state. Their "treaty" negotiations became the first step toward consolidating control over Ute lands, and their capacity to deploy violence to such ends contrasted with that of Santa Fe's earlier rulers.[30]

The first two years of Ute diplomacy with these new leaders held little portent of the revolutions to come. While Utes facilitated settlement in the San Luis, continued trading on the Arkansas, and even aided American explorers, including Frémont's ill-fated Fourth Expedition in the San Juan Mountains, the U.S. Army maintained a continental operation. In addition to occupying Mexico's capital and California, the army faced Indians throughout the West whose attacks plunged many newly conquered lands into chaos. Having pledged peace to Kearny and Doniphan, Ute leaders generally remained aloof from larger conflicts, choosing neutrality as a strategy for maintaining control over their mountain homelands. This policy potentially served Ute bands well; for the widening Indian wars drew many of the Utes' principal rivals—Arapahos and Cheyennes on the Plains, Navajos in the Southwest—into bitter campaigns of survival that would last until 1864, when, nearly simultaneously, Navajos were removed by the "Long Walk" to Bosque Redondo and Cheyenne blood ran deep at Sand Creek. Except for the easternmost Muache Utes, who raided with Jicarilla Apaches, most Ute bands understood that neutrality ensured continued autonomy. Besides, Ute dominion over breakaway New Mexican villagers seemed destined to increase the number of settlements that they could tax in times of need. For most Utes, maintaining peace with Americans while maintaining control over their homelands extended survival strategies forged in the early 1840s.[31]

But the new American prohibitions were broader than the Utes had realized. Although U.S. officials countenanced intertribal raids, they were not prepared to tolerate Indian attacks against white migrants or resident New Mexicans. In early 1849, after a winter attack by Arapahos, Utes escalated their raids upon El Rio Colorado in order to replace lost resources and honor. The practices of taxing New Mexicans had sustained them well following Martínez's attack and had led to the formation of breakaway communities in their midst. When needed, Utes made off with thousands of sheep and goats, dozens of cows, cat-

tle, and horses, as well as a few burros, leaving village pantries depleted. Unfortunately for the Utes, the new regime in Santa Fe had
created avenues of redress for even the most distant New Mexicans.
Upon hearing of Ute raids upon the territory, U.S. officials concluded
that the Utes had violated their pledge of peace, and in March 1849
they mobilized a reprisal force. As Janet Lecompte details, "Lieutenant
J. H. Whittlesey was sent out with fifty-seven soldiers to 'chastise' the
Utes . . . The soldiers surprised a village, killed ten braves, captured
two [women] and a chief's son, and destroyed fifty lodges with all
the provisions." The soldiers, according to another scholar, "drove the
remaining Indians like chickens in all directions through the snow"
as Ute survivors jettisoned supplies and stock needed to survive the
mountain winter. Later that month, when two of Frémont's guides returned to Colorado to retrieve cached supplies from their expedition
in the San Juans, Utes exacted prompt revenge, killing Dr. Benjamin
Kern and former trapper Bill Williams, whose familiarity with Ute ways
had once enabled him to navigate the borderlands to the northwest.[32]

In what was to become a common recurrence, the first military campaign between Utes and the U.S. Army stemmed from deep-seated
economic needs as well as misperceptions. Utes understood that their
leaders had pledged peace with U.S. officials, who threatened retaliation for Ute violence. They misunderstood, however, the new definitions of violence in the region. Visitors to El Rio Colorado such as
Ruxton, as well as the new villagers along the San Luis, all understood
that Utes' threats or uses of violence stemmed from economic need.
In the face of mounting economic pressure and intertribal warfare,
Utes taxed New Mexicans, as well as Euro-American migrants, within
their homelands by seizing crops, cattle, and goods. While Ruxton had
noted thousands of antelope along the Front Range, he also detailed
the region's dwindling bison population, as did chroniclers of Colorado's *Hispano* villages, whose herds ruptured bison ecologies. Colorado Utes were thus simultaneously fighting rivals for access to diminishing bison herds and raiding villagers in times of scarcity. Both
strategies were economic in nature, though violent in form, and now
U.S. officials insisted that Utes end such violence. Eliminate your raiding economies, curtail the forms of survival that you have developed,
and come to depend upon us for your community needs. Had Ute
leaders fully understood the nature of U.S. demands, their use of vio-

lence might have come much earlier or more selectively. Had U.S. leaders understood Ute economic challenges, Whittlesey's destruction of fifty Ute lodges in the winter of 1849 might have been averted.[33]

News of Whittlesey's attack spread throughout adjacent Ute communities. Fugitive survivors invariably detailed the rapidity with which the Americans advanced through the snow. The white newcomers' horses, efficient rifles, and uniformed cavalry units presented a sharp contrast with Mexican and Spanish forces. As harrowing tales fueled community debates about appropriate responses, Ute leaders quelled calls for reprisal. Now was not the time for violence, they insisted. The American numbers were already too great, and the next force might be even larger. The use of force must be a last resort, one that must be weighed against all other options. Besides, with Ute arms and ammunition so underprovisioned, there would be few chances of success against such might. A direct confrontation with this army, even in the face of such humiliation, was not warranted.[34]

Though undocumented, such logic undoubtedly circulated throughout Ute diplomatic channels in 1849; for in the months after the attack, Ute envoys, and not warriors, filtered into New Mexico, spreading reassuring words of their leaders' commitments to peace. By year's end, as they had for generations, Ute leaders assembled en masse and headed south to enter into what they believed would be a permanent agreement with Indian agents newly stationed in the region, the leader of whom, James S. Calhoun, possessed congressional authority to negotiate peace with the region's Indian powers. By responding to American military violence with diplomatic instead of military initiatives, Utes positioned themselves to create a more stable future, initiating a twenty-year ordeal to resolve their endemic subsistence and political problems.[35]

On New Year's Day 1850, after six months in office, New Mexico's Indian agent James Calhoun wrote to Commissioner of Indian Affairs Orlando Brown. Determined to secure peace treaties with Navajo, Ute, and Apache leaders, Calhoun noted that he had "not the slightest doubt" that many "have attempted a coalition for the purpose of overrunning and ravaging this territory." "If that purpose is abandoned, or has been defeated," he continued, "it is the result of the Utahs influence over the wild tribes." Despite constant efforts to convince them otherwise, Calhoun related, Apaches and Navajos "could not prevent the Utah Chiefs from meeting with me at Abiquiu."[36]

Reflecting his annoyance at earlier failures to cement negotiations with Utes, Calhoun's letter was written after an eventful seventy-two hours. Having sent messengers north in early December inviting Ute leaders to Abiquiu later in the month, the Indian agent arrived on December 28 and learned that Ute leaders were indeed only a few miles outside this gateway into New Mexico. Such proximity, however, also bred anxiety; for the Ute delegation did not come into the village on that day or the next, choosing instead to socialize with Abiquiu's *"traders,"* whose "influence" tested Calhoun's patience. On the evening of December 29, when a Ute leader "begged" Calhoun "to be patient," Calhoun responded with an ultimatum: "I would wait until the ensuing *midday, and not a moment longer,* for the Chiefs to come in," and "by 10 Oclk, on the next morning, they were present, and the enclosed treaty was fully and thoroughly explained to them."[37]

These brief glimpses of the creation of the first congressionally ratified treaty between Utes and the U.S. government underscore the challenges confronting American officials and Indian leaders after the U.S.-Mexican War. Fearing indigenous alliances and insurrections, anxious agents invited Indians to negotiate favorable conditions of peace rather than suffer through campaigns of war, while Indian leaders attempted to use agency resources for their needs. Despite Apache and Navajo appeals, Ute leaders understood the necessity and rewards of diplomacy. They could not, however, fully control their communities' actions; the familiar allures of trade, friendship, and holiday festivities almost compromised their primary intentions. Formalizing political and diplomatic agreements was an ordeal all its own. Doing so in concert with other community needs only deepened the challenge.

Ratified by Congress on September 9, 1850, the first Utah Treaty had twenty-nine "Principal and Subordinate" Ute chief signatories, and in the next weeks other Ute leaders came to New Mexico and signed on to the settlement. Unconditionally submitting to the "power and authority" of the U.S. government in Article 1, Utes agreed in the following articles to cease hostilities, to restore stolen property and captives, and to allow free white passage through their lands. In return, the U.S. government agreed to provide them with trading houses, military agencies, and annuities, as well as to establish clearly demarcated Ute territorial boundaries. Ute leaders agreed to this last provision reluctantly, for Article 7 called for more than the creation of Ute reservations; it also called for Utes' confinement within such boundaries and the cultivation of reservation lands. Utes were to become not only residents of a demarcated territory but also farmers upon it. They were, as the treaty dictated, "to cease the roving and rambling habits which have hitherto marked them as a people." When Ute leaders "expressed their *utter aversion to labor* and enquired what they would do, *to sustain life,* if so restricted," Calhoun "replied to them . . . if they behaved well, [the government] would take care of them . . . and that if they thought they ought not to agree to the terms of the treaty, that I would, at the peril of my life, secure them transit to their own Country unmolested and unharmed." Faced with Calhoun's assurances, Ute leaders accepted the overall tenor of the negotiations, understanding that future compromises would be necessary to retain control over their homelands.[38]

In retrospect, Ute acceptance of U.S. dominion in the 1850 Treaty appears as the first step in a long march toward dispossession, a fateful indigenous miscalculation of epic proportions. Such hindsight, however, is both misguided and unhelpful. Facing their own harrowing challenges, Ute signatories understood that fulfilling their treaty commitments was a key to survival, a willingness and commitment that Calhoun and others repeatedly noted. "The Utahs seem to be quiet, and no one has recently complained of their conduct," Calhoun wrote in October 1850. Utes accepted, by and large, the treaty's provisions and remained for four years, as Acting Superintendent of Indian Affairs John Greiner wrote in April 1852, "the easiest managed of any Indians in the Territory and with good treatment can always be relied upon." Even the most militant Muache leaders, including the notorious Chico Velasquez, who boasted of attacks against whites and Mexicans, aided New Mexican officials; Velasquez and seven other leaders promised in 1850 "never again to take up arms against the people of the United States, either Americans or Mexicans." Repeated and effusive remarks about Ute conduct, then, characterized American correspondence in the early 1850s and contrasted with officials' assessments of the territory's other Indian powers.[39]

Utes' compliance, however, went only so far. It taxed both their resolve and resources. Notwithstanding Calhoun's and Greiner's hopeful reports, the challenge of maintaining peace in the face of escalating economic pressures cast Ute leaders into a series of deepening dilemmas. While committed to peace and hopeful that promised annuities would be forthcoming, Utes watched as marauding Plains Indians continued their incursions into Ute homelands. They also saw uninvited settlers move farther up the Rio Grande onto disputed "land grants" established in the last years of Mexican rule. Most of all, they waited for the treaty's promised agencies, supplies, and provisions to arrive in their hungry communities, and Ute patience grew weaker with each season. At the end of 1850 Calhoun reported: "The Utahs seem to be perfectly quiet, and say they are waiting to ascertain what their Great Father . . . will do for them." Seven months later, in July 1851, he continued: "The Utahs, I have reason to believe are submissive, patiently waiting to see what our Government will do with them, and for them." Three months later Greiner pleaded to Calhoun: "The Eutaws are peaceable and kindly disposed towards our citizens, and have behaved well." Noting two earlier attacks by Kiowa and Arapahos and the Utes' subsequent preparations for reprisal, Greiner concluded: "I know of no remedy to check these outrages."[40]

Calhoun repeatedly requested additional military units to enforce U.S. Indian policy. One letter to the White House in 1850 pleading for assistance was cosigned by more than fifty New Mexicans. "We shall never have protection and quiet in this territory," it claimed, until equestrian Indians "are confined and forced to remain in certain fixed limits." Unfortunately for Calhoun and expectant Ute leaders, the messy aftermath of conquest overstretched the capacity of the federal government's Indian Office. Article 7's provision for a demarcated Ute homeland, for example, would take a generation to implement. An agent in an underfunded, overextended agency, Calhoun witnessed ebbs and flows in his attempts to channel the region's historical antagonists into the mainstream of U.S. governance. For Utes, rising expectations and government failures to fulfill fundamental American promises culminated in their abrogation of the landmark treaty.[41]

When exactly Utes abandoned diplomacy in favor of violence is unclear. Why they did so is not. Although Calhoun and Greiner noted occasional depredations by Ute raiders, most Colorado Utes remained committed to peace. American attention to Ute affairs, however, was too inconsistent, poorly planned, and uneven to assure that these commitments endured. Ute leaders were angered not only by the many years it took officials to establish promised forts, agencies, and annuity distributions but also by the perceived favoritism shown to their many rivals. In contrast to Calhoun, with his aversion to "bribery" and his perception that intentions, and not "presents," best oiled the wheels of Indian diplomacy, Indian agents on the Plains readily trafficked in powder, ammunition, and guns with the Utes' primary rivals, arming Kiowa, Arapaho, and Cheyenne warriors with the technologies of violence essential to warfare. In the Treaties of Fort Laramie (1851) and Fort Atkinson (1853), Plains Indian signatories received more "gifts," supplies, and annuities than had Utes, for whom powder and ammunition were harder to obtain. Furthermore, while traders on the Plains continued to trade with their many rivals, in New Mexico Calhoun moved to curtail unlicensed trading to the north, limiting the familiar "illicit" trade between northern villages and Ute communities. In short, American rule favored certain Indians over others, and American authority emanated north from Santa Fe in uneven waves.[42]

Signs of Ute disaffection were evident throughout 1854, particularly after the fateful death of Chico Velasquez, whose services on behalf of Governor David Meriwether had earned him accolades and gifts. Helping to retrieve stolen horses and cattle, Velasquez and his fellow tribesman Tamouche had also participated in a manhunt for a suspected murderer. Being paid "each a gray cloth coat . . . decorated handsomely with red and yellow braid," these Ute leaders returned home fashionably attired in tailored officer's clothing. They had also just contracted smallpox, and many "came to the conclusion that the Superintendent was the cause of the disease being among them . . . every one that received a coat died." The following spring, scattered and diseased Ute remains greeted travelers along the San Luis River.[43]

Combined with other grievances, such disaffection reached fever pitch on Christmas Eve 1854. Muache leader Tierra Blanco and 100 warriors rode roughshod over the Arkansas, killing twenty at El Pueblo and taking three captives before launching winter campaigns against Colorado's most vital artery. Enlisting the support of Arapaho and Cheyenne allies, William Bent endured months of Ute raids, while less protected settlements disbanded and fled. Conducting reprisals out of

Fort Massachusetts—the only fort in Colorado, which Utes had complained was too far south on the San Luis to protect them from Plains raiders—U.S. Army colonel Thomas Fauntleroy pursued Muache, Capote, and Jicarilla bands throughout 1855, destroying lodges, capturing more than fifty women and children, and burning tons of Ute saddles, robes, and matériel. Fauntleroy's men also disfigured Ute victims, while several Ute mothers reportedly made a greater sacrifice, painfully enduring the self-imposed deaths of their own children rather than see them lost to invaders. Such campaigns, Meriwether summarized, "caused these Indians great loss and suffering," and in August new treaties were signed at Abiquiu, treaties designed to ensure that the violent disagreements of the last half-decade would find other forms of resolution.[44]

Conducted under the shadow of American guns, the renewed nego-

Fort Massachusetts. Lithograph in Reports of Explorations and Surveys, to Ascertain the Most Practicable and Economical Route for a Railroad from the Mississippi River to the Pacific Ocean (1855). The first U.S. military outpost in Colorado, Fort Massachusetts in the San Luis Valley saw action against Utes in 1855, the last sustained military conflict between confederated Colorado Ute bands and the U.S. Army.

tiations did not proceed in the optimistic spirit that characterized Calhoun's efforts in 1849. Moreover, Senate failure to ratify the new agreements prolonged U.S. fulfillment of the 1850 treaty for another decade. Waiting for American officials to meet their commitments had fueled past violence; now more waiting seemingly augured more returns to the battlefield. Colorado Utes, however, chose a different path. Never again would they initiate concerted military campaigns against the American state; instead, their commitments to peace inaugurated a new era in Ute diplomacy. Ironically, U.S. military officials would soon create fertile avenues of service for Ute warriors, and Utes guided and rode alongside those who had just attacked them on the San Luis. After 1855, Ute diplomacy helped abate economic and ecological stresses. A new generation of Ute leaders came to know and even trust the authorities with whom they negotiated, and they believed them when in 1868 they finally said that the Utes' mountain homelands would remain theirs until the end of time.[45]

The Colorado Gold Rush and the Civil War

The events of 1855 did not bode well for U.S.-Ute relations. Many of the Ute signatories who had come to Abiquiu in 1849 had fallen out of favor as more bellicose leaders more readily drew warriors to their cause. Tierra Blanco had survived Fauntleroy's destruction along the San Luis River, but at considerable cost to his people and to their Jicarilla allies. In the months before winter, a time normally spent in hunting and harvesting, many Utes now found themselves, according to Abiquiu agent Lorenzo Labadi, in an "impoverished condition." They were, he reported in August, "dying from famine." On top of their ongoing warfare with Plains and Navajo rivals, U.S. failure to fulfill its 1855 promises further taxed Ute resolve. The difficulties they faced in the aftermath of war compounded existing problems and darkened an already uncertain future.[46]

In one sense, New Mexico had clearly not done much for northern Indians. The provisions of peace treaties signed in the first days of the U.S.-Mexican War had yet to be fulfilled. Select Ute agents at Taos and Abiquiu kept themselves apprised of Ute affairs, but no agencies, let alone mutually agreed-upon reservation lands, had been established. The first U.S. Army fort in Colorado had recently launched a punitive expedition against mainly women and children, yet it did not, as Ute leaders repeatedly complained, protect the San Luis Valley from Plains raiders. Confused efforts to resettle Jicarillas ran out of money or were arbitrarily discontinued, while all decried the paucity and poor quality of goods bestowed upon New Mexico's "friends." In 1856, for example, Governor Meriwether was nearly assaulted by a Ute leader who "tore up the blanket given him. It was old, had been worn, and he was dissatisfied." Ultimately, as Carson reflected, "I cannot see how the Superintendent can expect Indians to depart satisfied . . . They are given a meal . . . then the presents are given. Some get a blanket; those that get none are given . . . perhaps a few more trinkets . . . If presents are given them it should be taken to their own country." After a decade of rising expectations, none of the government's Ute policies had been implemented. As they mourned the loss of friends and family, Utes bitterly remembered Calhoun and now Meriwether's empty words.[47]

In another sense, U.S.-Ute relations paralleled the ups and downs of other western Indians, and the hostilities of 1855 and 1849 remain anomalies when juxtaposed with the larger patterns of fragile coexistence developed afterward. For between 1855 and 1868, the majority of Colorado Ute's interactions with American authorities centered not upon conflict, but upon securing access to their mountain homelands. These were the lands upon which several thousand Utes in half a dozen bands had raised their children, and these were the lands that Ute leaders fought to secure.[48]

Surprisingly, the Ute leader who best embodies this period and his people's commitments did not have a Ute father and had not been raised in Colorado. His name was Ouray—the spelling of which included many variations. Born in the early 1830s to a Jicarilla father and Tabeguache mother, Ouray spent much of his youth shepherding for New Mexicans before joining his mother's community in Colorado. A typically hybrid borderlands figure, he spoke at least four languages—Apache, Ute, Spanish, and, later, English—and grew up familiar with the cultural distinctions between the northern Pueblos and their *Hispano* neighbors. He also learned the Plains sign language, the lingua franca of the Indian trade, and well understood the polyglot composition of the Plains. Raised at Abiquiu, Taos, and points in between, Ouray as a teen worked with his brother Quenche as an indentured servant in the household of Taos' famous religious leader, Padre Antonio José Martínez, whose extended family had long-standing relations with the boys' parents. While little portended his rise as a regional and indeed national defender of "Indian" peoples, American presidents would soon welcome and bestow gifts upon the former shepherd from Taos.[49]

Ouray's political career soon became interlaced with that of another famous "New Mexican," Christopher "Kit" Carson. Carson's forty years in the West as a consummate guide, Indian agent, and cavalry leader overshadow his humble beginnings east of the Rockies. Like many former trappers, he married into a prominent *Hispaño* family, settling into a comfortable life of racial, economic, and gender privilege with his wife Josefa Jaramillo in Taos. The outcome of the U.S.-Mexican War catapulted Anglos into political positions, and after a stint at ranching, Carson accepted a job as Indian agent at Taos in December 1853, where he was responsible for handling Muache Ute and Jicarilla relations. His background with equestrian communities positioned him well to guide these bands into the currents of American rule, and except for an interlude during the Civil War Carson spent the rest of his life engaged in Indian affairs. Ouray and other Ute leaders were present with him at nearly every phase of his later career, constantly reminding their western compatriot of their experiences together and, most important, of their commitments to their mountain homelands. More than any other U.S. official, Carson understood these commitments, and his help in securing their reservation in 1868 momentarily heralded the rise of a semiautonomous Ute protectorate in western Colorado.[50]

Viewing the West's many Indian wars, historians often conclude that conflict between equestrian Indians and the U.S. Army was "inevitable," and that "no peaceful persuasion . . . could convince these tribes to give up" their lands in exchange for U.S. dominion. Violence in these narratives becomes the unfortunate and inexorable result of clashing, if not antithetical, difference, a regrettable counterpoint to American expansion. To some extent, such a perspective is useful; but the limitations of such conclusions are serious. For, as the first decade of U.S.-Ute relations reveals, these western Indians remained more than prepared to enter into diplomatic relations with U.S. representatives. They ventured hundreds of miles through inclement weather with hungry family and friends to hear agents instruct them on the virtues of American diplomacy. Ute leaders attempted to rein in renegade warriors, to broker and then to uphold teetering agreements, and to convince their people that American promises were not fleeting. The conflicts that did arise resulted from deep frustrations, and they sparked retaliatory blows that carried violence into the recesses of Ute homelands. Such campaigns targeted not only women and children but also the subsistence resources upon which Ute survival depended. As much as any others, then, Ute leaders held visions of peace and attempted to keep their societies from clashing with American newcomers.[51]

Ouray well understood the region's shifting balance of power. The extent of American power was impressed upon him in a series of seminal moments. A teenager at the time of Kearny's conquest, Ouray witnessed the bloody aftermath, if not the actual Taos Uprising of 1847, which culminated in Taos Pueblo's central plaza. He saw not only the violent repercussions meted out to Pueblo and *Hispano* insurgents but also the strength of the conquering forces. The number of soldiers, the quality of their guns, the size of their cavalry, and the reach of their artillery surpassed anything ever before assembled in the region. He understood moreover that these forces were tied to others that were conducting campaigns in the faraway Mexican capital as well as in California, where Kearny's army headed after Santa Fe. Such power contrasted sharply with the resources of Ute communities, whose subsistence and trading economies were increasingly threatened by the region's changing demographics. Ouray understood that the Utes' ability to continue their mountain ways rested to some degree on their relations with these conquerors. The war and its aftermath may even have influenced his decision in 1850 to forsake New Mexico altogether for his mother's community in Colorado, where following his father's death he inherited and began earning increased social standing.[52]

As agent, Carson for seven years welcomed Indians to Taos. Unlike other Indian agents, he literally worked out of his home and not out of a staffed agency, a fact that he drew much attention; even his efforts to use the funds allocated for his office's "translator" to hire a permanent secretary ran afoul of budget-conscious governors, who reasoned that Carson's oral fluency in many languages did not compensate for his illiteracy. Carson knew the limitations of the power of his office, and biographers often applaud his calm during visits from Indian leaders, who on occasion heaped scorn, threats, and even physical assaults upon the formerly popular trapper and guide. But the primary challenge confronting Carson, and the one to which he devoted the bulk of his time, was the growing twin crises of diminishing resources and escalating raids as American conquest compounded endemic Indian subsistence problems.[53]

Carson attempted to explain these cyclical problems to the rotating cast in the governor's office, emphasizing the need for "prompt and severe punishment" for Indian marauders. Himself unhesitant to use force against Indian peoples, Carson's vision of Indian affairs arose from glaring contradictions. Required to quell Indian raids while procuring resources to alleviate their hardships, he recognized the futility of early Indian policy: the greater the pressures for settlement of Indian lands, the greater the incentive was for Indian raids; the greater the delay in payments of annuities, the greater the likelihood was of Indian thefts; the greater the favoritism in allocating scarce resources to rival Indian groups, the greater the likelihood was of intertribal raids and warfare; the greater the delays in fulfilling treaty provisions, the greater the chances were of raids by hungry bands into the province. This downward spiral fueled the notion, held by Carson and others, that the only solution to Indian conflicts lay in land cessions and, if necessary, violence to impose them. As Superintendent James Collins rhetorically debated in his first annual report: the Utes and Jicarillas "should be removed from the settlements to the waters of the Rio San Juan, and located so as to bring them under one agency . . . It may be asked, will the Indians agree to this arrangement? I believe they will; but whether they agree to it or not, they should be *compelled* to submit to it."[54]

If the events of 1854–55 presaged a dark future, the pressures of the late 1850s cast an even more ominous shadow. The 1855 treaties had not been ratified, and raiding was becoming chronic. As game grew depleted, bands relied on raiding to supplement agency distributions. Some Jicarillas had taken to temporary farming experiments. Others retrieved stolen livestock for New Mexican ranchers. By and large, however, Muache and Jicarilla subsistence economies had ruptured, leaving hungry families to rely on raids, theft, and sporadic annuities. Social ills increased, tied to the gambling and alcohol consumption that often accompanied visits to Taos. Raids increased the likelihood of reprisals from army units, rival Indians, and settlers. "To keep the Indians from committing depredations on citizens," Carson summarized in 1858, "food by the government must be furnished them, and liberally, there being no game of any consequence in the country through which they roam."[55]

After 1855 Carson and others had noted a temporary rapprochement as Muache, Capote, Tabegauche, and Jicarilla leaders attempted to uphold their treaty provisions, to return stolen animals, and to work toward peace. As Collins reported in 1858, 1,200 Jicarillas and Capotes at Abiquiu "seemed to have increased confidence in the friendly purposes of the government . . . The Utahs seemed not only willing but anxious to make peace with all the Indians of the plains . . . provided Agent Carson would accompany them and be present in council." Ute leaders had even welcomed an Arapaho peace delegation in January 1858, receiving them at Fort Massachusetts before leaving together for Taos with hopes of having Carson mediate their historic antagonisms.[56]

The summer events of 1858 and 1859, however, threatened to overwhelm such efforts. Following the discovery of gold along the Front Range in July 1858, masses of white migrants trekked across the eastern Plains to the Rockies. Spurred by the effects of the national Panic of 1857, tens of thousands headed into the region, and by 1860 nearly 40,000 "able bodied men" lived in what was now known as Colorado. The gender imbalance, racial prejudices, and sheer numbers of whites pushed the region's Indians to a precipice of impoverishment and dependency.[57]

Whereas the first decade of U.S.-Ute relations brought a descent from hope into violence, the second witnessed surprising accommodations and cooperation. For the deluge of outside pressures brought by the Colorado gold rush was but one of two continental developments that recast Ute diplomacy in the second decade of American rule. Notwithstanding the burdens unleashed upon their homelands by Colorado miners, Utes saw and took the opportunities created by the American sectional crisis that culminated in the Civil War. The Union Army inflicted horrific defeats upon the Utes' Navajo, Cheyenne, and Arapaho rivals, while the Utes reaped political and economic rewards from serving the Union against both its Confederate and indigenous adversaries. They used the war to pursue their communities' interests, playing off internal white divisions to address both immediate and long-term needs. In 1863 and again in 1868, Ouray and allied Ute leaders traveled to the nation's capital to consolidate these gains, and on both occasions Carson first supported and later joined their delegation. By the second visit the man who was arguably the most famous western American also bore a Union general's title, incontestably adding luster to the Ute mission. By 1868, in short, an emergent confederation of Utes had endured multiple invasions of their homelands, witnessed the emergence of a political territory upon their borders, and served alongside Union soldiers. Such service, hardships, and loyalty brought what they and those who negotiated it believed would be a just solution to their prolonged suffering.[58]

Ten years before the ratification of their historic 1868 treaty, few would have believed it possible for Colorado Utes to reap such diplomatic gains. Colorado was not yet a territory, the Civil War had not begun, and Carson was still the Muache and Tabeguache agent. Though aware of their plight and committed to creating a reservation, Carson, like other officials, believed that small-scale farming, and not mountain hunting, remained their only recourse. "They are, at the present day, as uncivilized as when this government first took them," he reported in 1859, "and it is my opinion they will remain in the same state until they shall be settled on reserves, and compelled to cultivate the soil." Looking to earlier governors' dealings with the Jicarillas, Carson reasoned that similar efforts were needed to "reclaim" Utes "from their barbarous condition." Equating equestrian hunting with both poverty and savagery, he viewed the crisis confronting his charges through prisms of prejudice. He also misunderstood the depth of their rejection of such prescriptions. Unlike the Jicarillas, Utes had shown little inclination to practice agrarianism. On the contrary, they repeatedly expressed their reluctance to combine land cessions with expectant cultivation. These were mountain peoples who subsisted on a combination of hunting and gathering and who opposed treaties calling for a settled, sedentary existence. Access to available hunting grounds was intrinsic to Ute society and went against calls for "confining them to small agricultural districts." Despite his familiarity with their leaders, Carson did not yet grasp this firmly held Ute commandment.[59]

The events of the past year seemed only to confirm Carson's assessments. Hearing from both Indians and whites, Carson in 1859 reported a series of attacks along Colorado's gold rush frontier: "In July last hostilities were commenced by these Indians against the whites who were then entering the Valle Salada [South Park] in search of gold, and many murders, as well as other depredations, were committed by them . . . Nothing has been done . . . to teach them that when they rob and plunder our citizens they should expect a prompt and severe punishment." Expecting greater hostilities and calling for the army to impose order, he saw bloodshed looming; however, Carson had already predicted the aftermath. He assumed a priori that events in Colorado would further deteriorate and necessitate military force. He anticipated that Utes would be defeated and forced onto reservations where they were destined to become farmers. It appeared the single solution to their deepening dilemma, if not imminent destruction. It was only a matter of time before they recognized the inevitable or were "compelled" to do so.[60]

That Utes in Carson's lifetime did not agree to become sedentary cultivators nor were ever forced to do so testifies both to their resolve and to their rapidly changing world. The arrival of thousands of migrants each season brought with it the destruction of Colorado's Plains Indian economies as the gold rush extinguished equestrianism along the corridors to and from the mountains. Indian subsistence as well as many traders' economies collapsed under the weight of this influx. "In scarcely a blink," Elliot West argues, "the new order pushed aside the supporting economy of the plains tribes. The horse nomads were no longer just in trouble. They were irrelevant." Mushrooming settlements like Denver became commercial hubs that linked farms, ranches, and mines while stagecoach and soon railroad lines crisscrossed the region. Utes accustomed to finding game in South Park or along the San Luis retreated deeper into the mountains, while some bartered and begged in towns. Others starved. Many, as Carson wrote, decided to "remain in the vicinity of the agency," both "to prove their good faith" and also simply to receive food. Staying within their agent's jurisdiction provided temporary shelter but did little to solve their problems. These were years of great desperation and even greater loss as hunger bred theft and retribution, death and disease. "The two bands of the Muahuaches and Tobawatches," Carson noted, "are on the decline, and the causes of this decrease in population are disease and frequent conflicts with other warlike tribes." As Indian agent Henry Vaile wrote to Colorado's Governor Gilpin, "Let them remove from the presence of their white brethren, to a region a little further west."[61]

Unlike the torrent of migration to Colorado, the Anglo population in New Mexico rose but did not swell. By 1860, of New Mexico's 93,000 residents 6,300 were white Americans of whom nearly 50 percent were in the military; 3 percent of the territory's population wore U.S. Army uniforms. In contrast to Colorado, where bands of loosely organized men teemed across the prairie, in New Mexico if one saw a white man, he was probably a soldier or a military official. This likelihood only increased during the Civil War, when the events of national disunion marked both Indian and non-Indian peoples.[62]

Even before the war, the costs of supplying and maintaining such a force were enormous, and it is little wonder that governors complained so about their finances. In New Mexico, the vast preponderance of federal funds sustained military affairs, leaving few resources for domestic initiatives. At intermittent war with nearly all of the region's equestrians, the U.S. Army shaped New Mexico in fundamental ways. From the establishment of forts to the rise of military merchants and suppliers, the army, as one scholar argues, "was the single most significant factor in the economic development of the Southwest." The army also determined the region's Indian affairs, and not just through destructive military relations. To an underrecognized extent and in a semi-extralegal manner, military leaders provided opportunities for allied Indian auxiliaries to join campaigns in exchange for guns and ammunition, clothing, and food. As in the Spanish colonial period, such participation stemmed from the exigencies confronting Native communities and not from ideological conformity with U.S. colonialism, though through such joint initiatives Indian leaders acquired political capital.[63]

Utes had expressed intentions of joining army campaigns before. As part of their realization that diplomacy remained the key to survival, Ute leaders recognized that military affairs could be an arena in which they could pursue political goals. They could also exact revenge against rivals. As Superintendent Collins noted in 1858, "a war already exists with the Utahs and Navajos," and despite his intentions to "encourage a spirit of peace" between them, he "consented" to Colonel Benjamin Bonneville's request to "employ about twenty Utahs as guides and spies for the Navajo campaign." Anxious about fueling the wars raging around the province, Collins nonetheless instructed Carson to "assist the colonel in selecting the number required."[64]

Dozens of Ute warriors joined that November's campaign against Navajo encampments outside Fort Defiance. As Frank McNitt has detailed, Ute involvement, "all but ignored in the official reports," brought unintended results. After breaking away from the main column on November 9, a "defection" of a dozen under the Muache leader Kaniache attacked a Navajo *ranchería,* captured a captive and "forty horses and three hundred sheep and goats," and returned to Taos, where they sold their captive to Carson for $300. Carson, using scarce agency funds, "thought it better for [her] to be with me rather than with Mexicans or Utahs." Three hundred dollars, forty horses, 300 sheep, and honor on the battlefield—such were the benefits of riding alongside army soldiers. Although they risked government sanction for pursuing their own gain and glory, Utes took advantage of these opportunities, distributing their rivals' resources to hungry family and friends.[65]

Ute military service accelerated throughout the Civil War as both Indian and Confederate hostilities engulfed the region. Navajo campaigns, in particular, intensified as unfulfilled treaties, U.S. invasions, and Navajo reprisals broadened the conflict. In September 1860, when another Union Army expedition departed for Dinétah, the Navajo homeland, officials more than "consented" to Ute service; the governor even allowed five volunteer companies into the field alongside army regulars. With "500 to 600 Utahs" assembled behind him, Indian agent Albert Pfeiffer rode from Abiquiu to join in, as one merchant wrote, "a protracted war with those Navajos," the outcome of which would be forever seared into the region's history.[66]

U.S. officials attempting to determine the total number of Utes estimated that there were between 4,000 and 8,000 Muaches, Capotes, and Tabeguaches combined. Pfeiffer's expedition possibly also included warriors from more distant Ute communities in Colorado and in Utah. Collins' report the following year, for example, notes for the first time the presence of seven Ute bands in addition to the three originally named. It also includes his frank admission: "I have never been able to obtain satisfactory information in regard to their numbers." With their earlier Navajo assaults emboldening them, Utes had learned the value of joining army campaigns. They shared not only their spoils but also news of their success, and by 1861 Collins' reluctance to allow Utes into the field had vanished; he no longer set limits on the number of Ute participants. Soon, as Confederate forces advanced up the Rio Grande, New Mexico's "enemies" now included more than Indians.[67]

Union Indian allies did not alter or determine the course of the Civil War in New Mexico. As Collins suggested, however, New Mexico was "surrounded" by enemies, and the territory's future remained uncertain. Worry spread through Union ranks, and another agent bluntly reported that Muaches and Jicarillas "possess the balance of power in the Territory of New Mexico." Southern officers stationed at western forts had heeded Jefferson Davis' call to secede. Traders from Missouri and Texas severed supply lines, while many Indians increased their raids, interpreting white divisions as signs of weakness. The outbreak of war challenged an already unstable territorial order, and in the face of such difficulties, the Union's Indian wars temporarily lost immediacy. Following the redeployment of soldiers and the defection of officers, many Indian leaders militarily pursued community needs during the war. For others, white division provided opportunities for entrée into larger political arenas where they too also pursued strategic ends.[68]

Carson's resignation as Indian agent in May 1861 marked an end as well as a beginning in Ute diplomacy. With their annuity distributions relocated from Taos to Maxwell's Ranch on the Cimarron, Muaches now had a new agent to whom to turn. Colorado's territorial formation in 1860 had also created new agents and annuity sites for Tabeguaches and northern Ute bands, and soon the political levers used to facilitate treaty negotiations were pulled from New Mexico as well as from Colorado. Such diplomacy brewed constantly, filling agent reports and Ute meetings with territorial leaders. These local treaty discussions continued into 1861, when Ute leaders arrived in Santa Fe, but they fell momentarily upon unconcerned ears, for in the summer of 1861 New Mexican officials had little time for long-standing Indian tensions. Collins and former Abiquiu agents Pfeiffer and Diego Archuleta were now defending the region from invasion, and when Carson, a Missourian, learned of weakening Union ranks, he offered the Union not only his own services but also "those of the Utes." Heeding their agents' calls, then, Utes confirmed their loyalty to the Union, loyalties that for them carried certain expectations.[69]

Though smaller in scale and in duration than their eastern counterparts, the Civil War's New Mexican campaigns nonetheless critically shaped the national conflict. In 1862 Union victory was far from assured, and with overland links to California, New Mexico maintained strategic value within a potential western Dixie empire. After all, in the 1850s Jefferson Davis as secretary of war had orchestrated the mapping of possible railroad routes to the Pacific and thus knew the West's geography as well as anyone could at second hand. Breaking the Union blockade via a western corridor was a Confederate aspiration, particularly as Texas cotton rotted for lack of export possibilities. The potential for rebellion by the region's majority non-Anglo populations, as 1,500 had in 1847, and for their making common cause with other states'-rights proponents also became very real. Thus, when secessionist forces amassed along the Texas border in 1861, fear spread through Union quarters along the Rio Grande.[70]

In charge of raising New Mexican mounted volunteers, Carson also organized Utes to interdict supply trains, and throughout the summer of 1861 Ute warriors served as Union scouts. Patrolling trails in search of Confederate supplies, on at least five occasions Union commanders ordered Carson to "come on with your Ute Indians . . . to annoy and follow" enemy forces. On August 6, a week after a humiliating defeat outside Fort Stanton, where 500 exhausted Union soldiers had been captured by a force half their size, Edward Canby, New Mexico's leading officer, instructed commanders at Fort Union: "Urge the organization of the Utes as rapidly as possible and if any of them are in the immediate neighborhood of your post ask Col. Carson to send them out as spies and to annoy and cripple the Texans." Renowned for their equestrian capabilities, Ute warriors served with their former agents, who in turn understood the expectations and complexity attending such service. "Col. Carson thinks 100 will be sufficient," one officer reported; however, "he informs me the only terms upon which he can engage them will be to feed their families in their absence."[71]

A sense of urgency filled Union reports that summer, characterized by an abundance of imperative commands. In a territory home to thousands of expert Pueblo and *Hispano* horsemen, that 100 Ute warriors elicited such correspondence while also securing "provisions" for their "service" indicates both Union anxiety and the Utes' comparative power. For all intents and purposes, their purported possession of "the balance of power in the region" arose not simply from military prowess, but also from their demonstrated loyalty. Carson, Pfeiffer, Archuleta, and other territorial leaders had interacted with Utes since the bloody days of 1855. They had welcomed them, helped them secure resources, and tried to explain the agonizing delays in the fulfillment of treaty promises. Ute leaders, in turn, pledged to keep raids to a minimum, to rein in rogue warriors, and to participate in joint campaigns. In return, they expected provisions and eventual political redress. Such was the extent of this mutual recognition that when Union leaders wanted to harass Confederate supply lines, they envisioned Ute horseman. After all, in the excitement of the war's outbreak Carson had conjoined his offer to serve with "those of the Utes," recognizing a well of loyalty upon which he could draw.[72]

Such loyalties only went so far, however, and remained contingent upon food, family, and community. Carson, "authorized . . . to purchase flour and beef for them," understood the economics of Ute service, and in the coming weeks, as they rode hundreds of miles in search of Confederate supply trains, Ute warriors knew their families would not go hungry. Though often foul, army provisions met the needs of Ute lodges camped near Union outposts, as many Ute families had moved south from Colorado. Soon, however, Ute community demands superseded those of the Union, and after only three weeks in the field, one officer reported, "the Ute Indians have all gone home." Notwithstanding Carson's pleas, "nothing would induce them to stay. Sickness in the chief's family is the cause assigned for their departure." Ritual mourning ceremonies, potential leadership council decisions, or even subterfuge possibly underlay the Utes' withdrawal. Succeeded by a new "party of spies and guides" at Fort Union, Utes had nonetheless given their services in the territory's defense and would do so in even greater numbers as the region's most protracted Indian conflicts widened in the coming seasons.[73]

The Tragedy of American Indian Diplomacy

Unlike Colorado Utes, for whom military service became a means to economic and political ends, equestrian Indians throughout adjacent regions suffered immeasurably during the war. After initial unpreparedness, Union mobilization amassed volunteers, resources, and personnel on an unprecedented scale, and more often than not, such efforts spelled disaster for Indians. For, following the Confederate retreat from New Mexico in 1862, the western Union forces shifted their attention to Indian hostilities, and in rapid succession three of the most destructive chapters in western Indian history were written on the perimeters of Ute homelands. To the northwest, in January 1863 Union Army volunteers killed hundreds of Northern Shoshones along the Bear River on the Idaho border. To the southwest, concurrent Navajo campaigns in which Ute, Pueblo, and *Hispano* allies reaped bountiful spoils entered their final stage in 1864 with Carson's scorched-earth campaign at Canyon de Chelly. On the Plains, Black Kettle's band of Cheyennes were targeted by Colorado Union volunteers, culminating in a full-scale massacre at Sand Creek on November 29, 1864. Within this triangle of slaughter, Utes and Jicarilla allies remained the only unconquered equestrians, intermittently allied with Union forces but remaining aloof from the merciless Indian campaigns that dominated the Civil War in the West.[74]

By contrast with their rivals' sufferings, the future for Colorado's Utes appeared hopeful. While facing economic challenges as well as dependency on agency distributions, Utes maintained a distance from the violent turmoil that beset their rivals. They controlled vast lands between distant white settlements and alone determined their seasonal movements. Ute leaders deployed their power to pose both potential aid and potential threat, an astute strategy that demonstrated their sovereignty. Territorial as well as national officials, moreover, hoped that treaties would peacefully resolve outstanding Ute concerns. Echoing the sentiments of his many agents, Commissioner of Indian Affairs William Dole reported in 1863: "Establishing friendly relations with these intelligent, powerful, and warlike Indians . . . cannot be overestimated."[75]

Colorado Utes continued their service to the Union under Carson against Kiowa and Comanche forces at Adobe Walls in November 1864, and by war's end they had survived a violent era of punitive Indian policies pursued by military and civilian leaders in Utah, Colorado, Arizona, and New Mexico. As Robert Utley has detailed, the war contributed to the militarization of Indian policy as many western territories fell under the power of army commanders. Thus the primary proponent of Navajo removal, General James Carleton, arrived in New Mexico in 1862 with a column of California volunteers eager for battle. Having just missed the Confederate withdrawal, they turned instead to Apache and Navajo campaigns.[76]

In Colorado, military initiative was encouraged by civilian leaders eager to take advantage of popular Indian wars. With Utes in the mountains and Cheyenne, Arapaho, and their Lakota allies on the Plains, many of Colorado's white inhabitants rejoiced in the results of the Sand Creek Massacre, glad that Indians who had dared to interdict overland trains or invade white farms had finally felt the fury of white resentment. As Howard Lamar has suggested, the Indian-hating that accompanied Sand Creek stemmed in part from whites' perceptions that their nascent settlements were indeed surrounded by Indians. Furthermore, as Governor John Evans recalled, in Denver, "A great many had left," fueling speculation that the territory's largest "city" was as fleeting as the gold fever that attended its birth, and the transfer of the territorial capital to Colorado Springs had also sunk morale.[77]

Moreover, Colorado's leaders were inexperienced and uncomfortable dealing with Indians, and they often ignored advice from those who knew them best. A doctor from Chicago, territorial governor John Evans before his appointment in 1862 had never interacted with Indians; while Colonel John Chivington, who led the volunteers through the snow to Sand Creek, posted guards at William Bent's ranch on the Arkansas so that no word of his movement would reach Black Kettle's band beforehand, thus scotching any possibility of diplomatic resolution. In contrast to New Mexican authorities, then, Colorado's leaders remained uneasy about their nascent settlements and polity.[78]

Colorado Utes seemingly emerged from the war unscathed and on secure ground. A year after Appomattox, Manuelito and the last Navajo defenders surrendered to U.S. forces while Comanches and their allies waged the last of their unsuccessful military struggles. Furthermore, policymakers debated possible alternatives to Navajo imprison-

ment at Bosque Redondo that included ominous calls for their removal to Indian Territory, in Oklahoma. America's nineteenth-
century preferred catchall solution to the "Indian problem" appeared
headed to the Southwest. As with thousands of Apache, Cheyenne,
and Arapahos, forced displacement to Oklahoma appeared a likely
destiny for many, while Sand Creek signaled an alternate, final solution to Indian conflict. As Evans reminisced: "the benefit to Colorado,
of that massacre, as they call it, was very great, for it ridded the plains
of the Indians, for there was a sentiment that the Indians ought not
to be left in the midst of the community. It relieved us very much of
the roaming tribes of Indians." Dispossession, removal, forced internment, ethnic cleansing—these were the choices U.S. officials made to
deal with Ute rivals. For the moment, Ute fortunes followed a different, more promising path.[79]

A friend of Lincoln whose efforts on behalf of Northwestern University and the surrounding community named in his honor have overshadowed his Indian policies, John Evans presided over successes as
well as bloody failures. Often lost in his biography are his strides in Ute
diplomacy. During his brief and controversial tenure, Utes negotiated
agreements that attempted to resolve long-standing grievances. And,
as in other critical moments in Ute history, Ute diplomatic acumen
became apparent to all. As Evans remarked only weeks before Sand
Creek, "among the wild Indians of this Superintendency . . . there are
none whose general character and intelligence give so much promise
of future improvement as this band [Tabeguache] . . . Among their
chiefs are some of the most astute and intelligent Indians . . . anywhere."[80]

One of the first steps toward "future improvement" was a small one,
almost a vacation. Receiving approval "to send a deputation" of Ute
leaders to Washington in early 1863, Evans reported that this trip impressed upon Ouray and other Ute leaders the futility of military resistance, and upon their return Ouray persuaded a Ute council against
going to war following skirmishes with U.S. forces. Using his experiences from the East to counter call to arms, Ouray reportedly pro-
claimed: "The United States Government had soldiers enough under
arms to surround their entire country . . . and wipe them from the face
of the earth." Encompassing New York City, the Army of the Potomac,
and naval shipyards where "they saw a gun carry a ball five miles," the

journey to Washington increased Ute awareness of the rising power to their east. Ouray also met with the governor's busy benefactor from Springfield, Illinois, receiving a ceremonial cane that he carried during subsequent negotiations. Impressed by Ouray's political and linguistic fluency, Evans went so far as to give "him the salary that was allowed the interpreter . . . [making] him a kind of king among them, for he had some money, and through the influence of that elevation he became the great Ute chief." Now a paid official, Ouray moved to redress the Utes' long-standing concerns, and he, Evans, and Colorado's Indian agents all understood that Ute deliberations had entered a new diplomatic era.[81]

For the Utes, 1863 became a political watershed. Amidst the region's growing Indian wars, Ouray and Tabegauche leaders had restarted the stalled treaty process, negotiating a treaty for themselves with provisions for the Muaches and others to join them. Colorado's territorial formation in 1860 had created new Ute agencies and agents, and the emergence of Ute diplomatic initiatives within Colorado was not surprising. But the rapidity with which Ouray moved was. Negotiating with, among others, Lincoln's personal secretary, John Nicolay, Ouray and a small group of Ute leaders met at the Conejos Agency in southern Colorado and agreed to land cessions in what Commissioner Dole soon called "among the largest and most valuable tracts of land ever ceded to the United States"—no small feat in the history of Indian affairs. In return, Ouray's Tabegauches secured a reservation in the Gunnison Valley in addition to generous annuities. Though extinguishing Ute claims to New Mexico, the Front Range, and the San Luis Valley, the October 1863 treaty set in motion the creation of reservation lands in Colorado's mountain valleys, and it received congressional ratification in 1864.[82]

As in 1849 and 1855, implementation of the treaty stalled. Muache, Capote, Weenuche, and Uintah and Grand River bands, whose communities claimed portions of the ceded lands, had not been fully consulted. Concerned that the Tabeguache leader was orchestrating efforts without requisite counsel with elder statesmen, many Ute leaders did not recognize Ouray's "elevation" as a leader for bands other than his own. As New Mexican governor William Arny noted about the Ute delegation to Washington, "to take men who are not of influence either with our Indians or those in Colorado will . . . be of no benefit."

Unlike in 1849 and 1855, however, renewed negotiations soon followed as less enthusiastic leaders were incorporated into the diplomatic fold. Such incorporation, however, did not proceed easily. Attempts to resettle Muaches and their Jicarilla allies in Colorado encountered resistance, as did Evans' and others' suggestions that a single Ute reservation in the San Juan Valley would be sufficient for all Colorado Utes, whose combined range still extended from New Mexico through all of western Colorado.[83]

Muache leader Kaniache, a signatory of the 1849 treaty, presented the biggest obstacle to Ouray's efforts to secure a common Ute reservation. He and his followers did not attend the Conejos conference, instead remaining in New Mexico, where they had attached themselves to Union forces. They chose not to participate in the negotiations to their north, and they suffered for it. In early 1864 Commissioner Dole, anticipating the creation of a single reservation, transferred the Muache agency to Denver and combined it with the agency responsible for their Tabeguache kinsmen, who outnumbered them by four to one. Some Muaches had joined Ouray at Conejos, but most had remained in New Mexico, where army rations and remaining game sufficed for their needs. They also continued to help themselves to the region's growing livestock herds; according to one angry resident, "while *nominally* at peace they commit crimes and outrages of every kind with entire impunity, because there is *no law* which can reach them." Though remaining in familiar homelands, Kaniache's band found itself in a new political landscape; they remained outside the protection of their own agency while remaining dependent upon scarce resources. Having left Taos in 1861 for the Cimarron, they now heard that their agency had been transferred 300 miles away to Denver with the expectation that they would soon relocate to a reservation they had not agreed to. Such confusion bred unrest and nearly brought these Union allies to war.[84]

In August 1866, after Kaniache's son requested sheep from a *Hispano* herder, a fight ensued, leaving the Ute dead. Coming on the heels of rampant Ute sheep thefts and previous altercations, this killing threatened to explode into regional violence. While the elder Ute leader attempted to navigate the crisis, his sons, desperate to avenge their brother's death, did not. As the perpetrator hurried to Fort Union for protection, he ironically ran into the cavalry unit with whom Kaniache and his sons had just served. Unheeded Ute calls to turn over the killer created such an imbroglio that the matter was turned over to a grand jury in Mora that could not resolve the dispute. Not until New Mexico's superintendent of Indian affairs agreed to pay $400 to the brothers did tensions subside, but only briefly, as Muaches now felt more entitled to the region's livestock. In October, cavalry soldiers under A. J. Alexander "hastily" chased the band into the mountains, and only the arrival of Carson, Ouray's band, and subsequent diplomatic initiatives averted Carson's prediction that "this is bound to result in a general war with all the Utes," particularly if the cavalry mistook the arriving Tabeguaches for Muache allies, as he had feared. Convincing officials that he not only remained committed to peace but could also help resolve the tensions, Ouray led deliberations among 1,000 Utes encamped outside Fort Garland, which Carson, now an honorary general, commanded.[85]

Within such disputes lay the causes of as well as potential solutions to the Utes' dilemma. For, notwithstanding the Muaches' entitlement to livestock, Utes in New Mexico had become few and far between, having suffered irreversible demographic and subsistence declines. In 1868, only 881 Capote and Weenuche Utes were enumerated by Abiquiu's agent, who wrote: "their number has heretofore been overestimated." Although they had not borne the brunt of American campaigns, New Mexican Utes suffered with the war's end. Both their opportunities for service and their raiding economies declined. With many enemies exiled, their chances for captive, livestock, and horse seizures decreased, and they shifted to raiding against New Mexicans, whose protection the army attempted to assure. While forts still provided rations, an obvious truth was dawning: equestrianism had entered its twilight, leaving in its dim glow an impoverished and desperate people. As one official bemoaned their plight: "What am I to do? What is the cheapest food to give them? Write me immediately," he urged federal officials, "and tell me what to do. I'm lost."[86]

Securing legal protection became, then, a necessary step of survival, one that even the most militant Ute leaders came to understand. Unable to live outside the political and economic parameters established around them, Ute leaders moved to clarify their political status in order to secure territory and resources. For these unconquered and undefeated peoples, such legalities involved far more than marks on papers. They became avenues toward a more hopeful future, and, not-withstanding the poverty and disempowerment that soon beset Amer-ica's Indian reservations, many Utes had shown aptitude in shifting their economies away from equestrianism. They were becoming not farmers but ranchers. Many had taken to raising sheep. Ouray had several thousand and employed a Mexican herder. Indeed, as Evans later remembered, Ouray "became quite wealthy and he built him a fine house over near Ouray, the town named after him." Both territo-rial and Ute leaders thus recognized the economic potential of pas-toralism. "When I distributed to them individual sheep and cattle and horses," Evans continued, "I found that they were pleased with the idea wonderfully; that it was better than sugar and flour and blankets." As territorial governor Alexander Hunt later remarked, "I have no doubt that these people will in time . . . become a great stock-growing nation." As the Tabeguache example portended, securing territorial agreements remained an obvious step toward a more stable future. So too, however, was the necessity of transforming Ute economies.[87]

Multiple leaders like Kaniache had not agreed to the 1863 treaty, and Colorado's annuities became less frequent as Cheyenne-Lakota hostilities flared after Sand Creek. But despite tensions in New Mexico as well as sporadic Grand River and Uintah raids against overland stagecoaches in northern Colorado, it remained clear that most Ute bands were committed to peace. Equally important, agents and of-ficials recognized how rare and fragile such prospects remained, filling their reports with mounting urgency. Pleading in 1865, for example, for the annuities outlined in the Conejos treaty, Agent Lafayette Head related: "Although they have been grossly neglected by the govern-ment . . . [and] not one dollar of said promised annuities has yet been paid to them . . . their faith is not shaken in the least." He also worried, however, that reprisals for livestock thefts might prompt his charges to "follow their usual course of revenge." Such "faith," then, became strained under the pressures of white settlement, resource de-struction, and inconsistent annuity distribution. Yet the faith, and the peace, endured.[88]

Ute faith in diplomacy seemingly again reached fruition in 1868, when Ouray and a delegation of Ute leaders headed to Washington ac-companied by Head, Carson, and Colorado governor Hunt. Boarding a stagecoach to Cheyenne, where Union Pacific lines took them east,

Photograph of Chief Ouray (center, far-right panel) and the Ute delegation in Washington, 1868. Courtesy of the Colorado Historical Society, Denver (negative no. F-7809). Leading a group of Ute and other dignitaries to the nation's capital for the second time, through his determined diplomacy Ouray helped to achieve the March 1868 Ute Treaty, which created an immense reservation homeland for Colorado and remaining New Mexican Utes. The Utes' famous retired Indian agent, Christopher "Kit" Carson, accompanied Ouray but was unable to attend the negotiations because of illness. His death three months later would deprive Colorado's Utes of a trusted ally and advocate.

Utes again toured the White House. They attended the circus in New York and the ballet in Boston, where they were also received by a session of the Massachusetts legislature, and even felt the mist at Niagara Falls. These "Indians in unexpected places" were exceptional not only among Native peoples, but among Americans of any ilk. Whether he realized it or not, Ouray was one of few New Mexicans ever to have toured the East with such pomp and circumstance, and he would return again, twice, for further negotiations. After 1868, however, much would change. The studio photographs, fine meals, and clothes remained, but the shared commitments to diplomacy soon evaporated from the Colorado Territory.[89]

The 1868 Ute delegation is best known not for the momentous treaty, signed on March 2 in the Washington House Hotel, which created a reservation of fifteen million acres across western Colorado nor for the festivities honoring Ute leaders. Indians arrived in Washington every season, and the complicated diplomacy attending each of their visits was far too much for eastern audiences to follow. The most exciting aspect of the Utes' visit was the presence of their former agent in the delegation. Carson was one of the most famous Americans of his day, enjoying almost mythic status. More than twenty years had passed since he had last visited Washington, and the decommissioned brigadier general, now very ill, accepted Hunt's invitation to assist in the negotiations while seeking medical treatment. He succeeded in the former, but during his stay Carson's condition worsened, and the fifty-nine-year-old was confined to the hotel room that he shared with Ute leaders, including most likely Ouray.[90]

Carson's illness precipitated an early return to Colorado, where the family had recently relocated. Josepha was expecting their eighth child, and upon his return their family experienced two devastating blows. Josepha, who in her last trimester had hurried over rutted roads to receive her ill husband, died after the April birth of their daughter, and Carson's worsening aneurysm burst at Fort Lyon in May. Initially buried alongside each other in Boggsville, Colorado, they were re-interred the following year behind their home in Taos, while their orphaned children went to live with Josepha's family.[91]

Scenes of the Carsons' deaths, laden with understandable sadness and remorse, fill accounts of Colorado and New Mexican history. Seemingly signaling the end of an era, their lives evoke empathy as well as contemplation; both biographies appear to encapsulate much of the nineteenth-century West, with its legacies of individualism, conquest, and adaptation. Often lost in such accounts are the two Indian groups most affected by Carson's career, the Utes and the Navajos. For them, the year of his death proved to be a watershed.[92]

For the Utes, 1868 brought the loss of an experienced, trusted, and powerful ally whose support would be missed in the coming decade. Lacking employment, Carson had expressed interest in Colorado's Superintendency of Indian Affairs, while Hunt also considered him for agent at one of the two agencies to be created upon the treaty's ratification. His death, then, ended his expected service in Colorado's Indian affairs. Although his illiteracy would have ruined his chances for superintendent, as agent his influence over the treaty's enforcement would have been enormous. Indeed, he might have been able to prevent the tragedy that soon beset his closest and primary Indian allies.[93]

Enforcement of the treaty's provisions became, as always, an issue of contention. Utes felt frustration over the delayed arrival of livestock and other distributions; territorial leaders felt anxiety about the feasibility of settling seven different bands together on a single reservation. But the size of the new reservation soon assuaged such concerns. With two distant agencies, one in southern and the other in northwestern Colorado, the Utes' designated homeland extended more than 200 miles north of the New Mexican border and 100 miles east of the Utah border, forming an immense rectangle. Except for a 50-mile corridor between Wyoming and the reservation's northern border, all of western Colorado fell within reservation boundaries. This was to be the indisputable and federally protected home for Colorado and New Mexican Utes, as the latter had reluctantly agreed to cede their lands. As a result of recent treaties achieved with Plains Indians, Colorado's Indian affairs seemed to have reached resolution. Peaceful, pastoral, and seasonal Ute hunters in the mountains with Plains Indians elsewhere—this formula now defined Colorado, leaving the mineral- and soil-rich middle and eastern thirds of the state open for mining, ranching, farming, and settlement. The western third remained the Utes' recognized domain.[94]

For the Utes' Navajo rivals, 1868 also became a pivotal year. The misery, death, and disease at Bosque Redondo ended with a treaty establishing reservation homelands within the area bounded by the Four Sacred Mountains that traditionally demarcated Dinétah. The treaty was signed on June 1 and ratified on July 25, the same day as the Ute treaty. The Navajo observe June 1 as Treaty Day, making it an occasion both for remembrance of their imprisonment and for celebration of their renewal and perseverance. Further land agreements in the nineteenth century added more territory, eventually creating the largest Indian reservation within America's borders. As Peter Iverson notes, Treaty Day has become "as important in its own way as July 4, 1776, be-

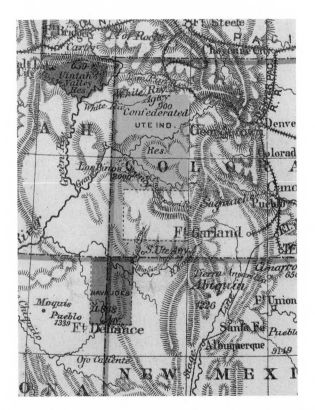

Map Showing Indian Reservations in the United States and Number of Indians Belonging Thereto. Lithograph in Annual Report of the Commissioner of Indian Affairs (Washington, D.C.: Office of Commissioner of Indian Affairs, 1879). Wisconsin Historical Society, image no. WHi-37716.

came to Americans." Their treaty, reservation, and homeland secured, the Navajos faced an arduous but hopeful return and readjustment to Dinétah.[95]

As late as 1879, federal publications included maps of the adjoining Navajo and Ute reservations, the latter dwarfing the former. However, just as their experiences as Union allies contrasted with those of the resistant Navajo, so too did Ute fortunes after 1868. There would be no permanent and extensive Ute reservation in western Colorado. Despite their service to the U.S. government, their commitments to peace, and their intelligent diplomacy, Ute families would not remain and flourish along the Western Slope; there would be no annual treaty day celebrations on March 2. Beginning five years after the treaty's ratification, a series of land seizures and abrogated treaty agreements rapidly diminished the Utes' once vast reservation homeland. Ultimately, Colorado Utes succumbed to waves of dispossession initiated in 1880.[96]

In 1873 the Brunot Agreement extracted four million acres from the southern parts of the reservation, establishing both a precedent and the mechanisms for taking the rest. Bands attached to the southern agency were forced onto a sliver of their former territory, while in 1879 and 1880 hostilities along the White River at the reservation's northern agency erupted into a larger conflict that turned deadly and was used by territorial leaders to justify abrogating the 1868 treaty. Mineral, ranching, and corporate interests soon combined with public sentiment to undermine Indian land claims, while bribery, alcohol, and intimidation facilitated Ute compliance. In 1881 Northern Ute bands, including Ouray's, were marched at gunpoint across the Green River into Utah to join other dispossessed Utes on the Uintah-Ouray Reservation. Ouray did not live to witness his people's permanent exile, though his wife Chipeta lived for another forty years in Utah.[97]

Unlike the massive loss of reservation lands that accompanied America's assimilation programs of the 1880s, the dispossession of Colorado's Utes did not include beneficent claims of "civilization's" uplifting capabilities. Rather, this removal, like that of Colorado's Plains Indians, revealed the triumphant capacity of white supremacy to eradicate forms of difference as the Indian-hating that had accompanied Sand Creek again fueled onslaughts against the territory's remaining Native people.

Historical geographer D. W. Meinig has compared the process of Indian removal east of the Mississippi to a giant bulldozer pushing Native peoples west. Western historians often relate the opening phases of American expansion across the continent as a pronged process, revealing how landmark treaties emptied the central Plains of Indians, driving equestrian communities both north and south while opening corridors across the land. Such narratives often end at the Rockies, implying that the waves of removal that swept across the Plains failed to subsume Navajo, Pueblo, and Apache nations, whose continued presence in the region represents a triumph of indigenous endurance as well as a failure of Manifest Destiny.[98]

The nineteenth-century history of Utes in New Mexico and Colorado belies such imagery and suggestion. Through compromise and accommodation with representatives of the American government, Colorado Utes achieved mutually agreed-upon constitutional protections. In the first three quarters of the nineteenth century, they withstood unrelenting pressures and positioned themselves to secure what they as well as American officials wanted, or at least were willing to provide: peace, land, and provisions. Despite sporadic hostilities, they remained committed to diplomatic recourse. Indeed, they continued into the U.S. period forms of adaptation initiated during the Spanish colonial era. In such perspective, their 1868 treaty represents the culmination of nearly two centuries of diplomacy. It is not happenstance that their most accomplished statesman personified such cultural and diplomatic connections. Ouray's and the Utes' ultimate tragedy, then, marks more than the passing of an era. It signals the final stages of resolute and successful indigenous struggles to withstand the turbulent currents engulfing their mountain communities. The bulldozer of American removal hit the Rockies hard, and it kept moving, scaling the nation's tallest peaks and descending into mountain valleys in search of the next Native community to uproot. The obstacles in its path were not just geographic, but also legal, political, and above all historical. Confronting Indians who had secured from national leaders multiple protections, the ravages of dispossession subsumed the most unlikely of communities.

✦ ✦ ✦

SEVEN

Utah's Indians and the
Crisis of Mormon Settlement

As a result of its war against Mexico, the American republic acquired the northern half of its southern neighbor's territory, including all of the Intermountain West south of the 42nd parallel. Before the war, the lands between the Rockies and Sierras, though officially claimed by Mexico, were outside the direct control of the Mexican state, and by war's end, aside from a sliver of Mormon settlement along the Utah Lake Valley, they remained Indian homelands. More specifically, as James Calhoun reported in March 1850, the territory "is called the Utah country," encompassing "all west of the Rio del Norte . . . to the very foot of the Sierra Nevada, and between the Navajo Country and the Great Salt Lake." Two great geographic axes running north–south between Salt Lake and Dinétah and east–west between the Rio Grande and the Sierras defined a massive region, first classified in 1844 by Frémont as a "Great Interior Basin," and by 1850 known by the familiar New Mexican appellation for the region's leading Indian people, "Yutas," or in English, Utahs.[1]

Calhoun, like earlier trappers and subsequent leaders, recognized Ute supremacy in the eastern half of the territory, and he differentiated between the region's "great tribes" and its lesser ones. "Great tribes" had horses, diplomats, and resources; lesser ones did not. So, while virtually all the Indians within this new national appendage spoke related Shoshone dialects, with some maintaining common territories and economies, important distinctions remained, and as the United States incorporated "Utah country" into its political sphere, such distinctions troubled federal and territorial officials. For what could be done with those smaller Indian communities who subsisted primarily on gathering and fell into conflict with the "great tribes" as well as with aggressive traders, migrants, and settlers? How best to handle these seemingly scattered groups who lacked horses, substantial numbers of warriors, or easily recognizable villages and territories? And how could federal Indian policy be implemented in lands so distant from centers of governance? Calhoun thought he knew the answers and offered Commissioner of Indian Affairs Orlando Brown the following suggestion:

> Let me remark, that the Pah Utahs, who inhabit the country east of the Sierra Nevada, are Utahs proper; benumbed by cold, and enfeebled . . . by the food upon which they subsist; it consisting only of roots, vermin, insects of all kinds, and everything that creeps, crawls, swims, flies, or bounds, they may chance to overtake; and when these resources fail them, and they can find no stranger, they feed upon their own children. Such a people should not be permitted to live within the limits of the United States, and must be elevated in the scale of human existence, or exterminated.

Taking pains to contrast these feeble, infanticidal cannibals with their "more adventurous and warlike brethren," Calhoun countered claims that might jeopardize ratification of his recently concluded negotiations at Abiquiu with leaders from the "great" Utah.[2]

"East of the Sierras" to the borders of Ute territories lay the "Pah Utahs," or Paiutes, "Piedes," and "diggers," generic designations for predominantly Northern and Southern Paiute as well as Western Shoshone bands; and throughout the turbulent decades of American conquest of the Intermountain West, many heeded Calhoun's calls for extermination. Either episodically or through state-sanctioned campaigns, these Indian peoples endured onslaughts into their homelands that indiscriminately targeted men, women, and children. Migrants on their way to California and Oregon often targeted *any* approaching Indians, while fur traders, Mormon legions, and U.S. Army forces more systematically deployed violence against these as well as the region's equestrians. In one of the earliest recorded incidents of such violence, Zenas Leonard recounted what happened to his trapping party of sixty under Joseph Walker's direction along the

Humboldt River in eastern Nevada in 1833. After some of Walker's men had killed Western Shoshone scouts, prompting pursuit from neighboring bands, Walker "gave his consent to chastise these Indians." Subsequently "32 of us mounted and surrounded this party of Indians . . . and fired, leaving thirty-nine dead on the field . . . Capt. Walker then gave orders to . . . put the wounded out of misery." While Leonard acknowledged that "the severity with which we dealt with these Indians may be revolting to the heart of the philanthropist," he went on to conclude: "These Indians . . . are generally small and weak." They lacked not only horses but also guns. "Small," "weak," and comparatively weaponless Indians confronting well-armed scores of mobile horsemen—such encounters encapsulate the comparative disadvantages facing these nonequestrians.[3]

Unbeknownst to Calhoun, Leonard, and those perpetrating these acts, such violence occurred within, and thus exacerbated, a larger constellation of colonial traumas. By 1833, as Leonard also noted, equestrian Shoshones in the northern Great Basin had been "almost annihilated" by gun-possessing Blackfeet raiders, while those Shoshones without horses "keep in the most retired recesses of the mountains and streams . . . living the most like animals of any race of beings." Before U.S. acquisition, then, equestrian Great Basin Indians in the region's northern and eastern portions and nonequestrians in the central, southern, and western parts endured waves of disruptions and cycles of violence from the New Mexican slave trade and Great Basin fur trade. Before U.S. territorial expansion colonial disruptions had already saturated the region.[4]

Such disruption particularly affected nonequestrian societies. From the south, New Mexican slavers came in search of women and children, while shortly thereafter British and American fur traders scrambled for the West's remaining furs. Such expansion disrupted families as well as ecologies, and subsequent American exploration and migratory routes entered not untouched lands, but disrupted ones. Calhoun, Leonard, and others' racist classifications of Great Basin nonequestrians as the "wretchedest type of mankind" mistook such existing trauma. Such assessments equated Indian impoverishment with humanity, thus often denying it. Within American racial hierarchies, materially poor Indians enjoyed little regard; as late as the 1940s prominent historians casually referred to these Native peoples as "red niggurs."[5]

Calhoun's appeals to "elevate or exterminate" Paiutes stemmed from immediate concerns. Though mistaken that the Ute signatories to his 1849 treaty would soon find secured homelands, Calhoun well understood the hazards accompanying Indian-white encounters outside the purview of state officials. He knew that white migration and settlement necessitated supervision, and his worries reflected a sobering realization. The Southwest's "four great tribes"—Utes, Comanches, Apaches, and Navajos—had long interacted with imperial envoys, and incorporating these Native powers into the U.S. dominion proceeded in accordance with preexisting diplomatic mechanisms: negotiations, treaties, land cessions, annuities, reservations, and agencies. When such initiatives failed, military force was deployed, either eradicating the troublesome Natives or reincorporating them into the framework of diplomacy. No such mechanisms existed, however, for dealing with nonequestrians. Migratory bands that "[kept] in the most retired recesses of the mountains" and lived in family and not confederated units defied political classifications. Lacking horses and guns, moreover, they remained less capable of seeking out the few authorities responsible for their "protection" and were also far more vulnerable to state use of violence. Nonequestrians did not visit the White House. Often retreating from the presence of white migrants, many Paiutes and Shoshones lived essentially beyond the scope of federal Indian policy, and notwithstanding Calhoun's urgency, no state fiat could "elevate" these desert peoples to a more convenient political status. On the margins of Calhoun's superintendency in lands still largely uncharted, "Of the Indians in Utah," Commissioner of Indian Affairs Luke Lea reported in November 1850, "we know but little."[6]

In contrast to their equestrian neighbors, then, nonequestrian societies in Utah (which until 1861 included Nevada) remained far more vulnerable to the onslaught of U.S. expansion. Many had heard of and interacted with members from these foreign worlds. Some, as Lewis and Clark learned, had stolen goods from equestrian travelers south of the Snake River, while others, as Leonard chronicled, bore the brunt of trappers' ire. Along the region's fertile waterways, Northern Paiutes in western Nevada and Timpanagos Utes in central Utah had developed successful fisheries at Pyramid Lake and Utah Lake, respectively, as well as trading economies; the former had traded with California Indian peoples, the latter with trappers in the eastern Great Basin. Still, none were prepared for the waves of migration and settler invasion during the 1840s and 1850s. Tens of thousands of outsiders and their herds traveled across these Indian homelands, wreaking incalculable social and ecological havoc. Having reached Oregon and California, many of these migrants were soon lured back into the region to work the growing number of mines. By 1864 much of the region would become another state in the Union.[7]

Astride the region's central corridor along Utah's Wasatch Front, Great Basin equestrians faced related ordeals. Beginning in the late 1840s, Utah's Ute and equestrian Shoshones had to contend not only with migrants but also with Mormon settlers seeking lands outside the American republic to await a celestial "gathering." Although Indian peoples enjoyed limited degrees of peaceful coexistence with the Latter-day Saints, Mormon-Indian conflicts erupted from the initial years of settlement in the late 1840s, becoming full-scale military campaigns in the 1850s. Combined with the Mormons' own struggles with the federal government, Utah's Indian wars were unique in that the settlers themselves became the initial agents of violence, followed by the U.S. Army. Whereas federal officials usually handled the messy process of Indian dispossession in the West, in Utah Mormon settlers challenged Native equestrians for control of the fertile portions of central Utah. Within one generation, equestrians lost control of their former territories and any role in shaping the region's future. The treaties that created many of the region's Indian reservations came on the heels of military campaigns and even massacres. Indeed, some of the most devastating Indian conflicts in western history occurred within the violent processes of state formation in the central Great Basin, as the January 1863 Bear River Massacre most clearly reveals.[8]

Utah's nonequestrian Indian experiences offer useful contrasts as well as parallels to the state's larger Indian wars. Influenced by the relations of enslavement that pervaded the Great Basin before U.S. expansion, Southern Paiute communities viewed Mormon settlements differently from their equestrian neighbors. For many, Mormons brought a reprieve from Ute dominion, and Paiute bands often allied themselves with Mormons in the region's conflicts. As the issue of Indian slavery became a primary source of tensions between Brigham Young and Ute leaders, who struggled to comprehend why these white newcomers forbade the familiar traffic in captives, many Paiute bands were drawn to Mormon settlements for protection. Unlike the fur trappers and New Mexicans of the previous half-century, these religious émigrés recoiled at the brutality of Indian slave trafficking. Generally viewing Paiutes, both young and old, as unredeemed children, Mormons initiated a series of household adoption programs that brought hundreds into the church as spiritual and figurative kin. Such paternalism, however, often bred its own forms of violence. When Paiutes attempted to gain opportunities within as well as outside Mormon society, the Saints attempted to control their movements. As in the case of other Basin Indians, Paiute efforts to gain autonomous spaces within settler society centered upon economics, and securing territories and resources to rebuild their communities became primary strategies of survival throughout the nineteenth century. With varying success, their struggles on the margins of Mormon society continued into the atomic age.[9]

The following pages survey the violent processes of American expansion in the central Great Basin in two crucial zones: the encounter between Utah's Utes and Mormon settlers, and the divergent paths followed by equestrian Shoshones in and around Utah. The first ends in Ute dispossession, and the other ends with the massacre of Northern Shoshones. In both cases the outcome arose from diminished resources for Great Basin Indians, prompting the use of violence.[10]

Mormon Settlement and Ute Reprisals

U.S. exploration west of the Rockies mushroomed after the Mexican-American War as vast territories came under the dominion of the United States. As the northern paths across the Rockies initiated by Lewis and Clark and Astoria-based traders gave way to central overland routes opened by fur traders, the Rocky Mountain fur trade brought growing access to the interior West. Even after the decline of the fur trade, the imperial utility of mountain trappers persisted, particularly as topographical expeditions streamed west, linking the Pacific Coast with the rest of the nation. As Robert Utley suggests, the role of Kit Carson, Jim Bridger, and other former trappers in facilitating the geographic consolidation of the West remains a critical aspect of their leg-acies.[11]

Antoine Leroux was like Carson in many ways. He lived in Taos, spoke Ute from his years in the mountains, and was also in demand by western explorers. In 1853, as Secretary of War Jefferson Davis orches-trated efforts to "lay before Congress printed reports of . . . the most practicable and economical route for a railroad from the Mississippi River to the Pacific Ocean," Leroux found employment in two of Da-vis' campaigns, the first headed by John W. Gunnison, the second by A. W. Whipple. Charged with crossing the central Rockies in search of potential railway routes, Gunnison moved west from Colorado's San Luis Valley, while Whipple followed a southern route across Arizona. Upon reaching Fort Massachusetts in August 1853, Gunnison realized the futility of traveling farther without guides, and, sending a search party to Taos, he turned to "that useful class of mountaineers who have spent many years . . . encountering the hardships and imminent dan-gers . . . in these fields of savage barbarity, short-lived gratitude and na-tive grandeur."[12]

Davis' choice of Gunnison to lead the central overland campaign came at the expense of John Frémont, whose failed fourth expedition had attempted a similar crossing; the nation's growing tensions over how best to integrate these western lands now shaped the selection of those leading these journeys of exploration. But it proved fortu-nate for both Frémont and Leroux that they were not with Gunnison on October 26, 1853. Leroux, who had guided Gunnison across the Rockies, had returned to New Mexico to await Whipple's arrival, while Frémont organized his fifth expedition before returning east for a campaign of a different kind, for president in 1856. At daybreak on October 26, Gunnison and several in his expedition lost their lives to suspected Pahvant Paiute raiders west of Utah's Sevier Lake. Gunni-son's subcommander E. G. Beckwith took command; others tried in vain to track the assailants. Unable to retrieve their lost comrades, the expedition retreated north to Salt Lake City to report its shocking news to Davis.[13]

Gunnison's death came at the end of two months of arduous travel that had bisected Ute territories in Colorado and Utah. From encamp-ment at Fort Massachusetts, the party left behind known peoples and places and headed west into the less inviting and less familiar territories of the eastern Great Basin. In the San Juan Mountains, where Frémont had met winter disaster during his fourth expedition, Gunnison navigated physical and cultural landscapes, gaining detailed knowledge of the region's labyrinth of valleys, passes, and basins. Upon reaching central Utah with its string of settlements known as the Mormon Corridor, Gunnison believed he had reentered hospitable lands.

Author of a sympathetic 1852 "treatise on the faith and condition of the Mormons," Gunnison understood that his mission in Utah was topographic, not military. Although he embodied federal authority in the nascent Mormon Kingdom, Gunnison anticipated little hostility from its settlers, many of whom he had previous interviewed. Nor did he fear the territory's Indians, whose "subjugation" he had also studied. In his 1852 work, for example, he had recounted the spread of epidemics to Utes and Shoshones as well as a series of "chastisement[s]" meted out to each, contrasting the violent swiftness of Mormon-Indian conflict with the federal government's protracted, costly wars against the Seminole. "Had public sentiment sanctioned a similar policy with the Seminoles," he concluded, "what sacrifices of blood and treasure would have been avoided!"[14]

The Mormons' use of force to establish political rule appeared to Gunnison a legitimate and necessary act of state formation. However, he found those involved in such violence hesitant to take ownership of their actions. One of his Mormon informants, who had participated in the 1850 winter campaign against the Timpanagos Utes, for example, "seemed disposed to paint it in as soft colors as possible." For Gunnison, such soft colors could not hide the obvious: Mormon settlement necessitated conflict with the region's Indians: the swifter the "sacrifices of blood and treasure," the better. As he described it, the Timpanagos were "induced to come down and surrender." When they were "ordered to give up their weapons . . . [and] refused . . . [they] were fired upon and nearly all killed immediately. A few broke through the line of sentinels . . . and were chased down by horsemen and 'ceased to breathe.'" For Gunnison, violence naturally and justly ordered this new settler society as Mormons and Indians competed for survival along this distant margin of the nation.[15]

Mormon and white settler supremacy, however, were not assured in 1853. Far from reaching a region of subjugated indigenous peoples,

Gunnison in fact entered violent and undetermined lands. On October 1, near the Colorado-Utah border, he heard Utes boast of raids against Mormon settlements. Once in Utah, he witnessed the sufferings of Mormon settlers at Manti City, but then failed to heed the warnings of those at Fillmore, choosing, for example, to camp along valley waterways rather than in elevated, defensive locations, as recommended. Even on the morning of his death, cautionary notices appeared in the Mormons' *Journal History* about a reckless emigrant party disturbing the region's settler-Indian relations. As Fillmore's bishop, Anson Call, reported:

> They came into Fillmore much excited in consequence of the Indians. They stated they had been shot at the night before. I informed the captain that the Indians hereabouts were friendly, although we kept a close guard, and it would be well for him to do the same. Inasmuch as he was fired upon I presumed it was Walker's Indians. He said he knew no difference in Indians and that the one that came into his camp, he swore, should die. I told him the practice of the Indians was to visit the camps for the purpose of begging and trading and that they would be sure to visit their camp. I tried to prevail on him not to molest them, but he and his men appeared very reckless in regard to Indian rights.[16]

Ultimately, Call failed to persuade either group's captain. Despite his accurate prediction that Paiute traders would approach them, when the emigrants did receive local Paiutes, they ordered them to disarm and when they refused opened fire, killing and wounding several. Retreating, the band's leaders vowed revenge, especially Moshoquop, whose father had been killed. Similar violence soon cost Gunnison his life.[17]

Throughout the Corridor, Mormon leaders like Call knew resident Indians like Moshoquop by name and grasped the violent complexities attending white settlement in the region. Paiute "begging and trading," for example, arose from mounting economic pressures that in turn helped to sustain "friendly" relations with Mormon providers. When Gunnison visited Call, whom he already knew, he heard warnings not only about Walkara's Utes, "who have killed several of the citizens, destroyed their mills, and driven off some of their stock," but also about Moshoquop's aggrieved band. Gunnison assured Call that he too knew Moshoquop, as well as Kanosh, the area's primary Paiute leader, as "firm friends," and continued to scout ahead, unconcerned about the volatile social landscape through which he traveled.[18]

Upon Gunnison's death, the region's Ute, Paiute, as well as Mormon leaders attempted to exonerate themselves, doing so for different though parallel reasons. Only six years had passed since Brigham Young first laid eyes upon the region, and a series of Indian raids had beleaguered settlements up and down the Mormon Corridor. However, Mormon leaders feared the power of the U.S. government more than they feared Indians, choosing instead to pursue their own methods of "subjugation." Some federal officials even suspected that Gunnison's death had Mormon fingerprints on it. The 1860 reprint edition of Gunnison's treatise, for example, includes an inflammatory letter to his widow from Judge W. W. Drummond, who worked in Utah during the trial of eight Indian suspects, including Kanosh. According to Drummond, despite "clear and conclusive" evidence, "the Mormon jury . . . found a verdict of not guilty"; three were convicted of manslaughter, with Kanosh and the rest acquitted. Drummond, who believed the deaths to be "a deep and maturely laid plan to murder the whole party of engineers," concluded his letter with the hope that Gunnison's widow would "see the day when the foul stain of Mormon oppression and tyranny shall be effectually checked in this our happy country, [and] your husband's untimely death vindicated by the courts and laws of this land." Soon federal-Mormon tensions would erupt into regional conflict.[19]

Unlike Drummond, those who recovered Gunnison's body concluded that the perpetrators were aggrieved "Parvain Indians" retaliating for murders upon their community. The climate of suspicion, the trial, and the diverse cast of Indian and white actors underscore the region's constellation of competing groups. Beckwith, Call, Young, and subsequent chroniclers all held Moshoquop responsible, if not "guilty." His band, according to Solomon Carvalho, "had, at different times, been wantonly and cruelly shot down, like so many wild beasts, by the American emigrants to California, [and] were now incited to revenge." In the spring of 1854, a gathering of Mormon and Indian leaders reached the same conclusion. Walkara, the region's leading slave and horse trafficker, insisted that he and his warriors had not been involved, since they had been away selling horses. They had also been selling seized Mormon livestock, raided during a series of 1853–54 attacks that soon bore the Ute leader's name as Walkara's War.[20]

As their eastern Ute brethren had learned, stealing from settlers was one thing, going to war against the U.S. Army another, and provoking the federal government was no one's intention. Even Kanosh had moved to quell the conflict. In the days after the attack, he repri-

Chief Walkara, possibly by Solomon Carvalho, 1854. Oil on canvas. Courtesy of the Utah State Historical Society, Salt Lake City. The "hawk of the mountains" or "greatest horse thief in history," Walkara occupied a command position astride the Old Spanish Trail that generated wealth and power for his band of equestrian Utes. Much of this dominion came at the expense of *Californio* ranchers, New Mexican villagers, and especially Paiute nonequestrians, whose servitude and enslavement by Utes remain poorly understood in the region's history.

manded his Paiute warriors, returned some of Gunnison's property and horses, and offered up a few tribesmen as culprits. Few Mormon or Indian leaders appeared willing to use the captain's death to lobby Washington for assistance of any kind. They all also wished to appear not culpable.[21]

Gunnison's death threatened the region's precarious equilibrium, in which Mormons, Utes, and the far less powerful Paiutes were all invested. Mormons held clear and growing advantages against Walkara and Ute equestrians, and they feared that Gunnison's death might increase the nation's anti-Mormon sentiments. They hoped to consolidate their position vis-à-vis the Utes before confronting other potential rivals. In a nation divided over states' rights versus the role of the federal government, Mormon anxieties arose from their own minority status. Their first leader, Joseph Smith, had lost his life fighting American persecution, and his successor, Brigham Young, had now secured a space for his Saints on the very margins of the nation. The last thing Young wanted was the expansion of federal authority in Utah, and Gunnison's death presaged such extension. Having clashed with Utah's first Indian agents, including Henry Day and Jacob Holeman, Young feared that a new superintendent of Indian Affairs or perhaps even governor might soon arrive. More Indian agents, treaties, reservations, and most ominously U.S. troops to enforce Indian policy all became possibilities in the aftermath of Gunnison's death.[22]

Walkara also feared that outside retaliation might jeopardize his bands' raiding economy, which had only accelerated after Mormon colonization. As settlements grew along the Wasatch Front, they undercut Ute subsistence patterns as the wetlands and valley ecologies in which Utah's Utes had customarily found fish and game ruptured. Such economics fueled nearly constant Mormon-Ute tensions throughout the first decade of settlement. Gunnison's death occurred within such ongoing conflicts. Mormon emigrants had also brought new diseases, particularly to Ute bands concentrated in valleys. As Jared Farmer remarks, "In the winter of 1848–49 . . . [t]he roughly three hundred natives who wintered [at Salt Lake] caught foreign diseases from their Mormon neighbors . . . The winter of 1849–50 was even worse. For Utes it marked the beginning of a devastating decade of disease." As one settler recalled: "That season a great number of Indians came to the Warm Springs suffering from Measles. They died off as fast as they went into the water. Some they buried and some they didn't bury. I helped bury those that were left unburied. We buried 36 in one grave."[23]

Like Colorado Utes, many Ute bands in Utah responded to such chaos with violence, first through a series of abortive campaigns in the winter of 1850, before settling into raiding economies that targeted Mormon as well as emigrant livestock. As in Colorado, such raids soon grew into "war" and prompted defensive retreat. Some fled valley homelands for mountain refuges, while others left the region altogether, sometimes for years on end. Mountains, however, offered limited resources, especially in the winter, forcing many to beg and especially to raid for food. Either way hunger altered Ute migratory patterns, while heightened mobility accelerated the increase in raiding. As Henry Day related, "The Indians complained bitterly of the treatment they had received from the Mormon settlers." Ute leaders, he continued, "expressed the wish . . . that [the Great Father] would not permit the Mormons to drive them out of the Vallies and into the Mountains where they must starve." In the first years of settlement, then, raiding, begging, and Mormon "presents" became intrinsic to Ute economics. Accordingly, in a context in which, as Jacob Holeman reported, "upon the slightest pretexts, they are shot down or driven to the mountain," being held responsible for killing Gunnison and seven members of his expedition would only further imperil Ute community survival.[24]

Paiute survival became even more precarious than that of their Ute neighbors. Subject to decades of enslavement, Paiutes had long endured colonialism's many traumas. Their relations with Mormon newcomers thus occurred within the context of larger hostilities, and as Martha Knack argues, Paiutes "may have sought alliance with Mormons to counterbalance regional Ute dominance." As Kanosh's example portended, by returning stolen property, offering up culprits, and participating in regional negotiations, Paiute leaders employed a range of conciliatory strategies that linked their bands to Mormon settlers. They did so, moreover, amidst the demographic deluge of Mormon settlement, and as Utes and Mormons vied for supremacy over central Utah, Paiutes found Mormons like Anson Call far more hospitable than either Ute warlords like Walkara or emigrants such as those who murdered Moshoquop's father. Utes also pressured Paiutes to join their raiding parties, using violent forms of persuasion. In times

of Mormon-Ute conflicts, then, many "friendly" Paiute bands fled to
Mormon towns.[25]

Always concerned about the financial burdens of Indian affairs,
Brigham Young's professed belief that it was "better for us to feed
the Indians . . . than it is to fight them" grew strained in times of war.
After the outbreak of Walkara's War in 1853, the region's multipolar
Indian relations forced the governor simultaneously to feed and to
fight. "The influence Walker and his band have exercised upon the
friendly Indians," he wrote in September 1853, "has caused this Superintendency an unusual and necessary expenditure in presents." "Ever
ready to be won over to the side of our enemies," he explained in his
next report, "I have made and ordered for the past quarter the small-
est am[oun]t of disbursement that my judgment would admit." The arrival of Paiute bands in settlements taxed Mormon resources. They all
expected provisions as well as protection. In return, "friendly" Paiutes
provided service as scouts, laborers, and auxiliaries both in these and
in later conflicts.[26]

Seeking an alliance with Mormons, however, was one thing, to receive one another. Alliance conveys a semblance of shared interest
and power that Paiutes never achieved. Stationing themselves within
Mormon settlements fulfilled only temporary needs and also exposed
them to the vagaries of Mormon dominion and to settlement diseases.
South of Sevier Lake in the traditional homelands of Southern Paiutes,
as Mormon households mushroomed, Indians struggled to survive.

Enslavement particularly imperiled Paiute survival. Unlike Utah's
equestrians, Paiutes confronted indigenous, New Mexican, as well as
Mormon captors. Such relations emerged during the Spanish colonial
period and extended into the U.S. territorial period. Whereas studies
of Great Basin Indian slavery have identified the centrality of Walkara
and various New Mexicans to these webs of violent exchange, Mormon
complicity remains less established. Often portrayed as those who mer-
cifully ended the region's traffic in Indians, Mormons in fact used
Paiute and to a lesser extent Ute captives as servants in their homes.
Indeed, among the earliest federal correspondences regarding Utah's
Indian affairs concern "about thirty Utah women and girls who were
taken prisoners in a war of extermination waged last winter by the
Mormons against two small bands of that tribe." Referring to the winter Timpanagos campaigns of 1850, which Gunnison's informers tried

to paint "in as soft colors as possible," Utah's first appointed Indian agent, Edward Cooper, reported: "It will be among my first efforts to give every attention to this subject."[27]

While Ute "prisoners" were returned or exchanged during military resolutions, Paiutes faced more enduring forms of servitude. They also suffered more at the hands of their traffickers. As both Sondra Jones and Martha Knack have detailed, Ute captive abuse was not only routine; it also became increasingly economical. The more pain inflicted upon captive children, the more likely Mormons were to purchase them. Threatening their captives' death, Ute slavers began in the late 1840s escalating their torture of Paiute captives, especially children, doing so with the expectation that Mormons would become more consistent buyers. As Jones relates, "The new settlers were not interested in purchasing any Indians, even though Baptiste [a Ute trader] threatened to kill his captives if they didn't. After he carried out his threat by killing one, Brigham Young's son-in-law, Charles Decker, purchased the second one for a gun. She was taken and raised in Brigham Young's home, where, according to Young, she 'fared as [did his] children.'" Other, more infamous accounts of Paiute executions include descriptions of Ute traffickers tossing children by their heels upon rocks when Mormons refused to bargain. Utes also camped outside settlements, where they tortured children with knives and hot metals to induce settlers to come to their slave markets. Sometimes these cruel strategies broke Mormons' resolve not to purchase slaves. At other times, when Mormons refused, Utes killed their cargo. As Young noted in June 1853, "one of Wacker's brothers, lately killed an Indian prisoner child, because the traders would not give him what he asked for it."[28]

That Mormons purchased Indian children is not debated. The extent to which such captives constituted a servile labor force is. In 1853, at the height of Walkara's War, "each of the one hundred households in Parowan," according to Martha Knack, "possessed one or more Paiute children." As she further notes, "the pragmatic labor value of these Paiute children cannot be underestimated for frontier settlements then constructing labor-intensive infrastructure." As many Mormon settlements fortified themselves against Ute raiders, refugee Paiute laborers and captive children assisted Mormon efforts through domestic and manual labor. Moreover, Mormon leaders consented to such practices; in 1851 some had initially wished Walkara "prosperity and good bargins" in his efforts to trade "Peide children."[29]

Failing to view Indian slavery as central to the West's territorial past, historians have only recently begun to examine the nature of indigenous enslavement. Some have even suggested that Paiute mothers willingly "pawned" their children to outsiders "in human exchanges both benign and hostile." On the contrary, as they faced predatory slave traffickers, Paiutes had little recourse but to attach themselves to settlements where their children served Mormon families. Utes who killed captives in front of reluctant buyers did worse to bands that refused their demands, and by 1860, as Indian agent Garland Hurt reported, "scarcely one-half of the Pyeed Children are permitted to grow up in the band." Notwithstanding his eventual efforts on their behalf, before Hurt's 1854 appointment Paiutes had received little assistance from federal agents. As Calhoun had worried in 1850, Paiutes remained removed from federal influence. During the first decade of colonization, then, Mormon newcomers were the Paiutes' only potential allies. As a Santa Clara Paiute headman was overheard shouting to suspected Ute raiders: "he said, they must not come now to steal their children; their white brothers—the Mormons—had come here, and would fight for them." And while white violence against Paiutes included public whippings, murders, and degrees of participation in Ute slave trafficking, Utah's Paiutes resorted to the few available strategies for survival. While such accommodation included the placement of children into Mormon households, there was nothing "benign" about their situation.[30]

The Utes who threw Paiute children upon rocks or stuck hot metal into their captives' open wounds also inhabited a world of desperation. With the U.S. conquest of New Mexico and California, Ute raiders faced diminishing markets for their stolen property and children. They also endured waves of Old World pathogens and faced constant threats to their subsistence resources. Confronting such challenges, Walkara and allied equestrians escalated their attacks against Mormon settlements in 1853. They did so, particularly, in response to Mormon efforts to curtail their slave trading, which, as John Alton Peterson argues, had become a centerpiece of their economies: "Young's attempts to terminate it were nearly as threatening to the Utes as was Mormon settlement in the first place." In April 1853, after New Mexican traders had again been imprisoned for traveling into Utah to purchase slaves, Utes confronted Young and "told me if we were to pay as high a price as the Mexicans offered and pay in horses, guns and ammunition, they would trade with us." Young, however, told the Utes "to raise their own children, and to refrain from stealing any from other tribes, and that ammunition sufficient for hunting would be traded to them for skins and peltry, as soon as it would be produced or procured." In a region of diminished game, the governor's solution to the crisis of Ute economics reverted to the logic of the fur trade. Worried that he would no longer be able to quell their demands, Young returned to Salt Lake, where "in the event of open collision I could operate more effectually."[31]

Open collisions did erupt in July as Ute warriors struck southern settlements. Utes attacked, however, not to drive out the teeming settlements along the Corridor but to terrorize them, using violence to destabilize outlying communities in order to procure stock, cattle, and horses. Such strategies had worked for Ute raiders against both Mormon settlers and Paiute bands; as in Colorado's San Luis Valley, Ute raiding economies necessitated consistent providers. This conflict, however, soon took on added dimensions. For, as Gunnison relayed, Utes had not only pushed settlers into fortifications and stolen their livestock; they also targeted crops and destroyed mills, attempting to impoverish Mormon settlers. As Young wrote in late July, "This occurring in the midst of our wheat harvest is causing as much inconvenience & loss and we do not as yet know, what amount of loss of life and destruction of property will be included in the final result." Outraged by Mormon interference in their slaving, then, Utes besieged southern Mormon communities, and by October, as Call suggested, even in his absence "Walker's Indians" seemed responsible for every Indian attack in the region. His name had become synonymous with a war as well as with latent Mormon fears about survival.[32]

During the war Young invoked Walkara from the pulpit, using him both as a foil to admonish wayward followers to mind their spiritual duties and as an impetus to secure church tithes, fortifications, and other earthly matters. "IT IS RIGHT, and perfectly calculated," he orated, "to chasten this people until they are willing to take counsel." Taking pains, however, not simply to reassure his followers but also to instruct them, Young singled out those parishioners who had not followed his previous warnings. "Do you not suppose people will now wish they had built forts when they were told? If they do not, it proves what they have been all the time, shall I say fools?" With the harvest upon them, Young balanced his objurgations with exhortations not to lose faith, to follow church instructions, and, above all, to "build forts." As with so many moments in their recent past, Walkara appeared a divine challenge to the followers of Mormonism. "The Lord," Young continued, "is making brother Walker an instrument to help me."[33]

Young could also become an instrument of power for his Ute rival, and Walkara understood and attempted to use his vilification to consolidate authority over subordinate Indian bands. Realizing that his warriors could not break fortified Mormon settlements and that subjugated Paiutes as well as other Ute bands had fled rather than join his cause, Walkara's Utes scaled back their hostilities. By January's end, the "war" was over, and by March signs of Ute accommodation filtered up to Salt Lake. Walkara, however, had not lost standing or stature within the region. Indeed, at the May treaty negotiations held near Fillmore that ended the conflict, the Ute leader detailed both his and others' renewed commitments to peace, commitments he claimed to have occasioned. After proclaiming his innocence in Gunnison's death, for example, the Ute leader turned and threatened the gathered Indian leaders: "'If [an] Indian kill[s] [another] white man again, Wakara [will] make that Indian howl.'" Speaking on behalf of all the region's Indians, Walkara recognized that while the war had diminished his authority vis-à-vis Mormons, he could continue his efforts to consolidate authority over Paiute and Ute bands. As the negotiations ended and the governor departed to tour the southern Corridor, Walkara informed him that "'he and his chiefs would accompany him . . . as a body-guard.'" Unable to dislodge Mormon power militarily, Walkara's Utes remained more than comfortable attaching themselves to it, shielding the region's emergent leaders as though they were their own, while communicating to Native as well as Mormon communities their continued, respected stature.[34]

In a "war" prompted by the politics and economics of Indian slavery, Walkara's band had unleashed their still resplendent raiding power, destabilizing settlements up and down the Corridor. After the May negotiations, Walkara returned to his familiar position astride the region's Indian affairs, publicly berating and punishing Indian subjects while attempting to stem his band's economic decline. He even re-initiated the traffic in Paiute captives, on one occasion prompting settlers to purchase eight children "rather" than see them killed. Despite sporadic conflicts, settler-Ute tensions subsided, aided in part by the mediating efforts of new Indian agents as well as by the Utes' sobering realization that Mormon fortifications were in fact more difficult to dismantle than they were to construct.[35]

Often portrayed as an irrational counter to Ouray's measured diplomacy, like his more famous Colorado Ute contemporary Walkara embodied the tumultuous social world that his community inherited. Unlike New Mexico, however, with its centuries-long relations between villagers and Indians, Utah remained an imperial crossroads into which outsiders ventured to profit, plunder, and enslave.

As in Colorado, Ute equestrians had positioned themselves within these networks, doing so at the expense of their nonequestrian neighbors. When Brigham Young arrived at Utah Lake in 1847, he and his followers believed they had found untouched lands. They in fact became the next wave of intrusion into Ute and Paiute homelands that had already been transformed by decades of slavery and fur trading. As with the 1850 Timpanagos War, the shaky détente that Mormon and Utes established in May 1854 would again fail, though Walkara would not live to see his people's forced displacement to the Uintah Basin east of the Wasatch Mountains, where Young had procured reservation lands for his "red children." Nor would he participate in their last guerrilla campaigns of the 1860s, when, facing endemic poverty and failed farming experiments, Utah's Utes staged their last military resistance in another misnamed "war," known after their leader Antogna, or Black Hawk. While attending the 1855 trial of Paiutes charged with Gunnison's murder, as Garland Hurt reported, a "violent epidemic" struck "among the Utahs," and like so many Native people throughout the hemisphere, Walkara "was among the victims." In a burial befitting the West's greatest horse thief and warlord, Walkara was buried with slain horses and Paiute captives, the twin economic bases for his once terrible power.[36]

Shoshone Equestrians and the Road to Bear River

Not all Utes mourned Walkara's passing, nor were all Paiutes freed from the tyranny of enslavement. Both indigenous populations, however, soon confronted ever-growing pressures south of Salt Lake as the tide of Mormon emigration subsumed all. As a Ute delegation returning to Provo after Walkara's death told agent George Armstrong: "they said [the city] had 'grown so very big' since they left two years ago that they hardly knew it was the same place." From across the seas, Mormon converts flocked to the Great Basin, seeking material and spiritual salvation. Some arrived overland from eastern entry ports, while others came via the Pacific and up the Corridor settlements once preyed upon by Ute warriors, now firmly secured. Southern Paiutes continued their precarious adjustment to Mormon colonization, migrating between mountain encampments and towns while attempting to navigate, in Martha Knack's analysis, the "complex triadic relationship" among themselves, Mormons, and federal representatives. Now, at least, they would not face indigenous oppressors, as Utah's Utes were forced onto reservation homelands that they would share after 1880 with Colorado's dispossessed Utes.[37]

North, northwest, and northeast of Salt Lake, in equestrian Shoshone homelands, Indian relations followed a different trajectory as larger national developments added new combustibles to the region's cauldron of Indian affairs. Had the Mormons ever achieved what they initially sought—a kingdom apart—Utah's northern Indian relations might have come to resemble the violent paternalism that Mormons enacted with Utes and Paiutes. However, as Mormon-federal tensions erupted in the 1850s, both the Mormon state and then, during the Civil War, the federal government retracted its power in the region. First, in 1857, as the U.S. Army marched for Utah, Mormon leaders recalled settlements from the far reaches of "Utah," including those from Carson Valley, Nevada, and Fort Limhi, Idaho, in a vain effort to prevent federal occupation. Eventually 20 percent of the Union Army would be used to reassert federal sovereignty during Utah's 1857–58 bloodless "Mormon War." Shortly thereafter, however, the federal government withdrew its soldiers to meet the crisis of union, leaving Utah in 1861 again semiautonomous. In 1862–63, as the war mobilized Union resources, the army again stationed troops in Utah, soon using violence to resolve Indian conflicts.

After ten years of chronic Mormon-Indian conflicts, in 1863 Utah's Indian wars took on a familiar as well as decisive federal form. As in Colorado, this western theater of the Civil War centered upon Indian subjugation; it also involved California volunteers eager for battle. To the lexicon of Indian wars more chapters of violence were soon added, as the January 1863 events along the Bear River on Utah's Idaho border preceded both Sand Creek and Wounded Knee as the Indian West's most traumatic day.[38]

Unlike Utah's Utes, who in 1844 had helped to dismantle Antoine Robidoux's regional forts and soon faced the tide of Mormon colonization, bands of equestrian Shoshones in Idaho and Wyoming had sustained relations with mountain men and emigrants within their homelands. Fort Bridger, after all, helped launch emigrant trains west while also becoming home to the hybrid social world of the post–fur trade era. While many trappers had lived among Ute bands, the familiar Green River country of the rendezvous remained a part of their world after the fur trade's heyday, as did remaining Hudson's Bay Company posts at Forts Hall and Boise. Farther north, on the Salmon River, even the Mormons' Fort Limhi briefly provided opportunities to Shoshone bands. Forts also held strategic and economic value astride emigrant trails to Oregon and California, and trading posts and river ferries sprouted up to accommodate the influx of travelers. Such familiarity, however, undercut Shoshone and trapper economies as their combined knowledge helped fuel outsiders' interests in the region. Paradoxically, Jim Bridger's advice to Brigham Young in 1847 about the oasis-like lands west of the Wasatch cost trappers and their Shoshone allies, as Mormon emigration accelerated the colonization of the Intermountain West.[39]

Part of the logic of Mormon settlement arose from Indian politics. Understanding that the northern portions of the Wasatch Front remained contested by hereditary Ute and Shoshone enemies, Mormon leaders seized on opportunities afforded by an indigenous political vacuum. Partially settling in the borderlands between equestrian Utes and Shoshones, Mormons moved to mitigate such animosities. While Indians were best fought by soldiers or in tandem with traditional rivals, the threat of constant warfare imperiled all; as Mormon settlers witnessed in 1853, such threats were particularly acute for families harvesting their fields. Only a year and a half after the 1850 Timpanagos War, Young encouraged Ute and Eastern Shoshone leaders to attend the 1851 Fort Laramie treaty negotiations, instructing agents Day and Holeman to gather and accompany respective delegations to the first assembly of northern Plains Indians and government leaders. Hoping to resolve Ute and Shoshone claims to the region as well as their mutual animosities, Young even agreed to purchase a stagecoach to carry Ute leaders "as privately as possible and in citizens dress" to allay the likelihood of Shoshone attack. Such inducements failed as Walkara and others grew suspicious. Worried about exposing themselves to potential attackers, Ute leaders remained in Utah. They would, however, still receive gifts for their initial willingness to attend the negotiations.[40]

Unfortunately for Shoshones, the momentous 1851 Fort Laramie Treaty excluded Indians from the newly formed Utah Territory. While initiating the "treaty process" with Shoshone rivals on the Plains, federal negotiators maintained that Utah's jurisdiction extended not only west to the Sierras but also into the northern reaches of the Rockies. It was, after all, Utah Indian agent Jacob Holeman who had accompanied sixty Shoshone delegates to the eastern Wyoming fort. While Oregon Territory technically extended east of the Cascades into the Snake River plain, there were no Indian agencies in the region, and for the time being Shoshone bands, whether they knew it or not, fell under Young's superintendency. In the swift currents of western diplomacy, they both became and remained attached to Utah.[41]

Initially such political liminality meant little to Shoshone delegates. Having viewed the splendor of the negotiations, Shoshone leaders, according to Holeman, "seem to have great confidence in and respect for whites" and remained "uniformly friendly." Like other delegates, they had been plied with presents. They had, however, also received expectations, leaving under the assumption that their comparable treaty negotiations were forthcoming. They were mistaken. For although the treaty process moved to establish federal authority vis-à-vis Plains Indians, Utah's Indian affairs went in divergent directions, becoming mired, according to Brigham Madsen, in a state of "almost hopeless confusion." Practicing intermittent placation, provisioning, and punishment, in its first decade Utah's Indian agency contrasted with others, where agents and superintendents lobbied on behalf of their charges. Utah's political secrecy, constant Mormon-federal infighting, and rotating cast of agents challenged any semblance of a national Indian policy. As Shoshone leaders gleaned at Fort Laramie, even the jurisdiction of Utah's superintendency was in doubt; seeing their agent fight with other officials hardly instilled confidence. For, where exactly did "Utah" begin, and who came under its jurisdiction, which ostensibly ranged from the Sierras in the west to the Rockies in the east, and from the Colorado River in the south to the Snake River in the north? Equally perplexing, the government had three (and soon just two) representatives, one agent and two subagents, charged with administering that huge expanse. To top it off, the superintendency was presided over by a governor and *ex officio* superintendent of Indian affairs whose hostility to federal authority was tempered only by the many costs of Indian affairs. The challenge of incorporating the interior West's Indians into the nation rested, then, on precarious as well as precariously few shoulders.[42]

Unlike Utah's Utes, for whom violence became the clearest response to the fallout from white settlement, equestrian Shoshones had trader and emigrant neighbors, particularly around Fort Bridger. Thus, when Mormons moved to control ferry crossings or encroached upon Green River lands, Indians as well as others responded. Whereas the multipolar world of central Utah revolved around Utes, Mormons, and Paiutes, from the Idaho-Oregon border, through the Snake River plain, and into Wyoming a constellation of Shoshone bands, mountain traders, other equestrian Indians, and soon thousands of emigrants coursed through the region. Additionally, whereas many Ute bands remained integrated into the political economy of the Spanish borderlands, epitomized by Walkara's command position on the Old Spanish Trail, equestrian Shoshones fought to secure resources from the northern Plains, especially from buffalo hunting grounds, gun-trading networks, and remaining pockets of the fur trade.[43]

Before Fort Laramie and the subsequent explosion of western emigration in the 1850s, Shoshones fought to mitigate their comparative disadvantages. As Zenas Leonard and early trappers noted, Shoshones faced rivals in multiple directions, particularly those who limited their access to the Plains. Intermarrying with traders became one strategy for ameliorating such isolation, seasonal trading another. Confronting such disadvantages had consumed nearly half a century of Shoshone diplomacy, and as Shoshone leaders at Fort Laramie suggested, clarifying their economic and political relationship with federal leaders remained high priorities. Straddling indigenous and economic realms that reached across half the continent, equestrian Shoshones coped with varying sets of regional challenges.[44]

Such challenges particularly affected the most remote Shoshone groups. Unlike Wyoming's Eastern Shoshones, who attended Fort Laramie and roamed the Plains under such distinguished chiefs as Washakie, Snake River Shoshones and their related Bannock allies suffered from their isolation, never more so than in 1863. The five primary bands that lived along Idaho's Snake and Salmon Rivers and their tributaries had fought to stem Mormon settlement. They had also increasingly taxed overland emigrants. In essence, they sought to keep whites from occupying their homelands while marauding those who ventured through them. Such conflict, as Brigham Madsen has argued, prefigured more widely studied Plains Indian wars: Shoshone impoverishment and white emigration went hand in hand, escalating into violent retribution. Shoshones had attracted white explorers and fur traders in order to address their comparative disadvantages vis-à-vis Plains rivals, and throughout the 1850s, when many Plains groups still controlled verdant horse and buffalo grasslands from which to secure subsistence and trade resources, Shoshones increasingly lacked both. Along the Oregon Trail, they faced tides of newcomers whose growing presence ruptured their economies. For them, with no state officials to hear, let alone act on, their many needs, the avenues of diplomatic resolution narrowed.[45]

The impact of westward emigrants upon the lands through which they traveled was both widespread and profound. Travel on the West's main emigrant routes, the Oregon and California Trails, devastated Shoshone ecologies. Emigrant parties, particularly their herds, consumed the grasses, seeds, and game that sustained these Great Basin Indians. Water sources also became jeopardized, not so much by outsiders' consumption as by their animals' defecation, while scarce timber and piñon pine fueled emigrant campfires. Moreover, emigrant parties not only feared approaching Indians but also often targeted them, as degenerative cycles of violence and reprisal between Shoshone and emigrants groups colored overland travel. Worse still, lawless bands of "renegades, deserters, and thieves," as Holeman reported, "who have had to fly from justice in California, have taken refuge in the mountains and have associated themselves with the Indians." They were, he reported, even "more savage than the Indians themselves by their cruelty to whites," often instigating cycles of thievery in order to buy from and then resupply those in need. Murder was common, and as Madsen relates, "ninety percent of all emigrant kill-ings took place beyond South Pass," particularly along the Snake River. As with the West's other Indian conflicts, the toll became even larger for Indian families through whose homelands emigrants passed.[46]

Like Utes west of the Wasatch, Shoshones between Forts Bridger and Boise lived within the nation's boundaries yet outside its control. Unlike Utes, Shoshones did not until the mid-1850s face aggressive Mormon settlement efforts, and despite interacting with streams of outsiders they encountered few actual representatives of the state. In-deed, all the talk they heard from emigrants, traders, and neighboring tribes of a powerful "great father" to the east appeared signs of weak-ness, not of strength. "They say the Americans have been continually telling them," reported Oregon agent R. R. Thompson in 1854, "that unless they cease their depredation, an army would come and destroy them, but no such thing has been done, and that the Americans are afraid of them." Confirmed in their sense of superiority as well as in the justness of their raids, Snake River Shoshones, Thompson contin-ued, "say that if we wish to fight them to come on."[47]

Organized with responsibility for Oregon's Columbia River and Pacific Coast tribes, Oregon's Indian superintendency barely reached east of the Cascades, let alone into the canyons of Idaho's Snake River. Within Superintendent Joel Palmer's jurisdiction Shoshone groups es-calated their attacks on emigrant parties in 1854. Stationed hundreds of miles away, at Oregon City, near Portland, Palmer awaited Thomp-son's September reports, complaining, "I remain wholly in the dark as to the state of affairs in the Interior."[48]

Shoshone raids on emigrant parties had taken a virulent form that summer. Simple cattle, horse, or property seizures had escalated into family killings while also occasioning their contempt. South of the Boise River twenty-five miles east of Fort Boise on August 20, thirty Shoshone warriors at noon attacked a Missouri emigrant party of five wagons and twenty-one persons, killing nineteen. The survivors in-cluded a teenage boy, along with another "still a lad." The younger "has since come into Fort Boise, having been wounded in the side with an arrow; he fled to the bushes and was 4 days in getting to the Fort during which time he was without food . . . the boy in his endeavors to draw it out broke it off at both ends, having about four inches [still] in the body." His parents, Alex Ward and his expectant wife, brothers,

and sisters, were less fortunate. After the men perished during an initial firefight, the women and children died in closer proximity to their
attackers, who used metals, axes, and fire to kill and mutilate. When an
unexpected scouting party returned, its attempted rescue failed. Afterward the victims' bodies littered over a quarter-mile of the trail.[49]

While spurring much correspondence and attempted retaliations,
the Ward Massacre, as it became known, more encapsulated regional
tensions than resolved them. Far from either stemming emigrant
travel or subsequently punishing Shoshone "miscreants," the August
attacks merely underscored the obvious: "the Interior" remained a
place of violence beyond the reach of agents. As heated reactions shut-
tled between Thompson, Palmer, and distant officials about these "barbarous" acts, no one paused to consider their potential symbolism.
Nor did anyone reflect on an obvious corollary: the region had become home to Indians desperate enough to maraud and antagonize.
Warriors who sacked emigrant parties, slaughtered women and children, and then taunted and welcomed reprisal clearly put little faith in
other forms of redress. Attacking at midday along trafficked summer
trails and strewing victims along at hundred-yard intervals were also
signs of weakness, not of strength. They became invitations for greater
calamity. Thus did Shoshone behavior reveal the extreme stresses precipitated by emigrant travel and by the inability of state officials to do
anything about them.[50]

Instead of opening and pursuing any avenues for resolution, Palmer
dispatched a new Indian agent, Nathan Olney, whose first mandate
was to attack. Palmer hoped that Olney's reprisals would come in concert with army forces stationed along the Columbia River in a campaign to "effectually awe and punish." Certain, if vague, limits were to
be remembered and "if possible" followed. "It should not be forgotten
that we are a civilized and Christian people and they savage and ignorant," Palmer instructed. "Women and children should if possible be
saved."[51]

The 1854 campaigns never fully materialized, nor were the Shoshones ever severely rebuked from Oregon, where other Indian conflicts
soon preoccupied Palmer, Thompson, and Olney. September reprisals
brought scattered Indian deaths and prisoners, while those targeted
for punishment eluded engagement. As tensions continued into 1855,
another campaign led by Major Granville Haller headed east and again

initiated select rather than communal killings. At Fort Boise on July 18, out of 200 Shoshones gathered to redress the Ward attack, 4 suspected "murderers . . . were seized, brought before a board of officers . . . three were hung on the graves of their victims; the fourth was shot by the guard in endeavoring to escape." Haller's outnumbered party adjudicated rather than engaged, their trial exacting little commensurate vengeance. Without artillery, reinforcements, and strategic advantages, U.S. Army officials would have to wait to conduct reprisals, and, not surprisingly, this small display of federal power failed to achieve resolution. "With the exception of the execution of the reputed murderers . . . by Major Haller, they have hitherto escaped with impunity." By 1860 Shoshone raiders had killed "at least a hundred whites, many of them women and children," and Oregon superintendents continued to complain of Shoshone raids, noting that before any policies could be implemented, "it will first be necessary that they feel the heavy hand of chastisement, and thus learn to respect our authority."[52]

Oregon's equestrian powers, the Cayuse and Nez Perce, consented to join in the federal campaign of retribution against the Shoshone. The Cayuse and Nez Perce not only remained Shoshone rivals but also had secured comparative power over them. Like Colorado's Utes, they sustained political and economic autonomy as their rivals' desperation grew. For example, in addition to the benefits of having Indian agents stationed among them, they had the two most important ingredients for survival: food for themselves and items to trade. As Thompson noted during his attempts to enlist auxiliaries, "I here found the greater portion of the Cayuse tribe, with about sixty Nez Perces, who had, as is their custom, come here for the purpose of trading with the immigrants, bringing with them peas, potatoes, melons, apples, and horses, to exchange for cattle, money, and such things as they might fancy . . . I had many conversations with them while here and was thereby enabled to gather a pretty good idea of the state of their feelings towards the Snakes, which was anything but friendly." Able scouts and allies, these Indians, like the Shoshones, depended upon and targeted summer emigrant parties; however, they sought to trade, not to plunder. Their cornucopia of "peas, potatoes, melons, apples, and horses" made them richer and more secure than their isolated Snake River neighbors.[53]

The Snake River remained, then, circumscribed in multiple directions. To their east and northwest, Shoshones faced equestrian rivals whose access to economic and political resources offered them wider potential avenues of survival. Columbian Plateau and northern Plains Indians had more subsistence resources procured through hunting, farming, and trade as well as greater access to government officials, who, notwithstanding subsequent processes of dispossession, momentarily provided provisions, annuities, and desperately needed matériel. In 1854 the tide of federal-Indian conflict had nowhere neared its height. The world of western wars, treaties, reservations, and their brutal aftermath still lay in the future. For now, Shoshone conflicts with their many neighbors escalated.[54]

Confronted with powerful rivals, Idaho's Shoshones faced to their south even more challenging adversaries, who by 1854 had achieved hegemony south of Salt Lake. After Walkara's death, Mormon-Indian relations appeared to have moved into a new, "pacific" phase. Garland Hurt's bustling, if costly, experimental Indian farms were taking hold, Ute raids had subsided, and although Young still complained to Washington that settlers must "surround their dwellings with earth walls to protect themselves," the governor's reports increasingly stressed the "friendly" nature of Indian relations. Fort Boise and the Snake River, however, remained unmentioned in the governor's communiqués.[55]

Deepening dilemmas underlay this apparent lull in Mormon-Indian conflict. Lacking other government advocates, Eastern Shoshones from the Wyoming Plains and particularly Northern Shoshones due north of Salt Lake continued to look to Mormons for consistent provisioning and compensation. Such accommodations were tested, however, as Mormon settlers pushed north into Shoshone lands. As Superintendent Jacob Forney noted upon his arrival in 1858, "There is no tribe of Indians in the Territory . . . that have been so much discommoded by the introduction of a white population as the Sho-sho-nes." In turn, as Hurt had earlier noted, Shoshone leaders expected Mormons to perform for them what were technically federal duties: "The Snakes complained that they had permitted the white people to make roads through their lands and travel upon them in safety, use the grass and drink the water, and had never received anything for it, all though the tribes around them had been getting presents." Expecting treaties and annuities, they "well understood," further, "that large appropriations had been made by Congress for the purpose of making presents to and treaties with them." As Mormon-Shoshone tensions simmered, Shoshone leaders attempted to gain what those "around them" had obtained.[56]

Though strategic in allaying federal supervision, Mormon optimism was as short-lived as it was shortsighted. As federal forces were gathering strength to quell Mormon separatism, conflict along the territory's northern and western boundaries intensified, not so much between settlers and Indians as between emigrants and Indians. As Snake River attacks increased, so too did Western Shoshone and Northern Paiute raids along the California Trail, and Jacob Holeman and Garland Hurt spent much of their time in "Utah" traveling back and forth along the Humboldt attempting to soothe Nevada's Indian tensions. Outside the Mormon settlements, equestrian and nonequestrian Indians increasingly used violence to supplement their livelihoods. Soon such violence would again erupt into warfare.[57]

Such tensions became others' responsibility as Washington, Nevada, and eventually Idaho territories claimed jurisdiction over these Native groups in the 1860s. However, beginning with the Mormon War of 1857–58 and through the Civil War, the U.S. Army dominated much of Utah. Whereas Oregon had few troops to deploy in September 1854, in the coming years army forces would be used to resolve regional conflicts. And, in contrast to Superintendent Palmer's prescription to spare, if possible, Indian women and children, army leaders and their volunteers often had little training in and patience for the protocols of Indian diplomacy. As their compatriots fought on eastern battlefields, Utah's Union soldiers also sought opportunities for glory.[58]

Ultimately, Shoshone raids on emigrants only partially fueled the fateful decisions that culminated on the Bear River. As the Ward attack revealed, Shoshone raids remained a source of tension that had prompted two campaigns of attempted destruction. These summer campaigns, however, failed to locate those who migrated seasonally and easily eluded pursuing forces. As Thompson reported after the attack, the summer was the wrong season to retaliate. "Winter and spring would be the time when they would be least able to make resistance," he suggested, "as they are then half famished, and would not find the same protection in the bush, they do in the summer when the leaves are on." But there were powerful impediments to winter reprisals. During the winter, Shoshones congregated in winter camps and did so in comparatively larger numbers than in the summer months, when bands broke off into smaller family units before making their annual travels onto the Plains. Their rivals were also less likely to join in winter campaigns, because with the exception of Utah's famed unit of settler forces, the Nauvoo Legion, provisioning winter scouts and soldiers remained beyond militia capabilities. Snow-covered trails, icy waters, and subzero temperatures awaited those who ventured into "the Interior." Larger, better-provisioned, and better-trained forces would be needed to subjugate these Native groups.[59]

Against this backdrop of raids and deteriorating Shoshone economics, the U.S. Army entered the region, wintering in 1857 outside Fort Bridger before marching unopposed into Utah in June 1858. With distant stations at San Francisco and on the Columbia, the army had scanty influence west of the Rockies. In 1855 the Department of War listed 1,365 officers and men in its "Department of the Pacific," encompassing the Pacific Coast and Intermountain West, versus a low estimate of 134,000 Indians, many of whom, Secretary of War Jefferson Davis reported, "are becoming formidable from concentration, from the acquisition of fire-arms and a knowledge of their use." The army's Mormon campaign, in contrast, utilized 3,000 soldiers, and unlike in the years ahead, these were "army regulars," not volunteers.[60]

Though limited in military scope, the Mormon War still wrought havoc over Utah, particularly in Indian affairs. In addition to the Mormon evacuation of Idaho and Nevada, where settlements had achieved a modicum of stable relations with resident Paiutes and Shoshones, the war altered the territory's boundaries and anointed new leaders. Brigham Young's ecclesiastical power continued, but a new governor, superintendent of Indian affairs, and Indian agents soon arrived, bringing with them new commitments as well as inexperience. Although renewed federalism seemingly augured well for Indians who resided outside of the federal system and had received only sporadic agents, annuities, and promises, the aftermath of the war brought as much chaos as before.

As was the case throughout much of western history, Utah's new leaders deferred to settlers and particularly to the military in matters of Indian affairs. They passed the challenge of incorporating Indians into the nation to others, and in the process of such incorporation, violence became a most expedient tool; within the military, as Durwood Ball notes, "There were almost no professional or political repercussions for the killing of Indian noncombatants in battle." As in Colorado before Sand Creek, territorial leaders abdicated their mandate for resolving Indian conflict. They relinquished authority and responsibility to military officers, for whom "armed violence was their specialty."[61]

As the region's western and northern expanses were politically recalibrated after the Mormon War, with Northern Paiute and Shoshone groups put under the jurisdiction of other territories, Utes and Southern Paiutes in Utah adjusted to a new era under Mormon dominion. During the Mormon War, Utes at Garland Hurt's string of farms lost both their agent and harvests. Fearing Mormon retaliation, Hurt and federal appointees fled the territory, and once-promising Indian farms lay empty with fallow untended fields; subsequent efforts to improve upon Hurt's initiatives languished through budgetary and political inattention. In 1865, following Young's recommendation, state officials removed Utes from Mormon jurisdiction, relocating them to largely unfertile lands east of the Wasatch in the Uintah Basin. Southern Paiutes found new state agents less approachable than Mormons and, ironically, fought to continue living within settler communities than fully outside of them. A life combining ranching and domestic labor with seasonal hunting and gathering remained more appealing than one isolated on reservation lands. The Mormon Church also afforded converted Indians select opportunities for social, economic, and spiritual mobility. Besides, bands of nonequestrians were of less concern than larger, potentially more militant groups, whom agents soon targeted directly.[62]

The arrival of federal forces enabled Indian superintendents to deploy force to achieve political ends. A prerequisite in the territory's attempts to monopolize the use of violence, the final stages of Utah's Indian wars again reflected common failures to achieve political resolution to the endemic crisis of Indian economics. Establishing treaty councils, securing tribal and congressional ratification, establishing reservation boundaries and agencies, and then provisioning them required sustained commitments and capital. And with the advent of civil war, the shifting sands of Utah's political institutions grew even less stable. As in other theaters, soldiers soon fought Indians whose leaders had once agreed to and been promised an equitable future. As these promises went unfulfilled and their families starved, settler and emigrant horses, crops, and livestock became the first casualties of such diplomatic failure, though not the last.

In Utah the earliest casualties became those encamped for the winter within closest range of Union soldiers. In the waning months of the Mormon War and amidst uncertainty about possible civil war, Indian conflicts now served to unite settlers and soldiers. The presence of the Union Army at Camp Floyd, south of Salt Lake, for example, fueled economic growth while fostering embryonic forms of nationalism. Initially assigned in 1858 to subdue Mormon separatists, the army was now drawn into and expected to settle Indian conflicts, and on the icy waters of the Bear River, many visions of community collided.

Since the army's arrival, Shoshones north and west of Salt Lake had escalated their raids both on emigrants and, ominously, on the communication routes known as the Overland Mail, which transported mail and wealth between distant stations. While emigrants may or may not have communicated their losses to state officials, mail company employees surely did. While the former included propertyless families, the latter were essential parts of powerful capitalist networks. Thus Shoshone raids fueled bursts of outrage not only from resident settlers but also from distant officials and from newsmen for whom atrocities fueled paper sales. Sometimes fictionalized, but mostly not, in combination such reports often made, as Madsen notes, a "series of small, impromptu attacks" seem like "an all-out war." And in this seeming context of war, the notoriously gambling, drinking, and carousing 3,000 Union soldiers stationed at Camp Floyd, according to one correspondent, were "doing nothing."[63]

Limited army reprisals had followed Shoshone raids in the summer of 1859. In 1860 deliberations began between Utah's governor, superintendent, and Shoshone leaders, but more militant warriors acted outside of political channels, particularly as Utah's political imbroglio continued. From the Mormon War to December 1861, no less than five different superintendents held office. Washakie's once-recognized authority over other Shoshone bands had weakened, as had the authority of hereditary chiefs, who increasingly complained of and apologized for the raids. As different Shoshone leaders faced increasing pressures, they became torn between the necessities of providing for their communities and averting deadly retribution. The promises of peace from Fort Laramie had now faded, and a decade of summer raids against emigrants had proved a viable strategy for feeding hungry communities. But, as Thompson indicated and everyone knew, the summer lasted only so long. Afterward, game hibernated, emigrants wintered, streams with fish froze, and "half famished" Indians struggled to survive.[64]

Of the many descriptions of Indian winter destitution sent to Washington, two stand out and suggest the crisis confronting Utah's Indians. In 1860 Agent A. Humphreys detailed his efforts to rehabilitate Hurt's agrarian project, reporting that Utah's Indian farms were now surrounded by 24,000 settlers, settlements that in effect "deprive them of all chances of killing game, even for their partial subsistence." Moreover, the crops that remained had been lost to recent plagues of insects. During the following winter "the sufferings . . . were horrible, many of them dying from starvation and exposure. It was a common circumstance to find them frozen to death." After reporting his failed attempts to secure additional supplies, Humphreys continued: "I was compelled to witness the[ir] sufferings and death . . . without money, provisions, or clothing wherewith to relieve them. On several occasions I parted with my own blankets to bury them in." The next fall, in November 1860, Superintendent Benjamin Davies detailed his winter travels among his new charges and made the following assessment: in Utah, he reported, "these are unquestionably the poorest Indians on the continent." After taking four wagonloads of goods to Shoshones west of Salt Lake, he struggled to convey, let alone make sense of, their "misery:" "the poverty . . . [of those] who crowded the wayside of my return to shake hands and beg me to 'come again soon with presents . . .' is beyond conception, much less description; and their number, I regret to say, is much larger than previously estimated."[65]

If subsistence procurement was not enough of a challenge, winter camps also became sites of disease exchange as the pandemics that befell Utah's Utes in the 1850s spread to Shoshones. In 1859, for example, Jacob Forney noted that the Bannock now numbered "about five hundred," a population staggeringly smaller than a generation before. Forney developed such conclusions in consultation with Jim Bridger, who "for the last thirty years [has] traded, almost yearly, with this tribe

. . . when he first knew them, they numbered about twelve hundred lodges." Even using conservative estimates of six people per lodge, one can approximate the Bannock's demographic collapse at 90 percent. While the winter brought the most deprivation, even in the summer Shoshone raiders were reportedly so hungry that upon attacking, they "eat the flour raw from the sacks." If they awaited government annuities or held out for other promises, then an entire season of potential emigrant herds and settler crops went unharvested. Many communities pursued a dual strategy, feigning peaceful compliance in order to procure provisions while continuing to raid.[66]

By 1860 such spiraling destitution had left Utah's Indian relations as violent as anywhere in North America. The summer witnessed Northern Paiute warfare and army reprisals, emigrant killings, and growing animosities. The 1859 discovery of gold in Virginia City had prompted the Pyramid Lake Indian War, in which nearly 100 miners perished to better-armed and disciplined Northern Paiutes along the Truckee River in western Nevada. Military response came from California, not Utah, and although Paiutes lost dozens in army reprisals, they also soon secured reservation lands at both Pyramid Lake and Walker River, two of their primary subsistence regions. For these populations on Utah's western borders, then, military involvement brought subjugation as well as a modicum of resolution as state pacification and paternalism proceeded hand in hand.[67]

In Utah, continued Mormon expansion north encroached further upon Northern Shoshone lands, while continued overland travel to Oregon and California precipitated more chaos. Utah's western and northern perimeters, in short, were engulfed in conflict. When army units from Fort Hall and Camp Floyd attempted to protect emigrant trains by accompanying them along part of the journey, Shoshone raiders often simply amassed farther west and fell upon emigrant trains when army convoys departed. Overland mail stations similarly contended with Shoshone raiders, who reportedly were "utterly indifferent to everything but the taste of food." In a representative example at Willow Creek Mail Post, as Madsen relates, "seven Indians came in asking for something to eat. Not satisfied with the twenty pounds of flour offered them . . . they shot a cow, which so angered the station keeper that he shot and killed two of them." Within such chaos, violence both relieved and deepened endemic problems. Once deployed, it spread in all directions, often returning with greater fury upon those who initially unleashed it.[68]

A casual survey of Shoshone raids reveals the economics driving Indian theft. In contrast to the Ward attack, for example, in 1860's most violent raid, known as the Otter Party Tragedy, after a thirty-six-hour firefight Shoshone warriors did not rush to molest white women and children. Instead, twenty-eight survivors fled the scene "while the Indians were ransacking the wagons" for provisions. The tragedy, however, deepened as the survivors now were also forced to subsist off the depleted ecologies of the Oregon Trail. Some went in search of soldiers. Others fell prey to unidentified captors, and upon rescue, as Madsen relates, the rest "revealed that they had sustained themselves by eating the flesh of those who had perished."[69]

As their raids continued to fall heaviest west of Utah, equestrian Shoshone bands had been pushed as well as drawn west, particularly in the summer as emigrants crossed the region. As in the case of the Otter attack, soldiers from Wyoming and Utah accompanied emigrants only so far, enticing Snake River raiders to await their passage out of Utah into Oregon. Akin to the buffalo commons formed by rival powers on the Plains, these unincorporated territories remained throughout the 1850s an emigrant commons for Shoshone raiders who targeted wagon trains for survival. Emigration and Indian economics had become interlocked, creating an intractable nexus of violence.

Understandings of the ethnic composition of these raiders, however, remain cloudy. Not only had "Snake" Indians become an amalgam for different raiding Shoshone and Northern Paiute bands; mentions of anti-Union Mormon and renegade white "instigators" also litter reports. Reports of raiders masquerading as Indians may have also missed the slight presence of Shoshone captives or adoptees, like Elijah Wilson, who as a boy had "run away" to and was raised by Shoshones. Besides offering a wealth of ethnographic and historical information in his memoir, *Among the Shoshones,* Wilson recalled that as settlers and army units expanded their defensive perimeters, Shoshones withdrew into more interior, mountainous, and desert regions in Nevada. They would have ended up in the Pacific, his tribesman Morogonai asserted, had conditions continued pushing them, an exaggerated fear that others also expressed.[70]

Conditions did not, however, continue pushing Shoshones west. Like other tribes throughout the region, Shoshones encamped during the winter along familiar watersheds, erecting defensive fortifications and fashioning new armaments, sheltered by the imagined protection of the cold, while anticipating a springtime harvest before returning to their summer hunts and raids. After April 1861, the thousands of Union soldiers stationed in the region returned east; in Utah, army leaders sold their supplies for a song before leaving. The army's inability to punish Shoshone raiders and now its withdrawal seemingly underscored the continued viability of Indian raiding, especially as state officials had done little to curtail Indian raids or alleviate the crisis of Indian economics. No treaties, reservations, or consistent annuities had been provided to these Native populations for whom raiding had become integral to survival.[71]

From Fort Bridger, the Mormon War had seemed a monumental conflagration. Many of Utah's non-Mormon leaders had retreated within its walls while 3,000 soldiers soon wintered nearby. Previously attacked and burned by Mormons and Paiute allies, the fort in 1858 became the launching pad for the retaking of Utah, and although no battles coincided with the fall of Salt Lake, supply trains had been taken, homes evacuated, and the central political figure in the region deposed. In California and the East, such conflict was newsworthy. For those who struggled to feed themselves amidst tides of newcomers, the war represented something larger—it redefined the region's balance of power. And now, in the summer of 1861, another conflict between whites raged, one reportedly larger than the Mormon War. East of the mountains, past the Crow, Lakota, Pawnee, and other Plains Indians, the fate of a nation hung in the balance.

If Shoshone raiders had endured the arrival of several thousand Union soldiers, surely they could survive their departure. The military withdrawal, however, did not last long. Although the body of western army regulars during the Civil War shrank, in Robert Utley's terms, "to a feeble skeleton," two million volunteers poured into Union ranks, strengthening the military and indeed the nation's corpus. By war's end, 20,000 were serving in the West, and nearly all of them, as in New Mexico and Colorado, became engaged in Indian conflicts. In short, the Civil War brought an unprecedented measure of military involvement in western Indian affairs as a conflict sparked by Confederate secession yielded increases in the state's capacity to police as well as punish Indians.[72]

Though constant, Shoshone raids did not escalate during the war, even as Mormon settlements encroached further north. Additionally, Nevada and soon Montana's growing mining districts accelerated the movement of men and herds while further jeopardizing Indian subsistence through their consumption of water, game, and timber. Snake River raiders undoubtedly would have increased their use of violence in response to such disruption had not the federal army moved to secure emigrant, telegraph, and mail crossings. Throughout 1862 the movement of goods, people, and animals now also included federal soldiers. From mid-June through October, for example, Captain Medorem Crawford's company crossed the continent from Omaha to Portland with the sole intent "of conducting an escort for the protection of emigrants." Furthermore, the expansion of western telegraph lines enabled the rapid communication and movement of army forces, some of which took to the field under less than violent pretexts. At Fort Ruby in northeastern Nevada, Major Patrick Gallagher in late November "started with a party, consisting of . . . forty-two men . . . with six days' rations." The outrage: "one of the herders . . . reported that 10 horses, 1 mule, and 1 head of beef had been stolen by the Indians." The fact that the loss of twelve animals drew nearly fifty Union soldiers across Nevada in early winter reveals both the growing power and presence of the federal government. Stationed Union soldiers, most of whom were California volunteers, stood ready to serve.[73]

The arrival of the federal army did not bring commensurate increases in power for the government's other institutions of state rule. For in 1862, potential signs of resolution to Utah's chaotic Indian relations emerged. After four superintendents in as many years, James Doty assumed the title (as well as the role of governor) in December 1861; within three years he would conduct four Shoshone treaties with which his name would become synonymous. Only five months before Bear River, he reported that "notwithstanding their destitution and hunger," Shoshones had "committed but few acts of violence . . . and received what was given them with many expressions of thankfulness." Additionally, Congress had appropriated funds for Shoshone treaty negotiations, which Doty, unlike previous officials, utilized. As Commissioner of Indian Affairs William Dole also reported, Indian affairs in Utah had reached critical levels, now necessitating national attention: "The Indian service in Utah cannot be otherwise than discreditable to the government, unless Congress shall, by liberal appropriations, enable our agents to conduct their operations upon a scale in some measure corresponding with the absolute necessities of the Indians under their charge." The leading Indian officers in both the territory and the nation, in short, understood how ineffective, mismanaged, and underfunded Utah's Indian policies had become. Both also attempted to remedy what they saw as a salvageable situation.[74]

Shoshone needs were not met in the months ahead, nor did Superintendent Doty negotiate treaties without duress. Rather, the growing presence of emboldened Union forces brought a violent escalation in Indian retribution; foreshadowing the carnage at Sand Creek and the misery of the Long Walk, Utah's Civil War theater in fact exceeded subsequent army atrocities. With 300 Shoshone warriors engaged in defense of over seventy lodges and estimates of nearly 300 killed and 160 surviving women and children, the Bear River Massacre involved at least 700 for an entire morning's battle on January 29, 1863. As commanding officer Colonel Patrick Edward Connor relayed, "It was not my intention to take any prisoners." Attacking in what is now Idaho, Connor's forces moved north from Utah and, much like Chivington before Sand Creek, disguised their movement from both Indians and settlers. They also came in the winter.[75]

While many point to recurring Shoshone raids on Utah's Cache Valley, to the still undetermined fate of captives from the Otter Party, or to the attacks of the preceding decade, the combination of a militarized Indian policy and aggressive volunteer forces better explains this moment of overwhelming state violence against unsuspecting Indian families. As Connor was at pains to explain, "I captured 175 horses, some arms, destroyed over seventy lodges, a large quantity of wheat and other provisions . . . [and] left a small quantity of wheat for the sustenance of 160 captive [women] and children, whom I left on the field." Emphasizing his military mastery as well as unconcern for survivors, Connor's forces not only killed at Bear River but also impoverished. Having destroyed Indian families, homes, and foodstuffs, the army left the survivors to a desperate and uncertain future. Connor's description of the battle ends with women and children standing alone on a corpse-littered field where they had recently slept, everything taken from them in the January snow except a "small quantity of wheat."[76]

Compared with the loss of life in other Civil War theaters, the outcome at Bear River appears of less potential import. One can argue that, though tragic, the killing of a few hundred Indians on a winter morning pales by comparison with the nation's other losses. Such an assessment is often reinforced by American history's prevailing silence: missing from most U.S. history texts and even from several American Indian histories, the Bear River Massacre often becomes an episodic aberration in the larger American narrative. Mostly, however, it simply falls into the margins and lies silent in the cold expanse of the past.[77]

Many Shoshone people have fought to obtain commemoration for those lost in 1863, particularly on behalf of the descendants of the victims. First designated an Idaho State Battle Ground in 1932, the massacre site near the confluence of Battle Creek and the Bear River dis-

Photograph of the Bear River Massacre site, 1991. Courtesy of Drex Brooks. Seen here as a dumping ground, the site of Colonel Edward Patrick Connor's raid against unsuspecting Northern Shoshone families in January 1863 has recently been renamed a historic "massacre" site.

turbingly became in the 1980s a dumping spot, notably profiled in western photo-surveys as an emblem of America's forgotten Indian past. As a result of Shoshone activism, the grounds have recently been renamed a "massacre" site while the remains of those lost have been repatriated. Most recently, the Fort Hall Shoshoni–Bannock Tribe of Idaho has assumed management of the site's preservation.[78]

The significance of the Bear River Massacre to Shoshone peoples and its absence from discussions of U.S. history illustrate the often extreme disconnects between Indians and non-Indians in contemporary America. Unknown to most while painful to others, Bear River can offer opportunities for bridging such divides. For the massacre's legacies include more than Shoshone peoples or the U.S. Army. Occurring within a larger context of violent social relations, the Bear River Massacre was not an aberration but the culmination of decades, indeed generations, of Indian destitution. Such destitution was not caused by white expansion but was deepened by it, the fragility and resiliency of Indian life, respectively, compounded and exacerbated by the many impoverishments of colonialism.

As many attempt to reconcile the hopeful promises of America with the traumatic acts discovered in our nation's past, attention to such violence may yield some insight. Surely, the history of the Great Basin is also a part of the American experience. Reconciliation must accompany resolution, and if one teaches or yearns for democratic aspirations, one must also recognize the genesis of such ideals. In large portions of America, Indian peoples found themselves engulfed in the chaotic storms of European expansion and responded in ways that refashioned themselves and those around them. Among such responses, violence became a necessary form of social, economic, and political survival, a practice that beleaguered as much as benefited. Though often presented without any mention of Native people, American history emerged from within, not outside of, such encounters.

Upon incorporation into distant empires and nations, Great Basin Indians witnessed continued and in many cases growing destitution, prompting the increased use of violence. Beginning in 1787 and for the first century of its existence, the U.S. government developed mechanisms for incorporating Indian peoples into the nation. Treaties, land cessions, state agents, annuities, and eventually reservations—these were the sinews that linked the state to the continent's indigenous populations. Though established and enshrined in constitutional law, these policies were often violated. As in the Great Basin, they were never fully funded or enforced, and were often only sporadically encouraged. Despite the efforts of superintendents and Indian agents, the nation-state's aspiration to simultaneously secure lands from and protect Indian peoples was never extended to Utah's Indians, who confronted the deluge of expansion without reliable or empowered agents of the state. Unlike in western Colorado, the crisis of Indian economics accelerated violence against settlers and emigrants. The ensuing progression of raiding, warfare, and ultimately massacre between these different social communities is not surprising. The lack of attention to them is, as the failures of the state to enact its own policies now approximate the struggles of subsequent generations to reconcile them.

Born on the Fourth of July, or Narrating Nevadan Indian Histories

According to Utah's Governor James Doty, Colonel Connor "justly punished" Shoshones at Bear River in the "severest and most bloody . . . [fight] which has ever occurred with the Indians west of the Mississippi." As the governor proudly added, "It struck terror into the heart" of Shoshone bands throughout the region. "They now acknowledge the Americans are the masters of this country." Eighteen sixty-three had become a triumphant year for Utah's Indian department, a year "so successful in restoring peace."[1]

On the heels of Shoshone massacre came Doty's vision of "peace." With one band of Northern Shoshones "almost exterminated," nearly all others soon confronted both the governor and now Brigadier General Connor in negotiations in which "treaties of peace and friendship" channeled the Great Basin's Northern, Western, Eastern, and Goshute Shoshones into the currents of state rule. In the months after Bear River, four treaties between Doty and Shoshone leaders were signed, establishing first steps toward federal recognition, land transfers, and promised annuities and reservations. From Fort Bridger, Wyoming, through Box Elder and Tuilla Valley, Utah, to Nevada's Ruby Valley, Doty's Shoshone treaties became political corollaries of Connor's violence as massacre and peace became interwoven.[2]

Much as the Bear River Massacre encapsulated decades of degenerative Indian-white relations in northern Utah, Doty's Ruby Valley Treaty has come to define an even longer conflict—the century-and-a-half political impasse between Western Shoshones and the federal government. Unlike Idaho's Fort Hall Reservation and Wyoming's Wind River Reservation, the majority of Nevada's Western Shoshones have never received the promised annuities or reservation lands mandated by the Treaty of Ruby Valley. Despite ratification by the U.S. Senate, Shoshone appeals through congressional bodies, and a series of legal battles, the U.S. government has failed to enact this agreement. As Steven Crum has revealed, even the treaty's negotiators "recognized the Western Shoshone peoples as the legal owners of a vast area in the Great Basin. Jacob Lockhart, Indian agent for Nevada . . . reported . . . 'the treaty is in no instance considered as extinguishing Indian title.'" Subsequent Shoshone appeals, however, have failed to secure compensation for this unconstitutional "taking," and more than 90 percent of Nevada is still "owned" by the federal government. Indian Claims Commission hearings in 1962 determined that Shoshone title "was extinguished by the gradual encroachment by whites," a finding challenged by Shoshone leaders. In a broad perspective, then, many strands of Great Basin Indian history converged in, culminated in, and sprang from the decisive events of 1863.[3]

Though separated by new jurisdictions and territorial boundaries, Nevada and Utah in 1863 retained common geographic and political features. Connor, for instance, had moved to Utah from Ruby Valley, where he had ordered his forces to kill indiscriminately. "You will also destroy every male Indian whom you encounter in the vicinity of the late massacres," he charged. When encountering suspected raiders, "immediately hang them, and leave their bodies thus exposed as an example of what evil-doers may expect while I command in this district." The triumphant conqueror of Bear River had earlier experiences with Shoshone families in northern Nevada.[4]

Composed of numerous basins and mountain ranges, the borders of eastern Nevada and western Utah remained until 1864, when Nevada emerged from the western half of Utah to become a political entity in its own right. A waystation to California, the Silver State linked Utah and California and soon surpassed all other mineral-producing regions in the world. Witnessing spectacular flows in specie, people, and resources, Nevada's boom, like the California gold rush, devastated Indian subsistence economies, rapidly propelling many into mines, settlements, and ranches as wage laborers.[5]

The rushed integration of Indians into mines and settlements contributed to the failed implementation of Doty's Nevada treaty. For the rest of the century, nonreservation Shoshones outnumbered those settled on the lone Shoshone reservation in Nevada at Duck Valley. Seasonally attached to white communities, many Shoshones fell beyond the reach of both national and state authorities, particularly the Bureau of Indian Affairs. Eleven Shoshone leaders, most of whom led autonomous political bands across Nevada's central and eastern valleys, had signed the Ruby Valley Treaty. Now "laboring" in white settlements, Western Shoshones held an ambiguous political status outside the established mechanisms of federal Indian policy. Securing reservations for Shoshones, as well as legal title to Shoshone lands, remained beyond the capacity, or at least commitments, of the federal government.[6]

Other state-designed Indian policies, however, still affected these communities, especially their children. Both reservation and off-reservation boarding schools targeted Shoshone children, several of which endured deep into the twentieth century; the Stewart Indian School in Carson City finally closed its doors in 1981. Indeed, policymakers viewed education—and not diplomatic negotiation—as the foundation for a shared future. Governor Nye went so far as to predict that "civilizing" pedagogy would transform Nevada's Indian people while also bringing renown to the state:

> I congratulate the country upon the success of the peaceful policy adopted for our tribes in this Territory . . . It will open up to them a new existence, and will make them not only a peaceful but useful class of inhabitants; the younger ones will be educated in all the useful branches of common education and ordinary agriculture, and transform them from savages to men and women adapted to all the employments necessary to self-subsistence . . . This great humanizing undertaking . . . will stand forth as one of the proudest achievements of the department, and will be looked at with wonder by nations and coming generations, that a nation, while struggling for its existence against a mighty rebellion, with one hand . . . stretches out the other with kindness over the long-neglected savage for his redemption.

By 1863 Nevada, particularly the Comstock mining district around Virginia City, had become the fast-growing, most profitable part of the West. Nye's optimism arose from the discovery of Nevada silver in the wake of California gold. Moreover, unlike California gold, many believed Nevada's silver to be "limitless."[7]

Despite such optimism, political resolution of Shoshone grievances has not been forthcoming. "Coming generations" have not marveled at the transcendent progress of Nevada's Indian affairs. The "great humanizing undertaking" that Nye foresaw never materialized. Nor has it percolated into the consciousness of nations. On the contrary, the most enduring images of Nevadan Indian history remain moments of contestation, cultural resistance, and abject dehumanization. A century and a half after Nevada attained statehood, its Shoshone Indians are best known for protesting their violated treaty and its attendant ecological deterioration as federal stewardship has allowed military and nuclear testing among other forms of land management. In the late nineteenth century, Northern Paiute author Sarah Winnemucca gained national prominence as a speaker, author, and critic of federal Indian policies, while the Paiute prophet Jack Wilson, known as Wovoka, foresaw a different future. In a series of visions, dances, and songs referred to as the Ghost Dance, he predicted that the tide of whites would recede and that deceased Indian family members would return to their loved ones.[8]

If the history of the Great Basin suggests anything, it is that America's regions and populations remain interconnected, often violently so. Emblematic of such connections, Wilson's teachings spread throughout the West and found fertile ground among reservation communities, particularly in South Dakota. Indeed, the Ghost Dance has become so iconographically attached to the Pine Ridge Indian Reservation that its Great Basin origins are often obscured. By the end of 1890 the Ghost Dance had brought spiritual hope as well as tragedy to the northern Plains. Days after Christmas, the Seventh Cavalry exacted revenge for Custer's defeat at the Little Big Horn and attacked 300 Lakota men, women, and children in the winter snow at Wounded Knee. Often portrayed as the quintessential moment of Indian victimization and even as the final chapter of Indian history, the links between the Wounded Knee Massacre and the Great Basin remain underexplored. For peoples unacknowledged in narratives of the nation's past, Utes, Paiutes, and Shoshones have surprisingly shaped many of the West's most traumatic chapters, moments that emerged from histories of violence while also challenging visions of a shared future.[9]

Photograph of Paiute prophet Wovoka, 1911. Courtesy of the Nevada Historical Society, Reno. The most famous Indian religious leader of the late
nineteenth century, Wovoka posed for this photograph at Nevada's Walker
River Reservation.

The challenges confronting many Paiute and Shoshones bordered upon the apocalyptic. Winnemucca's autobiography, *Life among the Piutes,* for example, is anchored in articulations of indigenous trauma, and a casual survey of its first chapter underscores the fear, anguish, and displacement that pervaded Sarah's youth. Forced into the Sierras in search of work, Winnemucca's mother lost many battles to her family's white employers, who "would come into our camp and ask my mother to give our sister to them. They would come in at night, and we would all scream and cry; but this did not stop them." The men in her community "would not dare to say a word, for fear they would be shot down," as rape and emasculinizaiton became everyday ordeals for Indians within mining communities. The only state west of the Mississippi without equestrian Indians, Nevada's Indian history remains underwritten, only recently pioneered by tribal scholars and anthropologists, many of whom are themselves participants in ongoing treaty rights negotiations.[10]

The Emptiness of Primitivity

Many American intellectuals who have sojourned in the region have looked askance at these Native peoples, since their wage labor and poverty have often conflicted with others' received knowledge of Indians. As in much of U.S. history, encounters with contemporary Native people tend to disturb others' expectations, and Indians remain among the least understood Americans. As many have suggested, "Indian" is a cultural category of such densities and incongruity of meaning that it has become arguably the most "empty signifier" in the discursive field of America's racial classifications. Accordingly, many have attempted to abandon the loaded, constraining meanings found within this powerful category, as "Native American," "First Nation," and "Native" intermix with Columbus' famous mistake.[11]

Of all North America's indigenous people, few have received as much intellectual disdain as Nevada's Shoshones. Not only have traders, travelers, and state officials questioned Shoshone humanity; they have also become the definitive "primitive" peoples of the world. Thanks in large part to the discipline of anthropology, Shoshones have been portrayed as "stone age" peoples and not as contemporary Americans. Historians, further, continue to discuss Great Basin history with-

Photograph of Paiute mother and children, early twentieth century. Courtesy of the Nevada Historical Society, Reno. Nevadan Indians adapted to American conquest in myriad ways. For those living outside reservations, survival necessitated integration into mining and ranching economies, as in the case of this Northern Paiute mother and children. The woven cradleboard and piñon winnower furnish evidence of continued cultural practices.

out reference to Indian experiences, let alone to the dialectics of colonialism central to the region's ongoing past. Ignored by history,
naturalized by anthropology, and mocked by travelers, Great Basin Indians maintain unnoticeable if not maligned roles in the pageant of
America.

Two of America's greatest literary and ethnographic writers began
their careers in Nevada; both commented on Shoshone culture and
humanity. One belittled Shoshone existence in passing; the other developed systematic theories of culture based on Shoshone economics.
Representative of the various strands of dehumanization that have
characterized narratives of Nevada's Indians, Samuel Clemens and anthropologist Julian Steward provide as much insight as any into the
ideological terrain in which Great Basin Indian history now operates.

Samuel Clemens is of course better known as Mark Twain, a pseud-
onym first deployed on February 3, 1863, in Virginia City's *Territorial
Enterprise*. Appointed secretary of Nevada Territory by the Lincoln
administration, Orion Clemens had invited his "young and ignorant"
brother Samuel to travel with him across the continent in 1861. A
twenty-six-year-old former steamboat pilot and onetime newspaper hand,
Samuel accepted at once. As he confessed in the opening paragraph
of *Roughing It,* "I never had been away from home, and that word
'travel' had a seductive charm."[12]

Traveling indeed propelled the younger Clemens' career. Stints in
Hawaii, the Middle East, and California formed the basis of his earliest
literary successes. Crafting an iconoclastic, jovial vernacular that has
become paradigmatic in American literature, Twain's gruff humor
aptly captured the ebbs and flows of life in a mining district in his descriptions of gunfighters, saloons, and itinerant politicians. Although
Roughing It (1871) failed to meet Twain's expectations, within a decade 100,000 copies in English as well as foreign editions took Twain's
only western novel into many hands, carrying with it the cultural
chauvinisms of his time while propelling the former Nevadan newsmen to greater prominence.[13]

Twelve of the last chapters of *Roughing It* chronicle the author's 1866
travels to Hawaii, where he covered the expansion of American sugar
plantations. Decades before the publication of his famous Mississippi
tales, Twain encountered in Hawaii, as Amy Kaplan suggests, not only
exotic and racialized others but also ethnographic subjects whose cul-

tural and political practices remained unintelligible, and thus discomforting, to the Missourian. Mockery, parody, and eroticization, Kaplan argues, fueled Twain's popularity: "By lecturing about 'savage' Hawaiians on stage, Twain could playfully cross the line between civilized and uncivilized . . . He merged the persona of the rough-hewn frontiersmen with that of the educated traveler through their shared difference from his nonwhite subjects." Derision, in particular, calmed and assured, masking his uncertainties while blunting the community practices and ambitions of Hawaiians whose kingdom had been transformed into plantation-style economies.[14]

Kaplan's suggestion that in Hawaii Twain both confronted and crafted ways of comprehending racial alterity restores a needed imperial perspective to discussions of America's most celebrated author. Far from remaining a regional or even continental writer, Twain traveled the Pacific, the Middle East, and Europe before settling in New York and then Connecticut. Such "imperial routes" enabled him later to return to his childhood for literary inspiration. That Twain first left Missouri for Nevada, however, and encountered indigenous "others" has not yet generated comparable reassessment. While many suggest that the frenetic, atomistic world of Virginia City allowed Clemens to reinvent and imagine himself anew—to become Mark Twain—few have considered where his discourse of Shoshone inhumanity resides. What may Twain's dehumanization of Great Basin Indians suggest about his emergent literary development? How might it recast Nevada's most celebrated, if adopted, author?[15]

"All right, then, I'll go to hell," Twain's most famous character, Huckleberry Finn, decides after deliberating on his friend Jim's continued enslavement; and generations have sought meaning in these hopeful, yearning sentiments. However, as with his portrait of Hawaiians, such visions of potential racial coexistence stand in contradistinction to the "nausea" that Clemens experienced upon encountering Goshute Shoshones. "They deserve pity, poor creatures; and they can have mine," he derided, "[but] at this distance. Nearer by, they never get anybody's." Distant pity and proximate revulsion—these related expressions encapsulate dominant visions of Nevadan Indians. Within a panoply of derisive labels, the most common has been "digger," a debasement of Shoshone gathering practices with strong homophonic resonance with America's most powerful racial epithet, "nigger."[16]

Twain believed that his revulsion revealed something larger, something universal. In his eyes, the Shoshone were not simply "inferior,"
but "the most wretchedest type of mankind . . . very considerably inferior to even the despised Digger Indians of California." Indeed, their
"degraded . . . rank" compelled the author to scour "bulky volumes" in
search of others to place alongside these Native peoples as the *ur*-prim-
itive peoples of the world. "I found but one," he concluded, "open to
that shameful verdict. It is the Bosjesmans [Bushmen] of South Africa." For Twain, always conscious of the racial landscapes in which he
traveled, the Shoshone would forever lurk behind his visions of American Indians, foreclosing remorse for the state of Indian-white relations
in America. Within every Indian, Twain maintained, were forms of debasement shared with and confirmed by the Goshute. "The nausea
that the Goshoots gave me," he concluded, "set me to examining authorities, to see if perchance I had been over-estimating the Red Man
. . . The revelations that came were disconcerting. It was curious to see
how quickly the paint and tinsel fell away from him and left him
treacherous, filthy, and repulsive." In sum, "whenever one finds an Indian tribe he has only found Goshoots more or less modified by circumstances and surroundings—but Goshoots, after all."[17]

That all Indians are Shoshone "after all" has become an implicit assumption in various strains of American intellectual history. Although
Twain remains the most telling example within this discursive field,
his perspective has not been the most influential. Indeed, few ever an-
alyze chapter 19 of *Roughing It*. What is clear is that Shoshone material
conditions have disturbed outsiders to such extent that supreme forms
of racial logic have been deployed to explain such difference. Twain's
"silent, sneaking, treacherous looking race . . . eating what a hog
would decline" has become the sediment for comparative assessments
of America's Indians. In the Great Basin, then, outsiders have both developed and had confirmed evolutionary typologies, most of which
have been devised under the guise of ethnographic observation.[18]

Anthropologists are generally known for the peoples and regions
they study, and as much as anyone dominates a region's ethnographic
universe, Julian Steward looms over the Great Basin. One can even
speak of Great Basin ethnography as pre- and post-Steward. Interested
as a teenager in the Indians of southern California, Steward studied
under ethnographic luminaries Robert Lowie and Alfred Kroeber at

Berkeley in the 1920s but departed from the cultural relativism popularized by their adviser Franz Boas. Steward sought to make anthropology more of a "science," one in which cultural models and comparisons could be developed and applied to all the world's people. He became, according to one assessment, "the greatest of synthesizers . . . the complete American anthropologist." And, in his search to derive meaning from cultural diversity, Great Basin Indians proved eminently useful.[19]

Much like Twain, Steward saw the Shoshone as exceptional. Their subsistence lifestyle, migratory routes, and political structures, he believed, contradicted established notions of "tribes." Living in arid and fragile environments, they appeared the most natural of America's Indians, but not in romantic or sentimental ways. As Twain had argued, other Indians remained more "modified by circumstances and surroundings" than the Shoshone, but underneath, fundamental commonalities remained. Steward expanded such links and attempted to understand the interplay between culture and "surroundings" in the evolving field of cultural ecology. Taking the "natural environment [as] a constant . . . [and] unalterable factor," Steward sought to establish links between behavior and ecology, and in the Great Basin he believed he had found America's simplest environment as well as its "simplest" people, for whom the "primitive family band" remained the primary political form. Shoshones, he argued, lived in a never-ending "food quest," perpetually on the verge of starvation in the most elemental form of human existence.[20]

Constructing elaborate models of culture change, Steward's work forever changed the study of America's Indians. As his work disseminated, broader causal assessments of culture could now be made based on correlations between ecological and cultural elements. Cultures could also be compared and equated. Across the ethnographic landscape of the Americas, common typologies emerged as hunters and gatherers, band-level societies, and chiefdoms challenged existing "culture area" definitions, filling in the remaining spaces of the anthropological universe. In sum, hierarchies of cultural difference informed by Steward's work provided an ethnographic lingua franca for analyzing North America's indigenous populations.[21]

Much as nineteenth-century cartographers rushed to identify "unknown" geographic locations, early anthropologists practiced various forms of ethnographic cartography. Many of those who charted the unincorporated West, for example, became prominent ethnographers, most notably John Wesley Powell, the great navigator of the Grand Canyon, who continued his fascination with the West at the Bureau of American Ethnography. At the BAE, Powell orchestrated collections and publications of ethnographic materials, making it the central nervous system of American anthropology. The links between American ethnography and empire have rarely been so personified.[22]

As director of the BAE from 1935 to 1946, Steward extended his ecological analyses to other parts of the world, particularly into Latin America through massive studies of South America's indigenous populations. Moving to Columbia University, he subsequently trained prominent postwar anthropologists, notably Eric Wolf and Sidney Mintz, directing three dozen dissertations in six years. Steward, in short, dominated the course of midcentury American anthropology, taking the field to a purportedly regimented and scientific plane, and by 1950 relativism, psychoanalysis, and personality studies had become less influential. Teaching in a department made famous by Boas, for example, Steward steered students away from Ruth Benedict and other relativist practitioners, as ecological and cultural variables, cross-cultural comparisons, and predictive models became hallmarks of his career. "Even to give summary treatment to the work carried out by those who have been directly influenced by Steward," Marvin Harris has argued, "could prove an exhausting task."[23]

The Great Basin, then, launched the career of America's most influential, if now forgotten, midcentury ethnographer. But although anthropological theory has moved away from neoevolutionary paradigms toward more discursive assessments of "culture," Steward's legacy still dominates studies of Great Basin nonequestrians. Problematic in its untainted notions of "culture" and "ecology," Steward's vision of timeless Shoshone "primitives" has consigned these Native peoples to the dusty shelves of "prehistory." Antitheses of modernity and "civilization," Shoshones have become intellectually synonymous with deprivation as the least "developed" peoples of the world. They and other "primitive people," as Elman Service once argued, "hover over thoughtful men like ancestral ghosts," apparitions of humanity's distant beginnings.[24]

Such debasement has had underrecognized political and moral consequences. For example, when Steward and some of his students arrived at the University of Illinois in 1952 to lead its anthropology program, they were temporarily housed in the college's agricultural school, where the Department of Meat served steak to its lunchtime employees. After losing their "best secretary" to this rival department, someone suggested that "her defection was a reaffirmation of his theories—there is indeed a Shoshoni in all of us." Unamused, Steward retorted: "We all need values that transcend our stomachs."[25]

Of Steward's thousands of pages of writing, none better captures the political unconscious of his work than an unpublished eighteen-page report submitted to Commissioner of Indian Affairs John Collier in 1936. Contacted by Collier's office to review efforts to bring federal resources to "landless" Shoshones, Steward recommended that the Bureau of Indian Affairs *not* grant federal recognition and small reservations to Nevada's Shoshones, who were fighting to secure land and autonomy in postconquest Nevada. Bestowing reservations and tribal governments, he believed, was "illogical," since governments and constitutions were antithetical to his view of Shoshone politics. They were Indians of course, but not tribes. Primitive family bands, for Steward, could not become tribal governments. Such efforts would only "baffle them."[26]

Largely integrated within white ranching and mining districts and without the guarantees mandated by the Treaty of Ruby Valley, under Collier's administration Shoshones were at last able to get their political grievances heard by the nation's highest policymakers. Attempting to reverse a half-century of state-designed assimilation programs, Collier weighed various options for rectifying Shoshone dispossession, and he sought additional advice from Indian agents working in Carson City. Fortunately for several Shoshone tribes, he did not heed the advice of his "consultant anthropologist." Siding with others' recommendations, Collier assisted many Western Shoshones in securing small reservations and federal recognition across portions of their still unceded homelands.[27]

That the region's most influential anthropologist lobbied against his informants' ambitions speaks volumes about the contested nature of Great Basin history. Much like Twain's, Steward's representations deny shared time, or contemporaneity, to his subjects. They also do more. To attribute Indian "values" to hunger or to fashion an aca-

demic career based on their "primitivity" is one thing, to curb their political options another. Debasing another's "culture" is not the same as
worsening their material or political circumstances. As scholars further expose the links between culture and imperialism, recognition is
still needed not only of how representations underpin colonial inequities, but also of how such ideas themselves can influence the conditions in which indigenous peoples must operate. How have everyday
settlers operating in new racial landscapes interacted with Native people? How have race and violence conditioned their relations with Indians? Most important, how have Native peoples fashioned responses to
such social and intellectual racism?[28]

The Everyday Challenges of Survival

The changes that followed U.S. incorporation did indeed threaten
Shoshone survival. Their material and ecological deprivations were,
however, far from "natural." They remained stark accompaniments to
colonial expansion, and the explosion of Nevada's mining districts
in the 1860s only deepened the crisis of indigenous subsistence. In
the fragile ecologies of Nevada, mines consumed water, piñon stands,
grasses, and game while ranches and farms helped feed the region's
mushrooming population. Timber stands, for example, used for both
fuel and construction, became exhausted, and soon logs had to be
brought east from the Sierras. The extent of such traffic east down the
Truckee River past the Northern Paiute Pyramid Lake Reservation led
even Governor Nye to propose the development of a Paiute mill.[29]

Paiute reservations provided a modicum of economic autonomy vis-
à-vis nonreservation Shoshones. Fishing, agriculture, annuities, and
limited game within reservation borders contrasted with the opportunities for Western and Goshute Shoshones in the central and eastern
thirds of the state. For example, just three seasons before Clemens encountered the Goshute, Utah's Superintendent Benjamin Davies decried the "poverty" of his most western charges, "who crowded the wayside of my return to shake hands and beg[ged] me to 'come again
soon with presents.'" Those who in November 1860 implored Davis to
return with provisions for their hungry families became the following
summer for Twain "prideless" beggars, and as overland stage, tele-

graph, and railway lines crossed the Great Basin, images of Shoshone deprivation abounded.[30]

Such impoverishment, as Davis suggested, had economic and political causes. Denied reservation lands and annuities while coping with interrelated ecological and demographic crises, Shoshones experienced a total reconfiguration of their economies as a direct result of U.S. expansion. "To survive," as Beth Sennett has shown for the Death Valley Timbisha Shoshone, "the Indians adapted to a wage labor economy." Mines, ranches, and towns now offered not only economic but also social opportunities, and throughout central and eastern Nevada, small Indian communities formed alongside white ranches and within urban settlements. Commonly referred to as "colonies" in towns, these attached Indian enclaves dotted the state, often rising and falling with the region's economies; in the early 1900s "colonies" even began securing federal recognition as federally sanctioned, urban Indian enclaves. Outside the state-designed framework of segregating Indians onto reservations, Shoshones integrated themselves into available economic channels in response to the changes unleashed by colonial expansion.[31]

In many settlements, Shoshones worked the lowest rungs of the economic ladder, performed menial domestic and ranching labor, and struggled to make ends meet. Some fashioned baskets, gloves, and riding gear to augment household income, while others adapted new modes of housing with more traditional "wickiup" designs. In Austin, for example, as the nineteenth-century silver boom tailed off and itinerant labor groups moved on, Shoshone families stayed and inhabited abandoned homes, living in the tarpaper shacks on "China Hill," first built by laboring Chinese immigrants, themselves targeted by anti-Chinese sentiments and organizations.[32]

Although survival necessitated wage labor, it also came on Shoshone terms. Shoshone families adapted their seasonal economies to the wage-labor and residential opportunities found alongside whites and continued to gather for celebrations and socializing at both traditional and new locations. Often they timed their gatherings to follow their wheat harvests and to coincide with pine-nut harvests, thus balancing the demands of their new labor markets with the familiar seasonal rounds that had long characterized their lives. Such practices, how-

ever, troubled state officials, who realized that the unmonitored proximity of Indians and whites undermined state-designed assimilation
programs while also engendering sporadic racial conflict. The more
Indians moved, officials reasoned, the less successful Indian policy
became; migration came to symbolize the persistence of Indian culture as well as a hindrance to transforming it. Accordingly, Indian
agents throughout the nineteenth century attempted to relocate Western Shoshones to Duck Valley, the lone Shoshone reservation in Nevada, as well as to Fort Hall in southern Idaho, where state agencies
could better monitor Indian families. Shoshone children, of course,
were already targeted for boarding schools, where notations of their
daily attendance recorded their now-fixed habitation.[33]

Not all families, however, wanted to relocate to distant reservations.
As Steward, Crum, Sennett, and others have shown, Nevadan Shoshones preferred living in the familiar environments of their local homelands, staying within range of known and demarcated hunting
grounds, piñon stands, and ancestral burials. Indeed, the cosmology
and cultural identities of Shoshone bands remain tied to localized
environments; band names evoke valley or mountain foods, terrains,
and cultural landmarks. While challenged by the voracious drive of
mining economies, Shoshone families nonetheless found niches
within settlement societies, choosing to remain in familiar landscapes
in their changing world.[34]

Some families did migrate to Duck Valley and Fort Hall. Given that
families, and not "tribes," remained the primary form of Western Shoshone sociopolitical organization, such migration arose from personal
and familial decisions. While on one level Shoshone grievances with
the federal government commonly linked bands together in shared
forms of supra- or pan-Shoshone politics, on another level individual
family bands interpreted and responded to the everyday demands of
Indian policy. So, whereas some Shoshones in the state's northern and
eastern portions choose to reside at Duck Valley, and eventually in the
1920s at the Goshute Indian Reservation on the Utah border, before
then many remained in their local environments or moved only temporarily to reservations.

Temporary migration, however, was not what state officials envisioned, because it undermined the processes of "inscription" that Indian agents were attempting in the region. Making Shoshones legible

to the state, in James Scott's terminology, remained a constant project throughout the nineteenth and twentieth centuries as policymakers continued to speculate about the precise nature of Shoshone demographics, locations, and politics. Nevada's colonies, Indian "farms," and unresolved Shoshone land claims all arose to some degree from the limited ability of the state to fold this vast region into established mechanisms of governance, and seemingly everyday challenges, such as enumerating Indian families, confounded Indian agents into the twentieth century. The diametrically opposed recommendations that arrived on John Collier's desk in 1936 were but another symptom of the state's limited ability to grasp Indian life.[35]

In more immediate ways, the state shaped Indian people's everyday lives. Indeed, it is hard to envision ways in which state policies—either in application or in absence—did not influence the course of Shoshone-white relations. The unfulfilled Ruby Valley Treaty stipulations, the limited federal protection of Indian lands, the encroachment of mines, ranches, and settlements into Shoshone homelands, and the subsequent entry of Shoshone laborers into white-run labor markets, all such phenomena occurred both in an amazingly short period—in some cases in less than a decade—and outside established avenues for Indian-white affairs. Treaties did not establish reservations, Indian agencies, or annual resource distributions. Once ratified, they were forgotten, their Indian signatories cast into the cauldron of white colonization without political allies.

With their rapid incorporation into the region's economy, Nevadan Shoshones resisted state formation in multiple aspects of their lives. While productive servants and laborers, agreeable neighbors, and even friends, Shoshone families remained dissatisfied with the economic, political, and social institutions that dictated the pace and scale of everyday life. Angered at the loss of traditional game and resources, concerned about the imposed cultural expectations for their children, and unsure about their ability to receive promised reparations for occupied lands, tensions characterized Indian-white relations long after statehood. Such tensions often erupted in violence, as minor thefts, poaching, and social conflicts percolated through mining and ranching communities, sometimes turning deadly. When assessed individually, such tensions belie the pervasive forms of state control and Native resistance that characterize this region's history. When assessed collectively, such conflicts underscore the attempts by state institutions to control the behavior, movement, and even ideas of Native peoples, while also revealing the everyday attempts by Native people to live within as well as outside of such impositions. This constant interplay, indeed dialectic, between autonomous Indian action and imposed state control characterizes the region's history in clear ways and does so into the twentieth century.

Of all the many attempts to live outside as well as within such impositions, the fate of two early twentieth-century Shoshone families illustrates such tensions. In northeastern Nevada, some families that temporarily migrated to Duck Valley as well as Fort Hall found themselves uncomfortable settling into reservation life, preferring the seasonal, migratory, wage-earning lifestyle fashioned in the decades after statehood. Though challenging, life on the margins of ranching and mining communities provided consistent economic and social opportunities while allowing proximity to familiar cultural and subsistence sites. Towns also offered forms of entertainment not found in more remote regions. The Duck Valley Indian Reservation, for example, straddles the Nevada-Idaho border, and its primary town, Owyhee, has historically remained farther from the railway and overland travel routes than other central and eastern Nevadan towns such as Elko, Ely, Austin, and Battle Mountain. Shoshone communities formed within each of these overland settlements.[36]

One family who briefly tried reservation life at Fort Hall returned to the Rock Creek region in northeastern Nevada astride the Idaho border. Organized under the leadership of headman Mike Daggett, "Shoshone Mike" had approximately a dozen family members in his band. His exact name, age, and origins remain uncertain, though his fate is better known. Like many other nonreservation Shoshones, Mike's band migrated between white ranches and settlements, combining hunting and gathering with seasonal wage labor. As Frank Bergon has most clearly suggested, Mike's dissatisfaction with reservation life probably stemmed from the loss of autonomy fostered by sedentary habitation as well as from a cultural malaise induced by seeing the old ways abandoned under pressure from reservation officials, whose commitments to preserving reservation boundaries diminished with each season's expansion of white settlements. Perhaps living at

Fort Hall among distant Northern Shoshone and Bannock groups also made adaptation difficult. Whatever the reasons, after leaving the reservation, Mike, his sons, and their wives and children returned to familiar lands in Elko County but soon found themselves in danger. After engaging in a shootout in May 1910 with a small band of horse rustlers—a parallel stateless group—Mike's band sojourned west across Nevada's deserts, traveling clandestinely until reaching California. One rustler had been killed, possibly in retaliation for the death of one of Mike's sons, and although both groups were living outside the reach of the law, one was white, the other Indian.[37]

Had they had a place to retreat to, Mike's family band might have eluded retaliation. However, Indians living in and off of unfamiliar lands attract attention, and when four ranchers in western Nevada turned up dead in January 1911, state authorities linked these deaths to Mike's band. The four had died while pursuing rustled livestock. Their bodies had been stripped and horses taken, and the testimonies of those from across the state in Elko suggested loose parallels to the 1910 shootout. News of Indians poaching horses, cattle, and sheep and fighting with cattlemen quickly mobilized two dozen officers and recently deputized settlers, charged with tracking down Mike's band. Two Paiutes agreed to serve as trackers.

On the cold morning of February 26, 1911, in Clover Valley, northeast of Winnemucca, the last documented massacre of Great Basin Indians occurred. Mike and all the adult members of his band refused surrender and vainly exchanged fire against a better-armed force before each falling dead. One deputy was killed, and had the leading officer not intervened and warned his men that they wanted "to find out everything," the surviving children would probably have also perished. According to one participant, "We caught up with 'em and killed the whole works except for one squaw and two kids. We'd [have] killed them too" but for their commander's orders.[38]

As at Bear River, the origins of the massacre of Shoshone Mike's band stemmed from ruptured Indian subsistence economies, the concomitant resort to violence, and the limited capacity of state officials to enforce policy objectives. Hostile racial attitudes and the loss of white life only further fueled the fires of aggression.

Not all of Mike's family was killed. Four children survived and were photographed upon capture. Of these, only one survived the subsequent attacks of disease, loneliness, and despair that accompanied their transportation back to Fort Hall, where all were enrolled as members of the Mosho family. By the end of 1913 only the youngest, Josephine, was still alive, though diagnosed with tuberculosis, and she had

Photograph of captured children after the Shoshone Mike Massacre, February 1911. Courtesy of the Nevada Historical Society, Reno. Of the children captured from Shoshone Mike's band, shown here in front of the Washoe County Court House with a Nevada State Police deputy, only the youngest, Josephine, would survive the bouts of loneliness, disease, and despair that followed her family's destruction.

been taken into the superintendent's home to be raised. This survivor of disease and massacre eventually moved to the Yakama Indian Reservation in Washington, where she became a teacher, dying in 1990.[39]

The killing of Indians by state authorities in the second decade of the twentieth century reveals darker and in many ways still unresolved moments from America's Indian past. Nearly three generations of a Shoshone family perished one morning as a result of the limited economic and political avenues available to Nevada's Indians, the lone survivor raised without parents by a non-Indian family. As with all the Ute and Paiute children placed in Utah's settler homes or sold into captivity, one wonders how many developed or sustained contact with their Indian families. Of the hundreds of children who arrived each year on the steps of Great Basin Indian boarding schools, how many maintained healthy lives within as well as after their departure from these institutions? What of their parents, siblings, and communities who saw them so infrequently during their formative periods? Surely, family bonds weakened for those who were taken away as well as for those who stayed behind.[40]

Examining select moments of violence from the pre-reservation history of the Great Basin is one way to raise such questions. For personal as well as intellectual reasons, I have attempted to survey these centuries of Indian-white relations, suggesting ways of approaching these difficult, and persisting, subjects. As many Indian people know all too well, reconciling the traumas found within our community and family pasts with the celebratory narratives of America remains an everyday and in many cases overwhelming challenge. One need not be an expert in psychology to grasp the psychological ordeals incumbent upon living with dignity amidst such hardships.

Many family histories highlight the resilient and in many ways triumphant capacity of Nevada and Idaho Shoshones to endure amidst trauma and racism. Western Shoshone historian Steven Crum, for example, has offered a meticulous account of his people's past without which this work would not have been possible, while Fort Hall Shoshone reporter Mark Trahant founded a reservation newspaper before becoming a nationally syndicated *Seattle Times* columnist. Recent Western Shoshone political developments have shined international attention upon Shoshone activists Mary and Carrie Dann while tribal leaders deliberate about how best to proceed with outstanding land claims.

Those who rarely appear in historical focus and whom Steward viewed as incapable of self-government now court counsel with international activists.[41]

To some degree, these currents have shaped my own intellectual development, but not as immediately as investigations into my own family's history. Unlike many Shoshone and other Indian people, none of my immediate family lives on a reservation, nor have they ever done so except at select and trying times. Ours in a sense is a nonreservation family history that both conforms to and defies the larger processes suggested above. Most of all, our family's past disrupts the staid and essential portraits of Indian life so common in the discourse of Great Basin primitivity. And finally, it suggests how quintessentially American our family remains, if the definition of American is broad enough to encompass triumphant as well as traumatic elements found within our nation's past.

One year after Shoshone Mike's death, reportedly on July 3, 1912, my grandmother Eva Charley was born in Nevada's Monitor Valley. Like Josephine Mosho, she never knew her mother or father. Eva's mother, Mamie Andrews, was taken away from her when Eva was eight, to the state mental hospital; her father, Sam Johnson, had already separated from the family. Mamie had three other children with Sam's half-brother, Bob Snooks, whose abuse many believe either caused or accelerated her mental illness.

Children who never know their parents often learn little about their family and are also reluctant to discuss it, and piecing together Mamie and Eva's lives still confounds their children and children's children. We have two known photographs of Mamie, one of which is in this book's introduction. The other is our only childhood photo of Eva, standing beside her mother and siblings under a tree. The first was taken in a studio after Mamie had styled her hair; the second is a personal snapshot, so small it is almost undecipherable. I received these photos from my grandmother's younger sister, Annie (Snooks) Maine. Upon Mamie's confinement, Annie and her two brothers were taken to Reese River Valley and raised by their father's family, while Eva was sent to Smoky Valley and raised by her father's relatives. The loss of her mother and the subsequent separation from her siblings appear the most defining moments of Eva's early life, at least as far as my father, aunts, and I have been able to determine.

Eva recalled working a great deal in Smoky Valley for relatives who generally did not care for her. Unlike her sister and one of her brothers, she never attended the Stewart Indian School in Carson City; starting in childhood, she would work for the rest of her life until physically unable. Traveling between ranches and towns such as Round Mountain and Tonopah, Eva eventually settled in Austin, Nevada, between the Smoky and Reese River Valleys, where she worked at the Interna-

Photograph of Eva Charley, ca. 1929. Eva Charley Family Collection. Born a year after Shoshone Mike's death, Eva Charley of Monitor Valley sent this photograph to her younger sister, Annie Snooks, who was attending the Stewart Indian School in Carson City.

tional Hotel on Main Street. By that time Austin's heyday, like that of many mining towns, had long since passed, and the small mountain community generally welcomed local Indians to live among them.

Moving out of China Hill's shacks into the home of the former undertaker, Eva seemed to have achieved some stability in her life by the time of the Second World War. She had had two children before coming to Austin, and she now lived with Bert Charley, another local Shoshone, whose Japanese father, a former shopkeeper, was interned during the war. He would never return. Fortunately for Bert and his two older siblings, they had a Shoshone mother and extended family and were generally never considered, nor considered themselves, anything but Shoshone. The politics of internment thus bypassed these "Indian" children.

Bert's service in the war along with Eva's two brothers made life more challenging for her family of what were now five children. Junior, the oldest, helped by cobbling together jobs around town, while in less public ways he hunted rabbit and deer, gathered wood and water, and in hungry times poached a calf or two. Beverly, Eva's oldest daughter, helped raise her three younger siblings while Eva worked. Poor but self-sufficient, the family endured during the war and after. Bert's return, however, was bittersweet, as distant employment in Ely eventually compromised his marriage with Eva, leaving her again the family's lone provider.

By 1952 Beverly had moved out of town to raise her own family, while the three youngest were all in Austin's schools. My father, Evan, then eleven, was the middle of the youngest three, and had it not been for the most traumatic event in Eva's life I imagine the family would have stayed in Austin, content as they generally recall. However, as in her earlier life, events beyond her control eroded Eva's stability, sending her and the children into despair.

Late one evening, Austin's sheriff awoke the family with sad news. Junior was dead, killed in an auto accident in the hills outside town. In a shock from which she would never fully recover, Eva's heart partially collapsed, and the family could not stay in their home. With their oldest brother now gone and Eva bedridden, someone would have to care for them, and they headed west 100 miles to Fallon, staying in the Indian colony there with distant family.

For Eva's children, Fallon was nearly as far from Austin as France, and life in the colony and later in a two-room house never approximated Austin's familiarity. The colony adjoined the city dump, and my father remembers the smell of burning trash upon coming home from his new school. Perched in Nevada's Toiyabe National Forest, Austin had offered a bounty of recreation, seasonal hunting and gathering, and forms of local knowledge passed on by Eva and her brothers. Fallon, by contrast, was larger, flatter, and more humid, located near the Humboldt River's sink in traditionally Northern Paiute homelands. Eva never fully recovered from her stroke and required regular medical attention. Such attention along with her children's departures from home soon took Eva farther west, to Reno, her lifetime in central Nevada now over.

Eva and her sister may have shared the same birthday, Annie reportedly being born on the Fourth of July, 1918. As with so many elements from our family's past, other than photos most of what we have are each other's stories, and sometimes, as in all families, accounts do not always conform. Not being from the region, I usually defer to my older relatives, who understand these subjects far better than I.

Sometimes disparities arise, and like the painful as well as humorous contingencies that appear to determine our fate, they stay with me. My grandfather, Bert Charley, for example, easily could have been named after his Japanese father. Had not his cousins the first day of school informed his teacher that Bert indeed shared their last name, he might have carried a Japanese surname. "He's one of us," Bert's slightly older cousins reportedly told his kindergarten teacher, the task of communicating this elemental social information carried by such young messengers.

Schools, in many remembrances, become places where names and ages become developed, adjudicated, and ultimately confirmed, experiences common for many Indian people. Luther Standing Bear's famous account of literally selecting his English first name off the blackboard at Carlisle Indian School resembles Bert's account. Often missing from assessments of such accounts, however, are the structural forces impinging upon young Indian children. For Native people, and especially for nonreservation Indians, schools were often the first institution of the state encountered. Inscribing the young into the public realm remains an essential component of state education.[42]

Most Americans often become inscribed into the state at an earlier, indeed, initial moment. At birth, children receive the commonplace markings of social identity: name, gender, lineage/race, and age. In the twentieth century, such inscription has largely occurred in hospitals, or in county and municipal registries soon thereafter.

Very few of my older Indian relatives were born in hospitals, and many of their births appear not to have been registered. Given that Eva and Annie were raised without parents, I have often wondered whether their birthdays were in fact so close together. Annie, in her eighties, once suggested that the Fourth of July was a logical birthday, given its larger meanings; and since then, I have wondered whether Shoshone people of their generation potentially selected their birthdays. My father insists that his mother and aunt did, and noticeably, many of the region's Indian cemeteries provide only years of birth.

Unlike so many other Americans, including other American Indians, nonreservation Great Basin Indians face myriad challenges in obtaining forms of legal documentation. Like the processes of obtaining birth certificates, passports, and social security cards, tribal enrollment remains a complicated endeavor, particularly when family members choose not to discuss their genealogies. Given the histories of displacement, captivity, and violence that characterize Indian-white relations, the idea of pinpointing biological, "racial" ancestry amidst such social turbulence seems counterproductive at best, and many have rightly decried the pernicious logic of American Indian "blood quantum" standards. Fewer, however, have noticed that many Indian families initially listed on government censuses—upon which most blood quantum enrollment standards are based—were in fact of mixed race to begin with, or had multiple or changing parents, particularly fathers. Ultimately, the legal currents in which impoverished and semi-stateless Indian peoples have been forced to swim necessitate deeper investigations into the different forms of American identity sustained by Indian peoples. Much like these two Shoshone sisters, claiming inclusion in, if not shared birthdays with, the nation characterizes many Indian families, whose connections to this country, despite their treatment by it, remain unsurpassed.[43]

American Indian history is filled with big and often tragic processes. European contact, invasion, and conquest; colonization, adaptation, and resistance; dispossession, warfare, and massacre; land loss, cultural revitalization, and community resurgence—these are among the many leitmotifs of the field, a language of interpretation used to understand the experiences of the first Americans. Standing in these professional currents as well as within the family history sketched above, I find reconciling the expediency with which so many Native lives are reduced to near caricature with the pressing need to communicate these underrecognized American truths a constant challenge. In the classroom, in faculty meetings, and mostly in front of the computer, the square pegs of Indian experiences so rarely fit the circular holes of received knowledge that the experiment can appear at times futile. Generations have viewed the history of America without understanding let alone appreciation of the continent's original inhabitants, while educational avenues remain hazardous to Indian students. Against such obstacles, the field of Indian history operates.

Yet this is a central battleground in a larger struggle, a contest for reconciliation, if not for coexistence and redemption. Much like a family bereft by tragedy, a nation unable to confront its past will surely compromise any sense of a shared civic culture. National histories need to be shared by all, not imposed from above, and finding ways of celebrating the endurance as well as ascendancy of contemporary Indian people appears a thread from which to weave potentially broader national narratives. For there are indigenous nations within the nation, peoples whose cultural identities and pride have been forged amidst much harder and imposed conditions, and, while the recent achievements of Indian peoples auspiciously herald the dawn of a new era, it still remains that the epic of America has not been equally shared or appropriately recognized. Five hundred and fourteen years later, we as a historical profession, if not as a nation, must still ask ourselves: Is there adequate space within the wellspring of American history to begin discussing the pain of America's indigenous peoples? Without recognition, first, of the magnitude of Europe's impact upon the Americas, histories of the nation will remain forever incomplete.[44]

Chronology

Select Great Basin Indian massacres, enslavements, and conflicts with Europeans and Euro-Americans

Date	Tribal group	Location	Reported number of lost/captured/ enslaved	Source
1637–1639	Rosas against Utacas		80 captured	*New Mexico Historical Review,* October 1936
1716	Serna against Utes			Thomas
1724	Bustamante against Utes			Thomas
1747	Rabal against "Yutas y Chapuapuas"	Chama River	107 killed; 206 captured; 4 executed	TC, II, reel 8; Bancroft
1813	Arze-García slave expedition for Paiutes	Southern Utah	12 female captives, of whom 5 perished	TC, II, reel 17
ca. 1830	Fur trappers against Bannocks	Wyoming-Utah Rendezvous	150–480 killed; 6–8 captured	Bonner

Date	Tribal group	Location	Reported number of lost/captured/ enslaved	Source
1833	Joseph Walker against Western Shoshones	Humboldt River, eastern Nevada	39 initially killed; untold put "out of misery"	Leonard
1844, summer	Mexican soldiers against Utes		7 killed; at least 4 captured	Weber
1844, September	Martínez against Ute delegation	Governor's Palace, Santa Fe	Untold killed and left dying	Weber
1845	Chavez against Utes	Southern Colorado		Sánchez
1849	Whittlesey against Utes	Southern Colorado	10 killed; 2 captured	Lecompte
1850	Mormon-Timapangos War	Utah Lake	Untold killed; "at least 30 women and girls" captured	NARG 75, reel 897
1853–54	Walkara's War	Mormon Corridor	Months of Ute raids and Mormon Reprisals	Peterson
1854–55	Oregon's summer campaigns against Shoshones	Snake River, Idaho	Limited engagements; 4 executions	NARG 75, reel 608
1855	Fauntleroy against Muache and Capote Utes	San Luis Valley, Colorado	Untold killed; 50 captured	Taylor
1859–60	U.S. Army–Shoshone Raids	Idaho-Utah border	Limited engagement	Madsen
1860	Pyramid Lake War	Pyramid Lake, Nevada	Dozens of losses on all sides	Knack and Stewart
1862	Connor's Western Shoshone Raids	Fort Ruby, Nevada	Unreported	*War of Rebellion*

Date	Tribal group	Location	Reported number of lost/captured/enslaved	Source
1863	Connor's Northern Shoshone Massacre	Bear River, Idaho	Nearly 300 killed	*War of Rebellion*
1881	Colorado Utes' removal to Utah	Western Colorado		Wilkinson
1911	Nevada police against Shoshone Mike's family	Clover Valley, Nevada	8 killed; 4 orphaned	Crum

Abbreviations

AB	Thomas D. Martínez, Abiquiu Baptisms, 1754–1866: Baptism Database of Archives Held by the Archdiocese of Santa Fe and the State Archive of New Mexico, New Mexico State Records Center and Archives, Santa Fe
ARCIA	*Annual Report of the Commissioner of Indian Affairs* (Washington, D.C.: U.S. Government Printing Office, 1850–1879)
Bancroft	Hubert Howe Bancroft, *History of Arizona and New Mexico* (San Francisco: History Company, 1889)
Bonner	Thomas D. Bonner, ed., *The Life and Adventures of James P. Beckwourth, Mountaineer, Scout, and Pioneer and Chief of the Crow Nation of Indians* (1856; reprint, Lincoln, Neb.: Bison Books, 1972)
Crum	Steven J. Crum, *The Road on Which We Came: A History of the Western Shoshone* (Salt Lake City: University of Utah Press, 1994)
HBNAI	William C. Sturtevant, gen. ed., *Handbook of North American Indians*, 20 vols. to date (Washington, D.C.: Smithsonian Institution, 1986–)
IA	Charles J. Kappler, ed., *Indian Affairs: Laws and Treaties*, 5 vols. (Washington, D.C.: U.S. Government Printing Office, 1904–1941)
JLC	Gary E. Moulton, ed., *The Journals of Lewis and Clark*, 13 vols. (Lincoln: University of Nebraska Press, 1983–2001)

KCP	Kit Carson Papers, 1847–1885, Bancroft Library, University of California, Berkeley
Knack and Stewart	Martha C. Knack and Omer C. Stewart, *As Long as the River Shall Run: An Ethnohistory of Pyramid Lake Indian Reservation* (1984; reprint, Reno: University of Nevada Press, 1999)
Lecompte	Janet Lecompte, *Pueblo, Hardscrabble, Greenhorn: The Upper Arkansas, 1832–1856* (Norman: University of Oklahoma Press, 1978)
Leonard	Zenas Leonard, *Narrative of the Adventures of Zenas Leonard* (1839; facsimile reprint, Ann Arbor: University Microfilms, 1966)
LFNMH	Ralph Emerson Twitchell, *The Leading Facts of New Mexican History,* 2 vols. (Cedar Rapids, Iowa: Torch, 1912)
Madsen	Brigham D. Madsen, *The Shoshoni Frontier and the Bear River Massacre* (Salt Lake City: University of Utah Press, 1985)
MMFTFW	Leroy R. Hafen, ed., *The Mountain Men and the Fur Trade of the Far West,* 10 vols. (Glendale, Calif.: Arthur H. Clark, 1965–1972)
MTMW	Carl I. Wheat, *Mapping the Transmississippi West,* 5 vols. (San Francisco: Institute of Historical Cartography, 1957–1963)
NARG 75	Letters Received by the Office of Indian Affairs, Record Group 75, Microcopy 234, National Archives, Washington, D.C.
Peterson	John Alton Peterson, *Utah's Black Hawk War* (Salt Lake City: University of Utah Press, 1998)
RES	*Reports of Explorations and Surveys, to Ascertain the Most Practicable and Economical Route for a Railroad from the Mississippi River to the Pacific Ocean,* Senate Executive Document No. 78, 33d Cong., 2d sess., 2 vols. (Washington, D.C.: U.S. Government Printing Office, 1856)
Sánchez	Joseph P. Sánchez, *Explorers, Traders, and Slavers: Forging the Old Spanish Trail, 1678–1850* (Salt Lake City: University of Utah Press, 1997)
SANM	Ralph Emerson Twitchell, *The Spanish Archives of New Mexico,* 2 vols. (Cedar Rapids, Iowa: Torch, 1914)

SDPUI   Selected Documents Pertaining to Ute Indians,
                         1851–1917, 27 reels, Bancroft Library, University of
                         California, Berkeley

Taylor   Morris F. Taylor, "Action at Fort Massachusetts: The
                         Indian Campaign of 1855," *Colorado Magazine* 42
                         (1965): 292–310

TC   Twitchell Collection, Series I and II, New Mexico
                         State Records Center and Archives, Santa Fe

Thomas   Alfred Barnaby Thomas, ed. and trans., *After
                         Coronado: Spanish Exploration Northeast of New Mexico,
                         1969–1727* (Norman: University of Oklahoma Press,
                         1935)

War of Rebellion   *The War of Rebellion: A Compilation of the Official Records
                         of the Union and Confederate Armies,* Series I, vol. 50,
                         part I (Washington, D.C.: Government Printing
                         Office, 1897)

Weber   David J. Weber, *The Mexican Frontier, 1821–1846: The
                         American Southwest under Mexico* (Albuquerque:
                         University of New Mexico Press, 1982)

Wilkinson   Charles Wilkinson, *Fire on the Plateau: Conflict and
                         Endurance in the American Southwest* (Washington,
                         D.C.: Island Press, 1999)

Notes

Introduction

1. Toni Morrison, *Playing in the Dark: Whiteness and the Literary Imagination* (Cambridge, Mass.: Harvard University Press, 1992), 91, 47, 52.
2. Studies of U.S. history have often maintained exceptional visions of the American experience, contradistinguishing the American past with other national histories. For surveys of recent challenges to such currents, see David W. Noble, *Death of a Nation: American Culture and the End of Exceptionalism* (Minneapolis: University of Minnesota Press, 2002), esp. 250–286. See also Kerwin Lee Klein, *Frontiers of Historical Imagination: Narrating the European Conquest of Native America, 1890–1990* (Berkeley: University of California Press, 1997).
3. Roland Barthes, *Mythologies,* trans. Annette Lavers (New York: Hill and Wang, 1972). As Joyce Appleby has argued, "For a long time American historical writing simply explained how the United States became the territorial embodiment of liberal truths." See Appleby, *Liberalism and Republicanism in the Historical Imagination* (Cambridge, Mass.: Harvard University Press, 1992), 2–3.
4. "Indian" is a problematic designation for the indigenous peoples of the Americas, one that has undergone critical interrogation and, in Canada, abandonment, where First Nations, Native, and Aboriginal commonly designate the status of Canada's First Peoples. In the United States, "Native American" has gained popularity, largely in an attempt to reject the homogenizing history of the term "Indian." While recognizing the constraining, contested usage of such terminology, this

301

study interchanges "Indian," "Native," and "indigenous" to describe aboriginal communities in North America, valuing the instructive past of
such terms in an attempt to recapture and revise their representational
power. While Indian history has recently become an honored subfield
in American history, the field remains largely tied to the U.S. colonial
period. See Ned Blackhawk, "Look How Far We've Come: How American Indian History Changed the Study of American History in the
1990s," *Organization of American Historians' Magazine of History* 19:6 (November 2005): 8–14.

5. Physiographically, the Great Basin begins west of the Wasatch Mountains in central Utah, while shared cultural traits, language, and historical experiences link Great Basin peoples to the Colorado Plateau and
Rocky Mountains. See Charles B. Hunt, *Physiography of the United States*
(San Francisco: W. H. Freeman, 1967), 308–347; Omer C. Stewart, *Indians of the Great Basin: A Critical Bibliography* (Bloomington: University
of Indiana Press, 1982); and Warren L. D'Azevedo, "Introduction,"
HBNAI, 11: 1–14.

6. Eric Wolf, *Europe and the Peoples without History* (Berkeley: University
of California Press, 1980). For Steward's legacies, see Richard O.
Clemmer, L. Daniel Myers, and Mary Elizabeth Rudden, *Julian Steward
and the Great Basin: The Making of an Anthropologist* (Salt Lake City: University of Utah Press, 1999), and citations therein for Steward's bibliography. For one example of Steward's influence in establishing Great Basin Indians as the evolutionary floor of human development, see Peter
Farb, *Man's Rise to Civilization as Shown by the Indians of North America*
(New York: E. P. Dutton, 1968).

7. For anthropology's imperialist legacies, see George W. Stocking Jr., *Colonial Situations: Essays on the Contextualization of Ethnographic Knowledge*
(Madison: University of Wisconsin Press, 1991).

8. Homi K. Bhabha theorizes the intellectual quandaries incumbent upon
being "amongst those whose very presence is both 'overlooked' and, at
the same time, overdetermined." See Bhabha, *The Location of Culture*
(New York: Routledge, 1994), 236. See also Linda Tuhiuai Smith, *Decolo-
nizing Methodologies: Research and Indigenous Peoples* (London: Zed Books,
1999), esp. 1–41.

9. See Vine Deloria Jr., *Custer Died for Your Sins: An Indian Manifesto* (New
York: Macmillan, 1969).

10. Max Weber pioneered the study of violence and state formation: "the
relation between the state and violence is an especially intimate one . . .
a state is a human community that (successfully) claims the *monopoly of*

the legitimate use of physical force within a given territory . . . The state is considered the sole source of the 'right' to use violence"; H. H. Gerth and C. Wright Mills, eds. and trans., *From Max Weber: Essays in Sociology* (New York: Oxford University Press, 1946), 78. The tensions between imperial historiographies and their simultaneous inabilities to grasp the colonial violence inherent in imperialism have forced reconsideration of innumerable national histories, especially in the aftermath of European decolonization and the enduring "postcolonial" challenge for former colonized populations. For a recent effort to expose such imperial currents in American cultural history, see Amy Kaplan, *The Anarchy of Empire in the Making of U.S. Culture* (Cambridge, Mass.: Harvard University Press, 2002).

11. For syntheses of Spanish colonialism in northern New Spain, see Thomas Hall, *Social Change in the Southwest, 1350–1880* (Lawrence: University of Kansas Press, 1988); and John L. Kessell, *Spain in the Southwest: A Narrative History of Colonial New Mexico, Arizona, Texas, and California* (Norman: University of Oklahoma Press, 2002).

12. For North American imperial-indigenous accommodation, see Richard White, *The Middle Ground: Indians, Empires, and Republics in the Great Lakes Region* (New York: Cambridge University Press, 1991). For a related attempt to complicate indigenous-state relations in Latin America as "no longer a simple celebration of subaltern agency," see Florencia E. Mallon, *Peasant and Nation: The Making of Postcolonial Mexico and Peru* (Berkeley: University of California Press, 1995), esp. 1–20.

13. Colin G. Calloway, *New Worlds for All: Indians, Europeans, and the Remaking of America* (Baltimore: Johns Hopkins University Press, 1997).

14. As R. Brian Ferguson and Neil L. Whitehead argue, "While the importance of history and the role of violent conflict may be readily seen, it is more difficult to know *what that recognition implies:* at the very least, it involves the need to revitalize our ideas about the ethnographic universe, going beyond the rejection of untenable notions of self-contained, stable local societies, *and instead developing a conceptual framework for understanding conflict and change as part of the historical process* underlying observed ethnographic patterns." See Ferguson and Whitehead, "The Violent Edge of Empire," in *War in the Tribal Zone: Expanding States and Indigenous Warfare,* ed. Ferguson and Whitehead (Santa Fe: School of American Research Press, 1992), 3 (emphasis added).

15. Physical pain, as Elaine Scarry argues, not only is "resistant to language but also actively destroys language," a notion suggesting that representations, in this case of indigenous trauma, are always partial and cannot

be fully measured. See Scarry, *The Body in Pain: The Making and Unmaking of the World* (New York: Oxford University Press, 1985), 172.

16. Barbara Young Welke, *Recasting American Liberty: Gender, Race, Law, and the Railroad Revolution, 1865–1920* (New York: Cambridge University Press, 2001), 126.

17. For reassessments of Frederick Jackson Turner's "frontier thesis," see Klein, *Frontiers of Historical Imagination*. See also Patricia Nelson Limerick, *The Legacy of Conquest: The Unbroken Past of the American West* (New York: W. W. Norton, 1987), esp. 17–32.

18. As Cole Harris suggests, "Claiming political control of a territory was an act of imperialism, coming to know it was often another, but using it was far more intrusive than either." See Harris, *The Resettlement of British Columbia: Essays on Colonialism and Geographic Change* (Vancouver: University of British Columbia Press, 1997), 182–183.

19. For the formulation of U.S. Indian policy, see Francis Paul Prucha, *American Indian Treaties: The History of a Political Anomaly* (Berkeley: University of California Press, 1994) and *The Great Father: The United States Government and the American Indians,* abridged ed. (Lincoln: University of Nebraska Press, 1986).

20. Franklin R. Rogers, ed., *The Works of Mark Twain: Roughing It* (Berkeley: University of California Press, 1972), 144.

21. See Clemmer et al., *Julian Steward and the Great Basin.*

22. Steven J. Crum provides the most complete assessment of Western Shoshone history. See Crum, *The Road on Which We Came: A History of the Western Shoshone* (Salt Lake City: University of Utah Press, 1994) (cited hereafter as Crum). For an overview of the development of nuclear testing in Nevada, see Howard Ball, *Justice Downwind: America's Atomic Testing Program in the 1950s* (New York: Oxford University Press, 1986), 20–83.

1. Spanish-Ute Relations to 1750

1. *LFNMH,* 2: 147. For additional references to Indian ears as trophies in New Spain, see Elizabeth A. H. John, *Storms Brewed in Other Men's Worlds: The Confrontation of Indians, Spanish, and French in the Southwest, 1540–1795,* 2d ed. (Norman: University of Oklahoma Press, 1996), 603; Ana Maria Alonso, *Thread of Blood: Colonialism, Revolution, and Gender on Mexico's Northern Frontier* (Tucson: University of Arizona Press, 1995), 38; Frank McNitt, *Navajo Wars: Military Campaigns, Slave Raids, and Reprisals* (Albuquerque: University of New Mexico Press, 1972), 51; and Zenas Leonard, *Narrative of the Adventures of Zenas Leonard* (1839; facsimile

reprint, Ann Arbor: University Microfilms, 1966) (cited hereafter as Leonard), 62. For links between equestrian raids and architectural design, see Frances Leon Swadesh, *Los Primeros Pobladores: Hispanic Americans of the Ute Frontier* (South Bend: University of Notre Dame Press, 1974), 32–33.

2. Thomas D. Hall argues that frontier relations established in New Mexico had antecedents in Spanish-Indian relations in northern Mexico along the "Chichimeca Frontier." See Hall, *Social Change in the Southwest, 1350–1880* (Lawrence: University of Kansas Press, 1989), 75–109. See also Gary Clayton Anderson, *The Indian Southwest: Ethnogenesis and Reinvention, 1580–1830* (Norman: University of Oklahoma Press, 1999).

3. See Hall, *Social Change in the Southwest*, 75–133; John, *Storms Brewed;* Charles L. Kenner, *A History of New Mexican–Plains Indian Relations* (Norman: University of Oklahoma Press, 1968); Anderson, *The Indian Southwest;* and James F. Brooks, *Captives and Cousins: Slavery, Kinship, and Community in the Southwest Borderlands* (Chapel Hill: University of North Carolina Press, 2002). For Comanche history, see also Ernest Wallace and E. Adamson Hoebel, *The Comanches: Lords of the South Plains* (Norman: University of Oklahoma Press, 1951); Morris W. Foster, *Being Comanche: A Social History of an American Indian Community* (Tucson: University of Arizona Press, 1991); and Thomas Kavanagh, *Comanche Political History: An Ethnohistorical Perspective, 1706–1875* (Lincoln: University of Nebraska Press, 1996). For Apache history, see Donald E. Worcester, *The Apaches: Eagles of the Southwest* (Norman: University of Oklahoma Press, 1979); and Jack D. Forbes, *Apache, Navaho, and Spaniard* (Norman: University of Oklahoma Press, 1960). For Spanish-Navajo relations, see ibid.; Edward H. Spicer, *Cycles of Conquest: The Impact of Spain, Mexico, and the United States on the Indians of the Southwest, 1533–1960* (Tucson: University of Arizona Press, 1962); David M. Brugge, *Navajos in the Catholic Church Records of New Mexico, 1964–1875*, 2d ed. (Tsaile, Ariz.: Navajo Community College Press, 1985); and McNitt, *Navajo Wars.*

4. For Comanche migration, see Demitri B. Shimkin, "The Introduction of the Horse," in *HBNAI,* 11: 517–524. See also Pekka Hämäläinen, "The Rise and Fall of Plains Indian Horse Cultures," *Journal of American History* 90 (December 2003): 835–845. For Spanish-Ute relations, see Marvin K. Opler, "The Southern Ute of Colorado," in *Acculturation in Seven American Indian Tribes*, ed. Ralph Linton (New York: D. Applegate Century, 1940), 122–128, 156–179; S. Lyman Tyler, "Before Escalante: An Early History of the Yuta Indians and the Area North of New Mexico" (Ph.D. diss., University of Utah, 1951); idem, "The Spaniard and

the Ute," *Utah Historical Quarterly* 22 (1954): 343–361; Albert H. Schroeder, "A Brief History of the Southern Utes," *Southwestern Lore* 30 (March 1965): 53–78; Robert W. Delaney, *The Ute Mountain Ute* (Albuquerque: University of New Mexico Press, 1989), 7–19; Virginia McConnell Simmons, *The Ute Indians of Utah, Colorado, and New Mexico* (Boulder: University of Colorado Press, 2000), 29–46; and Brooks, *Captives and Cousins*, 148–159. For Ute band classifications, see Opler, "The Southern Ute of Colorado," 126–127; Delaney, *The Ute Mountain Ute*, 6–7; Simmons, *The Ute Indians*, 17–24; and Donald G. Callaway, Joel C. Janetski, and Omer C. Stewart, "Ute," in *HBNAI*, 11: 336–340.

5. S. Lyman Tyler, "The Yuta Indians before 1680," *Western Humanities Review* 5 (Spring 1951): 158; Herbert Eugene Bolton, ed., *Spanish Exploration in the Southwest, 1542–1706* (New York: Charles Scribner's Sons, 1916), 224–230. See also John, *Storms Brewed*, 44–47. A league is approximately two and half miles.

6. Many classify both "Querecho" and "Vaquero" as Apaches. See, for instance, Bolton, *Spanish Exploration*, 183, 204; and John, *Storms Brewed*, 58–64. S. Lyman Tyler argues that "Querecho" was a more general term for mountain peoples who lived off buffalo and might be indicative of Ute encounters. See Tyler, "Yuta Indians before 1680," 158. For the references to "Yuttas" in Salmerón, Niel, and Posados, see Tyler, "The Spaniard and the Ute," 344–345; and idem, "Yuta Indians before 1680," 158. For the ties between Jemez and Pecos Pueblos, see John L. Kessell, *Kiva, Cross, and Crown: The Pecos Indians and New Mexico, 1540–1840* (Washington, D.C.: National Park Service, 1979).

7. See Colin G. Calloway, *One Vast Winter Count: The Native American West before Lewis and Clark* (Lincoln: University of Nebraska Press, 2003), 73–96 and notes.

8. Gaspar Pérez de Villagrá, *Historia de la Nueva México, 1610: A Critical and Annotated Spanish/English Edition*, ed. and trans. Miguel Encinias, Alfred Rodríguez, and Joseph P. Sánchez (Albuquerque: University of New Mexico Press, 1992), xxxvi–xxxix. John, *Storms Brewed*, 47–52, provides an overview of the Acoma revolt.

9. Spanish colonialism, as Cynthia Radding suggests, "implies political domination by the Spanish Crown over its American territories and peoples, economic exploitation and the transfer of wealth from the colonies to the metropole, cultural dislocation, and diverse responses from indigenous nations and enslaved workers. The concept is not simple, however, nor does it elicit the same meanings in different geographic regions and time periods." See Radding, *Wandering Peoples: Colonialism,*

Ethnic Spaces, and Ecological Frontiers in Northwestern Mexico, 1700–1850 (Durham: Duke University Press, 1997), xvii.

10. John L. Kessell, *Spain in the Southwest: A Narrative History of Colonial New Mexico, Arizona, Texas, and California* (Norman: University of Oklahoma Press, 2002), 107. For links between New Mexico and Mexico's early mining centers, see P. J. Bakewell, *Silver Mining and Society in Colonial Mexico: Zacatecas, 1546–1700* (New York: Cambridge University Press 1971), 32–39.

11. Ramón A. Gutiérrez, *When Jesus Came, the Corn Mothers Went Away: Marriage, Sexuality, and Power in New Mexico, 1500–1846* (Stanford: Stanford University Press, 1991), 105. For the origins of Indian slavery in New Mexico, see ibid., 101–127; John, *Storms Brewed*, 62–64, 69–71, 80, 84–85; Hall, *Social Change in the Southwest*, 83–86; and Brooks, *Captives and Cousins*, 3–40. Hall traces the origins of borderlands slavery to the economies of Mexico, while Brooks insists that pre-Columbian institutions of indigenous captivity meshed with those from Spain.

12. France V. Scholes, "Church and State in Colonial New Mexico, 1610–1650," *New Mexico Historical Review* 11 (October 1936): 297–349.

13. Ibid., 300–327. See also Gutiérrez, *When Jesus Came*, 112; and Forbes, *Apache, Navaho, and Spaniard*, 132–133.

14. Richard White, *The Middle Ground: Indians, Empires, and Republics in the Great Lakes Region, 1650–1815* (New York: Cambridge University Press, 1991). See also Amy Turner Bushnell and Jack P. Greene, "Peripheries, Centers, and the Construction of Early Modern American Empires," in *Negotiated Empires: Centers and Peripheries in the Americas, 1500–1820,* ed. Christine Daniels and Michael V. Kennedy (New York: Routledge, 2002), 1–14.

15. For an overview of New Mexico's eighteenth-century political economy, see Hall, *Social Change in the Southwest*, 75–99. This discussion of "bodies" and "technologies" is indebted to Elaine Scarry as well as Teresa de Lauretis, for whom "the representation of violence is inseparable from the notion of gender." See Lauretis, *Technologies of Gender: Essays on Theory, Film, and Fiction* (Bloomington: Indiana University Press, 1987), 33.

16. For an additional overview of Spanish-Indian relations, see Calloway, *One Vast Winter Count*, 165–211.

17. Hall, *Social Change in the Southwest*, 75–99.

18. John, *Storms Brewed*, 70–71. Distinctions often made between "weapons" and "tools" remain counterproductive, since, as Elaine Scarry notes, "The weapon and the tool seem at moments indistinguishable, for they may each reside in a single physical object . . . what differentiates them

is not the object itself but the surface upon which they fall. What we call a 'weapon' when it acts on a sentient surface we call a 'tool' when it acts on a nonsentient surface." See Scarry, *The Body in Pain: The Making and Unmaking of the World* (New York: Oxford University Press, 1985), 173.

19. John, *Storms Brewed*, 88–90.

20. Daniel Reff suggests that a series of "routes of contagion" developed throughout colonial New Spain as diseases harbored by trading parties, textiles, foods, and animals spread to Indian populations. Epidemics were reported in Santa Fe in 1623, 1636, 1641, and 1660 and, like most colonial influences, spread throughout northern societies. See Daniel T. Reff, *Disease, Depopulation, and Culture Change in Northwestern New Spain, 1518–1764* (Salt Lake City: University of Utah Press, 1991), esp. 97–178.

21. Quoted in Tyler, "The Yuta Indians before 1680," 161. See also S. Lyman Tyler, "The Myth of the Lake of Copala and Land of Teguayo," *Utah Historical Quarterly* 20 (October 1952): 323–324. Joseph P. Sánchez examines New Mexican chronicles of the northwest. See Sánchez, *Explorers, Traders, and Slavers: Forging the Old Spanish Trail, 1678–1850* (Salt Lake City: University of Utah Press, 1997) (cited hereafter as Sánchez), esp. 3–16.

22. Tyler, "The Yuta Indians before 1680," 158, 161. For an overview of the introduction of the horse in the eastern Great Basin, see Shimkin, "Introduction of the Horse"; and Hämäläinen, "Rise and Fall of Plains Indian Horse Cultures," 835–837.

23. For debates on precontact Great Basin social organization, see Julian H. Steward, "Native Cultures of the Intermontane (Great Basin) Area," in *Essays in Historical Anthropology of North America,* ed. Steward, Smithsonian Miscellaneous Collections, No. 100 (Washington, D.C.: Smithsonian Institution, 1940), 445–502; Omer C. Stewart, *Culture Element Distributions: XVIII Ute–Southern Paiute* (Berkeley: University of California Anthropological Records, 1942); and Opler, "The Southern Ute of Colorado."

24. Charles Wilson Hackett, ed., *Revolt of the Pueblo Indians of New Mexico and Otermín's Attempted Reconquest, 1680–1682,* trans. Charmion Clair Shelby (Albuquerque: University of New Mexico Press, 1942), 206. Otermín's letter is unclear about the exact date of the alliance; subsequent commentators identify it as 1678. See also John, *Storms Brewed*, 95.

25. Hubert Howe Bancroft, *History of Arizona and New Mexico* (San Francisco: History Company, 1889) (cited hereafter as Bancroft), 181. Utes had traded with northern Pueblos before Spanish settlement. See

Adolph F. Bandelier, *Final Report of Investigations among the Indians of the Southwestern United States, Part I* (Cambridge, Mass.: Archaeological Institute of America, 1890), 164.

26. The Pueblo Revolt is best understood, according to John Kessell, as a three-phased Spanish-Pueblo war lasting sixteen years. See Kessell, *Spain in the Southwest*, 119–124, 148–157, 201.

27. After the revolt, the need to reestablish the Spanish monopoly of violence was critical. Vargas, for example, in December 1693 executed all 70 Pueblo warriors in Santa Fe, enslaved the 400 women and children, and distributed them to the colonists as slaves. See Gutiérrez, *When Jesus Came*, 145. Recognizing the power of Spanish documents and records in their lives, Pueblo warriors, while allowing Spanish authorities and settlers to flee south, sacked the Governor's Palace and destroyed much of New Mexico's archives.

28. Håmålåinen, "Rise and Fall of Plains Indian Horse Cultures."

29. J. Manuel Espinosa, "Governor Vargas in Colorado," *New Mexico Historical Review* (1936): 179–187; and idem, *Crusaders on the Rio Grande: The Story of Don Diego de Vargas and the Reconquest and Refounding of New Mexico* (Chicago: Institute of Jesuit History, 1942), 197.

30. John L. Kessell, Rick Hendricks, and Meredith O. Daly, eds., *Blood on the Boulders: The Journals of don Diego de Vargas, New Mexico, 1694–1697,* 2 vols. (Albuquerque: University of New Mexico Press, 1998) 1: 307. For Ute-Pueblo hostilities during the Spanish absence, see Schroeder, "Brief History of Southern Utes," 56–57; and Tyler, "Before Escalante," 121–122.

31. Espinosa, "Governor Vargas in Colorado," 179–187.

32. Espinosa, *Crusaders on the Rio Grande*, 225–226, 354.

33. For unspecified Ute involvement in a potential 1690s Pueblo "conspiracy," see "Indians, Santa Fe," December 1704, Twitchell no. 104, in *SANM*, 2: 133.

34. The accelerated spread of Spanish influences after 1680 makes claims about Ute band designations only suggestive for this period. As R. Brian Ferguson and Neil L. Whitehead argue, "While the importance of history and the role of violent conflict may be readily seen, it is more difficult to know what that recognition implies: at the very least, it involves the need to revitalize our ideas about the ethnographic universe, going beyond the rejection of untenable notions of self-contained, stable local societies, and instead developing a conceptual framework for understanding conflict and change as part of the historical process underlying observed ethnographic patterns." See Ferguson and Whitehead,

"The Violent Edge of Empire," in *War in the Tribal Zone: Expanding States and Indigenous Warfare,* ed. Ferguson and Whitehead (Santa Fe: School of American Research Press, 1992), 3.

35. Alfred Barnaby Thomas, ed. and trans., *After Coronado: Spanish Exploration Northeast of New Mexico, 1969–1727* (Norman: University of Oklahoma Press, 1935) (cited hereafter as Thomas), 16–21. See also Kenner, *New Mexican–Plains Indian Relations,* 24–27.

36. Wallace and Hoebel, *The Comanches;* Foster, *Being Comanche,* 32–36; and Kavanagh, *Comanche Political History,* 57–65. For the Comanche's Great Basin origins, see also David Leedon Shaul, "Linguistic Adaptation and the Great Basin," *American Antiquity* 51 (1986): 415–416; Dan Flores, "Bison Ecology and Bison Diplomacy: The Southern Plains from 1800 to 1850," *Journal of American History* 78 (September 1991): 465–485; Galen Mark Buller, "Comanche Oral Narratives" (Ph.D. diss., University of Nebraska, Lincoln, 1977). Buller, esp. 82, uses Shoshone and Comanche tales at times interchangeably.

37. Thomas, 13–14.

38. McNitt, *Navajo Wars,* 23. See also Donald Emmet Worcester, "Early History of the Navaho Indians" (Ph.D. diss., University of California, Berkeley, 1947), 96–114; John, *Storms Brewed,* 238–245; and Rick Hendricks and John P. Wilson, eds. and trans., *The Navajos in 1705: Roque Madrid's Campaign Journal* (Albuquerque: University of New Mexico Press, 1996).

39. Bancroft, 232. David J. Weber provides overviews of northern trade fairs in *The Taos Trappers: The Fur Trade in the Far Southwest, 1540–1846* (Norman: University of Oklahoma Press, 1971).

40. "Archive 1347," TC, I, reel 4, frame [unclear]. An *alcalde* was "in general, a civil official with judicial, executive, and legislative functions," and an *alcalde mayor* was a "superior alcalde governing a district." See Marc Simmons, *Spanish Government in New Mexico* (Albuquerque: University of New Mexico Press, 1968), 219.

41. "Archive 1347"; Bancroft, 235. See also "Felix, Martinez," August 20–October 14, 1716, Twitchell no. 279, in *SANM,* 2: 184; and John, *Storms Brewed,* 241–242.

42. John, *Storms Brewed,* 242–243. See also "Flores, Mogollon, Don Juan Ygnacio," December 16, 1712, Twitchell no. 185, in *SANM,* 2: 169.

43. "Cruz to Valero [Taos, 1719]" and "Order of Valero, México, August 1, 1719," in Thomas, 137–139.

44. David J. Weber, *The Spanish Frontier in North America* (New Haven: Yale University Press, 1991), 168.

45. "Order of Council of War, Santa Fe, August 13, 1719," in Thomas, 99–100. "Coyote" refers to mixed-raced people in colonial New Mexico.

46. "Council of War, Santa Fe, August 19, 1719," ibid., 102–103, 104, 109–110. The estimated distance of 200 leagues is largely exaggerated, given the lack of Spanish exploration north of New Mexico.

47. "Diary of the Campaign of . . . Valverde," ibid., 126.

48. Ibid., 132. See also Weber, *Spanish Frontier*, 168.

49. Survivors of the Villasur campaign recorded a partial diary. See "A Portion of the Diary of the Reconnaissance Expedition of Colonel Don Pedro de Villasur along the Platte River, 1720," in Thomas, 133–137.

50. "Valverde to Valero, Santa Fé, October 8, 1720," ibid., 166.

51. "Revolledo to Valero, México, December, 9, 1720," and "Bustamante to Casa Fuerte, Santa Fé, May 30, 1724," ibid., 205–208. Bustamante briefly refers to a successful campaign he led against the Ute and Comanche to retake these captured Jicarillas: "Having set out to execute it, I had the fortune to restore sixty-four persons. They were gratified." He makes no mention of Ute-Comanche losses.

52. "Bustamante to Casa Fuerte, Santa Fé, May 30, 1724," and "Rivera to Casa Fuerte, presidio Del Paso Del Río Del Norte, September 26, 1727," ibid., 208, 209–212. See also "Revolledo to Casa Fuerte, México, March 31, 1727," and "Order of Casa Fuerte, México, April 1, 1727," ibid., 218–219, for final decisions on the potential Jicarilla presidio. For Navajo-Jicarilla relations, see Worcester, "Early History of the Navaho Indians," 100–113. For Rivera's full account, see Thomas H. Naylor and Charles W. Polzer, S.J., eds., *Pedro de Rivera and the Military Regulations for Northern new Spain, 1724–1729* (Tucson: University of Arizona Press, 1988). Cartographer and engineer Francisco Álvarez y Barreiro accompanied Rivera and made six maps of northern New Spain, including a 1727 map which detailed Ute *rancherías* in the north, over three decades before the first cartographic reference to Comanches. See *MTMW*, 1: 80–86.

53. Thomas, 46. See also "Bustamante, Juan Domingo," November 26, 1727, Twitchell no. 347, in *SANM*, 2: 196. Of course, horticultural Navajo settlements were tenable west of Santa Fe, though Ute-Comanche raids forced many Navajos into defensive locations. See W. W. Hill, "Some Navaho Culture Changes during Two Centuries (with a Translation of the Early Eighteenth Century Rabál Manuscript)," in Steward, *Essays in Historical Anthropology of North America*, 395–415.

54. Thomas, 45–46. As Elizabeth John writes: "Utes and Comanches had killed so many of their men and captured so many of their women and

children that all bands were gravely weakened, and they no longer knew anywhere that they could go to live in safety." She details the subsequent Apache diaspora south following the Ute-Comanche wars and notes the paradoxical nature of Rivera's legacies. In failing to colonize northern Apaches, Spanish leaders unwittingly fueled the subsequent rise of Apache raiding, which destabilized much of northern Mexico for generations. See John, *Storms Brewed,* 250–277.

55. See note 51 above for Bustamante's 1724 campaign against the Utes.

56. "Bustamante to Casa Fuerte, Santa Fé, April 30, 1727," in Thomas, 257–258.

57. Adolph F. Bandelier, "Contributions to the History of the Southwestern Portions of the United States," in *Papers of the Archaeological Institute of America,* American Series, No. 5 (Cambridge, Mass.: Archaeological Institute of America, 1890), 185–186; Malcolm Ebright, "Advocates for the Oppressed: Indians, Genízaros and Their Spanish Advocates in New Mexico, 1700–1786," *New Mexico Historical Review* 71 (October 1996): 315–317, and 336 for original Spanish quotes. Another Ute captive was baptized and probably purchased by Captain Sebastián Martín in March 1744 at San Juan Pueblo. See "Taos, Indians," Twitchell no. 361, in *SANM,* 2: 199. As Twitchell states, "There are several entries of this sort, all of the Indians being the property of this famous captain."

58. Quoted in Kavanagh, *Comanche Political History,* 66–67.

59. For Spanish godparent adoption, or *compadrazgo,* in New Mexico, see Brooks, *Captives and Cousins,* 124–125, 230, 236–237, 346–347; and Gutiérrez, *When Jesus Came,* 150–156. Brooks's claims about the "productive" nature of captive exchange and its capacity to mitigate violence between rivals have enriched the study of borderlands Indian social relations, pinpointing the internal stratification that flowed from captive exchanges while highlighting the extensiveness of captivity throughout the region. His arguments about the origins of these slave systems, however, remain less persuasive and eschew structural relations of power and inequity, particularly between equestrian and nonequestrian peoples. See Brooks, *Captives and Cousins,* 17–18; and Chapters 2, 3, and 7 of this volume for problems in assessing nonequestrian Indian captivity.

60. For New Mexico's eighteenth-century economic development, see Ross Frank, *From Settler to Citizen: New Mexican Economic Development and the Creation of Vecino Society, 1750–1820* (Berkeley: University of California Press, 2000). Regarding the tensions in assessing precontact versus postcontact Indian captive-taking, Colin Calloway offers the following observation: "Native peoples had raided each other for captives long be-

fore Europeans arrived, but as Indians began to participate in the Spanish slave trade, the taking and exchange of captives expanded in scope and assumed new meaning"; Calloway, *One Vast Winter Count,* 205.

61. "Council of War, Santa Fé, August 19, 1719," in Thomas, 103–104, 107.

62. French observers also failed to establish clear distinctions between Comanche and Ute bands, further confounding attempts to secure ethnographic certainty about these related groups. See, for instance, Charles Wilson Hackett, ed., *Pichardo's Treatise on the Limits of Louisiana and Texas,* 4 vols. (Austin: University of Texas Press, 1934), 2: 254.

63. "Joseph, Gomez, Roque Jacinto Jaramillo, Rosalia de Valdez, and Juan Manuel de Herrera," Twitchell no. 409, in *SANM,* 2: 208; and Swadesh, *Los Primeros Pobladores,* 47 and 215 n. 30.

64. Hill, "Some Navaho Culture Changes," 401, 406, 408.

65. "Año de 1747," TC, II, reel 8, frames 769–772. See also "Santistievan, Antonio," November 24, 1747, Twitchell no. 482, in *SANM,* 2: 219. Twitchell's spelling, "Santistievan," is inconsistent with the original. Santiestevan also lost his appointment in the army.

66. For the 1747 attack at Abiquiu, see "An Account of Lamentable Happenings in New Mexico, and of Losses Experienced Daily in Affairs Spiritual and Temporal; Written by Reverend Father Fray Juan Sanz de Lazaún, in the Year 1760," in *Historical Documents Relating to New Mexico, Nueva Vizcaya, and Approaches Thereto, to 1773,* ed. Charles Wilson Hackett, 3 vols. (Washington, D.C.: Carnegie Institute, 1937), 3: 477. See also "Codallos y Rabal," Twitchell no. 497, in *SANM,* 2: 227; and Lesley Poling-Kempes, *Valley of the Shining Stone: The Story of Abiquiu* (Tucson: University of Arizona Press, 1997), 36–37. For Comanche raids, see Bancroft, 249; John, *Storms Brewed,* 313–315; Kavanagh, *Comanche Political History,* 69; and Kessell, *Kiva, Cross, and Crown,* 372. There is disagreement about the extent of Comanche depredations during these years. See Frances Levine and Anna LaBauve, "Examining the Complexity of Historical Population Decline: A Case Study of Pecos Pueblo, New Mexico," *Ethnohistory* 44 (1997): 96–99.

67. As Santiesteven's trial (note 65 above) indicates, Comanches are not referred to after the return of Rabál's campaign, though Bancroft, 249–250, n. 48, includes Comanches. This inclusion contradicts both Sanz's account and Santiestevan's trial, though many use Bancroft's inclusion of the Comanche as well as his estimation of captive seizures and casualties. For Rabál's *bando,* see "Codallos y Rabal, Don Joachin," Twitchell no. 455, in *SANM,* 2: 213.

68. "Salazar, Pablo, December 2, 1748," TC, II, reel 8, frames 875–877. See also "Salazar, Pablo," Twitchell no. 500, in *SANM,* 2: 227.

69. "Salazar, Pablo," TC, II, reel 8, frame 877.
70. For 1748 Comanche raids at Pecos, see Kavanagh, *Comanche Political History,* 69; Kessell, *Kiva, Cross, and Crown,* 374–376; and Levine and LaBauve, "Examining the Complexity of Historical Population Decline," 96. For Chama raids, see "Inhabitants of Abiquiu and Ojo Caliente," trans. I. L. Chaves, TC, I, reel 1, frame 263. There are different spellings of "Beitta" provided. See also "Inhabitants of Abiquiu and Ojo Caliente," Twitchell no. 28, in *SANM,* 1: 25; and Swadesh, *Los Primeros Pobladores,* 33–37.
71. "Inhabitants of Abiquiu and Ojo Caliente," TC, I, reel 1, frame 264.
72. For the inefficiencies in Rabál's rule, see John, *Storms Brewed,* 314–315.
73. "Instruction of Don Thomas Vélez Cachupín, 1754," in *The Plains Indians and New Mexico, 1751–1778,* ed. and trans. Alfred Barnaby Thomas (Albuquerque: University of New Mexico Press, 1940), 130.
74. For Comanche economics, see Pekka Håmålåinen, "The Western Comanche Trade Center: Rethinking the Plains Indian Trade System," *Western Historical Quarterly* 29 (Winter 1998): 485–513.
75. For evidence of Ute-Comanche tensions, see Kavanagh, *Comanche Political History,* 68. See also "Cruzat y Gongora," Twitchell no. 403, in *SANM,* 2: 205; Tyler, "The Yuta Indians before 1680," 171–173; and Brooks, *Captives and Cousins,* 120. For Ute raids at Abiquiu, see "Codallos y Rabal," 227; Bancroft, 249; and Brooks, *Captives and Cousins,* 151.
76. "An Order Prohibiting the Abandonment of the Settlement of Chama, as Was Intended by Its Inhabitants, on Account of the Hostilities of the Utes," trans. José de Sena, TC, I, reel 1, frame 1339. See also "Partido de Chama," Twitchell no. 186, in *SANM,* 1: 74.
77. "Instructions of Don Thomas Vélez Cachupín, 1754," 131.

2. The Making of the New Mexican–Ute Borderlands

1. After 1750, as Ross Harold Frank argues, Indian raiders besieged New Mexico, threatening its "very existence as a Spanish province." See Frank, *From Settler to Citizen: New Mexican Economic Development and the Creation of Vecino Society, 1750–1820* (Berkeley: University of California Press, 2000), 13.
2. For Spanish expansion northwest of New Mexico, see Sánchez.
3. "A large proportion of the captives baptized as 'Yutas' were doubtless Paiutes, whose poverty and distance from settlements did not allow them much opportunity to retaliate"; David M. Brugge, *Navajos in the Catholic Church Records of New Mexico, 1964–1875,* 2d ed. (Tsaile, Ariz.: Navajo Community College Press, 1985), 31.
4. For overviews on *genízaro* relations, see James F. Brooks, *Captives and*

Cousins: Slavery, Kinship, and Community in the Southwest Borderlands (Chapel Hill: University of North Carolina Press, 2002); Ramón A. Gutiérrez, *When Jesus Came, the Corn Mothers Went Away: Marriage, Sexuality, and Power in New Mexico, 1500–1846* (Stanford: Stanford University Press, 1991); Gilberto Benito Córdova, "Missionization and Hispanicization of Santo Thomas Apostol de Abiquiu, 1750–1770" (Ph.D. diss., University of New Mexico, 1979); and Fray Angélico Chávez, "Genízaros," in *HBNAI,* 9: 198–200.

5. Martha C. Knack, *Boundaries Between: The Southern Paiutes, 1775–1995* (Lincoln: University of Nebraska Press, 2001), 30–47.

6. For the nineteenth-century Great Basin Indian slave trade, see Stephen P. Van Hoak, "And Who Shall Have the Children: The Indian Slave Trade in the Southern Great Basin, 1800–1865," *Nevada Historical Society Quarterly* 41 (1998): 3–25.

7. Elizabeth A. H. John, *Storms Brewed in Other Men's Worlds: The Confrontation of Indians, Spanish, and French in the Southwest, 1540–1795,* 2d ed. (Norman: University of Oklahoma Press, 1996), 315; "Order for Resettlement of Abiquiu, Abandoned Because of Ute War, Nov. 2, 1770," trans. I. L. Chaves, TC, I, reel 1, frames 289–292. See also "Town of Abiquiu," Twitchell no. 36, in *SANM,* 1: 27–28.

8. "Indian Policy in New Mexico, April 3, 1750," TC, I, reel 3, frames 1551–54. See also "El Marques de Altamira, Mexico," April 3, 1750, Twitchell no. 1098, in *SANM,* 1: 324. The Spanish had identified three primary Ute bands before 1750.

9. For overviews of French–New Mexican trading before Cachupín's rule, see John, *Storms Brewed,* 319–321; and David J. Weber, *The Spanish Frontier in American History* (New Haven: Yale University Press, 1991), 196–197.

10. For restrictions on foreign trade, see Alfred Barnaby Thomas, ed. and trans., *The Plains Indians and New Mexico, 1751–1778* (Albuquerque: University of New Mexico Press, 1940), 82–110.

11. Pekka Hämäläinen, "The Western Comanche Trade Center: Rethinking the Plains Indian Trade System," *Western Historical Quarterly* 29 (Winter 1998): 485–513. See also John, *Storms Brewed,* 316–321.

12. For ecological aspects of Comanche equestrianism, see Dan Flores, "Bison Ecology and Bison Diplomacy: The Southern Plains from 1800 to 1850," *Journal of American History* 78 (September 1991): 465–485; Elliot West, *The Contested Plains: Indians, Goldseekers, and the Rush to Colorado* (Lawrence: University of Kansas Press, 1998); and Pekka Hämäläinen, "The Rise and Fall of Plains Indian Horse Cultures," *Journal of American History* 90 (December 2003), esp. 835–845.

13. For the rise of Comanche economic power, see Hämäläinen, "The West-

ern Comanche Trade Center." For the paradoxical nature and instabil-
ity of Comanche equestrianism, see Flores, "Bison Ecology and Bison
Diplomacy." See also Hämäläinen, "Rise and Fall of Plains Indian Horse
Cultures."

14. "Instruction of Don Thomas Vélez Cachupín, 1754," "Revilla Gigedo
to the Marqués de Ensenada," and "The Marqués de la Ensenada to
Revilla Gigedo," in Thomas, *The Plains Indians and New Mexico*, 131, 122,
146. Cachupín also refers to Rabál's 1747 raid as a "scandalous indig-
nity"; ibid., 131.

15. For Comanche attempts to manipulate the new governor's peace initiative along with Cachupín's retaliatory measures, see "File of Papers on
the General Campaign," in Thomas, *The Plains Indians and New Mexico*,
68–74.

16. "Revilla Gigedo to the Marqués de Ensenada" and "Letter No. 2" from
Juan Joseph Lobato, ibid., 117.

17. "Revilla Gigedo to the Marqués de Ensenada," 117–118.

18. Ibid., 123.

19. Ibid.

20. "Instruction of Don Thomas Vélez Cachupín, 1754," 130. Efforts at repopulation had recurred following settler abandonment in 1748, and
not all settlers were as enthusiastic as Cachupín about allying with the
Utes. One prominent Chama Valley family "feared the 'faithlessness' of
'so cruel an enemy.'" See Frances Leon Swadesh, *Los Primeros Pobladores:
Hispanic Americans of the Ute Frontier* (South Bend: University of Notre
Dame Press, 1974), 35–37.

21. "Instruction of Don Thomas Vélez Cachupín, 1754," 131.

22. Donald Worcester, "Notes and Documents," *New Mexico Historical Review*
24 (1949): 236–254.

23. Eleanor B. Adams, ed., "Bishop Tamarón's Visitation of New Mexico,
1760," *New Mexico Historical Review* 28 (1953): 203, 217–220.

24. Frank's identification of 195 separate Comanche, Navajo, and Apache
raids from this decade includes no reference to any Ute raids. See
Frank, *From Settler to Citizen*, 37. For additional New Mexican campaigns
with Ute allies, see John, *Storms Brewed*, 330–331, 467–468.

25. "Instruction of Don Thomas Vélez Cachupín, 1754," 138.

26. Ibid., 132.

27. "Año de 1762," TC, II, reel 9, frames 256–261. See also "Valdez, Juan de
la Cruz," Twitchell no. 548, in *SANM*, 2: 237.

28. "Año de 1762," frame 261. The Hacienda of Encinillas was a labor camp
100 miles south of El Paso.

29. "Instruction of Don Thomas Vélez Cachupín, 1754," 131. In addition to

their degraded social status, *genízaros* and Indians were often considered minors in the court system. See Charles R. Cutter, *The Legal Culture of Northern New Spain* (Albuquerque: University of New Mexico Press, 1995), 117. For extended analysis of Spanish attitudes about unincorporated *bárbaros*, see David J. Weber, *Bárbaros: Spaniards and Their Savages in the Age of Enlightenment* (New Haven: Yale University Press, 2005).

30. Michel Foucault, *Discipline and Punish: The Birth of the Prison*, trans. Alan Sheridan (New York: Vintage, 1979), 216. On New Mexican hierarchies of race, gender, and honor, see Gutiérrez, *When Jesus Came*, esp. 176–240. For a related analysis, see Ana Maria Alonso, *Thread of Blood: Colonialism, Revolution, and Gender on Mexico's Northern Frontier* (Tucson: University of Arizona Press, 1995), esp. 15–103.

31. Adams, "Bishop Tamarón's Visitation," 216. For New Mexican economic development after 1750, see Frank, *From Settler to Citizen*, 176–222.

32. Eleanor B. Adams and Fray Angélico Chávez, eds. and trans., *The Missions of New Mexico, 1776: A Description by Fray Francisco Atanasio Domínguez with Other Contemporary Documents* (Albuquerque: University of New Mexico Press, 1956), 252–253. This assessment of Abiquiu's "Ute" captive baptisms is drawn from AB. See also Brugge, *Navajos in Catholic Church Records*.

33. Gutiérrez, *When Jesus Came*, 180–181. This claim of over 1,000 unidentified Indian captives is drawn from AB, in which unidentified "Indians" and children of various ages without known mothers or fathers appear more consistently than identified Utes or other tribal groups. The high number of unidentified Indian captives suggests that Brugge's demographic analyses reflect only those for identified or known tribes.

34. Brooks, *Captives and Cousins*, 244, 154. Chapters 4 and 7 also examine Ute slave trafficking.

35. For select studies of African and southern Indian slavery that emphasize imperial conflicts and growing economic dependency as factors in interindigenous enslavement, see Joseph C. Miller, *Way of Death: Merchant Capitalism and the Angolan Slave Trade, 1730–1830* (Madison: University of Wisconsin Press, 1988); and Alan Gallay, *The Indian Slave Trade: The Rise of the English Empire in the American South, 1670–1717* (New Haven: Yale University Press, 2002).

36. Brugge, *Navajos in Catholic Church Records*, 31. For an overview of Paiute and Ute linguistics, see Wick R. Miller, "Numic Languages," in *HBNAI*, 11: 98–106.

37. For Southern Paiute history and culture change, see Knack, *Boundaries Between*.

38. For Southern Paiute–Spanish relations, see ibid., 30–40.

39. For additional studies of Indian slavery that emphasize Ute dominion over Paiutes, see Van Hoak, "Who Shall Have the Children"; L. R. Bailey, *Indian Slave Trade in the Southwest: A Study of Slave-taking and the Traffic in Indian Captives* (Los Angeles: Westernlore, 1966), 139–172; Leland Hargrave Creer, "Spanish-American Slave Trade in the Great Basin, 1800–1853," *New Mexico Historical Review* 24 (July 1949): 171–183; and Carling Malouf and A. Arline Malouf, "The Effects of Spanish Slavery on the Indians of the Intermountain West," *Southwestern Journal of Anthropology* 1 (1945): 378–391. See also Chapter 7.

40. "Archive 1876, Aug. 18th, 1805," and "Archive 1877, Aug. 23rd, 1805," box 23, folder 429, Dorothy Woodward Collection, New Mexico State Records Center and Archives, Santa Fe. See also TC, II, reel 15, frame 780; and Brooks, *Captives and Cousins*, 155.

41. Charles Wilson Hackett, ed., *Historical Documents Relating to New Mexico, Nueva Vizcaya, and Approaches Thereto, to 1773*, 3 vols. (Washington, D.C.: Carnegie Institute, 1937), 3: 395–401, 497–487. For additional accounts of Indian women's rape as sanctioned by Spanish authorities, see ibid., 243–244, 425–429.

42. AB, 239, 380.

43. Gutiérrez, *When Jesus Came*, 153; AB, 282.

44. For eighteenth-century Abiquiu, see Lesley Poling-Kempes, *Valley of the Shining Stone: The Story of Abiquiu* (Tucson: University of Arizona Press, 1997), 30–48; Córdova, "Missionization and Hispanicization of Santo Thomas Apostol de Abiquiu"; and Swadesh, *Los Primeros Pobladores*, 27–58. See also Robert D. Martínez, "Fray Juan José Toledo and the Devil in Spanish New Mexico: A Story of Witchcraft and Cultural Conflict in Eighteenth-Century Abiquiu" (M.A. thesis, University of New Mexico, 1997).

45. Gilberto Benito Córdova, *Abiquiu and Don Cacahuate: A Folk History of a New Mexican Village* (Los Cerrillos, N.M.: San Marcos Press, 1973), 77–78, 18.

46. Swadesh, *Los Primeros Pobladores*, 42–46. For slightly lower estimates, see Adams and Chávez, *The Missions of New Mexico, 1776*, 126; and Adams, "Bishop Tamarón's Visitation," 292. See also Córdova, "Missionization and Hispanicization of Santo Thomas Apostol de Abiquiu," for various institutions of Hispanicization at Abiquiu after 1750.

47. "SANM II Translation 740 (Frances Swadesh Translation)," Dorothy Woodward Collection. See also TC, II, reel 10, frame 1055; Sánchez, 91–92; and David J. Weber, *The Taos Trappers: The Fur Trade in the Far Southwest, 1540–1846* (Norman: University of Oklahoma Press, 1971), 22–24.

48. Weber, *Taos Trappers*, 27; TC, II, reel 11, frames 520–523. See also

Sánchez, 93–94. For the trials of other illegal Ute trading expeditions, see TC, II, reel 11, frames 838, 845, and 853; and reel 14, frames 112–127. The primary goods traded were knives, tools, foods, horses, and mules. Weber, *Taos Trappers,* 27–28, suggests that slaves were purchased.

49. Sánchez, 21.

50. "Translation of Incomplete and Untitled Copy of Juan María Antonio Rivera's Original Diary of the First Expedition, 23 July 1765," trans. Joseph P. Sánchez, in Sánchez, 140–142.

51. Ibid., 142–147.

52. Ibid. The exact translations of Rivera's geological terminology refer to various types of lead and quicksilver.

53. Mythical waterways had excited Spanish explorers for generations; fantastic place-names—Quivira, Teguayo, Copala, and San Buenaventura—recur throughout Spanish chronicles. See Gloria Griffen Cline, *Exploring the Great Basin* (1963; reprint, Reno: University of Nevada Press, 1988), 18–32.

54. "Rivera's Original Diary," 146.

55. For a map of the spread of the horse, see "Dispersion of the Horse," in Warren A. Beck and Ynez D. Haase, *Historical Atlas of the American West* (Norman: University of Oklahoma Press, 1989), 9.

56. "Translation of Juan María Antonio Rivera's Second Diary, October 1765," trans. Joseph P. Sánchez, in Sánchez, 149–157.

57. Ibid., 150–151.

58. Ibid., 154–157. Rivera's second expedition had reached not the Colorado River, but the Gunnison, in western Colorado, and his incision was noticed by subsequent expeditions. As Elaine Scarry observes, "Marks on a series of trees register the marker's presence as through he stood in all those places: they allow him to inhabit a space much larger than the small circle of his immediately present body. Those marks are now part of the visual field of anyone else who approaches the grove of trees . . . the world is rebuilt or re-presented in such a way that it must be reseen." Utes and Paiutes recognized these and other Spanish alterations and became, in Scarry's terms, further "implicated in each other's sentience." See Elaine Scarry, *The Body in Pain: The Making and Unmaking of the World* (New York: Oxford University Press, 1985), 175–176.

3. The Enduring Spanish-Ute Alliance

1. See, for example, Hubert Howe Bancroft, *History of Utah, 1540–1886* (1890; reprint, Las Vegas: Nevada Publications, 1982), 1–18.

2. See Ross Harold Frank, *From Settler to Citizen: New Mexican Economic Devel-*

opment and the Creation of Vecino Society, 1750–1820 (Berkeley: University of California Press, 2000).

3. David J. Weber provides an overview of the "new politics" ushered in by Mexican independence in *The Mexican Frontier, 1821–1846: The American Southwest under Mexico* (Albuquerque: University of New Mexico Press, 1982) (cited hereafter as Weber). See also Andrés Reséndez, *Changing National Identities at the Frontier: Texas and New Mexico, 1800–1850* (New York: Cambridge University Press, 2005).

4. Elizabeth A. H. John, *Storms Brewed in Other Men's Worlds: The Confrontation of Indians, Spanish, and French in the Southwest, 1540–1795*, 2d ed. (Norman: University of Oklahoma Press, 1996), 432–442. See also Frank, *From Settler to Citizen*, 65–118.

5. As Elizabeth John argues, the failure of Spanish authorities to colonize Hopi, Yuma, and other southern Colorado River Indian communities initiated efforts to find alternate, northern routes between California and New Mexico. See John, *Storms Brewed*, 557–576.

6. Quoted in Sánchez, 47.

7. For the Domínguez-Escalante expedition, see ibid., 55–79; Herbert E. Bolton, *Pageant in the Wilderness: The Story of the Escalante Expedition to the Interior Basin, 1776* (Salt Lake City: Utah State Historical Society, 1950); Eleanor B. Adams, "Fray Francisco Atanasio Domínguez and Fray Silvestre Vélez de Escalante," *Utah Historical Quarterly* 44 (Winter 1976): 40–58; and Ted J. Warner, ed., and Fray Angélico Chávez, trans., *The Domínguez-Escalante Journal: Their Expedition through Colorado, Utah, Arizona, and New Mexico in 1776* (Salt Lake City: University of Utah Press, 1995). See also C. Gregory Crampton, "The Discovery of the Green River," *Utah Historical Quarterly* 20 (October 1952): 299–312.

8. Sánchez, 55–56. For translated copies of Miera's maps, see Bolton, *Pageant in the Wilderness;* and *MTMW,* 1: 94–116. See also Warner, *Domínguez-Escalante Journal.*

9. Sánchez, 57–59.

10. See Lesley Poling-Kempes, *Valley of the Shining Stone: The Story of Abiquiu* (Tucson: University of Arizona Press, 1997), xix.

11. Warner, *Domínguez-Escalante Journal,* 14–15, 18, 26–28.

12. Ibid., 33. Several more Ute parties had approached the expedition in the last days of August and were greeted warmly, "since," as Escalante noted, "they were our friends."

13. Ibid., 38.

14. Ibid., 39.

15. Ibid., 40.

16. Ibid., 42–57.

17. Ibid., 65. See Chapter 7 for further discussion of Utah Ute history.

18. Warner, *Domínguez-Escalante Journal*, 66, 67, 69.

19. Ibid., 91–93. For Southern Paiute band classifications and ethno-graphic geographies, see Martha C. Knack, *Boundaries Between: The Southern Paiutes, 1775–1995* (Lincoln: University of Nebraska Press, 2001); and Chapter 7.

20. Warner, *Domínguez-Escalante Journal*, 86.

21. Ibid., 79–80.

22. Ibid., 110.

23. Ibid., 108–109.

24. Chapter 5 examines Miera's cartographic legacies.

25. Warner, *Domínguez-Escalante Journal*, 122.

26. For Paiute corn cultivation and other evidences of trade relations with Havasupai, Hopi, and other Arizona peoples, see ibid., 95–127.

27. "Diary of Governor Anza's Expedition against the Comanche Nation, August 15–September 10, 1779," in *Forgotten Frontiers: A Study of the Spanish Indian Policy of Don Juan Bautista de Anza, Governor of New Mexico*, ed. and trans. Alfred Barnaby Thomas (1932; reprint, Norman: University of Oklahoma Press, 1968), 125–127.

28. "An Account of the Events Concerning the Comanche Peace, 1785–1786," ibid., 298–301. See also Alfred Barnaby Thomas, ed., "Governor Mendinueta's Proposals for the Defense of New Mexico, 1772–1778," *New Mexico Historical Review* (1931): 21–39.

29. "Events Concerning the Comanche Peace," 298, 301. Throughout Ecueracapa's visit to New Mexico, Ute leaders were "treated with equal distinction and esteem," and as word spread of the rapprochement between Spanish, Ute, and Comanche leaders, Ute and Comanche warriors at Pecos and Taos rejoiced, enacting rituals of reconciliation such as embracing, trading, smoking, and exchanging clothing. See ibid., 301–306.

30. "Urgate to Anza, October 5, 1786," in Thomas, *Forgotten Frontiers*, 332–336. See also TC, II, reel 11, frames 1058–65. For subsequent attempts to reconcile Spanish and Comanche leaders, see "Urgate y Loyola, Jan. 23, 1788," TC, II, reel 12, frame 35.

31. John, *Storms Brewed*, 714. For select correspondence regarding the peaceful and "good" conduct of unspecified Ute bands, see Twitchell nos. 1113, 1119, 1131, 1132, 1136, 1191, 1203, 1215, 1234, in *SANM*, 2: 326, 329, 331, 332, 343, 347, 349, 353. For Revilla Gigedo's replies, see nos. 1151, 1176, ibid., 335, 339. For continued Ute-Comanche con-

flicts, see "Fernando de la Concha to the Viceroy Conde de Revilla Gigedo," in *Border Comanches: Seven Spanish Colonial Documents,* ed. and trans. Marc Simmons (Santa Fe: Stagecoach Press, 1967), 25–26; and "NMSRCA, Spanish Archives #2304," trans. David M. Brugge, in "SANM II and MANM and Misc. Documents from Other Archives," Schroeder Collection, New Mexico State Records Center and Archives, Santa Fe; and Donald Jackson, ed., *The Journals of Zebulon Montgomery Pike,* 2 vols. (Norman: University of Oklahoma Press, 1966), 1: 52.

32. For New Mexico's economic development, see Frank, *From Settler to Citizen.*

33. "Urgate to Anza, October 5, 1786," in Thomas, 342.

34. "Indian Fund," box 1, folder 24, "SANM II Translations," Shishkin Collection, New Mexico State Records Center and Archives. See also Twitchell no. 2084, in *SANM,* 2: 517. The annual account totaled 526 pesos and 5 reales and included payments for "31 head of cattle," "41 fanegas of Flour," and "salaries of one woman servant to cook and make tortillas, and one boy to aid in the kitchen." See also Charles L. Kenner, *A History of New Mexican–Plains Indian Relations* (Norman: University of Oklahoma Press, 1968), 53–55; TC, II, reel 14, frames 718–719; and Twitchell no. 1533, in *SANM,* 2: 416.

35. David M. Brugge, *Navajos in the Catholic Church Records of New Mexico, 1964–1875,* 2d ed. (Tsaile, Ariz.: Navajo Community College Press, 1985), 22–23.

36. H. Bailey Carroll and J. Villasan Haggard, eds. and trans., *Three New Mexico Chronicles: The Exposición of Don Pedro Bautista Pino, 1812; the Ojeada of Lic. Antonio Barreiro, 1832; and the Additions by Don José Agustín de Escudero, 1849* (Albuquerque: Quivira Society, 1942), 134, 197; TC, II, reel 17, frames 554–556. See also Twitchell no. 2459, in *SANM,* 2: 571.

37. TC, II, reel 17, frames 783–795. See also Twitchell no. 2511, in *SANM,* 2: 577.

38. TC, II, reel 17, frames 783, 788–789.

39. Ibid., frames 789–790.

40. For the party's other testimonies, see ibid., frames 784–795.

41. TC, II, reel 15, frames 822–824. See also Twitchell no. 1881, in *SANM,* 2: 478. Mestas worked for fifty years as a translator among the Utes and was officially commissioned by Governor Real Alencaster in 1805. See TC, II, reel 15, frames 849–850. See also Twitchell no. 1886, in *SANM,* 2: 479.

42. For further discussion of Paiute slavery and its historiography, see Chapter 7.

43. Leroy R. Hafen and Ann W. Hafen, *Old Spanish Trail: Santa Fe to Los Angeles* (1954; reprint, Lincoln, Neb.: Bison Books, 1993), 86.

44. Joseph J. Hill, "Spanish and Mexican Exploration and Trade Northwest from New Mexico into the Great Basin, 1765–1853," *Utah Historical Quarterly* 3 (January 1930): 17–18; David J. Weber, *The Taos Trappers: The Fur Trade in the Far Southwest, 1540–1846* (Norman: University of Oklahoma Press, 1971), 27. See also Hafen and Hafen, *Old Spanish Trail*, 84–89.

45. From 1792 to 1810, four Indian captives, including two Ute children, were baptized at Abiquiu and placed in the homes of Juan Estevan Trujillo, Juan Pasqual Trujillo, and Juan Bautista Trujillo; AB, 380. See also Twitchell no. 2894, in *SANM*, 2: 625–626; and Frances Leon Swadesh, *Los Primeros Pobladores: Hispanic Americans of the Ute Frontier* (South Bend: University of Notre Dame Press, 1974), 174. "Caiguas" are often identified as Kiowas from the Plains, but as with references to undifferentiated "Comanches," such identified raiders are often of imprecise origin.

46. Quoted in Swadesh, *Los Primeros Pobladores*, 174. See also Twitchell no. 2894, in *SANM*, 2: 625–626.

47. For New Mexico's changing political economy, see Thomas Hall, *Social Change in the Southwest, 1350–1880* (Lawrence: University of Kansas Press, 1989), 135–184. For church and state control, see Weber, 18–82.

48. Ana Maria Alonso, *Thread of Blood: Colonialism, Revolution, and Gender on Mexico's Northern Frontier* (Tucson: University of Arizona Press, 1995), 39. See also Weber, 27, 107–121.

49. Alfred B. Thomas, ed., "Documents Bearing upon the Northern Frontier of New Mexico, 1818–1819," *New Mexico Historical Review* 4 (April 1929): 156; Kenner, *New Mexican–Plains Indian Relations*, 70.

50. Quoted in Elliot Coues, ed., *The Expeditions of Zebulon Montgomery Pike*, 2 vols. (Minneapolis: Ross and Haines, 1965), 2: 608.

51. For Spanish-American tensions and the Adams-Onis Treaty, see Weber, 11–13, 122–125; and D. W. Meinig, *The Shaping of America: A Geographical Perspective on 500 Years of History*, vol. 2: *Continental America, 1800–1867* (New Haven: Yale University Press 1993), 4–23, 71–78.

52. See Rex. W. Strickland, "Robert McKnight," in *MMFTFW*, 9: 259–268. See also Janet Lecompte, "Jules DeMun," in *MMFTFW*, 8: 96–105. For the 1818 campaign and "Diary of Second Lieutenant Don José María de Arce," see Thomas, "Documents Bearing upon the Northern Frontier of New Mexico," 158.

53. Hall, *Social Change in the Southwest*, 150–151; Weber, 13.

54. See Weber, 83–105.

4. Crisis in the New Mexican–Ute Borderlands

1. For Mexican land grants in Colorado, see Frances Leon Swadesh, *Los Primeros Pobladores: Hispanic Americans of the Ute Frontier* (South Bend: University of Notre Dame Press, 1974); Weber, 179–206; William Wyckoff, *Creating Colorado: The Making of a Western Landscape, 1860–1940* (New Haven: Yale University Press, 1999), 37–41; and Maria E. Montoya, *Translating Property: The Maxwell Land Grant and the Conflict over Land in the American West, 1840–1900* (Berkeley: University of California Press, 2002).

2. L. R. Bailey, *Indian Slave Trade in the Southwest: A Study of Slave-taking and the Traffic in Indian Captives* (Los Angeles: Westernlore, 1966), 152. Chapter 7 examines Walkara's relations with U.S. settlers as well as his band's dominion over Paiute vassals.

3. Chapter 5 traces Anglo and American trading rivalries in the northern Great Basin.

4. As Edward Said argues, "Neither imperialism nor colonialism is a simple act of accumulation and acquisition. Both are supported and perhaps even impelled by impressive ideological formulations that include notions that certain territories and peoples *require* and beseech domination." See Said, *Culture and Imperialism* (New York: Alfred A. Knopf, 1993), 9.

5. For Ute participation in 1818 raids in New Mexico, see Twitchell no. 2736, in *SANM,* 2: 606. For Ute-Jicarilla relations, see Chapter 6.

6. H. Bailey Carroll and J. Villasan Haggard, eds. and trans., *Three New Mexico Chronicles: The Exposición of Don Pedro Bautista Pino, 1812; the Ojeada of Lic. Antonio Barreiro, 1832; and the Additions by Don José Agustín de Escudero, 1849* (Albuquerque: Quivira Society, 1942), 134.

7. Andrés Reséndez, *Changing National Identities at the Frontier: Texas and New Mexico, 1800–1850* (New York: Cambridge University Press, 2005), 37. For traders' concentration of economic and political power, see Montoya, *Translating Property,* 30–77.

8. Thomas James, *Three Years among the Indians and Mexicans* (1846; reprint, Philadelphia: J. B. Lippincott, 1962). See also Frederick E. Voelker, "Thomas James," in *MMFTFW,* 4: 153–167.

9. James, *Three Years among the Indians and Mexicans,* 90.

10. Ibid., 92.

11. For Spanish gun-trading policy, see Charles L. Kenner, *A History of New Mexican–Plains Indian Relations* (Norman: University of Oklahoma Press, 1968), 54. For the Indian gun trade, see Louis A. Garavaglia and

Charles G. Worman, *Firearms of the American West, 1803–1865* (Albuquerque: University of New Mexico Press, 1984), 343–362. See also Charles Edward Chapel, *Guns of the Old West* (1961; reprint, Fairfax, Va.: Odysseus Editions, 1995).

12. James, *Three Years among the Indians and Mexicans*, 91–92.

13. Alfred B. Thomas, ed., "Documents Bearing upon the Northern Frontier of New Mexico, 1818–1819," *New Mexico Historical Review* 4 (April 1929): 156. For New Mexico's "economic boom," see Ross Harold Frank, *From Settler to Citizen: New Mexican Economic Development and the Creation of Vecino Society, 1750–1820* (Berkeley: University of California Press, 2000). For additional statistics on the decline in Spanish funding, see also Frank, "From Settler to Citizen: Economic Development and Cultural Change in Late Colonial New Mexico, 1750–1820" (Ph.D. diss., University of California, Berkeley, 1992), 433, 457. For the economic expansion of Indian groups after independence, see Reséndez, *Changing National Identities at the Frontier,* 50–55, who notes (51): "Undoubtedly, the Indian world was expanding at the expense of Mexico."

14. Weber, 11; James, *Three Years among the Indians and Mexicans,* 92–93. For Navajo–New Mexican hostilities, see Frank McNitt, *Navajo Wars: Military Campaigns, Slave Raids, and Reprisals* (Albuquerque: University of New Mexico Press, 1972); and J. Lee Correll, ed., *Through White Men's Eyes: A Contribution to Navajo History* (Window Rock, Ariz.: Navajo Heritage Center, 1976).

15. For attempts to link both New Mexico and Sonora with California, see Harlan Hague, *The Road to California: The Search for a Southern Overland Route, 1540–1848* (Glendale, Ill.: Arthur C. Clark, 1978), esp. 124–132.

16. Leroy R. Hafen and Ann W. Hafen, *Old Spanish Trail: Santa Fe to Los Angeles* (1954; reprint, Lincoln, Neb.: Bison Books, 1993), 93–94. See also Harvey L. Carter, "Ewing Young," in *MMFTFW,* 2: 379–380; and Iris Higbie Wilson, "Wilson Wolfskill," ibid., 351–353.

17. William S. Wallace, "Antoine Robidoux," in *MMFTFW,* 4: 268–269. For references to "Snake" Indians, see Virginia Cole Trenholm and Maurine Carley, *The Shoshonis: Sentinels of the Rockies* (Norman: University of Oklahoma Press, 1964). For Utes and the fur trade, see David J. Weber, *The Taos Trappers: The Fur Trade in the Far Southwest, 1540–1846* (Norman: University of Oklahoma Press, 1971), 90–95; and Gloria Griffen Cline, *Exploring the Great Basin* (1963; Reno: University of Nevada Press, 1988), 132–163.

18. For overviews of the Great Basin fur trade, see Trenholm and Carley, *The Shoshonis,* 56–96; Hafen and Hafen, *Old Spanish Trail,* 95–129; and

Cline, *Exploring the Great Basin,* 93–132. The classic treatment of Smith remains Dale L. Morgan's *Jedediah Smith and the Opening of the West* (1953; reprint, Lincoln, Neb.: Bison Books, 1964).

19. Correll, *Through White Men's Eyes,* 120–150, presents a compilation of Navajo-Mexican relations with extensive Ute references. During one retaliatory campaign against the Navajo in 1823, Governor José Antonio Vizcarra attacked a Paiute *ranchería* in northern Arizona in the belief that it was a Navajo encampment; ibid., 116. Navajo–New Mexican conflicts thereafter became so severe that Navajos for the first time in half a century constituted the majority of captive baptisms. See David M. Brugge, *Navajos in the Catholic Church Records of New Mexico, 1694–1875,* 2d ed. (Tsaile, Ariz.: Navajo Community College Press, 1985), 22–23. Brugge identifies 259 known Navajo baptisms out of a total 363 for the decade, or 71 percent.

20. Josiah Gregg, *Commerce of the Prairies* (1844; reprint, Philadelphia: J. B. Lippincott, 1962), 161–163.

21. Ibid., 162. Ralph Emerson Twitchell identifies Archuleta as the Mexican officer referred to by Gregg. See *LFNMH,* 2: 48.

22. Correll, *Through White Men's Eyes,* 143–145, 154–156.

23. Quoted in Weber, 36.

24. Ibid., 92–93. See also James F. Brooks, *Captives and Cousins: Slavery, Kinship, and Community in the Southwest Borderlands* (Chapel Hill: University of North Carolina Press, 2002), 301; Lesley Poling-Kempes, *Valley of the Shining Stone: The Story of Abiquiu* (Tucson: University of Arizona Press 1997), 84–85; and Ward Alan Minge, "Mexican Independence Day and a Ute Tragedy in Santa Fe, 1844," in *The Changing Ways of Southwestern Indians: A Historic Perspective,* ed. Albert H. Schroeder (Glorieta, N.M.: Rio Grande, 1973).

25. Weber, 92–93; and Poling-Kempes, *Valley of the Shining Stone,* 85. See also Albert H. Schroeder, "A Brief History of the Southern Utes," *Southwestern Lore* 30 (March 1965): 64. Before the attack, Martínez had received numerous accounts of Ute-Navajo raids and depredations that contributed to his fear and reactionary Indian policy. See Correll, *Through White Men's Eyes,* 154–158. For the course of Ute-Mexican warfare after the incident at the *Palacio,* see Chapter 6. See also Sánchez, 115; David J. Weber, "American Westward Expansion and the Breakdown of Relations between Pobladores and 'Indios Bárbaros' on Mexico's Far Northern Frontier, 1821–1846," *New Mexico Historical Review* 56 (July 1981): 224; and Daniel Tyler, "Mexican Indian Policy in New Mexico," ibid., 55 (April 1980): 101–120.

26. See Chapter 6 for further discussion of Ute responses to Martínez's attack.

27. For changing *genízaro* settlement patterns, see Swadesh, *Los Primeros Pobladores;* Brooks, *Captives and Cousins;* Gilberto Benito Córdova, "Missionization and Hispanicization of Santo Thomas Apostol de Abiquiu, 1750–1770" (Ph.D. diss., University of New Mexico, 1979); and Robert D. Martínez, "Fray Juan José Toledo and the Devil in Spanish New Mexico: A Story of Witchcraft and Cultural Conflict in Eighteenth-Century Abiquiu" (M.A. thesis, University of New Mexico, 1997).

28. David J. Weber, "Introduction," in Hafen and Hafen, *Old Spanish Trail*, 11.

29. Hafen and Hafen's classic treatment of the "opening" and course of the Old Spanish Trail mostly chronicles Anglo-American expeditions. The authors often fail to recognize the hybrid composition of these parties or to assess fully the effects of such trade and travel on Great Basin Indians. Joseph Sánchez redresses this anglocentrism and identifies the centrality of Hispanic traders to the Old Spanish Trail.

30. Quoted in Hafen and Hafen, *Old Spanish Trail*, 149–151. See also ibid., 139–154, for overviews of the expedition, its members, and likely route.

31. J. Cecil Alter, ed., "Journal of Orange Clark and George Yount," *California Historical Quarterly* 2 (April 1923): 13.

32. Ibid.

33. Quoted in Hafen and Hafen, *Old Spanish Trail*, 163–164. See ibid., 155–169, for overviews of Armijo's expedition, Armijo's diary, and Mexican national reports about the voyage. See also ibid., 187, for prevailing terms of trade.

34. For Southern Paiute band classifications, see Martha C. Knack, *Boundaries Between: The Southern Paiutes, 1775–1995* (Lincoln: University of Nebraska Press, 2001). See also Robert A. Manners, *Southern Paiute and Chemehuevi: An Ethnohistorical Report* (New York: Garland, 1974), 34–48.

35. For Southern Paiute history and political organization, see Knack, *Boundaries Between.*

36. For Great Basin ecological history, see Donald K. Grayson, *The Desert's Past: A Natural Prehistory of the Great Basin* (Washington, D.C.: Smithsonian Institution Press, 1993), esp. 270–276, 299–303.

37. Eleanor Lawrence, "Mexican Trade between Santa Fe and Los Angeles, 1830–1848," *California Historical Society Quarterly* 10 (July 1931): 27–39. See also Hafen and Hafen, *Old Spanish Trail*, 174–194, for additional regulations. For population comparisons, see Weber, 6. For California horse herds, see George Harwood Phillips, *Indians and Intruders in*

Central California, 1769–1849 (Norman: University of Oklahoma Press, 1993), esp. 95–106; and idem, *Chiefs and Challengers: Indian Resistance and Cooperation in Southern California* (Berkeley: University of California Press, 1975). Hafen and Hafen, *Old Spanish Trail*, 226, cite an additional, extraordinary account of the killings of thousands of feral horses in Los Angeles. For former California mission Indians traveling to Abiquiu and becoming *genízaros*, see Reséndez, *Changing National Identities at the Frontier*, 52–53.

38. Phillips, *Indians and Intruders*, 95. For horse raiding on the Old Spanish Trail, see Hafen and Hafen, *Old Spanish Trail*, 227–257. The effects of secularization on interior Californian Indian communities require further research and interpretation, as the suggestion that former mission Indians raided along the Old Spanish Trail raises additional questions about the exact identities of the many "Indian" horse raiders in southern California.

39. Hafen and Hafen, *Old Spanish Trail*, 236–242.

40. Ibid. Pursuing parties often came upon dying animals, and later expeditions often identified bleached animal skeletons. See ibid.; and Thomas D. Bonner, ed., *The Life and Adventures of James P. Beckwourth, Mountaineer, Scout, and Pioneer and Chief of the Crow Nation of Indians* (1856; reprint, Lincoln, Neb.: Bison Books, 1972) (cited hereafter as Bonner). For problems in using Beckwourth's text, see Chapter 5.

41. Quoted in Hafen and Hafen, *Old Spanish Trail*, 243. "Sozones" probably refers to unspecified Shoshone or misidentified Indian groups. For Ute band designations, see Chapter 1. For Walkara's involvement in California raids, see Chapter 7. Hafen and Hafen discount Ute influence upon the California horse trade, calling this 1840 raiding party "American" although no sources cited suggest so. Moreover, their suggestion that after 1848 Walkara's Utes became "effective operators (thieves), having received excellent coaching from their late white associates," overly glorifies "mountain men." In contrast, an understanding of Spanish-Ute relations reveals countless examples of Ute power attributable not to "white coaching" but to Ute adaptations to the region's relations of violence.

42. Quoted in Hafen and Hafen, *Old Spanish Trail*, 185–186.

43. Quoted in Gerald A. Smith and Clifford J. Walker, *Indian Slave Trade along the Mojave* (San Bernardino, Calif.: San Bernardino Country Museum, 1965); Daniel W. Jones, *Forty Years among the Indians* (Los Angeles: Westernlore, 1960), 45–48; and Gustive O. Larson, "Walkara, Ute Chief," in *MMFTFW*, 2: 339–359.

44. William R. Palmer, "Pahute Indian Government and Laws," *Utah Histori-*

cal Quarterly 2 (April 1929): 35–42. The Shivwits are a Southern Paiute band from southeastern Utah.

45. "An Interview with Mr. Toney Tillohash, Southern Paiute, Recorded on June 16, 1967, in the Home of His Son, Arthur Tillohash, St. George, Utah. Kay S. Fowler, Interviewer," in The American Indian History Project Supported by Miss Doris Duke, Western History Center, Duke no. 119, Special Collections, University of Utah. For additional accounts of Paiute oral histories, see LaVan Martineau, *The Southern Paiutes: Legends, Lore, Languages, and Lineage* (Las Vegas: KC Publications, 1992).

46. H. L. Conrad, *Uncle Dick Wotton: Pioneer Frontiersman* (Chicago: W. E. Dibble, 1890), 75–76. Brugge, *Navajos in Catholic Church Records,* 22–23.

47. Brugge, *Navajos in Catholic Church Records,* 22–23.

48. Quoted in Hafen and Hafen, *Old Spanish Trail,* 267–268; Jones, *Forty Years among the Indians,* 47–48.

49. Smith and Walker, *Indian Slave Trade along the Mojave,* 13–15; Hafen and Hafen, *Old Spanish Trail,* 269–270. For overviews of Indians within California's mission economy, see Steven W. Hackel, "Land, Labor, and Production: The Colonial Economy of Spanish and Mexican California," in *Contested Eden: California before the Gold Rush,* ed. Ramón A. Gutiérrez and Richard J. Orsi (Berkeley: University of California Press, 1998), 111–146.

50. Jones, *Forty Years among the Indians,* 48; Palmer, "Pahute Indian Government and Laws," 40.

51. See Bailey, *Indian Slave Trade in the Southwest,* 147–164.

5. Great Basin Indians in the Era of Lewis and Clark

1. For studies of the Intermountain West fur trade, see David J. Weber, *The Taos Trappers: The Fur Trade in the Far Southwest, 1540–1846* (Norman: University of Oklahoma Press, 1971), 52–111, 134–175; David J. Wishart, *The Fur Trade of the American West, 1807–1840* (1979; reprint, Lincoln: University of Nebraska Press, 1992), 115–204; and Gloria Griffen Cline, *Exploring the Great Basin* (1963; reprint, Reno: University of Nevada Press, 1988), 60–188.

2. D. W. Meinig examines American expansion in *The Shaping of America: A Geographical Perspective on 500 Years of History,* vol. 2: *Continental America, 1800–1867* (New Haven: Yale University Press, 1993).

3. For the centrality of territorial accumulation to Jeffersonian democracy, see Drew McCoy, *The Elusive Republic: Political Economy in Jeffersonian America* (Chapel Hill: University of North Carolina Press, 1980).

4. For competing Anglo and American western trading policies, see Meinig,

Continental America, 41–58, 103–128; and Cline, *Exploring the Great Basin,*
77–131. See also Gloria Griffen Cline, *Peter Skene Ogden and the Hudson's
Bay Company* (Norman: University of Oklahoma Press, 1974). For an al-
ternative assessment of the Anglo-American economic rivalry in the
Intermountain West, see John Phillip Reid, *Contested Empire: Peter Skene
Ogden and the Snake River Expeditions* (Norman: University of Oklahoma
Press, 2002).

5. For captivity in the New Mexican borderlands, see James F. Brooks, *Captives and Cousins: Slavery, Kinship, and Community in the Southwest Borderlands* (Chapel Hill: University of North Carolina Press, 2002).

6. For water in the making of the imperial West, see Donald Worster,
Rivers of Empire: Water, Aridity, and the Growth of the American West (New
York: Pantheon Books, 1985).

7. Humboldt does not identify or cite Miera in the extended "Geographic
Introduction" to his massive *Political Essay on the Kingdom of New Spain,*
4 vols. (1822; reprint, New York: AMS Press, 1966). He does, however,
reference Mexican mapmakers, who, according to Cline, "had appropriated the Miera geography." See Cline, *Exploring the Great Basin,*
67. For Miera's influences on Humboldt and subsequent New Mexican
cartography, see also *MTMW,* 1: 117–138; and C. Gregory Crampton,
"Humboldt's Utah, 1811," *Utah Historical Quarterly* 26 (July 1958): 269–
281.

8. For the changing relationship between geography and state power in
the Age of Revolution, see Ann Marie Claire Godlewska, *Geography Un-
bound: French Cartographic Science from Cassini to Humboldt* (Chicago: University of Chicago Press, 1999).

9. For the place of Indian groups in the Lewis and Clark expedition as well
as an appendix on the changing biographical details and spellings of
Sacagawea, see James P. Ronda, *Lewis and Clark among the Indians* (Lincoln: University of Nebraska Press, 1984). For English antecedents to
Great Basin expansion, see Cline, *Exploring the Great Basin,* 60–64. For
cartographic achievements of Lewis and Clark, see *JLC,* 1: 3–13. For
a differentiation between the "Mountainous West" and the "Intermountain West," see William Wyckoff and Lary M. Dilsaver, eds., *The
Mountainous West: Explorations in Historical Geography* (Lincoln: University of Nebraska Press, 1995), 1–59.

10. Donald Jackson, ed., *Letters of the Lewis and Clark Expedition with Related
Documents, 1783–1854* (Urbana: University of Illinois Press, 1962), 61.

11. Humboldt arrived in Philadelphia from Cuba and visited Jefferson both
in Washington and at Monticello. After receiving his letter of introduction, Jefferson replied, "The countries you have visited are of those least

known and most interesting, and a lively desire will be felt generally to receive the information you have to give"; quoted in L. Kellner, *Alexander von Humboldt* (New York: Oxford University Press, 1963), 61. See also Helmut de Terra, *Humboldt: The Life and Times of Alexander von Humboldt, 1769–1859* (New York: Alfred A. Knopf, 1955), 172–189. Regarding his maps of Mexico, Humboldt later wrote: "I left a copy, in 1804, at the secretary of state's office in Washington"; subsequent scholars, most notably Carl Wheat, have been unable to find this copy and believe it was destroyed during the War of 1812. Quoted in *MTMW,* 1: 137.

12. See Cline, *Exploring the Great Basin,* 64–67; *JLC,* 1: maps 123, 125, 125; and *MTMW,* 2: 49–60.

13. John L. Allen, "Lands of Myth, Waters of Wonder: The Place of Imagination in the History of Geographical Expansion," in *Geographies of Mind,* ed. David Lowenthal and Martyn Bowden (New York, 1976), 57. See also Thongchai Winichakul, *Siam Mapped: A History of the Geo-Body of a Nation* (Honolulu: University of Hawaii Press, 1994); and Matthew H. Edney, *Mapping an Empire: The Geographical Construction of British India, 1765–1843* (Chicago: University of Chicago Press, 1997).

14. *JLC,* 5: 59; Ronda, *Lewis and Clark among the Indians,* 137.

15. *JLC,* 5: 119, 103.

16. Ibid., 91–92.

17. John C. Ewers, *Indian Life on the Upper Missouri* (Norman: University of Oklahoma Press, 1968), 35–36. For an overview of Lakota expansion, see Richard White, "Winning the West: The Expansion of the Western Sioux in the Eighteenth and Nineteenth Centuries," *Journal of American History* 65 (Summer 1978): 319–343. See also Ronda, *Lewis and Clark among the Indians,* 148–156. For Blackfoot and Piegan distinctions, see Hugh A. Dempsey, "Blackfoot," in *HBNAI,* 13: 604–637.

18. *JLC,* 5: 89.

19. *JLC,* 9: 205, 208; 5: 178; and Ronda, *Lewis and Clark among the Indians,* 154. For firearms in the early West, see Louis A. Garavaglia and Charles G. Worman, *Firearms of the American West, 1803–1865* (Albuquerque: University of New Mexico Press, 1984); and Charles Edward Chapel, *Guns of the Old West* (1961; reprint, Fairfax, Va.: Odysseus Editions, 1995).

20. *JLC,* 5: 126.

21. Wishart, *Fur Trade of American West,* 41–174.

22. James P. Ronda, *Astoria and Empire* (Lincoln: University of Nebraska Press, 1990), 190, 165–195. Hunt's original diary has been lost, and Ronda's reconstructed account is based largely on redactions from

translated French accounts. See also Philip Ashton Rollins, ed., *The Discovery of the Oregon Trail: Robert Stuart's Narratives of His Overland Trips Eastward from Astoria in 1812–13* (New York: Charles Scribner's Sons, 1935), 281–308.

23. Quoted in D. W. Meinig, *The Great Columbia Plain: A Historical Geography, 1805–1910* (1968; reprint, Seattle: University of Washington Press, 1995), 52.

24. Meinig, *The Great Columbia Plain,* 62–65.

25. For the Treaty of Ghent and the Joint Occupancy Treaty of 1818, see Bradford Perkins, *The Creation of a Republican Empire, 1776–1865* (New York: Cambridge University Press, 1993), 140–146, 208–211.

26. Alexander Ross, *The Fur Hunters of the Far West,* ed. Kenneth A. Spaulding (Norman: University of Oklahoma Press, 1956), 135. For an overview of McKenzie's career, see Edward I. Stewart, "Donald McKenzie," in *MMFTFW,* 5: 227–238.

27. Ross, *Fur Hunters of Far West,* 135.

28. Ibid., 127, 136.

29. Cole Harris, *The Resettlement of British Columbia: Essays on Colonialism and Geographic Change* (Vancouver: University of British Columbia Press, 1997), 33. For studies of Indian women's authority within the fur trade, see Sylvia Van Kirk, *"Many Tender Ties": Women in Fur-Trade Society, 1670–1870* (Winnipeg: University of Manitoba Press, 1980); and Jennifer S. H. Brown, *Strangers in Blood: Fur Trade Company Families in Indian Country* (Vancouver: University of British Columbia Press, 1980). See also Elizabeth Vibert, *Traders' Tales: Narratives of Cultural Encounters in the Columbia Plateau, 1807–1846* (Norman: University of Oklahoma Press, 1997).

30. Ross, *Fur Hunters of Far West,* 168, 169. Ross estimates that the "Snake country therefore contains an area . . . of about 150,000 square miles . . . and may contain 36,000 souls or nearly one person to every four mile square"; ibid., 167.

31. Ibid., 171–172.

32. Ibid., 175, 172.

33. Stewart, "Donald McKenzie," 237.

34. See Cline, *Peter Skene Ogden and Hudson's Bay Company,* 52–96.

35. For Ogden's Snake River campaigns, see E. E. Rich, ed., *Peter Skene Ogden's Snake Country Journals, 1824–25 and 1825–26* (London: Hudson's Bay Record Society, 1950), xi–lxxix; and Ted J. Warner, "Peter Skene Ogden," in *MMFTFW,* 3: 213–232. See also Cline, *Peter Skene Ogden and Hudson's Bay Company;* and Reid, *Contested Empire,* 49–203.

36. For accounts of Ogden's daily fur tally, see Rich, *Ogden's Snake Country Journals*, 42–56.
37. Ibid., 41, 51, 234. For a biographical sketch of Johnson Gardner, see Aubrey L. Haines, "Johnson Gardner," in *MMFTFW*, 2: 157–159.
38. Rich, *Ogden's Snake Country Journals*, 54.
39. For Crow involvement in the fur trade, see Frederick E. Hoxie, *Parading through History: The Making of the Crow Nation in America, 1805–1935* (New York: Cambridge University Press, 1995), 60–78.
40. Rich, *Ogden's Snake Country Journals*, 233; Haines, "Johnson Gardner," 158; and Wishart, *Fur Trade of American West*, 115–174.
41. Virginia Cole Trenholm and Maurine Carley, *The Shoshonis: Sentinels of the Rockies* (Norman: University of Oklahoma Press, 1964), 67.
42. Rich, *Ogden's Snake Country Journals*, 233, 50; Dale L. Morgan, *Jedediah Smith and the Opening of the West* (1953; reprint, Lincoln, Neb.: Bison Books, 1964), 168; Rich, *Ogden's Snake Country Journals*, 175. The Bannock are Snake River peoples who became co-residents with Northern Shoshones on the Fort Hall Indian Reservation and have been mistakenly considered Shoshones. See Brigham D. Madsen, *The Bannock of Idaho* (Caldwell, Iowa: Caxton Printers, 1958).
43. Bonner, 134–137. For challenges in using Beckwourth's narrative, see Delmont R. Oswald, "Introduction," in *Life and Adventures of James P. Beckwourth*, ed. Oswald (1856; reprint, Lincoln: University of Nebraska Press, 1972), vii, ix–x. See also idem, "James P. Beckwourth," in *MMFTFW*, 6: 37–60. Despite such challenges, numerous Great Basin and Shoshone historians deploy his narrative while recognizing his hyperbolic tendencies. See, for instance, Madsen, *The Bannock of Idaho*, 50–51.
44. Bonner, 99–100, 139.
45. Ibid., 137–138; F. A. Wislizenius, *A Journey to the Rocky Mountains in the Year 1839* (St. Louis: State Historical Society of Missouri, 1912), 90.
46. Morgan, *Jedediah Smith*, 171–172.
47. Glyndwr Williams, ed., *Peter Skene Ogden's Snake Country Journals, 1827–28 and 1828–29* (London: Hudson's Bay Record Society, 1971), 65, 51–52.

6. Colorado Utes and the Traumatic Storms of Expansion

1. D. W. Meinig, *The Shaping of America: A Geographical Perspective on 500 Years of History*, vol. 2: *Continental America, 1800–1867* (New Haven: Yale University Press, 1993), 128–144. For overviews of Mexico's Indian pol-

icy, see Weber, 83–121, 242–272; and James F. Brooks, *Captives and Cousins: Slavery, Kinship, and Community in the Southwest Borderlands* (Chapel Hill: University of North Carolina Press, 2002), 273–292.

2. For assessments of the Frémont Second Expedition's cartographic legacies, see Gloria Griffen Cline, *Exploring the Great Basin* (1963; reprint, Reno: University of Nevada Press, 1988), 214–215; Mary Lee Spence and Donald Jackson, eds., "Map Portfolio," in *The Expeditions of John Charles Frémont* (Urbana: University of Illinois Press, 1970); and *MTMW*, 2: 194–200. Wheat suggests that Frémont's map "changed the entire picture of the West"; ibid., 194. For California equestrian Indian societies, see George Harwood Phillips, *Indians and Intruders in Central California, 1769–1849* (Norman: University of Oklahoma Press, 1993). For Colorado River colonial Indian history, see Jack D. Forbes, *Warriors of the Colorado: The Yumas of the Quechan Nation and Their Neighbors* (Norman: University of Oklahoma Press, 1965).

3. For the origins of U.S. Indian policy, see Francis Paul Prucha, *American Indian Treaties: The History of a Political Anomaly* (Berkeley: University of California Press, 1994) and *The Great Father: The United States Government and the American Indians,* abridged ed. (Lincoln: University of Nebraska Press, 1986).

4. Brooks, *Captives and Cousins,* 157–257; Ross Harold Frank, *From Settler to Citizen: New Mexican Economic Development and the Creation of Vecino Society, 1750–1820* (Berkeley: University of California Press, 2000), esp. 176–233. See also Andrés Reséndez, *Changing National Identities at the Frontier: Texas and New Mexico, 1800–1850* (New York: Cambridge University Press, 2005).

5. Elliot West, *The Contested Plains: Indians, Goldseekers, and the Rush to Colorado* (Lawrence: University of Kansas Press, 1998), 78. For Plains Indian relations with southeastern Indians forced west by removal, see David La Vere, *Contrary Neighbors: Southern Plains and Removed Indians in Indian Territory* (Norman: University of Oklahoma Press, 2000). For *comanchero* and *cibolero* relations, see Brooks, *Captives and Cousins.*

6. For Arkansas River trading settlements, see Janet Lecompte, *Pueblo, Hardscrabble, Greenhorn: The Upper Arkansas, 1832–1856* (Norman: University of Oklahoma Press, 1978) (cited hereafter as Lecompte). For Alexander Barclay's trading among the Utes, see George P. Hammond, ed., *The Adventures of Alexander Barclay, Mountain Man* (Denver: Old West Publishing, 1976).

7. Virginia McConnell Simmons, *The Ute Indians of Utah, Colorado, and New Mexico* (Boulder: University Press of Colorado, 2000), 62. See also Vir-

ginia McConnell, *Ute Pass: Route of the Blue Sky People* (Denver: Sage Books, 1963), 9–11.

8. West, *The Contested Plains,* 192; and Elliot West, *The Way to the West: Essays on the Central Plains* (Albuquerque: University of New Mexico Press, 1995), 43. For the collapse of the western fur trade, see David J. Wishart, *The Fur Trade of the American West, 1807–1840* (1979; reprint, Lincoln: University of Nebraska Press, 1992), 115–174.

9. Loretta Fowler, *Arapahoe Politics, 1851–1978: Symbols in Crises of Authority* (Lincoln: University of Nebraska Press, 1982).

10. John C. Frémont, *The Exploring Expedition to the Rocky Mountains* (1845; reprint, Washington, D.C.: Smithsonian Institution Press, 1988), 283–286; Charles Preuss, *Exploring with Frémont: The Private Diaries of Charles Preuss, Cartographer for John C. Frémont on His First, Second, and Fourth Expeditions to the Far West,* trans. and ed. Erwin G. and Elisabeth K. Gudde (Norman: University of Oklahoma Press, 1958), 137. For other accounts of Arapahoe-Ute hostilities, see Fowler, *Arapahoe Politics,* 37–38; Hammond, *The Adventures of Alexander Barclay,* 150; Simmons, *Ute Indians,* 55–56, 61–62; and LeRoy R. Hafen, ed., *Ruxton of the Rockies* (Norman: University of Oklahoma Press, 1950), 213–215, 231–232, 236–237.

11. Preuss, *Exploring with Frémont,* 137. For Carson's experiences in the Great Basin before 1844, see Harvey Lewis Carter, ed., *"Dear Old Kit": The Historical Christopher Carson* (Norman: University of Oklahoma Press, 1968), 44–83. See also Tom Dunlay, *Kit Carson and the Indians* (Lincoln: University of Nebraska Press, 2000), 48–84.

12. Brooks, *Captives and Cousins,* 300–301. For Cheyenne-Bent relations, see also Joseph Jablow, *The Cheyenne in Plains Indian Trade Relations, 1795–1840* (1951; reprint, Lincoln: University of Nebraska Press, 1994); West, *The Contested Plains;* and Lecompte.

13. For the Indian gun trade in the nineteenth-century West, see Louis A. Garavaglia and Charles G. Warren, *Firearms of the American West, 1803–1865* (Albuquerque: University of New Mexico Press, 1984), 343–362.

14. For Antoine Robidoux's forts within Ute territories, see Ken Reyher, *Antoine Robidoux and Fort Uncompahgre: The Story of a Western Colorado Fur Trader* (Ouray, Colo.: Western Reflections, 1998). See also William S. Wallace, "Antoine Robidoux," in *MMFTFW,* 4: 261–273.

15. Frémont, *The Exploring Expedition,* 286.

16. Hammond, *The Adventures of Alexander Barclay,* 142–143; Dunlay, *Kit Carson and the Indians,* 97. For Carson's accounts of his Ute altercation, see ibid., 96–97.

17. "The depreciation in the value of beaver skins has thrown the great

body of trappers out of employment," George Ruxton noted in 1847, "and there is a general tendency amongst the mountain men to settle in the fruitful valleys of the Rocky Mountains"; Hafen, *Ruxton of the Rockies,* 209. See also ibid., 225–228, for the decline of beaver values and subsequent trapper settlement patterns as well as rebounding beaver populations.

18. Frémont, *The Exploring Expedition,* 279; Hafen, *Ruxton of the Rockies,* 198. See also Lecompte, 135–138, 301; Brooks, *Captives and Cousins,* 301–302; Wallace, "Antoine Robidoux," 271–272; Reyher, *Antoine Robidoux and Fort Uncompahgre;* and David J. Weber, *The Taos Trappers: the Fur Trade in the Far Southwest, 1540–1846* (Norman: University of Oklahoma Press, 1971), 216. Robidoux had also constructed a temporary third fort in Utah. See Reyher, *Antoine Robidoux and Fort Uncompahgre,* 51–53; and Joseph J. Hill, "Antoine Robidoux, Kingpin in the Colorado River Fur Trade, 1824–1844," *Colorado Magazine* 7 (July 1930): 131–132.

19. Brooks, *Captives and Cousins,* 301. For additional sketches of Ute–New Mexican hostilities, see also Reyher, *Antoine Robidoux and Fort Uncompahgre,* 61–66; and Chapter 4.

20. For Archuleta's Ute campaign in 1845, see Lecompte, 162–163 and nn. 306–307.

21. See Hammond, *The Adventures of Alexander Barclay,* 135. For U.S. Indian trading policies on alcohol, see Prucha, *The Great Father,* 105–107.

22. For Arkansas River–Ute trading relations, see Lecompte, 162–166. For the shift to seasonal alcohol trade, see ibid., 74–97.

23. For Ute economic changes during the 1840s, see Thomas G. Andrews, "Tata Atanasio Trujillo's Unlikely Tale of Utes, Nuevomexicanos, and the Settling of Colorado's San Luis Valley," *New Mexico Historical Review* 75 (January 2000): 5–41.

24. For the Taos Uprising of 1847, see Brooks, *Captives and Cousins,* 281–292.

25. Hafen, *Ruxton of the Rockies,* 198.

26. Ibid.

27. Brooks, *Captives and Cousins,* 79.

28. Andrews, "Tata Atanasio Trujillo's Unlikely Tale," 11–20. See also Thomas G. Andrews, "Settling the San Luis Valley: Ecology, Society, and 'Beautiful Roads' in the Hispanic Colonization of Conejos and Costilla Counties, Colorado" (M.A. thesis, University of Wisconsin, Madison, 1997).

29. "Recuerdos de Tata Atanasio Trujillo," *San Luis Valley Historian* 8 (1976): 15.

30. Lecompte, 237; Simmons, *Ute Indians,* 83–84.

31. For overviews of the many Indian conflicts after the U.S.-Mexican War, see Robert M. Utley, *The Indian Frontier of the American West, 1846–1890* (Albuquerque: University of New Mexico Press, 1984).

32. Lecompte, 238; Robert V. Hine, *In the Shadow of Frémont: Edward Kern and the Art of American Exploration, 1845–1860* (1962; reprint, Norman: University of Oklahoma Press, 1982), 65; Alpheus H. Favour, *Old Bill Williams, Mountain Man* (Chapel Hill: University of North Carolina Press, 1936), 179. For the extent of Ute livestock raids, see note 42 below. See also "James S. Calhoun to Commissioner of Indian Affairs Orlando Brown," November 15, 1849, in *The Official Correspondence of James S. Calhoun, While Indian Agent in Santa Fe and Superintendent of Indian Affairs in New Mexico,* ed. Annie Heloise Abel (Washington, D.C.: Government Printing Office, 1915), 77; and "Carson, Christopher, Bounty Land Papers," MSS P-E 64, box 3, folders 1–3, KCP.

33. For changing ecologies and herds in the San Luis Valley, see Hafen, *Ruxton of the Rockies,* 200, 210; and Andrews, "Tata Atanasio Trujillo's Unlikely Tale."

34. See note 37 below for evidence of Ute leaders' diplomatic reactions to Whittlesey's "murders."

35. In October 1849 Jicarilla Apaches and possibly Muache Ute allies attacked James White's caravan, capturing Ann White, her daughter, and an African American servant, all of whom were killed. As with Kern's and Williams' murders, such Ute involvement may have been a response to Whittlesey's spring raid. See Simmons, *Ute Indians,* 86; and Veronica E. Velarde Tiller, *The Jicarilla Apache Tribe: A History, 1846–1970* (Lincoln: University of Nebraska Press, 1983), 34–36. Carson participated in the subsequent cavalry pursuit and made no mention of Utes. See Carter, *"Dear Old Kit,"* 124–126. See also Dunlay, *Kit Carson and the Indians,* 138–140.

36. "Calhoun to Brown," January 1, 1850, in Abel, *Official Correspondence of James Calhoun,* 96.

37. Ibid., 96–97. See also "Calhoun to the Utah Chiefs," December 3, 1849; and "Calhoun to the Prefect of Abiqui[u]," December 20, 1849, ibid., 90, 92. For earlier signs of Ute "disposition" to enter treaty negotiations, see "Calhoun to Commander of Indian Affairs W. Medill," October 15, 1849, ibid., 55.

38. "Treaty between the United States of America and the Utah Indians," ibid., 127–132; "Calhoun to Brown," January 1, 1850, 97. See also "Treaty with the Utah, 1849," in *IA,* 2: 585–587. For subsequent attempts by Ute

leaders to attach themselves to the treaty, see "Alcalde Mariano Valdez to the Prefect of Taos," January 26, 1850; and "Calhoun to Brown," June 12, 1850, in Abel, *Official Correspondence of James Calhoun,* 126–127, 208.

39. "Report of Agent J. S. Calhoun, Oct. 12, 1850—Santa Fé," *ARCIA,* 1850, 110; "John Greiner, Acting Superintendent of Indian Affairs, New Mexico, to Commissioner of Indian Affairs Luke Lea," April 30, 1852; and "Report of Auguste Lacome to Colonel J. S. Calhoun U.S. Agent for the Territory New Mexico," March 16, 1850, in Abel, *Official Correspondence of James Calhoun,* 530, 169–170. For Chico Velasquez's amity with New Mexican officials, see also David Meriwether, *My Life in the Mountains and on the Plains: The Newly Discovered Autobiography,* ed. Robert A. Griffen (Norman: University of Oklahoma Press, 1965), 195–202.

40. "Calhoun to Lea," December 28, 1850, in Abel, *Official Correspondence of James Calhoun,* 281; "Calhoun to Lea," July 25, 1851, ibid., 389; and "Greiner to Calhoun," October 20, 1851, ibid., 438. See also "Letter of Agent J. S. Calhoun, July 25, 1851," *ARCIA,* 1851, 462. For Ute resistance to Mexican settlement, see "Calhoun to Secretary of State Daniel Webster," October 29, 1851; and "Grenier to Lea," April 30, 1852, in Abel, *Official Correspondence of James Calhoun,* 441, 530.

41. "To the President of the United States," February 27, 1850, in Abel, *Official Correspondence of James Calhoun,* 158.

42. For references to Calhoun's aversion to gift-giving, see "Calhoun to Brown," January 1, 1850; and "Calhoun to Indian Agent Cyrus Choice," May 10, 1850, ibid., 97, 201. For select Ute depredations against Arkansas River settlements after 1850, see "Calhoun to Lea," February 2, 1851, ibid., 288. An earlier dispute between Utes and residents at Abiquiu had left seven dead as Utes also stole 2,425 sheep, 518 goats, 43 cows, 29 oxen, 4 burros, and 3 horses. See "Choice to Calhoun," February 5, 1850, ibid., 142–144. For contrasts between Ute and Arapaho, Cheyenne, and Kiowa treaty provisions, see Lecompte, 239; and "Report of Supt. Mitchell, Transmitting Treaty with Prairie and Mountain Tribes at Fort Laramie," *ARCIA,* 1851, 288–290.

43. Carter, *"Dear Old Kit,"* 143; "Report of Governor David Meriwether," *ARCIA,* 1855, 187. See also Meriwether, *My Life in the Mountains and on the Plains,* 201–202.

44. For the "Pueblo Massacre," see Lecompte, 248–252, 270–274. For U.S. Army reprisals, see Morris F. Taylor, "Action at Fort Massachusetts: The Indian Campaign of 1855," *Colorado Magazine* 42 (1965): 292–310. See also Carter, *"Dear Old Kit,"* 144–146; Meriwether, *My Life in the Mountains and on the Plains,* 201–202; LeRoy R. Hafen, "The Fort Pueblo Massacre and the Punitive Expedition against the Utes," *Colorado Magazine* 4

(1927): 49–58; Rafael Chacon, "Campaign against Utes and Apaches in Southern Colorado, 1855," ibid., 11 (1934): 108–112; and "Mexican Colorado by P. R. Thombs," 2–3, MSS P-L 64, H. H. Bancroft Collection, Bancroft Library, University of California, Berkeley. For other Ute raids, see *RES*, 2: 35; "Carson, Christopher, Outgoing Letters, 1849–1865," box 1, folder 1, KCP. In a February 28, 1855, letter, Carson reports more than 4,000 sheep and goats taken from northern New Mexico.

45. See "Articles of Agreement and Convention made . . . by David Meriwether . . . U.S. Commissioner, and Chiefs of the Capote Band of the Ute Nation" and "Articles of Agreement and Convention Made . . . by David Meriwether . . . U.S. Commissioner, and Chiefs of the Moache band of the Ute Nation," MSS P-E 239, Bancroft Library. See also "Report of Governor David Meriwether," *ARCIA*, 1855, 188–189; "Report of Agent Christopher Carson," ibid., 191–192; Prucha, *American Indian Treaties*, 258–259; Simmons, *Ute Indians*, 102–103; and Carter, *"Dear Old Kit,"* 146–147.

46. "Report of Agent Lorenzo Labadi," *ARCIA*, 1855, 190–191. For Jicarilla-U.S. relations, see Tiller, *Jicarilla Apache Tribe*, 37–55.

47. Carter, *"Dear Old Kit,"* 147–149. Carson's criticisms are informed by his strained relationship with Meriwether. See also Meriwether, *My Life in the Mountains and on the Plains*, 226–232; and Dunlay, *Kit Carson and the Indians*, 168–189. For further evidence of Utes "waiting patiently," see "Report of Governor David Meriwether," *ARCIA*, 1856, 182.

48. For Ute willingness to "commence farming next spring, provided permanent homes are assigned to them," see "Report of Governor David Meriwether," *ARCIA*, 1856, 182. For population estimates of the three southern Colorado Ute bands—"Copotes, Mohuaches, and Tobawaches"—see "Report of J. L. Collins," *ARCIA*, 1857, 273–274. Collins also notes: "I found it impossible to form anything like a correct estimate of their respective numbers"; ibid., 273.

49. For biographies of Ouray, see P. David Smith, *Ouray: Chief of the Utes* (Ridgway, Colo.: Wayfinder, 1990); and Marshall Sprague, *Massacre: The Tragedy at White River* (Boston: Little Brown, 1957), 75–99. See also Simmons, *Ute Indians*, 59–63; Dunlay, *Kit Carson and the Indians*, 379–380; S. F. Stacher, "Ouray and the Utes," *Colorado Magazine* 27 (April 1950): 134–140; and Terry G. Knight Sr., "Ute Leaders of the Past," and Richard N. Ellis, "The Ute Indians in Southern Colorado since 1850," in *Ute Indian Arts and Culture: From Prehistory to the New Millennium*, ed. William Worth (Colorado Springs: Colorado Springs Fine Arts Center, 2000), 21–25, 73–87.

50. Dunlay, *Kit Carson and the Indians,* 133–147. See also "U.S. Office of Indian Affairs, 1853–1860," box 1, folder 34, KCP.

51. Dunlay, *Kit Carson and the Indians,* 156; and Robert Trennert, *Alternative to Extinction: Federal Indian Policy and the Beginnings of the Reservation System, 1846–1851* (Philadelphia: Temple University Press, 1975), quoted in ibid., 155.

52. Smith, *Ouray,* 37–43; Sprague, *Massacre,* 76.

53. Carter, *"Dear Old Kit,"* 149. For Carson's agency finances, see Dunlay, *Kit Carson and the Indians,* 177–180. See also "U.S. Office of Indian Affairs, 1853–1860," box 1, folder 34, KCP; "U.S. Treasury Dept, 1856–1861," box 1, folder 36, KCP; and "Carson, Christopher, Outgoing Letters, 1849–1865," box 1, folder 1, KCP.

54. "Report of J. L. Collins," *ARCIA,* 1857, 277–278. For examples of Carson's calls for violent punishment, see "Report of Christopher Carson," *ARCIA,* 1859, 343; Dunlay, *Kit Carson and the Indians,* 162–163; 211–212; and Carter, *"Dear Old Kit,"* 154.

55. "Report of Christopher Carson," *ARCIA,* 1858, 195. For gambling and alcohol use as well as the difficulties in getting Utes to leave settlements, see "Report of J. L. Collins," *ARCIA,* 1858, 186. For dwindling game and escalating raids, see Dunlay, *Kit Carson and the Indians,* 210–221.

56. "Report of J. L. Collins," *ARCIA,* 1858, 184–185; "Report of William Gilpin," *ARCIA,* 1861, 100. See also "Report of Diego Archuleta," *ARCIA,* 1857, 284–285. For the Ute-Arapaho peace delegation, see "Bowman, A. W., Jan. 17, 1858," box 1, folder 2, KCP.

57. "William Gilpin to William P. Dole, Commissioner of Indian Affairs, June 19, 1861," SDPUI, MSS P-L 805 Film, reel 1. For the origins of the Colorado gold rush, see West, *The Contested Plains,* 105–170.

58. For Carson's generalship, see "U.S. War Dept, 1861–1865," box 1, folder 37, KCP.

59. "Report of Christopher Carson," *ARCIA,* 1859, 343; "Report of J. L. Collins," *ARCIA,* 1858, 186. See also "Report of Governor Evans," *ARCIA,* 1863, 126; and "Gilpin to Dole," June 19, 1861, SDPUI, reel 1.

60. "Report of Christopher Carson," *ARCIA,* 1859, 343. See also "William Gilpin to William Dole," October 8, 1861, SDPUI, reel 1. In 1863 Colorado Governor John Evans recommended relocating all of Colorado's Utes onto farms in the San Luis Valley. See "Evans to Dole," March 4, 1863, ibid.

61. "Report of Christopher Carson," *ARCIA,* 1859, 342–343; West, *The Contested Plains,* 260; "Henry M. Vaile to William Gilpin," December 31, 1861, SDPUI, reel 1. See also Wyckoff, *Creating Colorado,* 42–72. For Ute raids and Colorado miners' attempts to receive compensation, see

"Clark Gayford to William Dole," June 26, 1862, SDPUI, reel 1. For Ute bartering in settlements, see Simmons, *Ute Indians*, 108–109.

62. Jane Lenz Elder and David J. Weber, eds., *Trading in Santa Fe: John M. Kingbury's Correspondence with James Josiah Webb, 1853–1861* (Dallas: Southern Methodist University Press, 1996), xx. For white population estimates, see "Letter of Agent J. S. Calhoun, Feb. 16, 1851," *ARCIA,* 1851, 453; and Howard Lamar, *The Far Southwest: A Territorial History,* rev. ed. (Albuquerque: University of New Mexico Press, 2000), 92.

63. Robert W. Frazer, *Fort and Suppliers: The Role of the Army in the Economy of the Southwest, 1846–1861* (Albuquerque: University of New Mexico Press, 1983), ix.

64. "Report of J. L. Collins," *ARCIA,* 1858, 192. For Navajo-Ute conflicts in 1855, see L. R. Bailey, *The Long Walk: A History of the Navajo Wars, 1846–1868* (Pasadena: Westernlore Publications, 1964), 72–74.

65. Frank McNitt, *Navajo Wars: Military Campaigns, Slave Raids, and Reprisals* (Albuquerque: University of New Mexico Press, 1990), 350–356; Carson quoted in Dunlay, *Kit Carson and the Indians,* 200. McNitt details a subsequent Ute attack on another Navajo encampment.

66. "Kingsbury to Webb," in Elder and Weber, *Trading in Santa Fe,* 254. For U.S.-Navajo campaigns and the formation of volunteer companies, see McNitt, *Navajo Wars,* 386–399.

67. "Report of J. L. Collins," *ARCIA,* 1861, 124–126. For higher estimates of Utes, see "Report of Lafayette Head," ibid., 101–102. Sprague is considerably off in his population estimates. See Sprague, *Massacre,* 77–78; and "Vaile to William Gilpin," July 5, 1861, SDPUI, reel 1.

68. For the Civil War in New Mexico, see Lamar, *The Far Southwest,* 97–120; and Martin Hardwick Hall, *Sibley's New Mexico Campaign* (Albuquerque: University of New Mexico Press, 2000).

69. Chris Emmett, *Fort Union and the Winning of the Southwest* (Norman: University of Oklahoma Press, 1965), 228. For Carson's appointment as "Lieutenant Colonel of the First Regiment of New Mexican Volunteers," see "U.S. War Dept., 1861–1865," box 1, folder 37, KCP.

70. Hall, *Sibley's New Mexico Campaign,* 3–19.

71. "Headquarters and Fort Union Correspondence, August 1861," in *When the Texans Came: Missing Records from the Civil War in the Southwest,* ed. John P. Wilson (Albuquerque: University of New Mexico Press, 2001), 76, 73, 74. See also ibid., 67, 71–72, 80–81, 84, 87–88.

72. Ibid., 76.

73. Ibid., 74, 88.

74. Utley, *Indian Frontier of American West,* 65–98. See also Peter Iverson, *Diné: A History of the Navajos* (Albuquerque: University of New Mexico

Press, 2002), 37–65; and Bailey, *The Long Walk*, 131–197. For Ute involvement in the Navajo wars, see ibid., 156–160; and Dunlay, *Kit Carson and the Indians*, 275–300.

75. "Report of the Commissioner of Indian Affairs," *ARCIA*, 1863, 17. For agent and Ute "complaints," see "Vaile to William Gilpin," July 5, 1861, SDPUI, reel 1.

76. Utley, *Indian Frontier of American West*, 93–98. See also Lamar, *The Far Southwest*, 106–117. For Ute service at Adobe Walls, see Dunlay, *Kit Carson and the Indians*, 325–336; and "Carson, Christopher, Army Accounts and Returns, 1862–1865," box 3, folder 7, KCP.

77. "Evans, John, 1814–1897, Statement," 11, MSS P-L 329, folder II, H. H. Bancroft Collection, Bancroft Library; Lamar, *The Far Southwest*, 207–208. See also Harry E. Kelsey Jr., *Frontier Capitalist: The Life of John Evans* (Denver: Colorado Historical Society, 1969), 115–136.

78. "See West, *The Contested Plains*, esp. 297–307; Lamar, *The Far Southwest*, 209–215; and Utley, *Indian Frontier of American West*, 86–93. See also "Evans, John, 1814–1897, Statement," 17–22. Evans did enlist some former trappers who had married Arapahos. See Edgar Carlisle McMechen, *Life of Governor Evans, Second Territorial Governor of Colorado* (Denver: Wahlgreen Publishing, 1924), 116–117.

79. "Evans, Interview with, 1884," 20, MSS P-L 23, Bancroft Library; Utley, *Indian Frontier of American West*, 84–86. Evans was asked to resign following reactions to Sand Creek, a national response that did not accompany, as Brigham D. Madsen notes, the Bear River Massacre of 1863. See Madsen, *The Shoshoni Frontier and the Bear River Massacre* (Salt Lake City: University of Utah Press, 1985) (cited hereafter as Madsen), 20–24. For policy deliberations during Navajo internment, see Iverson, *Diné*, 51–65.

80. "Report of Governor Evans," *ARCIA*, 1864, 224. For views of Evans' career that exclude mention of Sand Creek, see Walter Dill Scott, *John Evans, 1814–1897: An Appreciation* (St. Charles, Ill.: Chronicle Publishing, 1939).

81. "Evans, John, 1814–1897, Statement," 11–13; "Evans, Interview with, 1884," 14. See also Kelsey, *Frontier Capitalist*, 132–133; Smith, *Ouray*, 59–65; McMechen, *Life of Governor Evans*, 119–120; and Finis E. Downing, "With the Ute Peace Delegation of 1863, across the Plains and at Conejos," *Colorado Magazine* 22 (September 1945): 193–205.

82. "Report of the Commissioner of Indian Affairs," *ARCIA*, 1863, 17; "Treaty with the Utah—Tabeguache Band, 1863," in *IA*, 2: 856–859. See also Smith, *Ouray*, 59–71; "Report of Governor Evans," *ARCIA*, 1863,

125–126; "Report of Simeon Whitely," ibid., 133–134; and "Report of John G. Nicolay," ibid., 148–151.

83. "W. F. M. Arny to William Dole," February 21, 1863, SDPUI, reel 1. See also "J. L. Collins to William Dole," February 23, 1863, ibid. For Ute signatories to the 1863 and 1868 treaties, see "Treaty with the Utah—Tabeguache Band, 1863," and "Treaty with the Ute, 1868," in *IA*, 2: 858, 994–995. For Utes' concern about Ouray's political ascendancy, see Smith, *Ouray*, 62–71; Morris F. Taylor, "Ka-ni-ache/2," *Colorado Magazine* 44 (Spring 1967): 139–161; and Frank D. Reeve, "The Federal Indian Policy in New Mexico, 1858–1880, III," *New Mexican Historical Review* 8 (1938): 146–191. For the migratory range of Uintah, Grand River, and Elk Mountain Utes, See "Vaile to William Gilpin," July 5, 1861, SDPUI, reel 1.

84. Quoted in Reeve, "Federal Indian Policy in New Mexico," 168. See also "Report of John G. Nicolay," *ARCIA*, 1863, 148–151; and Taylor, "Ka-ni-ache," 285–291.

85. Quoted in Taylor, "Ka-ni-ache," 299. See also "Superintendent North's Report Relative to Hostilities by Utes," *ARCIA*, 1866, 152; "Correspondence Relative to Recent Hostilities," ibid., 160–161; and Reeve, "Federal Indian Policy in New Mexico," 168–172. For Carson's changing military titles, see Marc Simmons, *Kit Carson and His Three Wives: A Family History* (Albuquerque: University of New Mexico Press, 2003), 128.

86. "Annual Report of William F. M. Anry, Agent Abiquiu Agency," *ARCIA*, 1868, 166; Norton quoted in Reeve, "Federal Indian Policy in New Mexico," 168. For Jicarillas' parallel ambiguity, see Tiller, *Jicarilla Apache Tribe*, 56–75.

87. "Evans, Interview with, 1884," 14; "Evans, John, 1814–1897, Statement," 14; "Annual Report of Governor A. C. Hunt," *ARCIA*, 1868, 182. For Ute pastoralism, see also "Report of Governor Evans," *ARCIA*, 1864, 223; and "Annual Report of Governor Cummings," *ARCIA*, 1866, 154–155. Northern Colorado Ute bands were also interested in augmenting hunting with farming and ranching. See "Vaile to William Gilpin," July 5, 1861, SDPUI, reel 1.

88. "Report of Lafayette Head," *ARCIA*, 1865, 178. For Grand River and Uintah raids as well as their peace commitments, see "Report of Governor Evans," *ARCIA*, 1864, 224; "Report of S. Whitely," ibid., 241–242; and "Report of D. C. Oakes," *ARCIA*, 1865, 179. For Weenuche and Capote raids, see "Annual Report of William F. M. Anry, Agent Abiquiu Agency," *ARCIA*, 1868, 166–171.

89. Smith, *Ouray*, 72–75; Taylor, "Ka-ni-ache/2," 141–142; and Simmons, *Kit*

Carson and His Three Wives, 135–139. Philip J. Deloria, *Indians in Un-expected Places* (Lawrence: University of Kansas Press, 2004). For studies of Indian delegations to Washington, see Herman J. Viola, *Diplomats in Buckskins: A History of Indian Delegations in Washington City* (Washington, D.C.: Smithsonian Institution Press, 1981); and Katharine C. Turner, *Red Men Calling on the Great White Father* (Norman: University of Oklahoma Press, 1951).

90. Simmons, *Kit Carson and His Three Wives,* 136–139. For the 1868 treaty, see *IA,* 2: 990–996. See also Sprague, *Massacre,* 92.

91. Simmons, *Kit Carson and His Three Wives,* 140–146. For the Carsons' estate, see "Boggs, Thomas, Papers Related to the Estate of Christopher Carson, 1868–1874," box 3, KCP.

92. For studies of Carson's "Indian policies" that generally end with his death, see Dunlay, *Kit Carson and the Indians;* and R. C. Gordon-McCutchan, *Kit Carson: Indian Fighter or Indian Killer?* (Niwot: University Press of Colorado, 1996). For a biography of Maria Josepha Jaramillio, see Simmons, *Kit Carson and His Three Wives,* 55–146.

93. Simmons, *Kit Carson and His Three Wives,* 130–131.

94. For problems of treaty enforcement, see "Report of Governor A. C. Hunt," *ARCIA,* 1869, 258–261; "Report of Governor Edward M. McCook," ibid., 262–264; and "Report of Daniel C. Oakes," ibid., 264–265. For the dimensions of the reservation, see *IA,* 2: 990. See also Sprague, *Massacre,* 92–93; Simmons, *Ute Indians,* 132–133; and Wyckoff, *Creating Colorado,* 223.

95. Iverson, *Diné,* 37. For the Navajo treaty, see *IA,* 2: 1015–20.

96. For a map of Navajo-Ute reservations, see *ARCIA,* 1879, frontispiece inset.

97. For Colorado Utes' removal to Utah, see Charles Wilkinson, *Fire on the Plateau: Conflict and Endurance in the American Southwest* (Washington, D.C.: Island Press, 1999), 124–147; and Dee Brown, *Bury My Heart at Wounded Knee: An Indian History of the American West,* 30th anniversary ed. (New York: Henry Holt, 2000), 367–390.

98. Meinig, *Continental America,* 78–103.

7. Utah's Indians and the Crisis of Mormon Settlement

1. "Report of Agent J. S. Calhoun," *ARCIA,* 1850, 98.

2. Ibid., 99.

3. Leonard, 37. For the "indiscriminate" killing of nonequestrian Indians by white travelers, see Madsen, 30–36.

4. Leonard, 25.

5. Dale L. Morgan, *The Humboldt: Highroad of the West* (New York: Farrar and Rinehart, 1943), 49, 51. See also S. N. Carvalho, *Incidents of Travel and Adventure in the Far West* (New York: Derby & Jackson, 1857), 266, who calls a Paiute band "a dirty degraded set of beings, scarcely deserving of the name human."

6. "Report of the Commissioner of Indian Affairs," *ARCIA*, 1850, 12.

7. For links between Nevadan and Californian Indian societies, see Martha C. Knack and Omer C. Stewart, *As Long as the River Shall Run: An Ethnohistory of Pyramid Lake Indian Reservation* (1984; reprint, Reno: University of Nevada Press, 1999) (cited hereafter as Knack and Stewart), 29–30; and John C. Frémont, *The Exploring Expedition to the Rocky Mountains* (1845; reprint, Washington, D.C.: Smithsonian Institution Press, 1988), 226–228. For Utah Lake Indian fishing, see Jared Farmer, "American Land Mark: A History of Place and Displacement" (Ph.D. diss., Stanford University, 2005). See also David Rich Lewis, *Neither Wolf nor Dog: American Indians, Environment, and Agrarian Change* (New York: Oxford University Press, 1994), 35–36.

8. For Utah's Ute Indian wars, see Madsen; and John Alton Peterson, *Utah's Black Hawk War* (Salt Lake City: University of Utah Press, 1998) (cited hereafter as Peterson).

9. For Southern Paiute–Mormon relations, see Martha C. Knack, *Boundaries Between: The Southern Paiutes, 1775–1995* (Lincoln: University of Nebraska Press, 2001), 48–94.

10. For equestrian Shoshone history, see Virginia Cole Trenholm and Maurine Carley, *The Shoshonis: Sentinels of the Rockies* (Norman: University of Oklahoma Press, 1964); and Madsen.

11. For trappers and U.S. western expansion, see Robert M. Utley, *A Life Wild and Perilous: Mountain Men and the Paths to the Pacific* (New York: Henry Holt, 1997).

12. *RES*, 1: 3; 2: 39. See also Forbes Parkhill, *The Blazed Trail of Antoine Leroux* (Los Angeles: Westernlore, 1965), 181–183.

13. Lieut. E. G. Beckwith, "Report of Explorations for a Route for the Pacific Railroad," in *RES*, 2: 66–74. See also "An Account of the Massacre of Captain J. W. Gunnison and Seven of His Party on the Sevier River on the 26th of October 1853," in Brigham Young to George Maypenny, Commissioner of Indian Affairs, November 30, 1853, NARG 75, reel 897, "Utah Superintendency, 1849–1855." For Ute and Paiute distinctions, see Knack, *Boundaries Between*, 30–31, 59–62, and 73–74. See also William R. Palmer, "Pahute Indian Homelands," *Utah Historical Quarterly* 6 (April 1933): 88–102; and Isabel T. Kelly, *Southern Paiute Ethnography*, University of Utah Anthropological Papers No. 69 (Salt Lake

City: University of Utah Press, 1964). This work follows Knack's assessment, identifying Parvain, or Pahvant, Indians as Paiutes.

14. J. W. Gunnison, *The Mormons, or, Latter-day Saints, in the Valley of the Great Salt Lake: A History of the Rise and Progress, Peculiar Doctrines, Present Condition, and Prospects, Derived from Personal Observation, during a Residence among Them* (1852; reprint, Philadelphia: J. B. Lippincott, 1860), v, 146–147. For disease and demographic assessments, see Richard W. Stoffle, Kristina L. Jones, and Henry F. Dobyns, "Direct European Immigrant Transmissions of Old World Pathogens to Numic Indians during the Nineteenth Century," *American Indian Quarterly* 19 (1995): 181–203.

15. Gunnison, *The Mormons*, 147. For Mormon colonizing designs, see Milton R. Hunter, *Brigham Young: The Colonizer*, 3d ed. (Independence, Mo.: Zion's Printing and Publishing, 1945); Leonard J. Arrington, *Great Basin Kingdom: An Economic History of the Latter-day Saints* (Cambridge, Mass.: Harvard University Press, 1958), 39–194; and Eugene E. Campbell, "Brigham Young's Outer Cordon—A Reappraisal," *Utah Historical Quarterly* 41 (Summer 1973): 220–253. For the 1850 campaign, see also Holeman to Day, November 28, 1851, NARG 75, reel 897.

16. Quoted in Conway B. Sonne, *World of Wakara* (San Antonio: Naylor, 1962), 174–175. See also Brigham Young to George Maypenny, Commissioner of Indian Affairs, September 30, 1853, NARG 75, reel 897; and "Daniel H. Well's Narrative," *Utah State Historical Quarterly* 6 (October 1933): 127–129.

17. *RES*, 2: 71–74.

18. Ibid. See also Josiah F. Gibbs, "Gunnison Massacre—1853—Millard County, Utah—Indian Mereer's Version of the Tragedy—1894," *Utah Historical Quarterly* 1 (July 1928): 68–75. See also Sonne, *World of Wakara*, 175; and Knack, *Boundaries Between*, 59–62.

19. Gunnison, *The Mormons*, vi–xiv. For Mormon-federal tensions, see Howard Roberts Lamar, *The Far Southwest: A Territorial History*, rev. ed. (Albuquerque: University of New Mexico Press, 2000), 285–306. For Thomas Kane's counter to Drummond, see Oscar Osburn Winther, ed., *A Friend of the Mormons: The Private Papers and Diary of Thomas Leiper Kane* (San Francisco: Gelber-Lilienthal, 1937); "Preliminary Copy of Letter from Kane to High Official on Drummond's Accusation against Mormons, 1857," Thomas Leiper Kane Papers, 1846–1883, Department of Special Collections, Stanford University Library.

20. Carvalho, *Incidents of Travel and Adventure*, 253. For Walkara's proclamation of innocence and whereabouts in October 1853, see *RES*, 2: 73–76; Carvalho, *Incidents of Travel and Adventure*, 259; and Sonne, *World of Wakara*, 188–189.

21. For the immediate reactions of Kanosh, see *RES*, 2: 73–76.

22. As governor, Young held the title of *ex officio* superintendent of Indian affairs, and after Day's departure in September 1851, only two federal Indian agents, Jacob H. Holeman and Stephen A. Rose, remained. Governor Young and subagent Rose, according to Holeman, worked against federal initiatives. See Jacob Holeman to Luke Lea, Commissioner of Indian Affairs, February 2, 1852, NARG 75, reel 897. For the extent of Holeman's jurisdiction, see "Report of Agent Jacob H. Holeman," *ARCIA*, 1852, 149–155. For Day's resignation, see Henry R. Day to Luke Lea, January 2, January 9, February 19, and June 2, 1852, NARG 75, reel 897. For Young's request for Indian agents and treaties to extinguish Indian title in Utah, see Young to Maypenny, December 31, 1853, ibid.

23. Farmer, "American Land Mark," chap. 1. See also Stoffle, Jones, and Dobyns, "Direct Transmissions of Old World Pathogens."

24. Henry R. Day to Luke Lea, January 2, 1852, NARG 75, reel 897; and Jacob Holeman to Luke Lea, November 28, 1851, ibid. See also "Report of J. H. Holeman," September 21, 1851, *ARCIA*, 1851. For Mormon leaders' concerns over the "expenses" of Indian presents, see A. W. Babbitt to Luke Lea, February 26, 1851, NARG 75, reel 897; and Brigham Young to Luke Lea, October 20, 1851, ibid. For evidence of the resettlement to New Mexico of one Ute band of "seventy lodge[s]" as well as their plea for "presents," see George M. Armstrong to Brigham Young, September 30, 1855, ibid.

25. Knack, *Boundaries Between*, 54.

26. Young to Maypenny, June 30, 1854; and September 30 and December 31, 1853, NARG 75, reel 897.

27. G. E. Montgomery to Ardavan S. Loughery, Commissioner of Indian Affairs, July 26, 1850, NARG 75, reel 897; Edward Cooper to Ardavan Loughery, September 10, 1850, ibid.

28. Sondra Jones, *The Trial of Don Pedro Leon Lujan: The Attack against Indian Slavery and Mexican Traders in Utah* (Salt Lake City: University of Utah Press, 2000), 47–48; Brigham Young to Commissioner of Indian Affairs, June 28, 1853, NARG 75, reel 897. See also Knack, *Boundaries Between*, 55–59.

29. Knack, *Boundaries Between*, 54–57; quotation on 56.

30. James F. Brooks, *Captives and Cousins: Slavery, Kinship, and Community in the Southwest Borderlands* (Chapel Hill: University of North Carolina Press, 2002), 244, 154; quoted in Knack, *Boundaries Between*, 57. Hurt accepted his position as Utah's Indian agent in September 1854. See Garland Hurt to Charles E. Mix, Commissioner of Indian Affairs, September 7, 1854, NARG 75, reel 897.

31. Brigham Young to Commissioner of Indian Affairs, June 28, 1853,

NARG 75, reel 897; Peterson, 65. For the crisis of Ute economics, see Lewis, *Neither Wolf nor Dog*, 35–38. For Utah's decade of diseases, see Stoffle, Jones, and Dobyns, "Direct Transmissions of Old World Pathogens."

32. Young to Maypenny, July 25, 1853, NARG 75, reel 897. See also "Report of Brigham Young," September 30, 1853, *ARCIA*, 1853. For the Walkara War, see Peterson, 63–71.

33. "Indian Hostilities and Treachery—Mormon Policy towards Them: An Address Delivered by President Brigham Young, in the Tabernacle, Great Salt Lake City," in Carvalho, *Incidents of Travel and Adventure*, 39–54.

34. Carvalho, *Incidents of Travel and Adventure*, 259–260. See also Sonne, *World of Wakara*, 194–205. For the 1854 Ute rapprochement, see Rose to Young and Young to Maypenny, March 31, 1854, NARG 75, reel 897.

35. For Walkara's continued slave trafficking as well as abuses of Paiutes, see Sonne, *World of Wakara*, 194–205. For mediating efforts by new Indian agents, see George M. Armstrong to Brigham Young and Hurt to Young, June 30, 1855, NARG 75, reel 897; and "George A. Smith, Home Correspondence," newspaper clipping, June 12, 1855, ibid.

36. Hurt to Maypenny, April 2, 1855, NARG 75, reel 897. For the aftermath of Walkara's death, subsequent conflict, and Ute relocation to the Uintah Basin, see Lewis, *Neither Wolf nor Dog*, 36–39; Peterson, esp. 69–208; and Farmer, "American Land Mark," chap. 2. There are few accounts of Walkara's death, and even fewer mention the prevalence of diseases. Sonne, *World of Wakara*, 219–221, provides the best-documented account of his burial.

37. Armstrong to Young, September 30, 1855, NARG 75, reel 897; Knack, *Boundaries Between*, 73. For an overview of nineteenth-century Mormon international migration, see Conway B. Sonne, *Saints on the Seas: A Maritime History of Mormon Migration, 1830–1890* (Salt Lake City: University of Utah Press, 1983). For the history of the Uintah-Ouray reservation, see Floyd O'Neil and Kathryn L. MacKay, *A History of the Uintah-Ouray Ute Lands* (Salt Lake City: University of Utah Press, 1977).

38. For federal-Mormon tensions from 1857 to 1861, see Lamar, *The Far Southwest*, 293–310; and Durwood Ball, *Army Regulars on the Western Frontier, 1848–1861* (Norman: University of Oklahoma Press, 2001), 160–171. For Mormon missionary efforts at Fort Limhi, see David Bigler, *Fort Limhi: Mormon Adventure in Oregon Territory, 1855–1858* (Spokane: Arthur H. Clark, 2003). See also John W. W. Mann, *Sacajawea's People: The Lemhi Shoshones and the Salmon River Country* (Lincoln: University of Nebraska Press, 2004), 22–25. The "Mormon War" originated partly in

the aftermath of Utah's most famous "massacre" at Mountain Meadows, in which Mormon settlers, including John D. Lee and "his [Paiute] Indian son" as well as other Paiute allies attacked an emigrant party. Paiutes were also mobilized during the Mormon War. See Will Bagley, *Blood of the Prophets: Brigham Young and the Massacre at Mountain Meadows* (Norman: University of Oklahoma Press, 2002), 83–87, 156–164.

39. For Shoshone-trader relations, see Henry E. Stamm IV, *People of the Wind River: The Eastern Shoshones, 1825–1900* (Norman: University of Oklahoma Press, 1999), 19–28; and Mann, *Sacajawea's People*, 16–23.

40. Day to Luke Lea, Commissioner of Indian Affairs, August 12, 1851, NARG 75, reel 897. See also Young to Lea, October 20, 1851, ibid.; and Day to Lea, January 2, 1852, ibid.

41. "Report of J. H. Holeman," September 21, 1851, *ARCIA*, 1851. For overlapping jurisdictions, see Madsen, 41–62. See also "Report of Anson Dart, Superintendent of Indian Affairs for Oregon Territory," *ARCIA*, 1851. For the Fort Laramie Treaty, see "Treaty of Fort Laramie with Sioux, Etc., 1851," in *IA*, 2: 594–596.

42. "Report of J. H. Holeman," September 21, 1851, *ARCIA*, 1851; Madsen, 25. See also "Proclamation" and Young to Day, July 21, 1851, NARG 75, reel 897.

43. Trenholm and Carley, *The Shoshonis*, 94–110; Madsen, 41–56.

44. For Shoshone-trader intermarriage and Mormon encroachments on the Green River, see J. M. Hackaday to Maypenny, June 17 and August 15, 1854, NARG 75, reel 897. There were also some marriages between Mormons and Lemhi Shoshone women; Mann, *Sacajawea's People*, 23–24.

45. Madsen, 41–73.

46. Holeman to Lea, May 8, 1852, NARG 75, reel 897; Madsen, 17. For white bandits masquerading as Indians, see Holeman to Lea, March 29, 1852, NARG 75, reel 897; "Report of Jacob H. Holeman," September 25, 1852, *ARCIA*, 1852; and Madsen, 55–60, 100–113.

47. R. R. Thompson, Indian Agent Middle Oregon, to Joel Palmer, Superintendent of Indian Affairs, September 3, 1854, NARG 75, reel 608, "Oregon Superintendency, 1853–1855."

48. Palmer to Thompson, September 28, 1854, ibid.

49. Thompson to Palmer, September 3 and 6, 1854, ibid. See also Madsen, 58–59; and Thompson to Palmer, October 11, 1854, NARG 75, reel 608.

50. Palmer to Thompson and Palmer to Nathan Olney, Special Agent, September 28, 1854, NARG 75, reel 608.

51. Palmer to Thompson, September 28, 1854.

52. "Headquarters Department of the Pacific," September 4, 1855, in *An-*

nual Report of the Secretary of War, Senate Executive Document, 34th Cong., 1st sess., vol. 2, no. 1, part 2 (Washington, D.C.: U.S. Government Printing Office, 1855), 78–79; "Report of Edward R. Geary," *ARCIA,* 1859, 389. For 1854 campaigns, see also Thompson to Palmer, October 18, 1854, NARG 75, reel 608; Madsen, 59–63; and Palmer to Nathan Olney, Special Agent, September 28, 1854.

53. For Cayuse, Nez Perce, and "Sandwich Islander" auxiliaries, see Thompson to Palmer, October 11 and 18, 1854, NARG 75, reel 608. For Nez Perce–Shoshone relations in 1854, see Thompson to Palmer, September 6, 1854; and Palmer to Thompson, September 28, 1854. See also *HBNAI,* 12: 149–173, 395–419, 420–438; and Alvin M. Josephy Jr., *The Nez Perce Indians and the Opening of the Northwest* (New Haven: Yale University Press, 1965).

54. For Western Indian policy before the Civil War, see Francis Paul Prucha, *The Great Father: The United States Government and the American Indians,* abridged ed. (Lincoln: University of Nebraska Press, 1986), 122–135.

55. "Report of Brigham Young," *ARCIA,* 1855; Young to Maypenny, December 31, 1854, NARG 75, reel 897. See also Young to Maypenny, September 30, 1854, ibid., which includes reports of Shoshone horse raids but makes no mention of the Ward attacks or other Snake River raids. For Hurt's costly farming efforts, see Madsen, 63–64.

56. "Report of Jacob Forney," *ARCIA,* 1858; "Report of Agent Garland Hurt," *ARCIA,* 1855.

57. Both Hurt and Holeman crisscrossed Utah and Nevada. See "Report of Garland Hurt, Agent for Indians in Utah," *ARCIA,* 1856; and "Report of Agent Jacob H. Holeman," *ARCIA,* 1852.

58. For the U.S. Army's influences in Utah before the Civil War, see Ball, *Army Regulars on the Western Frontier,* 153–171. See also Brigham D. Madsen, *Glory Hunter: A Biography of Patrick Edward Connor* (Salt Lake City: University of Utah Press, 1990).

59. Thompson to Palmer, September 6, 1854, NARG 75, reel 897.

60. "Report of the Secretary of War," December 4, 1854, in *Annual Report of the Secretary of War,* 1854, part 2 (Washington, D.C.: U.S. Government Printing Office, 1854), 6. See also Ball, *Army Regulars on the Western Frontier,* 89–106.

61. Ball, *Army Regulars on the Western Frontier,* 55.

62. For Utah's Indian farms, see Lewis, *Neither Wolf nor Dog,* 36–38; Knack, *Boundaries Between,* 62–72; and Pearson H. Corbett, *Jacob Hamblin: The Peacemaker* (Salt Lake City: Deseret Book, 1973), 48–131.

63. Madsen, 108–109. See also John M. Townley, *The Overland Stage: A History and Guidebook* (Reno: Great Basin Studies Center, 1994).

64. For army reprisals, see Madsen, 104–105, 107, 111, 115, 125. From the Mormon War through December 1861, Utah's superintendents included Brigham Young, Jacob Forney, Benjamin Davies, Henry Martin, and James Duane Doty, though from September 1859 to Davies' arrival in November 1860 there was no one in office. For the inability of Shoshone leaders, including Washakie, to rein in recalcitrant warriors, see "Report of Luther Man, Jr.," *ARCIA*, 1862, 204–205; Elijah Nicholas Wilson, *Among the Shoshones* (1910; reprint, Medford, Ore.: Pine Cone Publishers, 1971), 30–31; and Brigham D. Madsen, *Chief Pocatello: The "White Plume"* (Salt Lake City: University of Utah Press, 1986), 29–42.

65. "Report of A. Humphreys," *ARCIA*, 1860, 169–170; "Report of Benjamin Davies," *ARCIA*, 1861, 129–130. For additional winter impoverishment, see "Report of F. W. Hatch," *ARCIA*, 1862, 207.

66. "Report of Jacob Forney," *ARCIA*, 1859, 363; quoted in Madsen, 121.

67. For Northern Paiute–U.S. relations and the Pyramid Lake Indian War, see Madsen; and Knack and Stewart.

68. Quoted in Madsen, 124–125.

69. Ibid., 116–117.

70. Wilson, *Among the Shoshones*, 119. See also "Annual Report of Benjamin Davies," *ARCIA*, 1861, 131.

71. See Ball, *Army Regulars on the Western Frontier*, 189–203; and Robert M. Utley, *The Indian Frontier of the American West, 1846–1890* (Albuquerque: University of New Mexico Press, 1984), 65–72. For Utah during the Civil War, see E. B. Long, *The Saints and the Union: Utah Territory during the Civil War* (Urbana: University of Illinois Press, 1981).

72. Utley, *Indian Frontier of American West*, 70.

73. "Report of Capt. Medorem Crawford" and "Report of Maj. Patrick A. Gallagher," in *The War of Rebellion: A Compilation of the Official Records of the Union and Confederate Armies*, Series I, vol. 50, part I (Washington, D.C.: U.S. Government Printing Office, 1897) (cited hereafter as *War of Rebellion*), 153–155, 183–184.

74. "Report of James Duane Doty" and "Report of the Commissioner of Indian Affairs," *ARCIA*, 1862, 198, 33. For Doty's Shoshone treaties, see *IA*, 2: 848–853.

75. "Report of Col. P. Edward Connor," in *War of Rebellion*, 187. For overviews of the massacre, see Madsen, 177–200; and Scott R. Christensen, *Sagwitch: Shoshone Chieftain, Mormon Elder, 1822–1887* (Logan: Utah State University Press, 1999), 41–76. See also Kass Fleisher, *The Bear*

River Massacre and the Making of History (Albany: State University of New York Press, 2004).

76. "Report of Col. Edward P. Connor," 187. See also "Report of James Duane Doty," *ARCIA*, 1863, 419–420.

77. See, for example, Dee Brown, *Bury My Heart at Wounded Knee: An Indian History of the American West*, 30th anniversary ed. (New York: Henry Holt, 2000,), 104, who mistakes those lost as "a camp of Paiutes."

78. For Bear River's changing forms of commemoration, see Fleisher, *The Bear River Massacre.*

Epilogue

1. "Report of James Duane Doty," *ARCIA*, 1863, 419–420.

2. Between July 2 and October 12, 1863, Doty negotiated four treaties with "Eastern," "Northwestern," "Western," and "Goship" Shoshones. See *IA*, 2: 848–853, 859–860. For Connor's promotion, see "H. W. Halleck to Connor," March 29, 1863, in *War of Rebellion*, 187. See also "Expedition to the Snake Indian Country, Idaho Ter., Reports" and "Expedition from Camp Douglas, Utah Ter., to Soda Springs, on the Bear River, Idaho Ter.," ibid., 214–229.

3. Steven J. Crum, *The Road on Which We Came: A History of the Western Shoshone* (Salt Lake: University of Utah Press, 1994) (cited hereafter as Crum), 25–26; *Shoshone Nation or Tribe of Indians v. The United States of America*, Docket No. 367, 11th Indian Claims Commission 387; cited in David Agee Horr, ed., *Shoshone Indians* (New York: Garland, 1974), 290. For the creation of the Wind River and Fort Hall Reservations, see ibid., 260–262.

4. "Connor to Edward McGarry," September 29, 1862, in *War of Rebellion*, 144. See also Crum, 23–32.

5. See "Report of James W. Nye," *ARCIA*, 1863, 416. For Nevada's nineteenth-century history, see Robert Laxalt, *Nevada: A History* (New York: W. W. Norton, 1977); Eugene P. Moehring, *Urbanism and Empire in the Far West, 1840–1890* (Reno: University of Nevada Press, 2004), 121–166; and David Alan Johnson, *Founding the Far West: California, Oregon, and Nevada, 1840–1890* (Berkeley: University of California Press, 1992), 71–97, 189–230, 313–348. For Indian laborers in Virginia City, see Eugene M. Hattori, "'And Some of Them Swear like Pirates': Acculturation of American Indian Women in Nineteenth-Century Virginia City," in *Comstock Women: The Making of a Mining Community*, ed. Ronald M. James and Elizabeth Raymond (Reno: University of Nevada Press, 1998), 229–245.

6. Crum, 43–84. See also Whitney McKinney, *A History of the Shoshone-Paiutes of the Duck Valley Indian Reservation* (Duck Valley, Nev.: Institute of the American West, 1983), 33–56.

7. "Report of James Nye," *ARCIA,* 1863, 418–419. See also Johnson, *Founding the Far West,* 75–97, 189–230.

8. For Nevada's nuclear testing in the context of violated Shoshone treaty rights, see Rebecca Solnit, *Savage Dreams: A Journey into the Hidden Wars of the American West* (San Francisco: Sierra Club Books, 1994), esp. 68–212; and Ward Churchill, *A Little Matter of Genocide: Holocaust and Denial in the Americas, 1492 to the Present* (San Francisco: City Light Books, 1997), 324–332. See also Crum, 176–183. For an overview of Winnemucca's career, see Sally Zanjani, *Sarah Winnemucca* (Lincoln: University of Nebraska Press, 2001). For an assessment of Wilson's Ghost Dance, see Michael Hittman, *Wovoka and the Ghost Dance,* ed. Don Lynch, rev. ed. (Lincoln: University of Nebraska Press, 1997).

9. For Wounded Knee as a final chapter to Indian history, see Dee Brown, *Bury My Heart at Wounded Knee: An Indian History of the American West,* 30th anniversary ed. (New York: Henry Holt, 2000). For a study of the Ghost Dance that emphasizes its Great Basin origins, see Jeffrey Ostler, *The Plains Sioux and U.S. Colonialism from Lewis and Clark to Wounded Knee* (New York: Cambridge University Press, 2004), 243–288.

10. Sarah Winnemucca Hopkins, *Life among the Piutes* (1883; reprint, Reno: University of Nevada Press, 1994), 34. The Inter-Tribal Council of Nevada (ITCN) pioneered Nevadan Indian history with its series on Nevadan Indian tribes. See, for example, *Nuwuvi: A Southern Paiute History* (Reno: ITCN, 1976); *Newe: A Western Shoshone History* (Reno: ITCN, 1976); and *Numa: A Northern Paiute History* (Reno: ITCN, 1976). See also *Newe Sogobia: The Western Shoshone People and their Lands* (Battle Mountain, Nev.: Western Shoshone Sacred Lands Association, 1982); Crum; Knack and Stewart; and Martha C. Knack, *Boundaries Between: The Southern Paiutes, 1775–1995* (Lincoln: University of Nebraska Press, 2001). Ferol Egan, *Sand in a Whirlwind: The Paiute Indian War of 1860* (1972; reprint, Reno: University of Nevada Press, 1985), provides the most thorough study of a single conflict in Nevadan Indian history.

11. This discussion of signification is drawn from Jacob Torfing's readings of Ernesto Laclau and Chantal Mouffe in Torfing, *New Theories of Discourse: Laclau, Mouffe, and Zizek* (Oxford: Blackwell Publishers, 1999), esp. 84–100. For discussions of Indians and "expectation," see Philip J. Deloria, *Indians in Unexpected Places* (Lawrence: University of Kansas Press, 2004), 3–14. See also idem, *Playing Indian* (New Haven: Yale University Press, 1995); and Gerald Vizenor, *Manifest Manners: Post-Indian*

Warriors of Survivance (Hanover, N.H.: Wesleyan University Press, 1994). For Paiute wage labor, see Martha C. Knack, "Nineteenth-Century Great Basin Indian Wage Labor," in *Native Americans and Wage Labor,* ed. Knack and Alice Littlefield (Norman: University of Oklahoma Press, 1996), 144–176; and Hattori, "'And Some of Them Swear like Pirates.'"

12. Mark Twain, *The Works of Mark Twain: Roughing It,* ed. Franklin R. Rogers (Berkeley: University of California Press, 1972), 43. For a summary of Twain's career in Nevada, see Brian Scot Hagen, "The Making of Mark Twain," *Nevada Historical Society Quarterly* 41 (Spring 1998): 26–39.

13. Franklin R. Rogers, "Introduction," in *The Works of Mark Twain: Roughing It,* 1–25.

14. Amy Kaplan, *The Anarchy of Empire in the Making of U.S. Culture* (Cambridge, Mass.: Harvard University Press, 2002), 59. For Hawaiian responses to U.S. expansion, see Noenoe K. Silva, *Aloha Betrayed: Native Hawaiian Resistance to American Colonization* (Durham, N.C.: Duke University Press, 2004). See also David E. Stannard, *Before the Horror: The Population of Hawai'i on the Eve of Western Contact* (Honolulu: Social Science Research Institute of Hawai'i Press, 1989).

15. Kaplan, *The Anarchy of Empire,* 51–91. Select analyses of Twain's Goshute imagery are found in J. R. LeMaster and James D. Wilson, eds., *The Mark Twain Encyclopedia* (New York: Garland, 1993), 182, 393, 422, and 695. For the romantic embrace of Twain in Nevada, see George D. Lyman, *The Saga of the Comstock Lode* (New York: Charles Scribner's Sons, 1937), 212–215, 246–250, 293–304.

16. Twain, *The Works of Mark Twain: Roughing It,* 144–146. For discussion of African American influences on Twain, see Shelley Fisher Fishkin, *Was Huck Black? Mark Twain and African-American Voices* (New York: Oxford University Press, 1993). See also idem, "Mark Twain and Race," in *A Historical Guide to Mark Twain,* ed. Fisher Fishkin (New York: Oxford University Press, 2002), 127–162, though her discussion of race rests on a black-white binary. Steven Andrews of Grinnell College's English Department provided guidance on this discussion of homophony.

17. Twain, *The Works of Mark Twain: Roughing It,* 144–146.

18. Ibid., 144–145.

19. Robert F. Murphy, "Introduction: The Anthropological Theories of Julian H. Steward," in *Evolution and Ecology: Essays on Social Transformation by Julian Steward,* ed. Jane C. Steward and Robert F. Murphy (Urbana: University of Illinois Press, 1977), 1–39. See also Virginia Kerns, *Scenes from the High Desert: Julian Steward's Life and Theory* (Urbana: University of Illinois Press, 2003); Ned Blackhawk, "Julian Steward and the Politics of Representation: A Critique of Anthropologist Julian Stew-

ard's Ethnographic Portrayals of the American Indians of the Great Basin," *American Indian Culture and Research Journal* 21 (1997): 61–81; Marvin Harris, *The Rise of Anthropological Theory: A History of Theories of Culture* (New York: Thomas Crowell, 1968); and Richard O. Clemmer, L. Daniel Myers, and Mary Elizabeth Rudden, eds., *Julian Steward and the Great Basin: The Making of an Anthropologist* (Salt Lake City: University of Utah Press, 1999). For "Boasian Culturalism," see George W. Stocking Jr., *Delimiting Anthropology: Occasional Essays and Reflections* (Madison: University of Wisconsin Press, 2001), 24–48.

20. For the classic formulation of this hypothesis, see Julian H. Steward, *Basin-Plateau Aboriginal Sociopolitical Groups* (1938; reprint, Salt Lake City: University of Utah Press, 1970), esp. 1–3, 230–262. For its most recognized elaboration, see idem, *Theory of Culture Change: The Methodology of Multilinear Evolution* (Urbana: University of Illinois Press, 1955), esp. 101–142. See also Murphy, "Introduction: The Anthropological Theories of Julian H. Steward"; Harris, *The Rise of Anthropological Theory,* esp. 654–667; and Kerns, *Scenes from the High Desert.*

21. For Steward's challenge to "cultural area" definitions, see Harris, *The Rise of Anthropological Theory,* 373–377.

22. See Donald Worcester, *A River Running West: The Life of John Wesley Powell* (New York: Oxford University Press, 2001), esp. 383–532; and Don D. Fowler, *A Laboratory for Anthropology: Science and Romanticism in the American Southwest, 1846–1890* (Albuquerque: University of New Mexico Press, 2000), esp. 79–147.

23. Harris, *The Rise of Anthropological Theory,* 654–655. See also Murphy, "Introduction: The Anthropological Theories of Julian H. Steward"; and Kerns, *Scenes from the High Desert,* 206–262, in which Kerns emphasizes Steward's "liminal" and "outsider" "sense of being" at Columbia; ibid., 237–240.

24. Elman R. Service, *The Hunters* (Englewood Cliffs, N.J.: Prentice-Hall, 1966), v. For critiques of the "myth of cultural purity," see James Clifford and George E. Marcus, eds., *Writing Culture: The Poetics and Politics of Ethnography* (Berkeley: University of California Press, 1986); Renato Rosaldo, *Culture and Truth: The Remaking of Social Analysis* (Boston: Beacon, 1993); and Vijay Prashad, *everybody was kung fu fighting: Afro-Asian Connections and the Myth of Cultural Purity* (Boston: Beacon, 2001).

25. Murphy, "Introduction: The Anthropological Theories of Julian H. Steward," 13.

26. Julian H. Steward, "Shoshonean Tribes: Utah, Idaho, Nevada, and Eastern California," Report Prepared for the Bureau of Indian Affairs, box 10, Papers of Julian H. Steward, University Archives, University Library,

University of Illinois, Champaign-Urbana. See also Elmer R. Rusco, "Julian Steward, the Western Shoshones, and the Bureau of Indian Affairs: A Failure to Communicate"; and Steven J. Crum, "Julian Steward's Vision of the Great Basin: A Critique and Response," both in Clemmer, Myers, and Rudden, *Julian Steward and the Great Basin.*

27. For Collier's reforms, see Lawrence C. Kelly, *The Assault on Assimilation: John Collier and the Origins of Indian Policy Reform* (Albuquerque: University of New Mexico Press, 1983).

28. For the denial of shared time to ethnographic subjects, see Johannes Fabian, *Time and the Other: How Anthropology Makes Its Object* (New York: Columbia University Press, 1983). For the centrality of "the imperial experience" to modern intellectual history, see also Edward W. Said, *Culture and Imperialism* (New York: Alfred A. Knopf, 1993).

29. "Report of James Nye," *ARCIA,* 1863, 417.

30. "Report of Benjamin Davies," *ARCIA,* 1861, 129–130. For Northern Paiute reservation economics, see Knack, "Nineteenth-Century Great Basin Indian Wage Labor."

31. Beth Sennett, "Wage Labor: Survival for the Death Valley Timbisha," in Knack and Littlefield, *Native Americans and Wage Labor,* 230. See also Crum, 30–41; Robert B. Campbell, "Newlands, Old Lands: Native American Labor, Agrarian Ideology, and the Progressive-Era State in the Making of the Newlands Reclamation Project, 1902–1926," *Pacific Historical Review* 71 (May 2002): 203–238; and John Walton, *Western Times, Water Wars* (Berkeley: University of California Press, 1988). For the colony program, see also Elmer R. Rusco, "Purchasing Lands for Nevada Indian Colonies, 1916–1917," *Nevada Historical Society Quarterly* 32 (Spring 1989): 1–19.

32. For Western Shoshone nonreservation economics, see Crum, 30–31, 63–67. For central Nevada's mining industry, see Donald R. Abbe, *Austin and the Reese River Mining District: Nevada's Forgotten Frontier* (Reno: University of Nevada Press, 1986).

33. For creation of the Duck Valley Indian Reservation and attempts to resettle nonreservation Shoshones, see Crum, 33–48; and McKinney, *Shoshone-Paiutes of Duck Valley Reservation,* 49–78.

34. For overviews of Shoshone band classifications, see Steward, *Basin-Plateau Aboriginal Sociopolitical Groups;* and Crum.

35. For recent theories of state formation as applied to Indian-white relations, see Cole Harris, *The Resettlement of British Columbia: Essays on Geographic Change and Colonialism* (Vancouver: University of British Columbia Press, 1997); Thomas Biolsi, *Organizing the Lakota: The Political Economy of the New Deal on the Pine Ridge and Rosebud Reservations* (Tuc-

son: University of Arizona Press, 1992); and Ostler, *Plains Sioux and U.S. Colonialism*. See also James C. Scott, *Seeing like a State: How Certain Schemes to Improve the Human Condition Have Failed* (New Haven: Yale University Press, 1998), 1–8.

36. McKinney, *Shoshone-Paiutes of Duck Valley Reservation*.

37. For Shoshone Mike's demise, see Crum, 70; and McKinney, *Shoshone-Paiutes of Duck Valley Reservation*, 103–105. Frank Bergon has provided the most extended narrative of Mike's life based upon archival and newspaper research, oral histories, and interviews of the lone survivor, Josephine Mosho Estep. See Bergon, *Shoshone Mike* (New York: Viking Penguin, 1987). Although the narrative is a work of fiction, extended communication with Professor Bergon has clarified his exhaustive documentary methodology.

38. Quoted in McKinney, *Shoshone-Paiutes of Duck Valley Reservation*, 105.

39. Bergon, "Afterword," in *Shoshone Mike*, 287–288; and personal communication with the author, August–September 2005.

40. For select biographies of Stewart Shoshone graduates, see Crum, 65, 67. Annie Maime also attended Stewart and remembers her brother Richard Birchum's many attempts to run away; author's interviews with Annie Maime, Napa, California, 1997–1999; notes and tape recordings in author's possession.

41. For assessments of recent Western Shoshone history, see Crum; and Solnit, *Savage Dreams*, 27–212. As of September 2005, there had been no settlement of land claims.

42. Luther Standing Bear, *Land of the Spotted Eagle* (1933; reprint, Lincoln: University of Nebraska Press, 1978), 229–237.

43. For the quandaries of blood quantum, see Circe Sturm, *Blood Politics: Race, Culture, and Identity in the Cherokee Nation of Oklahoma* (Berkeley: University of California Press, 2002).

44. Charles Wilkinson, *Blood Struggle: The Rise of Modern Indian Nations* (New York: W. W. Norton, 2005).

Acknowledgments

The making of this book began when I decided to enter graduate school in American history, and its completion would not have been possible without the guidance of many individuals as well generous research support from several institutions.

First and foremost, my parents, Terry and Evan Blackhawk, from an early age instilled in me a sense of the possible, and they have my eternal respect and love. My mother's forty years of commitment to public education in Detroit's schools have provided constant inspiration, while my father's ability to simultaneously share with and shelter me from aspects of his youth has left me appreciative and awed. As the introduction and epilogue suggest, this book is linked to my father's home, and there is simply no way for me to express adequately my debt of gratitude for his and our family's enduring sacrifices. My aunts Beverly Stone and Versa Menendez and my great-aunt Annie Maine provided endless hours of insight into the nature of Indian life in Nevada. The transcribed notes of interviews, video recordings, and family photographs that together now form the Eva Charley Family Collection remain in my possession through Annie, Versa, and Beverly's continuing generosity.

Within academia, three individuals in particular have helped guide this project to fruition. At the American Indian Studies Center at the University of California at Los Angeles, Director Duane Champagne's sustained commitment to academic excellence illuminated my path. Indeed, coupled with the outstanding cadre of Ethnic Studies faculty

359

and programs, the UCLA History Department in the early 1990s remained the most vibrant graduate program that I have yet to encounter, and I would like to thank the many students and faculty who made that environment enriching, particularly Professors Valerie Matsumoto, George Sanchez, and Brenda Stevenson and my cohorts Jamie Cardenas, Arlene Devera, Augusto Espiritu, Bob Myers Jr., Brian O'Neil, and Andrew Smith. Ernesto Chávez, Miroslava Chávez-García, Cathy Choy, Kerwin Klein, and Omar Valerio-Jiménez provided excellent peer mentoring, as did Dwight McBride.

At the University of Washington, where I completed my doctoral studies, Richard White's commitment to my project never wavered, and his supportive and forceful responses have proved invaluable again and again. James Gregory, Sasha Harmon, and Laurie Sears all helped guide my dissertation to completion, while fellow Danforth-Compton Scholar Steven Andrews pushed me to engage literary theory. Steve's explication of Elaine Scarry's work enabled me to broaden the project's reach. Many thanks to Julius Debro, the Danforth Program, and members of UW's Native community, particularly Scott and Vicki Pinkham, for their support and friendship. A resident fellowship at the School of American Research in Santa Fe enabled me to research New Mexican history, while coaching at the Santa Fe Indian School introduced me to New Mexico. Father Thomas J. Steele offered invaluable translation help early on. Dr. Svetlana T. Karpe has also provided critical translation support.

The transition from graduate student to faculty member is not an easy one, and combining scholarship and teaching with community service has remained a constant and rewarding challenge. I owe enormous thanks to those who helped steer the Big Ten's American Indian Studies Consortium into being, and especially to Fred Hoxie. The Consortium remains an exemplary forum of interdisciplinary cooperation. Under its auspices, I was privileged to help organize the "Narrating Native Histories in the Americas" conference in Madison, for which I owe thanks to Florenica Mallon and to all who participated.

The Ford Foundation and Stanford University's Center for the Comparative Study of Race and Ethnicity provided direly needed research support, while the University of Wisconsin provided ample teaching leaves. My colleagues at the University of Wisconsin in History, American Indian Studies, and Chicano/a and Latino/a Studies, particularly

Charles Cohen, Bill Cronon, Susan Johnson, and Steve Stern, have all offered valuable feedback. As directors of the American Indian Studies Program, Roberta Hill and Ada Deer have guided many campus initiatives to fruition, while Nan Enstad, Gayle Plummer, James Schlender Jr., and Jeremi Suri of the History Department's Diversity Committee helped initiate important changes. Lori Curley of Delavan Enterprises assisted with the index.

One of the most fulfilling pleasures of academic life is teaching engaged students. Casey Brown, Amanda Bruegl, Tol Foster, Doug Kiel, Leah Lapointe, Collette Montoya-Humphreys, David O'Connor, Erik Redix, Amanda Rockman, and James Washinawatok are a few of the Native students who have enriched my understandings of Indian history. The Madison Indian community has welcomed my family and me, and Sheryl Baker, Aaron and Marianne Bird Bear, Ken Cornelius, Lana Fox, Derek Jennings, Michelle Johnson, and Lea Wolf share our joy in seeing our children play and grow together. Aaron's friendship means to the world to me, and Erik Schultz and Michael Walsh remain close friends despite the distance.

I owe a great debt of thanks to those whose commitments to multiculturalism have guided me, in particular Zoltan Grossman, Jonathan Holloway, and Audra Simpson. I am also indebted beyond measure to those who have helped craft the histories of Utah, Colorado, New Mexico, and Nevada, many of them devoting decades to the effort. I see bringing these histories together to shape a larger vision as one of my tasks as their successor.

My wife, Birgit, and daughter, Eva, have sustained and nourished the production of this work in countless ways while coping with sacrifices along the way. My deepest appreciation remains for them. Their joyous love is the most powerful force in my life.

Index